MENTAL HEALTH
IN THE
WORKPLACE

A Practical Psychiatric Guide

Edited by

Jeffrey P. Kahn, M.D.

 VAN NOSTRAND REINHOLD
New York

Copyright © 1993 by Van Nostrand Reinhold
Library of Congress Catalog Card Number 92-49362
ISBN 0-442-00632-2

Printed in the United States of America.

Van Nostrand Reinhold
115 Fifth Avenue
New York, New York 10003

Chapman and Hall
2-6 Boundary Row
London, SE1 8HN, England

Thomas Nelson Australia
102 Dodds Street
South Melbourne 3205
Victoria, Australia

Nelson Canada
120 Birchmount Road
Scarborough, Ontario MIK 5G4, Canada

16 15 14 13 12 11 10 9 8 7 6 5 4 3 2 1

Library of Congress Cataloging-in-Publication Data

Mental health in the workplace : a practical psychiatric guide / edited
   by Jeffrey P. Kahn.
         p.   cm.
   Includes bibliographical references and index.
   ISBN 0-442-00632-2
   1. Industrial psychiatry.   I. Kahn, Jeffrey P. [DNLM: 1. Mental
Health. 2. Psychology, Industrial. WA 495 M5513]
RC967.5.M464   1993
616.89—dc20
DNLM/DLC
for Library of Congress   92-49362
                                                                      CIP

Contents

Part III: Common Employee Problems

Foreword

Psychiatric knowledge and skills are increasingly important tools for addressing the daily problems and challenges faced by organizations and their employees. While emotional problems have always been a pressing concern, stressful times and economic change have led to a steady increase in their prevalence and effects.

Mental Health in the Workplace makes clear the usefulness of psychiatry for workplace problems. Books on occupational stress reflect neither the complexity of mental health problems nor the effectiveness of specific solutions. Books about organizational change focus primarily on systems' problems without fully considering the influence of key individuals, important emotional reactions, or the intricacies of organizational interactions. And other psychiatric books describe emotional problems with very limited attention to career issues, productivity, and interactions on the job. This book bridges the gap between psychiatry and the workplace. It addresses workplace aspects of common psychiatric disorders, emotional problems caused by organizational events such as job loss, and also problems that face the organization as a whole. Not merely theoretical, this book is a practical guide to essential and common concerns. For example:

1. How can employee problems be specifically understood and effectively resolved?
2. How do psychiatric disorders manifest themselves in the workplace?
3. How can organizational structure and development problems be addressed in logical and practical ways?
4. How and when should management, and human-resources and employee-health professionals intervene?
5. What treatments are most effective and practical, how do they work, and how do you get it done right the first time around?
6. How do employees with psychiatric problems or disabilities reintegrate into the workplace?

I think that most managers would agree that the employee mental health, morale, organizational health, and productivity are closely linked. But finding effective strategies to enhance employee and organizational mental health can be a very difficult problem. Superficial solutions yield superficial results, and just throwing money at a problem won't always make it go away either. This book offers specific guidance for improving the health of both employees and organizations. It is a valuable guide that will be read by professionals from management, human resources, occupational health, employee assistance programs, psychiatry, and many others fields. *Mental*

Health in the Workplace should be kept within easy reach for reference as problems arise. And once it is read, the relevance of psychiatric knowledge and logic to everyday corporate problems will become clear. Problems that had once looked impossible will become more easily understood, and practical solutions will be easier to find.

STEPHEN H. HEIDEL, M.D.
President, Academy of Organizational and
Occupational Psychiatry (Dallas, Texas)
Associate Clinical Professor of Psychiatry,
University of California at San Diego

Preface

Emotional problems can have profound effects on individuals, families, and employers. Those effects can range from hidden internal distress, to outwardly obvious emotional, drug abuse, and behavioral problems, to effects on families or organizations as a whole. The complex interplay of individual emotions and organizational function has long been a focus of attention. Recent years, though, have seen an enormous growth in that attention.

There has been greater awareness of the considerable emotional, financial, and organizational costs of these problems, and of the need for thorough understanding of causes and solutions. Good managers have always known the importance of maintaining individual and group morale. Such long-standing concerns have been highlighted recently by the major restructuring of many U.S. industries and by implementation of the Americans with Disabilities Act, which mandates nondiscriminatory employment for people with mental health problems. Organizational effectiveness requires careful attention to both individuals and to organizational functioning. And, outside mental health issues are increasingly felt in the workplace. Drug abuse, breakdown of family supports (the subject of a *Fortune* magazine cover article as I write this preface), and increasing questions about cost and quality of mental health care are just a few examples.

This book reviews common individual and organizational mental health concerns at a relatively sophisticated level of discussion, but in nontechnical language. Discussions include a particular focus on workplace considerations and solutions. Workplace emotional problems can be understood and resolved, with benefits for patient, family, and the workplace itself. There is no substitute for comprehensive understanding of problems and careful implementation of practical and effective solutions.

Part I of the book reviews such general psychiatric topics as diagnosis, treatment, ethics, mental health providers and systems, and a history of occupational psychiatry. Part II addresses major organizational concerns about organizational structure and change, job loss, disability, executive distress, executive development, organizational effects of family problems, and emotional crises in the workplace. Finally, Part III reviews selected psychiatric diagnoses in chapters on anxiety, depression, personality, alcoholism, drug abuse, psychosis, and psychosomatic illnesses.

The potential audience for this book is broad. Psychiatrists and other mental health professionals can learn about specific organizational problems (Part II), as well as about workplace considerations for syndromes that they may already know well (Part III). Managers, Occupational Health professionals, Human Resource professionals, business students, and others who are concerned with workplace mental health and organizational development will also find this book of value. It is an introduction to a comprehensive psychiatric perspective on the emotional problems and issues that are so important for effective management and organizational success.

However, this book should not be used as a layperson's manual for the provision of mental health care. Comprehensive and appropriate professional training are essential for accurate diagnosis and effective treatment of any distressed individual. Similarly, proper training and experience are also required when addressing the issues of organizational concern described in Part II. While diagnoses, medication dosages, and medical considerations are discussed in various parts of the book, decisions about such issues should always be made by a qualified medical professional with full knowledge of the specifics of any given case. All case material in this book is either fictitious or a fictionalized composite. Similarity of characters presented in the text to any person living or dead is coincidental.

There is a nearly endless list of teachers, colleagues, students, patients and friends whose teachings, guidance or support have made this book possible. Donald Klein, Roger MacKinnon, and David Peretz have each had a lasting effect on my understanding of emotional problems and solutions. Richard Cantor, Paul Brandt-Rauf, Clint Weiman, Elizabeth Ramos, Edward Anselm, MaryEllen Guroy, and Howard Leaman have offered valuable insights into mental health aspects of occupational medicine. Marcia Scott, Harvey Barten, Jeffrey Speller, Leonard Moss, Norman Wyloge, and all of the indefatigable contributors to this book have offered a wealth of knowledge and skill in organizational and occupational psychiatry. Alan McLean, in particular, has been a mentor and a source of inspiration since the inception of this project so long ago. Ira Glick and many others at Cornell have been a steady source of support. Stephen Zollo, Robert Esposito, Thomas Phillips, and Bernice Pettinato have offered wise and tolerant editorial guidance.

Most of the contributors are members of the Academy of Organizational and Occupational Psychiatry (AOOP; Dallas, Texas, telephone 214-392-0552). Founded in 1990 to address the contributions of psychiatry to workplace mental health solutions, the rapid growth and strength of AOOP is testimony to the current importance of those issues. AOOP offers information and collegial support to interested psychiatrists, and provides a referral service to corporations concerned about the broad range of employee or larger organizational problems.

Most important, I am forever indebted for the warm affection and wise counsel of Nancy, Jessica, and Tara.

About the Contributors

Peter L. Brill, M.D., is a board-certified psychiatrist with over 20 years of experience in psychiatry and organizational consulting. He is founder and chairman/CEO of Integra, Inc., a company that offers a range of mental health services to organizations. Dr. Brill is also director of the Center for the Study of Adult Development, affiliated with the departments of psychiatry at the University of Pennsylvania, Northwestern University, and the Medical College of Wisconsin.

Dr. Brill has served on the faculties of the University of Pennsylvania School of Medicine (since 1972), Hahnemann Medical School, the Management and Behavioral Science Center, and the National Health Care Management Center at Wharton. Presently, he is an assistant professor in the Department of Psychiatry at the University of Pennsylvania and is chairman of the Committee on Occupational Psychiatry of the American Psychiatric Association. He has written many papers and articles, and has lectured and consulted at more than 150 corporations. He has spoken on radio and television, and lectured around the country on issues such as corporate culture, the empowerment of the HR professional, work stress, mental health and substance abuse, adult development, and psychiatric case management.

Dr. Brill received the M.D. from the University of California, Los Angeles, and served his residency in psychiatry at the University of Pennsylvania, where he also studied at the Wharton School.

David A. Deacon, M.B.A., joined Morrison Associates in 1989. After a nearly 15-year career with a major money center bank in varied line and staff functions, he is now involved with the spectrum of Morrison Associates' consultation services. He undertook doctoral work in philosophy at Duke University, then completed an M.B.A. at the University of Chicago. He is currently a clinical psychology doctoral candidate at the Illinois School of Professional Psychology.

Richard H. Gabel, M.D., F.A.P.A., completed his psychiatric training at the Massachusetts General Hospital, a Harvard Medical School program. He is currently chief of psychiatric services and medical director of the substance abuse program at White Plains Hospital Center, New York. He is clinical assistant professor of psychiatry at New York Medical College, and attending psychiatrist at the St. Vincent's Hospital and Medical Center of New York. As legislative representative of the Westchester District Branch of the American Psychiatric Association, he educates state and federal legislators about psychiatric issues. He maintains a private practice of psychiatry in White Plains, New York.

Brian L. Grant, M.D., is clinical associate professor in the University of Washington Department of Psychiatry and Behavioral Sciences, and a clinical associate in the Seattle Institute for Psycho-analysis. He completed his psychiatric residency training in 1982 at the University of Washington and is in the private practice of psychiatry in Seattle. In addition, he is the president and medical director of Medical Consultants Northwest, Inc., a company that provides multidisciplinary evaluations of industrial injuries in various cities on the West Coast.

Barrie S. Greiff, M.D., is currently consultant to the Harvard University Health Services, and visiting professor of occupational psychiatry at the Institute of Living in Hartford, Connecticut. From 1968 to 1984, he was the psychiatrist to the Harvard Business School. In 1970, he pioneered a unique course at the business school, entitled *The Executive Family,* addressing the relationships of self, family, and work life, and leading to coauthorship of the book *Tradeoffs* (New American Library, 1980). He has consulted and lectured to a wide range of organizations including IBM, General Foods, Pepsico, Digital Equipment Corporation, AT&T, Corning, First National Bank of Boston, Toyota, several Big 8 Accounting Firms, and the MIT Sloan School. He chairs a committee of psychiatrists consulting to industry, and he founded the Center for the Study of Work. He is a fellow of the American Psychiatric Association and a diplomate of the American Board of Psychiatry and Neurology. He is presently a private practitioner and organizational consultant in Cambridge, Massachusetts. He is married and has three children.

Duane Q. Hagen, M.D., is chairperson of the Department of Psychiatry at St. John's Mercy Medical Center in St. Louis, and has been the recipient of a National Institute of Mental Health Career Teacher's Award. He has worked full-time as a psychiatric consultant to various federal government agencies, and has consulted to such corporations as Southwestern Bell, AT&T, and McDonnell Douglas. He serves as chairperson of the American Psychiatric Association Committee on Occupational Psychiatry, and was chairperson of the Group for the Advance of Psychiatry Committee on Psychiatry in Industry during the preparation of *Job Loss—A Psychiatric Perspective,* published in 1982 (Mental Health Materials Center).

Stephen H. Heidel, M.D., is the founder and president of the Health and Human Resource Center, which provides psychiatric services, employee assistance programs, and managed care to organizations throughout the United States. He is a board-certified psychiatrist, certified by the American Society of Addiction Medicine, a fellow in the American Psychiatric Association, president of the Academy of Organizational and Occupational Psychiatry, and associate clinical professor at the University of California San Diego Medical School.

Eric Hollander, M.D., is associate professor of clinical psychiatry at the College of Physicians and Surgeons of Columbia University. At the New York State Psychiatric Institute, he is director of the Obsessive-Compulsive Disorder Biological Studies Program, and of the Anxiety Diagnostic and Recruitment Unit. Dr. Hollander has spoken and published extensively on obsessive-compulsive and other anxiety disorders. He is a recipient of the American Psychiatric Association/Wisniewski Young Psychiatrist Research Award, the CINP Rafaelsen Scholar Award, and a National Institute of Mental Health Research Scientist Development Award (MH-OO750).

Jeffrey P. Kahn, M.D., is a board-certified psychiatrist, with offices in New York City and Scarsdale, New York. Raised in a business family, he is the founder of Kahn Associates, workplace mental health consultants. He has consulted to major corporations, smaller organizations, and individuals. Following Swarthmore College, he completed medical school, psychiatric residency, and fellowship training at the

Columbia University College of Physicians and Surgeons. After starting in practice, he completed eight years of faculty research and teaching at Columbia, and is currently clinical assistant professor of psychiatry at the Cornell University Medical College, New York City. He has spoken widely at national meetings and has published extensively in leading journals about executive distress, anxiety disorders, and emotional aspects of heart disease. He is a founding member of the Academy of Organizational and Occupational Psychiatry.

Nick Kates, M.B.B.S., is the director of East Region Mental Health Services in Hamilton, Ontario. He is an associate professor of psychiatry at McMaster University, and is director of the psychiatry residency program there. He has consulted to many local organizations on work-related issues, and is currently involved as a consultant with a labor-sponsored plant closure adjustment program. He has made many presentations on the psychological impact of job loss, and recently coauthored a book titled *The Psychosocial Impact of Job Loss* (American Psychiatric Press, 1990) with Barrie S. Greiff and Duane Q. Hagen.

Robert C. Larsen, M.D., M.P.H., is a board-certified psychiatrist in San Francisco. He is the director of the Center for Occupational Psychiatry, Inc. This outpatient mental health group provides services with a focus on career and job concerns. Dr. Larsen frequently evaluates the treatment decisions of other clinical professionals. This experience has sensitized him to the handling of consultative clinical situations. He frequently lectures on topics of stress, injury, and disability in the work force.

Alan A. McLean, M.D., has been a consultant in occupational psychiatry since 1985. Based in Westport, Connecticut, and Gig Harbor, Washington, his bicoastal professional life currently includes positions as chair of IBM's Mental Health Advisory Board, clinical associate professor of psychiatry at Cornell University Medical College (where he has been on the faculty since 1954), and part owner of Integra, Inc., an integrated mental health services company in Radnor, Pennsylvania.

He is past president of the American College of Occupational and Environmental Medicine, a member of the World Health Organization's Expert Advisory Panel on Occupational Health, and, for 10 years, a delegate in the House of Delegates of the American Medical Association. He is a life fellow of the American Psychiatric Association, where his many tasks have included chair of the Committee on Occupational Psychiatry, and vice-chair of the Committee on Confidentiality. From 1957 to 1985, he was associated with IBM in positions that included chief psychiatric consultant and manager of medical programs.

In addition to 75 articles in professional journals and textbooks, he is author of 9 books, the most recent of which are *Work Stress* (Addison-Wesley) and *High Tech Survival Kit* (Wiley).

David E. Morrison, M.D., has been a private consultant to major corporations and government groups since 1970. After medical school at the University of Southern California, he completed psychiatric residency at the Menninger School of Psychiatry. He is currently on the faculty of Rush Medical School. The thrust of his work has been with leaders who are stressed by numerous and complex pressures. Morrison

Associates, Ltd., in Palatine, Illinois, examines personal, emotional, and business factors that interfere with or contribute to effective work. Services include individual consultations for executives and middle managers, organizational consultations (including team building), seminars on a variety of topics (including change, stress, and balancing work, family, and self), and speeches.

David B. Robbins, M.D., M.P.H., is clinical associate professor of psychiatry at New York Medical College, and psychiatric consultant to the IBM Corporation. He completed Cornell University Medical College, psychiatric residency at New York Hospital-Cornell Medical Center (Westchester division), and the master's of public health from New York Medical College. As a principal consultant with IBM, he currently provides clinical services for the Westchester County medical region, serves as an advisor to the medical disability insurance plan panel, and offers employee training sessions on various topics. Other industry and local government clients have included AT&T, New York Telephone, Texaco, and the Chappaqua (New York) School District. His publication subjects have included the assessment and management of psychiatric disability. He is a fellow of the American College of Occupational and Environmental Medicine; a member of the Committee on Psychiatry in Industry of the Group for the Advancement of Psychiatry; and a member of the Academy of Organizational and Occupational Psychiatry.

Jeffrey S. Rosecan, M.D., is the founder and director of the Cocaine Abuse and Chemical Dependency Treatment Program at the Columbia University College of Physicians and Surgeons, where he is also assistant clinical professor of psychiatry. He is coauthor of the textbook *Cocaine Abuse: New Directions in Treatment and Research* (Brunner-Mazel, 1987). He has been a drug abuse consultant to many corporations and organizations, including the National Football League, and he has served as a professional-in-residence at the Betty Ford Center in Rancho Mirage, California.

Carlotta L. Schuster, M.D., is a graduate of Barnard College, Columbia University, and of the New York University School of Medicine. She is chief of the Substance Abuse Service at Silver Hill Hospital, New Canaan, Connecticut, and teaches on the faculty of the Columbia University College of Physicians and Surgeons. She is chair of the Treatment Committee of the American Academy of Psychiatrists in Alcohol and Addiction, and a member of the Substance Abuse Subcommittee of the Connecticut Psychiatric Society. She has coauthored papers and book chapters on alcoholism, and is the author of a monograph on alcohol and sexuality. Her clinical experience includes many years of working with corporations and employee assistance programs in the treatment of alcoholism.

Steven Sharfstein, M.D., is president, CEO, and medical director of Sheppard and Enoch Pratt Hospital in Baltimore. He holds faculty appointments at Johns Hopkins University and at Georgetown University. He worked for 9 years at the National Institute of Mental Health in Rockville, Maryland, and for 3 years at the American Psychiatric Association as deputy medical director. He was elected secretary of the

American Psychiatric Association in 1991. He is the author of numerous books and articles on mental health policy issues. Among his many activities, he serves as editor of the quarterly economic grand rounds column for the journal *Hospital and Community Psychiatry.*

Dan J. Stein, M.D., received the undergraduate medical degree from the University of Cape Town, and completed his residency in psychiatry at the New York State Psychiatric Institute and the Columbia-Presbyterian Medical Center. He is currently a postdoctoral research fellow in psychiatry there, with a focus on anxiety disorders. He has also received a NARSAD Young Investigator Award for psychiatric research.

Anne Stoline, M.D., has just completed residency training in psychiatry at Johns Hopkins University in Baltimore, Maryland. She is currently in private practice in Baltimore, and is a staff psychiatrist at Springfield Hospital Center in Sykesville, Maryland. Her book, *The New Medical Marketplace: A Physician's Guide to the Health Care Revolution* (Johns Hopkins University Press), currently in its second edition, is a text that is intended as an introduction to health care economics for medical professionals. She has also written several other pieces on health policy issues.

Charles W. Swearingen, M.D., is a psychiatrist and psychoanalyst who has been a management consultant with the Levinson Institute. A graduate of Harvard College, Yale University School of Medicine, and the Boston Psychoanalytic Institute, he has also studied management at the Boston College Graduate School of Management. He has been program chairperson for the International Society for the Psychoanalytic Study of Organizations. His private practice in Cambridge, Massachusetts, focuses on the career and family issues of executives and professionals. He has consulted on a wide range of organizational problems to Fortune 500 companies, smaller family firms, and medical institutions.

Mark P. Unterberg, M.D., is a board-certified psychiatrist and a fellow of the American Psychiatric Association. He is executive medical director of Green Oaks Hospital, Dallas, Texas, where he also directs a specialized inpatient unit for professionals and executives. In addition, he is clinical assistant professor of psychiatry at the University of Texas Southwestern Medical School. Besides private practice, he is director of the psychiatric department of the Cooper Clinic, team psychiatrist to the Dallas Cowboys football team, and senior analytic candidate at the Dallas Psychoanalytic Institute. Currently he is president-elect of the Academy of Organizational and Occupational Psychiatry, as well as vice president of the Texas district branch of the American Psychiatric Association.

David A. Van Liew, M.D., is president of Van Liew and Associates, a professional psychiatric service corporation in Seattle dedicated to maximizing personal and organizational development. His specialized practice emphasizes addressing conflicts of both individuals and companies from a practical, solution-oriented perspective. His ability to creatively solve people problems has earned him the respect of many clients in business and industry. His services have been retained by many professional organizations, including medicine, law, sports, and commerce. Van Liew is assistant clinical professor at the University of Washington, a board member of the Occupational Psychiatry Committee of the American Psychiatric Association, and a founding member of the Academy of Occupational and Organizational Psychiatry. He is also active in the Rotary, United Good Neighbors, Leadership Tomorrow, and the Chamber of Commerce. He finds that his penchant for painting vivid watercolors, coupled with a lively interest in the visual and expressive arts, has proved an effective means of averting depression.

MENTAL HEALTH
IN THE WORKPLACE

I

Problems in Adaptation: Symptoms, Reasons, and Treatment

1

Workplace Mental Health Problems: Recognition, Management, Assessment, and Treatment

Jeffrey P. Kahn, M.D.

ABSTRACT

Workplace mental health problems pose special challenges for management and human resource, occupational health, and mental health professionals. Recognition and management of emotional problems requires careful attention. Referral and proper initial evaluation of personal and organizational problems involves awareness of the complex and often hidden causes of surface symptoms. Once causal factors are identified, then defined treatment can effect helpful solutions. The many different types of therapy include educational, supportive, behavioral, cognitive, insight-oriented, organizational, and medication approaches. Basic principles of psychoanalytic thought are useful for understanding many of these approaches. Without considered attention, it can be hard to distinguish treatment response from treatment resistance. As with other organizational tasks, a thorough initial approach will reduce future costs and complications.

INTRODUCTION

The scientific principles that define psychiatric thought are not always obvious to the casual observer. Common belief often suggests that psychiatric illness is largely willful or hopeless. Psychiatric treatment is sometimes dismissed as nonspecific hand-holding, as based on outdated and rigid psychoanalytic theory, or else as inappropriate or abusive use of dangerous medications. Such views are reinforced by media representations of psychiatrists and other mental health professionals as treating only the most disturbed and untreatable patients, as themselves disturbed, or as unnecessarily confusing patients no more eccentric than themselves. And unfortunately, some of mental health care is truly much less than it could be.

Actually, psychiatric knowledge and skills have changed enormously since the work of Sigmund Freud and his predecessors. While Freud was perhaps the first to offer a systematic approach to understanding mental processes and underlying hidden emotions, there are few today who would directly emulate his specific techniques. Freud himself predicted that psychiatric knowledge would require an understanding of biological underpinnings, and even the most orthodox of psychoanalysts today would offer far more refined and flexible psychotherapeutic principles than Freud. Today's complex blend of scientific skills in diagnosis, psychotherapy, medicine, and medication use make it possible for patient and psychiatrist to resolve distressing problems. Syndromes once considered untreatable are now readily brought under the patient's control, often with short-term methods.

What does all this have to do with work? Well, psychiatry has focused much of its attention on interpersonal interactions and specific illnesses as the centerpiece of treatment. Less attention has been given to the personal meanings of work, and to the role of emotional issues in the workplace. In fact, while home life usually has a greater emotional significance to people, working people often spend more waking hours at the job than at home. And, workplace problems are to some extent determined by the emotions, personalities, and problems of the people who work there.

As companies adapt to changing markets, new economic conditions, and increasing work force diversity, mental health issues are easily overlooked until they cause overriding interpersonal, performance, or organizational problems. This oversight is not surprising, because emotional issues typically are more complex than they seem, involve hidden and deeply personal emotions, and can be uncomfortable to address. At first glance, they do not look like they can be understood, much less effectively resolved. And there are good reasons to avoid dealing directly with personal problems in the workplace. It is usually more appropriate for managers to address issues of work performance, and to suggest effective outside attention for contributory personal problems. Informed, specific, and empathic interventions benefit worker and company alike, and require scientific understanding of both people and their distress, and of organizational contexts and problems. Superficial attempts at remedy yield disappointingly superficial results.

RECOGNITION, MANAGEMENT, AND REFERRAL

Problems need to be recognized before they can be helped, and even that recognition can be a difficult task. Less enmeshed in the personal emotional turmoil, workplace colleagues and management often recognize problems before the family does. Problems at work will often show up only in such subtle ways as decreased productivity, ambition, quality, or interpersonal effectiveness. And larger scale problems of the organization itself can creep up gradually, invisible to management until the organizational effects are pressing or severe. The first step toward a remedy is to realize that a problem exists. Effective resolution also requires technical skill to know when and how to manage the problem, and when to look for outside help.

Management and Mental Health

Management plays many roles in fostering the emotional health of worker and workplace. Perhaps most of all, management structure and style defines interactions at all levels, and what sort of an emotional environment will exist (see Chapter 7). Recent years have seen increasing attention to the role of organizational structure on employee morale and productivity. Major emotional problems in managers themselves are sometimes obvious, but more subtle distress can alter the emotional culture of a division or of an entire company (see Chapter 6). Management also plays the largest role in determining mental health insurance benefits, and thus the availability and quality of mental health care for employees (see Chapter 2).

Managers are in a position to notice and point out employee and organizational problems that can be helped by treatment. They can create a climate where appropriate psychiatric care is encouraged, and its benefits recognized. Last, but not least, managers are in a position to counsel employees about performance problems in a way that points out any need for outside help. Many companies have a psychiatric consultant on call for emergencies, available for specific employee problems, and offering consultation on more general organizational concerns.

Human Resources and Mental Health

In most large companies, much of management's attention to employee mental health problems is through the Human Resources Department (commonly called Personnel in the past). Human Resources (HR) professionals help determine insurance coverage. They often play a major role in sorting out workplace problems, and in the development of improved organizational models. HR professionals are thus often the first to be presented with a distressed employee, a dysfunctional supervisor, or a problematic work area. Recognition and correction of problems is a difficult task, always further complicated by complex office politics. Still, HR in many companies is very well situated to help manage mental health issues, and often has established relationships with outside consultants.

Workplace Employee Counseling

Many companies offer limited counseling at the workplace, often through an employee assistance program (EAP; see Chapter 2). Counseling can cover issues that range from eldercare to substance abuse to financial planning to emotional problems. Such programs can help identify employees in particular distress and at risk, and are valuable benefits for those employees who use them. Many in-house programs have ongoing consultation arrangements with outside mental health providers. There are a few that have part-time psychiatrists who supervise or work directly with the program.

In-house programs must be very careful in what services they offer, and with what degree of training their staff has. There is a natural tendency to operate such programs at minimum cost, and with attention largely to immediate and obvious crises. Insufficient attention or professional skill often results in failures of assessment and treatment, and consequent increases in long-term costs. And prompt attention to less obvious problems can also be cost efficient in the long run. There can be real or perceived problems of conflict of interest and confidentiality when in-house treatment is provided by someone who works for the same employer (see Chapter 3).

Psychiatry in the Medical Department

Medical departments are another common site for presentation of emotional problems. Many large companies have medical departments that offer services that include employee examinations, disability reviews, urgent medical care, health promotion programs, and referral for quality medical treatment. Employees on disability or medical leave will commonly have concurrent depressive or anxiety disorders that often remain unrecognized and untreated (see Chapters 12 and 13). The emotional component can prolong absence from work long after an actual physical impairment has improved (see Chapters 5 and 18). A psychiatric consultant to the medical department can offer direct consultation and make treatment referrals. On-site consultation is often more acceptable to employees reporting physical symptoms or workplace causes. Even when an employee assistance program is in place, many employees will often make discreet requests for psychiatric referral through the medical department.

Outside Consultation

There are advantages and disadvantages to outside referral for consultation. The advantages lie largely in the availability of greater expertise and improved outcome, and in diminished concern about confidentiality and potential conflicts of interest. As with outside management consultants and advertising agencies, an outside psychiatric consultant may have a higher fee, but offer advantages in quality, independence from company politics, and reduced long-term costs. Effective consultation to any part of a company requires identification of skilled clinicians and a comfortable working relationship. The consultant must be able to conduct rapid and thorough assessments of functioning individuals in an organizational setting, must be able to communicate that understanding to employee or manager, and must be committed to preserving function in the workplace. In addition, it is imperative to know the difference between a consultation for the company and a confidential treatment relationship (see Chapter 3).

Barriers to Effective Treatment and Referral

Even with the best of intentions, it is often difficult to bring about effective referrals for treatment. The reasons are varied, but mostly not surprising.

Fears of Stigma, Employment Effects, and Punishment

For one thing, employees and managers are often afraid that seeking any sort of mental health care will stigmatize them and adversely affect their careers. In the midst of emotional distress, it is hard for people to realize that much of their concern may come from their own inner fears of rejection or of failure. And those inner fears are readily sensed by concerned managers and co-workers, who are naturally reluctant to seem insensitive. Employees with severe depressions can even convince others of the hopelessness of their situation, and therefore of the pointlessness of treatment. Employees who are especially sensitive may see a supervisor's suggestion as punitive rather than helpful. In reality, effective treatment will most often improve workplace performance and contentment, and psychotherapy is commonplace in the culture.

Low Treatment Expectations and Previous Ineffective Treatment

Even aside from low expectations that derive from the distress itself, employees, families, and managers may think that treatment will not help much. Low expectation can be caused by an absence of obviously treatable causes of distress. It can also be caused by a conscious conviction or wish that the distress has a single and emotionally acceptable cause, such as workplace unfairness or physical illness. In fact, emotional distress is usually multiply determined, and the major contributors are often inapparent. A careful diagnostic evaluation sorts out the various contributors, and allows for treatment that specifically addresses actual causes.

Low expectations can also stem from previously ineffective treatment and from awareness of the great variations in the quality of mental health care. Many clinicians are not as effective as they could be. Some have limited skills or training (or sometimes no training at all). Others' training or temperament lead them to stereotype illness and treatment. They fail to focus on individualized evaluation, diagnosis, and treatment (see Chapter 2). Employees are also sometimes more comfortable with treatments that reinforce beliefs in irremediable external causes for distress, but that offer only limited symptomatic improvement.

Concerns about Self-Reliance, Time, and Money

While effective treatment does require some commitment of emotional, financial, and time resources, magnified concerns about those costs can also reflect inner emotional concerns. For instance, many people think of themselves as self-reliant and find distasteful the idea of making an emotional investment in seeking help from someone else. While self-reliant abilities are generally adaptive, they can be used in self-defeating ways to deny emotional or adaptational problems. Exaggerated self-reliance reflects a heightened natural reluctance to address painful hidden fears and emotions. For instance, self-reliance can be a protection against hidden fears that other people are unreliable. Those fears can make employees feel that any attempt at resolving them will only make the fears come true. In a very similar way, people who would benefit from treatment can have disproportionate concerns about investing time and money in their emotional well-being. Any investment can seem unwise when there is a hidden expectation of certain disappointment.

Effective Management and Referral of Mental Health Problems

The art of effective management always involves understanding and responding to people's personal characteristics. In the case of mental health problems, the management issue is those personal characteristics themselves. Emotional problems at work can pose a dilemma for managers. On the one hand, there is a natural tendency to leave intense emotions untouched. And on the other hand, there is an equally natural urge to help the employee. In addition, there are corresponding managerial responsibilities to stay out of personal matters and to maximize employee performance. Emotional problems evident in the workplace are best addressed with discretion, respect for privacy, and with genuine concern. Every employee and circumstance is different, so the usefulness of the following suggestions differ for each case.

Timing is important, and it is never easy to tell the difference between early recognition of a real problem and exaggerated concern about a minor issue. Some basic considerations include evidence of significant emotional distress, maladaptation at work, or references to major personal problems or concerns. Often it is helpful just to ask an employee whether he or she would like to talk to someone about the problem. At other times, effective treatment referral requires skillful management.

Most important, people respond to empathic advice. Empathy reflects awareness of inner feelings and is not the same as sympathy for expressed concerns. The best approach is nonintrusive, nonthreatening, and nonconfrontational. Look for an opening in what employees say. When they refer to a problem, point out their concern about it. Even when other problems or causes are obvious, referrals are most readily accepted for conscious concerns, rather than for hidden causes, or for management's purposes. At the same time, though, indicate any specific workplace problems. Point out that all emotional distress is complex, and that careful psychiatric consultation can help sort out the details. Know that catch phrases like stress and burnout are useful shorthand that often reflect problems requiring a skillful initial evaluation. Major depression, panic disorder, and other common problems have medical causes, and should not be a cause for shame. Acceptance of a consultation does not require any commitment to treatment.

Be reassuring. Proper treatment does make problems better, and while genuine life problems may exist, emotional distress makes everything look even worse than the reality. Point out that therapy is confidential and commonplace. Note explicitly that referral is not evidence of rejection, a hopeless situation, or punishment. Be sensitive to the possibility of conscious or unwitting emotional reactions to employee distress. Depressed employees often leave other people sharing their hopelessness (see Chapter 12), while other employees may generate hostility toward themselves. Most of all, do not be frustrated if the employee cannot easily recognize a need for help.

Review available referral resources, what kinds of credentials to look for, and be aware of the advantages and disadvantages of the different kinds of treatments and clinicians. Where possible, offer flexible work schedules to accommodate treatment. Within legal and ethical limits, it is sometimes appropriate to use authority to encourage treatment. For instance, grossly disruptive or dysfunctional workplace behavior may require treatment to allow continued employment. Lesser problems may limit an employee's potential for future promotion. Such referrals can at first be colored by resentment that impedes treatment response. Ultimately, though, employees often feel grateful after effective treatment. Some problems are so serious or acute that intervention is mandatory. Employees with significant suicidal, violent, or psychotic features often need immediate attention, and perhaps police assistance during a crisis (see Chapter 10).

ASSESSMENT: DEFINE THE PROBLEM TO DEFINE THE TREATMENT

Effective solutions for medical, business, and emotional problems all require skillful assessment, detailed understanding, and focused implementation. All are multiply determined, but emotional problems nearly always involve unpleasant feelings that hide important causes from view.

Stress and Burnout

There is a natural reluctance to directly address intense feelings such as fear, sadness, and anger that typically underlie emotional distress and organizational dysfunction. Instead, less threatening words are more useful to describe certain kinds of problems in ordinary language. *Stress* is certainly the most familiar such word and has a variety of meanings. Perhaps most often, it is used as a catchall for forms and degrees of anxiety (see Chapter 12). But the useful vagueness of its meaning fails to convey useful understanding of the problem, and it also fails to differentiate unpleasant stress (*distress*) from less disagreeable pressures of work and circumstance (*eustress*).

Burnout, another familiar catch phrase, most commonly refers to various forms and degrees of depression (see Chapter 13). Here, too, ordinary language has found a less threatening word for a set of distressing problems. While these common phrases make initial recognition of emotional problems easier, effective resolution ultimately requires more careful assessment.

Complex and Obscure Causes of Maladaptation

The causes of emotional and adaptational problems are always more complex than they appear. Feeling unhappy at home, for instance, individual employees may be more readily aware of long work hours or interpersonal conflicts at the office. The more pressing family concerns are too overwhelming to really think about (see Chapter 11). In fact, people sometimes get so wrapped up in what otherwise might be a minor concern, that they become almost unaware of things that really distress or frighten them. This shifting of attention is common, especially when past emotional experiences leave the belief that family problems are essentially unresolvable. The reverse shift is equally common, as in the common metaphor of "kicking the dog" in response to unacceptable angry feelings toward the boss.

Finding the true causes of distress is a complex and demanding process that is essential for gaining control of feelings and solving problems. People may be aware of some causes for their distress, but ferreting out others requires careful assessment of personal history, experience, and style. Distressed employees usually have experienced a recent event of emotional significance. Both positive and negative life events can be significant, including family births, deaths, marriages, and retirements. The most emotionally important events are often overlooked ("You mean I never told you that my best friend died last month?"), hidden ("Our relationship hasn't changed in three years. Well, okay, so now he's pressing me to marry him."), or their significance denied ("How could a new baby bring anything but happiness?"). Similarly, people are largely unaware of personality traits that can contribute to their distress. Because the traits were a way of adapting to early emotional environments, people are not aware when those traits sometimes cause problems in adulthood (see Chapter 14).

An employee may deliberately overemphasize specific issues in an honest attempt to make sure that they are not disregarded. For example, fears of stigma, or honest belief that work factors caused disability can lead an employee to focus only on workplace issues (see Chapter 5). Unscrupulous employees may deliberately hide details so as to mask substance abuse (see Chapters 15 and 16), hide dishonest behavior, or abuse disability entitlements.

Deliberate and skilled effort is needed to make accurate psychiatric diagnoses in both medical and psychosocial contexts. Patients with common syndromes such as major depression or panic disorder will not usually present themselves specifically for treatment of those conditions. Instead, their conscious concerns will be about distressing events in their lives. Faced with any depressive or anxiety disorder, psychiatrists will routinely take a brief medical history and, if necessary, arrange for further medical evaluation. Medical problems themselves can be present with emotional symptoms, or with exacerbation of existing emotional problems (see Chapter 18).

Psychiatrists also need to evaluate the organizational culture and the more specific work context of an individual's distress. Organizations are collections of people with complicated goals, motivations, and methods. While an employee who feels stymied in his or her career may have disadvantageous personality traits or mixed feelings about advancement, consultants must acknowledge the organizational context as well as hidden organizational impediments (see Chapter 9).

Organizations can be highly political and do not always operate on meritocratic, rational, or even obvious principles (see Chapter 7). Problems of the organization itself are also demanding to assess. While the emotions and goals of key individuals are always important, much of the problem can lie in corporate culture, idiosyncratic group process, or changing economic circumstances.

Value of Defined Treatment

Specific evaluation is important because it allows for carefully defined treatment. The most effective approaches for individual and organizational problems are those that resolve underlying causes. While not all such problems require resolution of underlying causes, it is always useful to know what those causes are, and it is essential to know the difference between treatment of causes and treatment of symptoms. Nonspecific treatments for individuals (such as relaxation therapy and some kinds of support groups) can offer some temporary relief of symptoms, but leave unaddressed the underlying family problems, work conflicts, or significant medical psychiatric problems (such as anxiety disorders). Specific treatments include psychotherapy aimed at uncovering sources of distress and overreaction, problem solving to facilitate adaptation, and medication for some syndromes that are not treated well by psychotherapy alone. Organizational programs that encourage effective communication and appropriate workplace interactions can stimulate individual problem solving and recognition of personal dysfunction. Sometimes just the process of careful evaluation will make underlying causes more apparent, and thus effect a partial resolution of the immediate problem.

The DSM-III-R Diagnostic System

Personality and adaptability are a result of thoughts and feelings derived from experience. Illness is the dysfunction that occurs when adaptation fails in the face of internal or external change. Diagnosis simply defines the nature of dysfunctions that can include adjustment, anxiety, and depressive or personality disorders. Historically, psychiatric diagnosis has sometimes been viewed as vague, nonspecific, and of limited practical value. Since the early 1980s, though, the *Diagnostic and Statistical Manual of Mental Disorders,* third edition, now revised (DSM-III and DSM-III-R; developed by the American Psychiatric Association) has become a standard for psychiatric diagnosis. DSM-III-R criteria allow emotional diagnoses to have specific meanings and clearer implications for treatment and prognosis (see the chapters in Part III of this volume). By design, DSM-III-R describes discreetly recognizable syndromes and avoids reliance on psychodynamic, biological, and sociological theories. The continuing efforts at diagnostic specificity have led to greater knowledge about the psychotherapeutic and medication responsiveness of diagnoses, and have spurred interest in still further improvements. DSM-IV is currently in preparation.

DSM-III-R has become an invaluable tool for the recognition and treatment of both mild and severe emotional problems. It is not, however, a replacement for clinical skills in general, or knowledge of individual, family, and organizational interactions in particular. And diagnosis itself is not as important in predicting future functioning as are an individual's ability to recognize and tolerate distress, and to seek and accept emotional support and the most effective treatment.

TREATMENT: TECHNIQUES OF PSYCHOTHERAPY AND CONSULTATION

Psychotherapy can be many different things, but it is always based on a therapeutic relationship that is intended to address emotional distress or maladaptive traits. There are many varieties of psychotherapeutic ideology, and no matter how hard they tried, no two therapists could use exactly the same technique. Within limits, variety in technique allows therapists to find effective approaches that mesh with their own personalities, and with those of their patients. Selecting a therapist or consultant requires attention to diagnostic and psychotherapeutic training, ability, and integrity (see Chapter 2). Depending on the nature of the problem, treatment goals, economic constraints, and individual preference, there are many different psychotherapeutic approaches that are commonly used.

Education: Awareness Programs and Stress Management

All psychotherapy is education of a sort, and some problems call for a straightforward didactic approach. For instance, there are often educational programs in the workplace that increase awareness of problems such as depression and substance abuse. The goal of the program is to increase knowledge and recognition of the problem, with the intent of encouraging early treatment. Many stress management programs also use an educational approach. Increased awareness of the stresses of work, family, and holidays allows some relief. Other common techniques include relaxation therapy and biofeedback. Such approaches can be beneficial for mild situational anxiety that is largely related to a specific stressor, but should not be a replacement for focused assessment.

Support: Counseling and Self-Help Groups

Supportive counseling and self-help groups may include problem recognition, advice about specific problems, and direction to available community resources. They can be useful for guidance through a stressful period. In contrast to purely educational approaches, the process of discussing a practical problem and its solutions offers indirect emotional support from a therapist or from other group members. Supportive approaches are most useful for helping people adapt in crisis situations (such as initial treatment after a major trauma), for long-term support (such as people with chronic illness that make stable adaptation difficult, or who prefer supportive therapy), and for group interventions (such as large numbers of employees who need to address shared concerns about organizational change). Some self-help groups offer this kind of support, while others focus more simply on members' mutual troubles.

Supportive therapies are not designed to address or recognize underlying emotional, medical, or organizational problems. Supportive therapy is not a replacement for more reflective therapy. But, its more limited goals can improve individual adaptation where distress is overwhelming, or where a more limited approach is initially preferred. Effectiveness depends on the skill of the therapist and the receptiveness of the patient. The most distressed patients are often least able to feel emotionally supported, while less distressed patients may feel frustrated by the circumscribed approach. It is not always easy to give useful advice. Most people are intelligent and knowledgable enough to look for solutions to their interpersonal problems. When they are unaware of practical solutions, it may be because their emotions have unwittingly hidden solutions from view. Helping people to overcome their emotions and use suggested solutions is a challenging task in supportive therapy.

Surface Behavior and Thought:
Behavioral and Cognitive Therapy

Behavior therapy focuses on problematic external behaviors and attempts to modify them through instruction and practice of new behavioral techniques. For example, a behavioral approach to an elevator phobia in a patient with panic disorder might attempt progressively longer periods of time in an open elevator, leading ultimately to an elevator ride. Strictly applied, behavioral approaches do not directly address underlying emotions or associated psychiatric syndromes. The hope is that tolerating unpleasant feelings in small doses will allow the maladaptive behavior to cease.

Cognitive therapy focuses on reworking unrealistic thoughts (*cognitive distortions*) that are associated with emotional distress and maladaptive behaviors. For instance, a cognitive approach to depression would involve identification of recurring thoughts of worthlessness and hopelessness, and an attempt to replace them with more rationally accurate thoughts of self worth and future possibility. In its pure form, cognitive therapy also does not attempt to directly address underlying emotions or associated psychiatric syndromes. Rather, the focus is on developing adaptive new cognitions. Behavior therapy and cognitive therapy are often used together. Recent research has suggested that such approaches may have benefits for some depressive and anxiety disorders.

Relationship Patterns and Inner Emotions: Insight-Oriented Therapy

Insight-oriented psychotherapy is a more thorough form of psychotherapy, often used for patients who already have generally high levels of social functioning. Low-functioning patients, and those in severe acute distress, are less likely to benefit from the goal of understanding the hidden long-term emotional determinants of their relationship patterns. In some cases, looking for such feelings can increase distress and dysfunction. The names for the many different forms of insight-oriented therapy are derived largely from psychoanalytic theories, but they can be very similar in clinical practice. As a group, they are also called psychoanalytic, psychodynamic, and uncovering psychotherapies.

In contemporary psychiatric practice, insight-oriented psychotherapy is often combined with other forms of therapy for specific purposes. Supportive therapy may be used just after an emotional crisis, or behavior therapy used for phobic avoidance. Medication may be used for problems where psychotherapy alone is not fully effective (such as panic disorder and social phobia), or where its benefits are not reliable, prompt, or complete (such as major depression). Insight-oriented therapy relies on a set of basic concepts and techniques. The further significance of these concepts for organizational interactions is discussed elsewhere in this volume (see Chapter 7).

Session Frequency and Goals of Insight-Oriented Psychotherapy

The extent to which psychoanalytic techniques are used depends on the nature of the insight-oriented therapy employed. Generally speaking, more intensive forms are suitable for patients who are already psychologically minded and functioning at least reasonably well. Formal psychoanalysis is an intensive treatment for certain deep-seated personality problems. Typically conducted four times per week on a couch, treatment may last for several years. Only a few patients opt for this major commitment of time, money, and emotional effort. Psychoanalytic psychotherapy is conducted once or twice a week. While using similar basic principles, the goal is limited to uncovering maladaptive emotions and perceptions that are hidden from conscious awareness. Recent years have seen the increasing use of short-term psychotherapy. These ten- to twenty-session treatments are primarily aimed at short-term crisis resolution. In addition, similar principles are essential to understanding even the most supportive psychotherapy.

Treatment should not continue indefinitely. Rather, certain goals are sought, and a continuing process of reevaluation is part of the treatment itself. At a certain point in time, continuing benefits for the patient are outweighed by the costs, and a specific termination phase of therapy is started. That does not mean that therapy should stop any time the question comes up. In fact, the question will often arise at exactly those times when anxiety rises as important issues start to emerge. Care must be taken not to see these signs of impending therapeutic progress as evidence for termination of therapy.

Emotional Development, Unconscious Expectation, and Conflict

Basically, people grow up in some particular emotional environment, usually their biological family. From their early relationships, they unconsciously acquire direct and indirect expectations about what relationships are like and about how best to interact with other people. These expectations derive from experience and observation of family behavior, and from inner experience of personal emotional reactions. The expectations remain unconsciously present into adulthood; they color perceptions of other people and they influence behavior and emotion. Without realizing it, all people thus have certain expectations about what the world is like and are limited in their ability to see people and situations for what they really are. Depending on the strength and kind of these unconscious expectations, they can have detrimental effects on social adaptation and on emotional well-being. An example might be a manager who has trouble completing a prestigious project because he unwittingly fears the envy of his peers. The fear may derive from his experience of envious siblings in childhood. It may also derive from projection onto peers of his own defiant anger about anticipated lack of recognition. Similarly, avoidance of success may be an unconscious attempt at avoiding punishment from a powerful authority figure. Such concerns about intergenerational competition (*oedipal conflict*) are particularly well known in psychoanalytic and popular culture (see Chapter 6).

Transference and Countertransference

People experience varying degrees of unconscious expectation and feeling with all other people, and they can have relationship problems as a result. In the particular setting of psychotherapy, persistent expectations and feelings can become focused on the therapist (*transference*), without any real basis in the therapeutic relationship itself. In the psychotherapeutic setting, transference can be more readily recognized and understood than in social relationships. The psychotherapeutic relationship is designed to allow transferential expectations and feelings to become evident and therapeutically useful. Transference thus becomes a major tool in understanding the hidden factors that adversely influence relationships.

Therapists, too, have hidden expectations and feelings in the therapeutic setting (*countertransference*). For this reason, psychotherapy training programs always include direct individual supervision. Programs should also include a primary focus on keeping trainees constantly aware of their own inappropriate expectations and feelings that would otherwise impose limitations on psychotherapeutic progress. Many psychiatric resident and other training programs encourage trainees to complete a formal personal psychoanalysis. Such treatment is a requirement for psychoanalytic certification.

Defense, Resistance, Interpretation, and Insight

Since hidden emotional dilemmas (*unconscious conflicts*) can be distressing, people develop a variety of unwitting mechanisms (*psychological defenses*) to protect themselves from emotional pain. For example, repression is a process of removing a painful thought from awareness (such as failure to remember childhood sadness or angry impulses). Counterphobia involves attempts at conquering a feared situation in order to hide the fear itself from awareness (such as hidden competitive fears of success leading to ever more intense drive for accomplishment). These two mechanisms are among the mature defenses that are ordinary parts of adult personality function. Recent decades have also seen increasing attention to other defenses that protect against more primitive fears of an overwhelmingly inattentive world. Splitting, for instance, seeing all people as either all good or all bad, is a way of avoiding a perception of rejection by everyone.

These emotional defenses also operate within the psychotherapeutic setting (*resistance*). Resistance is the largely unwitting process of keeping transferential feelings toward the therapist out of awareness. From one perspective, psychoanalytic process involves an empathic and progressive interpretation of resistance. The process thus allows awareness of transferential expectations and feelings, corresponding hidden emotional dilemmas, and painful childhood experiences. At the same time, other current relationships are examined for evidence of similar emotional and behavioral patterns. The same patterns are reviewed many times, and from different perspectives (*working through*). As a result, there is increased awareness of relationship patterns and their emotional determinants (*insight*). Newly alerted to unwitting expectations and feelings, patients feel less distressed and more able to change their circumstances and relationships. Introspective self-awareness, in contrast to insight, rarely brings either the same kind of emotional relief or the capacity for personal change.

Therapeutic Alliance, Neutrality, Advice, Free Association, and Dreams

As therapy begins, one of the first tasks is development of a therapeutic alliance. Therapy is not a social relationship, and the therapeutic alliance calls for recognition of the therapist's role in offering insight into self-defeating unconscious expectations and feelings. In that capacity, the therapist maintains therapeutic neutrality. This does not mean neutrality toward the well-being of the patient. Rather, the therapist is neutral toward patients' conflicting hidden motivations. The assumption is made that inability to make choices is usually a function of unconscious emotional conflict. Understanding those conflicts is the most important goal, and specific practical advice is sometimes counterproductive. Instead, attempts are made to uncover the emotional dilemma and to allow comfortable conscious decisions to emerge. When advice is given, or other deliberate breaks in therapeutic neutrality occur (*parameters*), there are specific emotional meanings for patients that should be understood. For instance, some patients might feel that they are not permitted to solve their own problems.

Once therapy is underway, patients are encouraged to say whatever comes to mind, no matter how irrelevant, disconnected, painful, or silly it might seem (*free association*). The idea is that a common emotional thread ties the thoughts together, and that free association allows recognition and interpretation of that thread. Since this process is so different from normal social conversation, it takes some effort and practice. Difficulty in free association also reflects expectations and feelings about the therapist and thus also becomes useful information for the therapy. The therapist allows free association and transference to emerge by saying comparatively little and by maintaining an attentive nonjudgemental attitude. Dreams are another source of useful information in this type of therapy. Since dreams are put together by the mind (presumably for some physiologic purpose), they symbolically reflect the kinds of relationship patterns that people unwittingly perceive in the world around them. There are no textbook or mystical explanations for dreams. The patterns of the dream become clear in the overall context of relationships, but particularly those in childhood, family, and the therapy itself.

Career Enhancement: Executive Development

While the process of psychotherapy can offer many kinds of personal advantages, one particular area of interest is career success and satisfaction. Transference, emotional conflict, and personality style have major effects in the workplace. There are many different psychotherapeutic methods of enhancing career development (see Chapter 9). They range from educational models that are like business courses, to supportive advice and mentoring models, to a form that has become known as executive coaching. This last approach will often rely on both standardized skill assessment and on a modified form of psychotherapy. While many of the techniques are similar to insight-oriented psychotherapy, there are important differences. Less attention is paid to inner emotional life, and more to the effects of expectations, feelings, and behaviors on business skills and relationships. Executive coaching is sometimes preferred by people who are primarily interested in improving their management or sales skills. At the same time, though, resulting career benefits may be accompanied by heightened tension. That tension is often responsive to appropriate interpretation and may thus lead to further benefits beyond career advancement alone.

Organizational Development:
Organizational Consulting

There are also emotional and interpersonal factors that affect the organization as a whole, and that managers may recognize as needing outside consultation. On the largest scale, there are often concerns about issues of organizational structure (see Chapter 7), especially in times of change. For example, changing external circumstances can include increased competition, shifting customer preferences, or a major lawsuit. Changing internal organizational circumstances include mergers and acquisitions, growth, and downsizing (see Chapter 8). Stagnation in the face of change is a problem that needs attention. There are also many smaller scale issues, including team building, conflict resolution, fostering "intrapreneurship" and creativity, succession planning, and general aspects of employee motivation and management.

Addressing these problems requires a wide variety of psychiatric skills. Behavioral approaches are useful for understanding surface effects of performance evaluation and promotional systems. Psychometric approaches use interviews and questionnaires to develop a detailed perspective on management and interactional problems. Group process and family systems theory are useful in further understanding interactions within the organization. More psychodynamic approaches help explore and improve management and employee morale and motivations. True employee empowerment comes about through creation of a healthy organizational culture. But any change in emotional environment can be threatening to entrenched interests and to hidden emotions. Changing organizational culture is a true challenge for managers and consultants. Perhaps most important, a psychiatric perspective is essential for understanding the organizational and individual behavior of key personnel. Consultation to an organization often results in identification and referral of a distressed executive. Sometimes the distress is most obvious through its organizational effects (see Chapter 6).

Medication and Therapy

Optimal treatment of emotional problems often requires more than psychotherapy alone, and the importance of adding medication is not always obvious. For instance, there are several common syndromes that psychotherapy alone does not treat well, and that respond much better when appropriate medication is added. Notable among these are chronic low-grade problems such as dysthymia, panic disorder, social phobia, and obsessive compulsive disorder (see Chapters 12 and 13). These problems can be easily overlooked, unless specific history is sought by a skilled clinician. Ineffective psychotherapies commonly result from failure to diagnose and treat such conditions. Major depression is a more acute syndrome, which may show a delayed, partial, or unreliable response to psychotherapy alone. Recent studies have shown that the fastest and most complete response is achieved through combined medication and psychotherapy. The need for medication is most obvious in patients with overt mania or psychosis (see Chapter 17).

The process of prescribing medication for emotional problems is complex. Even beyond issues of careful diagnosis, specific and adequate treatment, and medication side effects, there are issues of the emotional meaning of the medication itself. The medication is seen both consciously and unconsciously in many different ways. It can be seen as a gift, a penalty, an opportunity, or an impediment. Some patients will jump at the chance to use medication instead of psychotherapy, while others will fear that medication will be a "crutch" that prevents self-reliance or psychotherapeutic benefit. Most patients will react to effective medication with relief, although some will experience that relief mixed with anxiety and even treatment non-compliance.

Appropriate medication is not usually an alternative to some equally effective psychotherapy. Specific medications should be used for specific syndromes. They should not be used just because psychotherapy does not seem to be working, because a patient is considered hopeless, or because of some feelings toward the patient of which the therapist is not aware. And neither should medication be withheld because of some need to make psychotherapy work where it cannot, failure or inability to recognize medication responsive syndromes, or some unwitting feelings toward the patient. Psychotherapy and medication work together, each of them primarily addressing symptoms unresponsive to the other. Once medication-responsive syndromes are treated, patients often find it easier to understand the emotional issues that confront them and find solutions for their practical and interpersonal problems.

ASSESSING TREATMENT AND CONSULTATION RESPONSE

Just as optimal psychiatric evaluation and treatment require focused approaches, assessing treatment response requires equally careful attention. Changes are often gradual or subtle. And, people do not usually tell co-workers when symptoms or conflicts are newly improved, nor should they. Only occasionally is it appropriate for colleagues or supervisors to receive direct feedback from a treating psychiatrist (see Chapter 2). So, though subtle improvements are easy to overlook, it is important for everyone to recognize workplace changes when they occur.

Employee Changes: Symptoms, Demeanor, Style, and Family

Some changes are relatively easy to see. For instance, return to work after a major depression or the absence of intoxication on the job are evidence of symptomatic improvement. But even for those more overt problems, improvement may become evident only as subtle changes in demeanor. The always reserved but now depressed worker who stays on the job may seem only more reserved than usual. When the depression resolves (typically after three weeks of medication), he or she will seem more alert and well rested. Less obvious to co-workers will be the resolution of unremitting sadness, insomnia, and suicidal thoughts. Similarly, the alcoholic worker who had always been sober on the job may show a subtle decrease in irritability once he or she stops drinking.

More subtle still are changes in interpersonal style. These kinds of changes can occur gradually after treatment of chronic mild depressive and anxiety disorders, and after effective insight-oriented psychotherapy. Subtle style changes are followed by gradual self-awareness and gradual recognition by others. For instance, an employee with social phobia might have been tense and withdrawn in meetings, and even at lunch. Initial treatment effects might include relief of the tension. Only later is there greater social interaction, and increasingly comfortable efforts at meeting participation. And when those changes do occur, it may take a while before anyone recognizes them.

Personality changes through psychotherapy are often the most subtle of all. Insight-oriented psychotherapy has the potential for gradually effecting substantial change in rigid and self-defeating styles (see Chapter 14). Even once change has occurred, it may take close attention to see that personality style has become more flexible, and that workplace interactions have become more productive. Effective treatment benefits family life as well. Those changes will typically be inapparent at work, although often with secondary benefits for workplace functioning.

Workplace Changes: Productivity, Decisions, Interactions, and Leadership

Beyond benefits for the individual worker, personal treatment and organizational consultation can bring about changes for the organization as a whole. Some changes are readily apparent. For instance, treatment or consultation can produce changes in productivity, reductions in infighting, or beneficial organizational streamlining. But less tangible changes can have just as important effects on the workplace. Careful observation is needed to recognize such benefits as wise planning, recognition of both short- and long-term effects of decisions, effective management style, and visionary leadership. The better people feel inside about themselves and their work, the better the job they will do for themselves, co-workers, and the organization as a whole. At the same time, there are limits to the benefits that can accrue. Productivity, decisions, interactions and leadership are functions of individuals, organizational structure and style, and of external economic and social factors.

Treatment Resistance and Entrenched Reputation

When people do not seem to get better, there are many possible explanations. Commonly, there is real improvement that is not very apparent. Sometimes people even have trouble seeing improvement in themselves. For instance, shortly after resolution of a depression, some hopeless thoughts may persist despite a more cheerful mood. Or a pessimistic outlook makes outward acknowledgment of improvement uncomfortable. Within an organization, people often develop entrenched reputations. Even when there is definite change in both acute problems and long-term style, the old reputation can linger. The same is true for changing the organization. Even if effective changes are brought about, plainly the old images may linger for a while within the organization, and longer still to customers on the outside.

It is important to allow enough time for treatment to work. Medications might take effect in days or weeks (sometimes months), but psychotherapy is often more gradual. Still, treatment quality varies considerably, and questions about ineffectiveness are sometimes appropriate. In those cases where contact with the clinician is appropriate, his or her opinion and the employee's can be sought. Alternatively, there are some situations where a consultation with a nontreating psychiatrist can provide useful reevaluation of diagnosis, treatment, and prognosis. When treatment does not seem to be going well, there are certain kinds of questions to keep in mind.

Incorrect Diagnosis, Therapy, or Goals

The first question is whether there was a complete and accurate evaluation before treatment began. Frequently, important problems are overlooked. For example, treatment might have focused on reducing stress in the office when problems at home were a more pressing issue. Or, depressive or anxiety disorders may have gone undiagnosed and untreated. It is also possible that the treatment used was unsuited for the goals at hand, or that the therapist is insufficiently skilled. For instance, supportive therapy may not be sufficient for helping to uncover and change maladaptive personality styles. Also, insight-oriented therapy by itself may not be sufficient for acute family crises, sudden job loss, or panic disorder. And even appropriate medication, without psychotherapy, is usually insufficient for most problems. Less frequently, treatment may be impaired by noncompliance or by deliberate misrepresentation.

Family, Organizational, Medication, or Medical Problems

Even if the evaluation and treatment seem appropriate, there may be other factors that keep progress at a minimum. For instance, families often develop habitual patterns of interaction that can impede progress. As the employee starts to feel better, relatives may unwittingly protect the family structure by discouraging further change. The same thing can happen within an organization, where people get used to certain patterns of behavior. When a colleague starts to feel or act differently, that demeanor threatens the organizational equilibrium. Similarly, when efforts are made to change the organization itself, individuals will feel threatened and resist the change.

Both mild and serious medication-responsive symptoms are often overlooked, and their treatment can require specific expertise. Different kinds or combinations of medication are often tried, and proper integration with psychotherapy is important. Medical illness is commonly mistaken for emotional problems. Even demoralization at work can sometimes be a surface presentation of undetected illnesses such as thyroid disease, anemia, and many others.

SUMMARY

Understanding and resolving mental health problems in the workplace requires careful attention by management, human resource, occupational health, and mental health professionals. Both individual and organizational problems have multiple causes, some of which may be hidden from casual observation. Referral for proper initial evaluation calls for special knowledge and skills. Once underlying causal factors are identified, then defined treatment can effect helpful solutions. The many different types of therapy include educational, supportive, behavioral, cognitive, insight-oriented, organizational, and medication approaches. These approaches are often combined, and basic principles of psychoanalytic thought are useful for understanding many of them. Once treatment is underway, special attention is needed to assess changes in workplace performance. The best results and lowest long-term costs are obtained through careful initial assessment, followed by optimal treatment.

Bibliography
American Psychiatric Association. 1987. *Diagnostic and Statistical Manual of Mental Disorders,* 3d ed. rev. Washington, D.C.: American Psychiatric Association.
American Psychiatric Association. 1989. *Treatments of Psychiatric Disorders.* Washington, D.C.: American Psychiatric Association.
Beitman, Bernard D., and Gerald L. Klerman. 1991. *Integrating Pharmacotherapy and Psychotherapy.* Washington, D.C.: American Psychiatric Press.
Bernstein, Anne E., and Gloria Marmar Warner. 1981. *An Introduction to Contemporary Psychoanalysis.* New York: Jason Aronson.
McLean, Alan A. 1979. *Work Stress.* Reading, Mass.: Addison Wesley.
Schatzberg, Alan F., and Jonathan O. Cole (eds.). 1991. *Manual of Clinical Psychopharmacology,* 2d ed. Washington, D.C.: American Psychiatric Press.
Sperry, Len. 1993. *Psychiatric Consultation in the Workplace.* Washington, D.C.: American Psychiatric Press.

2

Mental Health Care: Providers, Delivery Systems, and Cost Containment

Anne Stoline, M.D., and Steven Sharfstein, M.D.

ABSTRACT

A variety of professionals are available within the mental health care system for employees who seek or need mental health evaluation. Choice of health care provider will depend on the employee's particular problem, as well as goals for the evaluation or treatment. Selecting a provider will be constrained by financial considerations, including whether or not the employee has mental health insurance benefits. Some health insurance programs constrain provider selection. Employees without mental health insurance benefits can receive evaluation or treatment in the public-sector mental health care system. Rising health care expenditures motivated third-party payers, including government, corporations, and insurance companies, to implement cost-containment approaches, including programs to oversee resource use. Many managed care systems and employee assistance programs (EAPs) employ gatekeepers (with variable training) to regulate use of mental health care resources. These oversight methods have uncertain effects on quality of care. Their potential impact on employees' care are described, as are methods for coping with their negative effects.

INTRODUCTION

Employers may wish to refer a troubled employee for mental health evaluation or treatment, at which point they will confront the complex and diverse U.S. mental health care system. This chapter provides basic information about the types of health care professionals available to perform mental health evaluations and to provide treatment. Psychiatrists, psychologists, and social workers are described in greater detail than are others in the field. The employer who is aware of the training, educational philosophy, unique skills, and scope of practice of each type of professional is better able to make an appropriate referral.

The U.S. mental health care system is funded through myriad sources, including government programs, private insurance companies, and out-of-pocket payment from individuals. Many people receive insurance coverage through their place of employment, whereby the employer becomes the payer either directly (with self-insurance) or indirectly (through an insurance company).

The private sector has various reimbursement mechanisms, including the traditional method of fee-for-service (FFS), discounted FFS such as preferred provider organizations (PPOs), and prospective arrangements such as health maintenance organizations (HMOs). Employees without insurance coverage pay for mental health care services out-of-pocket.

There are a number of alternatives for those who are unable to afford these costs. The public mental health care sector includes a network of state hospitals for inpatient care. State and local clinics provide income-adjusted outpatient care to the population. In large cities such as New York, city-funded hospital clinics provide low-fee care to the poor. Private agencies, often run by religious groups, are another low-fee alternative found in most urban areas. Additional sources of reduced-fee care include teaching clinics staffed by physicians in training, research clinics treating people with designated conditions, and psychoanalytic training institutes. These services are sought by the uninsured, including those whose traditional policy does not include mental health care or who exhaust their mental health coverage.

The provision of mental health care in the United States has been heavily influenced in the 1980s and 1990s by a crisis in health care costs that has been caused by a number of factors, including general price inflation, an aging and expanding population, and the inflationary incentives of FFS reimbursement. Specific to the mental health care sector, inpatient adolescent units and treatment of substance abuse are the main additional causes of rising expenditures. Greater use of these services reflects increases in societal stress from a relative breakdown in family structure, as well as a weakening of church and work relationships that formerly provided channels for handling personal problems. A growth of for-profit hospitals is a result, many of which specialize in these services.

The health care cost crisis motivated payers to implement a number of cost-containment strategies. These include restrictions on health insurance benefits, in many cases resulting in severe constraints on mental health care coverage. Cost sharing by employees has been increased, usually with greater copayments and deductibles for mental health care than for other conditions.

Several methods of resource management at the level of the patient/provider encounter have been implemented. These include case management, gatekeeper programs, and utilization review. The effects of these programs on mental health care are explored in this chapter. Through this discussion of the U.S. mental health care system from the perspective of its care providers, payment, and current oversight methods, it is hoped that the employer will be able to optimize treatment choices for the troubled employee.

PROVIDERS

A wide variety of health care professionals are available within the mental health care system. Care is provided in diverse settings. Selecting a professional will depend on the employee's particular problem, as well as on the goals of evaluation or treatment. In today's era of managed care, gatekeepers often refer employees to mental health care providers. Many gatekeepers tend to have minimal (if any) clinical training. This is a problem because whoever refers a troubled employee with a low mood *should* be able to distinguish between major depression, demoralization, and other possible underlying emotional and medical conditions. Distinguishing these causes of low mood will affect the selection of an appropriate professional to evaluate the employee. In selecting a professional, it is often best to rely on the quality and depth of training, as well as on an impressionistic opinion of the person's skills.

Substitutability of the various provider types is a hotly debated issue because little basic research to compare treatment outcomes between various providers has been done. A gatekeeper may be charged with finding the most economical provider, allowing quality of care to be a secondary concern (if that). Similarly, little information is available about the benefits of the different types of treatment (such as those endorsed by the various schools of psychotherapy). However, lack of data does not mean that a certain therapy is ineffective, but instead may reflect the difficulty inherent in studying this type of treatment. In fact, studies of psychotherapy reveal its economic benefits (reflected in improved productivity and lower costs of other types of medical care), in addition to its clinical benefits.

Clergy, social welfare agencies, teachers, and medical care providers without specialized training in mental health may interact with a troubled employee. However, this chapter focuses on those professionals who typically provide initial clinical evaluation. Other professionals may be called on as specialized services are needed, including marital and family counselors, expressive art therapists, occupational therapists, group therapists, vocational rehabilitation counselors, and nurses.

Each type of education in mental health has a particular emphasis, which then partly characterizes the professionals it prepares to provide mental health care. There are also areas common to every mental health professional, as the following discussion highlights. To varying extents, the knowledge of all mental health professionals broadens and deepens with time, clinical experience, and contact with other health care professionals.

The issue of market value influences the decision process. While psychiatric care is sometimes more expensive than care by other mental health professionals, higher price generally reflects higher perceived quality. The concept of "doing it right the first time" also applies. Without realizing it, those with lesser training may be in over their head on a particular case, not recognizing their own clinical limitations. At risk is the lack of recognition by a lesser-trained professional of the need for more sophisticated psychotherapeutic approaches, the need for medication, or the presence of a medical or psychiatric diagnosis. False starts delay or prevent effective treatment, while increasing eventual total cost. It is incumbent upon all health care professionals to know their limitations and to refer to or consult with another clinician when appropriate.

Psychiatrists

A psychiatrist is a physician, and has thus obtained an undergraduate degree with a number of basic science course requirements, followed by medical school where the M.D. or D.O. degree is obtained. Extensive patient care and medical skills are developed in this training, under the supervision of both experienced physicians and those in residency training. The physician then spends 4 years in postgraduate specialty training in an approved psychiatry residency program. The overall length of training before independent practice is at least 8 years after the undergraduate degree is obtained.

Psychiatrists are the only mental health specialists with medical school training. As a result, they have a number of unique skills, including the education required to prescribe medications. They are trained to recognize and treat unsuspected organic or physical causes of mental disorders. Of all the mental health professionals, they receive the most training in diagnosing mental disorders through a systematic examination of the patient's thoughts, emotions, mental life, and relationships. This process of systematic conversation, known as the mental status examination, is in many ways analogous to physical examination of the body. Psychiatrists are extensively trained to perform individual, group, and family psychotherapy. Psychotherapy training includes academic course work, supervised clinical experience, seminars, and often personal psychotherapy.

Many elect to seek further training within specific areas of psychiatry in a fellowship. Potential areas of specialization include psychopharmacology (the use of medications), geriatrics, forensics (concerning psychiatry and the law), research, psychotherapy, addictions, consultation liaison (evaluating inpatients on medical and surgical units with suspected psychiatric conditions), and child/adolescent psychiatry. Some fellows focus on the treatment of a particular disease, such as depression or eating disorders: Such work is often combined with basic scientific research on the condition. Psychiatrists may undergo an extended training to practice psychoanalysis, a form of intensive psychotherapy. Many psychiatrists undergo personal psychoanalysis to further enhance their own psychotherapeutic skills.

Psychiatrists are credentialed at a number of steps in the educational process. During medical school and residency they must pass either the National Board Exams or the Federation Licensing Examination (FLEX), both of which encompass basic science knowledge and general clinical knowledge. Passage of one of these tests permits the physician to qualify for licensure by the state to practice medicine. State requirements for licensure vary. In order to remain licensed, physicians must complete a predetermined number of hours of continuing medical education (earning CME credits toward recertification).

One year after completing residency, psychiatrists may take an optional two-stage board certification exam that includes written and oral components. The latter requires interviewing a patient, followed by an examination of the results of the interview with two board-certified psychiatrists. Psychiatrists who pass both phases are board-certified. Until recently, there was no requirement for recertification. However, this regulation has been changed, and psychiatrists tested after 1993 will be required to take a written test every 10 years.

Nearly all patients treated by psychiatrists receive some type of psychotherapy, depending on their diagnosis and the goals of treatment. In addition, surveys by the American Psychiatric Association indicate that about two thirds of the people treated by psychiatrists receive care that depends in some way on the clinician's medical skills. Such treatment includes medication management, and evaluation or consultation (often for patients being treated on hospital medical or surgical units). The other one third of the psychiatric patient population receive psychotherapy or psychoanalysis without medication.

Ideally, a well-trained psychiatrist provides the best initial evaluation for any troubled employee. Several directories are available that list physicians in active practice, facilitating selection of a provider. An example of such a guide is the *American Psychiatric Association Biographical Directory.* The *APA Directory* lists psychiatrists by state and city, as well as alphabetically. The citation includes the psychiatrist's name, address, type of practice, birthdate, professional titles, education, and special interests. Such guides will often note whether the psychiatrist is board-certified. The local chapter of the American Psychiatric Association or the state psychiatric association can also assist with private referrals. The Academy of Organizational and Occupational Psychiatry (AOOP; Dallas, TX) was established in 1990 by psychiatrists with special interests and expertise in organizational mental health issues. Many of the contributors to *Mental Health in the Workplace* are AOOP members.

Psychiatrists are available in nearly every area of the United States. A local practitioner can be found in the *Who's Who Directory of Medical Specialists,* which lists information similar to that described above. APA surveys reveal that about half of U.S. mental health services are provided by nonpsychiatric physicians, including general practitioners, family physicians, emergency room physicians, neurologists, internists, and pediatricians. Of note, where there is a shortage of psychiatrists, there is an equal shortage of other mental health professionals.

Selection of a psychiatrist is based on several other factors, such as availability. Of approximately 220,000 mental health professionals in the United States, only about 50,000 are psychiatrists. Psychiatry is one of the few undersupplied medical specialties in the United States, and waiting lists for treatment in many areas (particularly rural) can be long. Another consideration is whether the psychiatrist has specialized in a particular type of treatment or particular group of patients. Certain considerations become important when obtaining treatment for employees with some conditions, as is clear in Part III of this book. For example, an employee with a known medical condition or suspected illness should be evaluated by a psychiatrist. Furthermore, since only a psychiatrist is trained to recognize these conditions, a decision to refer the employee to another type of specialist for evaluation or treatment may preclude accurate diagnosis and appropriate treatment. Similarly, an employee already taking prescribed medication or who might require medication as part of treatment should be evaluated by a psychiatrist, the only medical specialist trained in mental disorders and the only mental health professional trained to prescribe medications. Optimal evaluation includes an integrated review of emotional, interpersonal, diagnostic, and medical issues.

Psychologists

A clinical psychologist is a mental health professional who has first obtained an undergraduate degree, and then completed requirements for a Ph.D. in clinical or counseling psychology (exceptions include psychology associates, licensed in some states with a master's degree), or for an Ed.D. Graduate programs in psychology are diverse, but most include course work, practica or clerkships in the various areas of psychology, followed by a 1-2-year internship. A thesis is required by most programs, an exception being the Psy.D. degree in applied psychology, which has no requirement for original research. Psychologists receive a significant amount of systematic training in psychotherapy. Psychologists are also trained to perform tests on patients, including tests of intelligence, memory, and personality. Psychology is a broad field, including training in education and industrial organization. Supervision is generally provided by experienced psychologists, as well as by psychiatrists. Following completion of a basic program, psychologists may further specialize in cognitive-behavioral therapy, psychoanalysis, neuropsychology (focusing on the impact of brain disease on human behavior and mental life), and other areas. The overall length of training after the undergraduate degree before qualifying for independent practice is 4 years.

Just as a major part of a psychiatric evaluation focuses on inner conflicts and relationship problems, psychological evaluation of a patient focuses primarily on inner conflicts or problems within the individual. Psychologists are also trained to be attuned to the quality of relationships at work, as well as with family and friends. It could be said that nonphysician mental health professionals study "dis-ease," not disease per se in the sense of physical illness. Psychologists do not prescribe medication, nor are they trained to diagnose physical conditions that can influence a patient's mental state.

As Sharfstein and Koran (1990) note,

> Psychologists have . . . been pressing for hospital admitting privileges, and they debate with psychiatrists the qualifications necessary for practicing psychotherapy. On the one hand, a medical education is not needed to be a skilled psychotherapist or to counsel or treat physically well individuals whose mental disorders

do not require medications. On the other hand, only psychiatric physicians can prescribe indicated psychotherapeutic drugs, knowledgeably treat the large proportion of mentally disordered patients who suffer from both physical disease and mental disorder, and be relied on to recognize organic diseases masquerading behind mental symptoms.

Psychologists are licensed by forty-eight states, with unregulated practice in the remaining two states. Licensure requires that the psychologist complete the necessary educational requirements, then pass a national written examination, followed by a separate state examination. The content and form of this exam varies by state, and may be written or oral. State licenses generally permit the psychologist to perform psychological services, including psychotherapy and testing. Licenses are renewable every 2 years and include continuing education requirements. Whether psychologists can bill third-party payers independently varies by state. Medicare accepts claims for financial reimbursement from psychologists.

Several directories are available that list psychologists in active practice. These guides include the *American Psychological Association Directory* and the *National Register of Health Services Providers in Psychotherapy.* These directories list psychologists separately by geographic area and alphabetically. Citations include the education, experience, and professional membership of the clinician, as well as any areas of specialization or particular expertise. The local chapter of the American Psychological Association or the state psychological association (almost every state has one) can also assist with private referrals.

Selection of a psychologist is based on several factors, including availability. Of approximately 220,000 U.S. mental health practitioners, about 75,000 are psychologists, of which about one third are clinical psychologists. Other considerations include the type of treatment anticipated for the employee, and the specialization or expertise of the psychologist. Again, it is important to note that employees who might need medication, those with complicated medical histories, or those suspected of having a medical condition contributing to their problem should be referred for evaluation by a psychiatrist instead. Furthermore, it is not usually initially obvious which patients have an illness or need medication.

Social Workers

Social workers in the mental health system have completed an undergraduate degree, usually in a social sciences major, followed by a master's (M.S.W.) or doctoral (D.S.W.) degree in social work. Their education focuses on interventions in the social system, from the individual in the family to a group in the community or greater society. This discipline draws on sociology and most of the behavioral sciences, such as psychology. After completing this broadly based degree, social workers obtain specialty training, pursuing either a clinical or a policy/community-level track. Education of clinical social workers in mental health includes an internship. Some obtain advanced training in a particular school of psychotherapy or family treatment. The overall length of training after obtaining the B.S. degree before a social worker qualifies for independent practice is at least 3 years. Supervision is provided by experienced social workers, as well as by psychologists and psychiatrists.

While sharing skills with other mental health professionals, such as the ability to perform psychotherapy, clinical social workers strongly emphasize the interaction of the person within his or her environment, whether it be the individual's job, family, community, or other social system (factors also considered in evaluation by psychiatrists and psychologists). The social worker focuses heavily on the family and on the community system's impact on the individual. Thus, social workers are uniquely skilled to interface with community resources such as health and welfare agencies, often assisting their clients in obtaining social services such as medical assistance, housing, and food stamps.

The process for credentialing social workers is only 25 years old. In most states, social workers obtain licensure by passing a test. Many states have different levels of licensure, depending on the clinician's degree and amount of experience. Most states have continuing social work education requirements. In most states they can be licensed for independent practice. Social workers are able to submit claims for financial reimbursement to Medicare.

Referral to a social worker can be facilitated by use of a directory such as the *1991 Diplomate Directory,* published by the American Board of Examiners in Clinical Social Work, which lists practicing clinicians by geographic area, licensure, type of practice, and so forth. Of approximately 220,000 U.S. mental health professionals, about half that number are social workers.

Considerations in the selection of a social worker include the focus of treatment. A social worker is particularly appropriate for work with the family or conflicts on the job. As with any professional, licensure is an important sign of quality, as it indicates that the individual has met the standards set by his or her profession. Cost may be a consideration as well: Social workers' fees are generally lower than psychologists or psychiatrists, which is particularly important for employees who will be paying for treatment out-of-pocket. Psychologists, and to a lesser extent psychiatrists, find themselves in competition with social workers (and family and marital counselors), who believe that they provide the same psychotherapy and counseling services at less cost.

Other Providers

There are a number of other mental health professionals to whom an employee can be referred for initial evaluation. These professionals may be employed by hospitals, clinics, or clinicians such as psychiatrists (who can provide the supervision required by law, medical backup, and prescriptions for medication). These clinicians are generally supervised by other mental health professionals, primarily psychologists and psychiatrists (as well as other physicians), although some are licensed for independent practice. The length of training following the undergraduate degree varies by specialty.

Psychiatric nurses and psychiatric nurse practitioners have completed requirements for a nursing degree, the latter obtaining additional specialized training and certification in mental health. They may provide counseling or therapy. With their nursing training, they can also administer medications both orally and by injection, when that medication has been prescribed by a physician.

Mental health counselors represent a small, diverse group of professionals who received training as a result of programs established in the 1960s in response to the shortage of psychiatrists and other therapists in the United States. Their training programs vary from 1 to 3 years following undergraduate work. Most obtain master's or doctoral degrees, although some clinicians have associate degrees. Their education focuses strongly on psychotherapy and includes a clinical internship. Other clinicians include certified alcoholism counselors and marriage and family counselors, whose training and orientation are reflected in their titles.

Although none of these clinician types can bill for services provided to Medicare enrollees, licensure to practice independently or to receive reimbursement from insurance companies is available to some of these clinician types in some states. These practice privileges have been brought about mainly as a result of lobbying efforts of professional organizations representing these clinicians. For example, nurses have recently begun following the lead of social workers in lobbying for increased autonomous practice privileges such as the right to bill independently for services. To date, however, their scope of practice remains quite limited.

Selection of one of these professionals will be dependent, as with other professionals, on the employee's presenting problem, the availability of the most appropriately trained provider, licensure of available professionals, and costs. Most of these providers have state or local associations that can be contacted for referrals.

DELIVERY SYSTEMS

This section provides an overview of the major reimbursement methods and delivery organizations in the public and private mental health care sectors. Just as there is a spectrum of mental health professionals, there are various organizational settings in which individuals receiving treatment for mental disorders are seen. Similarly, payment for treatment can be arranged in various ways. The choice of setting will be determined by a number of factors, including insurance coverage, type of professional assessed to be most likely needed, prior arrangements between health care organizations and corporate representatives, and employee choice.

Many insurance and other financing arrangements may restrict selection of a provider. Some policies exclude mental health care, in which case the employee must be able to afford to pay for treatment out-of-pocket in the private sector, or otherwise must be willing to seek treatment in the public sector.

Payment issues are often central to treatment of mental disorders. Mental health professionals, in contrast to many other health professionals, often prefer that their patients deal directly with their insurance companies. Under this arrangement, the patient receives reimbursement for covered services from the insurance company and the patient pays the clinician. This arrangement is more common in mental health for several reasons, including the greater degree of confidentiality possible for the patient, and also because in psychotherapy payment of the fee is often a central emotional issue in the therapy itself. It is thus important that the payment relationship between patient and therapist be pure rather than "contaminated" by third-party payers.

Fee-For-Service

Since health insurance began in the United States in the late 1930s, FFS has been the traditional reimbursement method and is still the method most commonly used today. Under this system, the mental health professional bills for services after they are provided. For example, a fee is charged for each separate service provided, such as a therapy session.

Employees may have coverage for mental health services under a number of arrangements that use FFS reimbursement. In what is likely the most common arrangement in large corporations, the business insures their employees through the purchase of private indemnity coverage. Most private insurance companies use FFS reimbursement. Employees in corporations that do not provide health insurance can purchase such coverage independently (at a much higher premium price).

In addition, FFS is also used by many corporations that self-insure medical care for their employees. Self-insuring corporations commonly pay an insurance company to provide administrative services for the business, the insurance company then processing claims and serving as a conduit for payment. The corporation pays for these administrative services, but does not pay policy premiums to the insurance company. Instead, the business takes on the financial risk for its employees and pays medical bills as they are incurred.

Under FFS reimbursement for covered benefits, the bill (or more commonly some portion of it) is paid by the insurance company. Under some arrangements, the patient is responsible for the portion of the bill the insurance company does not pay. Under other arrangements, the care provider accepts insurance company reimbursement as payment in full.

Costs under an FFS system are not wholly predictable: They are dependent on the incidence of problems and the services received in treating them. The insurance industry profits by charging higher premiums than estimated payouts. Such prediction, based on the methods of actuarial science, is sophisticated, complicated, and not easily replicated. Insurance premiums under this type of reimbursement tend to be more expensive than for other payment methods, because the clinician's incentive is to provide all the care that the patient could logically need. This *can* have optimal treatment potential, but can also have potential for cost escalation.

The setting in which care is delivered is not restricted under this arrangement. Likewise, any clinician who is licensed to bill independently or who is working under the supervision of a billing professional can provide services to an employee under FFS reimbursement. In general, there is unlimited flexibility under this system for choice of provider.

There are pros and cons to FFS reimbursement, as is true with any form of reimbursement. One potential disadvantage is the possibility of higher expenditures under this system. Another disadvantage for the risk-taking entity, whether it be the self-insuring business or the insurance company, is the inability to predict costs in advance. Yet another disadvantage of FFS is that employees may be billed for costs not reimbursed by the insurance company; leeway for fee negotiation is variable.

However, optimal initial psychiatric care may reduce both psychiatric and medical costs, as well as having productivity benefits. In a true free market, higher fees reflect a higher perceived value. There are other advantages in FFS payment as well: Corporate management can be assured that the mental health professional has no financial incentive to skimp on the care provided to employees. In addition, FFS offers the most flexibility in choice of provider.

Self-insurance under FFS has other nuances: With a population of healthy employees, a self-insured company will not pay out much for medical care. This contrasts with methods described below: If the corporation pays in advance for care, expenditures for the same hypothetical group of healthy employees could be greater than necessary. Conversely, if the employee population of a self-insured corporation has a high incidence of illness and treatment, medical expenditures will be high, with insurance reducing the out-of-pocket costs to the employee who receives services. In a company with choice of coverage types, healthy individuals will seek coverage under PPOs, HMOs, and similar systems. Those who expect to need treatment are more likely to stay with conventional insurance coverage (termed *adverse selection*), which can create an artificial appearance of cost reduction in non-FFS systems.

The effects of adverse selection on health care costs created the need for mandated benefits for insurance coverage that specify legal limits for minimum coverage of psychiatric conditions and substance abuse. To date, twenty-eight states have passed such legislation. Requirements vary widely between states, ranging from parity with coverage for medical and surgical conditions to very limited coverage. Drug abuse treatment is covered by nearly all, and alcohol treatment by all but one. Of note, self-insured corporations are exempt from state mandates; as more and more Americans are employed by a self-insured business or are uninsured, the mandates are having less of an impact on access to care than was originally hoped.

Preferred Provider Organizations

Another reimbursement method is discounted FFS payment, which has become possible in the era of cost control as a result of a confluence of factors, including the recent oversupply of mental health care providers and payers' desire to minimize expenditures. As a result, third-party payers and self-insuring corporations have been able to negotiate discounted FFS reimbursement with providers.

One type of discounted FFS arrangement is the PPO, in which a group of providers agrees to accept a discounted fee (typically 10% to 30% below customary charges) as reimbursement for a group of employees. They also agree to accept this fee as payment in full and to not bill patients for the balance. PPO managers seek providers who give resource efficient care and the providers they enroll agree to utilization management oversight by PPO administrators.

The discounted FFS method does not usually restrict the setting in which care is provided. However, it does restrict the employee to receiving care from the preferred providers, as enrollees agree not to see providers outside the PPO, on penalty of paying a large portion or the full fee. Physicians are the mental health professionals most commonly involved in PPO arrangements.

The mental health care provider's advantage in this arrangement is the guarantee of a potential patient population. The disadvantage to the provider is a reduced fee for caring for these patients.

The patient's disadvantage is limited choice of providers. The advantage is financial, in that the arrangement creates reduced fees and eliminates the need for copayments. However, the personal cost of this arrangement may be steep if the employee leaves an established relationship with a provider outside the PPO. The financial cost can be substantial if the employee elects to seek treatment outside the PPO roster of providers. It should be remembered that preferred providers often are those clinicians who meet minimal qualifications and agree to accept reduced fees.

Health Maintenance Organizations

Capitation is another reimbursement method, in which the self-insured corporation or the insurer pays a provider organization in advance on a per head or "capitated" basis for the care of a group of employees. In return for this payment, the provider organization agrees to provide all necessary care to the group for a predetermined period of time; thus, total payment is independent of the amount of services eventually given.

Such an arrangement usually occurs only within nontraditional delivery settings such as HMOs. From the provider's perspective, capitation is often viewed more as an organizational arrangement than as an insurance program. From the business or employee perspective, however, capitation is an insurance mechanism, as it protects the enrollees against financial loss from illness, with the prepayment analogous to purchasing an insurance premium.

Capitation plans rarely require cost sharing except for small copayments for some services. Services are usually comprehensive in scope, although with limited depth. HMOs usually offer a broader benefit package than conventional private insurance policies, including preventive care, immunizations, and annual checkups. The enrollee has no financial disincentive to use the HMO, as there is no significant additional cost once the capitation payment is made. Therefore, financial survival of the HMO requires that services be limited. Nonfinancial barriers may include time delays between appointment and visit, telephone triage using gatekeepers (see next section), and visit limits. Since all psychotherapy depends on development of a therapeutic alliance, many mental health patients will be put off by bureaucratic procedures, in many cases opting to forego treatment.

Federal standards have been developed for HMOs. Minimal mental health care benefits include short-term (up to twenty visits) outpatient evaluation and crisis intervention mental health services, medical treatment, and referral services for alcohol and drug abuse or addiction. Of note, it is thus possible to meet federal standards without offering inpatient psychiatric coverage. Furthermore, the federally legislated benefits do not entitle the enrollee to care; while gatekeepers and other bureaucratic procedures concurrently used to minimize resource use do not technically prohibit the use of services, in reality that is often the result.

The financial incentives facing the HMO organization may be different from the incentives facing the providers it employs. However, these incentives may be tightly linked through contractual arrangements that pass along financial risk to the provider. Alternatively, the link may be quite loose, with the organization absorbing the financial risk. It is therefore difficult to generalize about the effects of financing on care received within an HMO. However, it is clear that because the HMO receives lump payment in advance for the care of all patients, the incentive is to provide as few services as possible, so as to maximize revenue. The provider organization and its practitioners (depending on the contractual financial arrangement) bear the financial risk instead of the third-party payer or enrollee. Because the capitation payment depends only on the number of people cared for, rather than on the quantity of services, there is no incentive to maximize the volume of services provided. In fact, there is some incentive to enroll more members and provide fewer services for each.

As a result of this potential for compromise, much has been written about HMOs concerning their financial incentives and the resulting quality of care that patients receive compared to other health care delivery systems. Opinions about quality of care differ, although anecdotal evidence would suggest that at least some enrollees receive suboptimal care. However, the main conclusion is that HMOs save money over FFS systems because of the low rate of patient hospitalization (for medical and surgical conditions)—about 40 percent lower than within FFS systems. The lower rate of hospitalization within HMOs does not represent a higher quality of medical care. Apart from the financial incentive not to hospitalize, healthier enrollees self-select into HMOs. Given that HMOs are not mandated to provide inpatient psychiatric care, their rate of hospitalization for these conditions is likely even less than 40 percent of the rate within FFS systems.

Treatment sites depend on the arrangement between the provider and the HMO. Care may be rendered in a private office or in a central site. Choice of clinician is limited to those employed by or on staff of the HMO. To save money, many HMOs use lowest-cost nonphysician providers, particularly to provide psychotherapy. While this may be adequate for some patients, often it results in suboptimal care. Because of the nonfinancial barriers alluded to above, employees may have difficulty getting an appointment with a staff psychiatrist (assuming there is one). Alternatively, primary mental health care may be provided by a family or general practitioner. These arrangements keep costs (but probably also quality) down. Enrollees may receive fewer visits than they think they need.

This discussion has alluded to the advantages and disadvantages of employee care in an HMO. For a healthy employee population with good overall mental health, an HMO may be a good option. Additionally, because the corporation will know in advance just how much they will be paying for employee care, there are yearly budgeting advantages to using an HMO.

The major disadvantages are a consequence of the HMO's financial incentives to minimize care and to the existence of nonfinancial barriers to care. It is generally agreed that most HMOs have problems providing care for psychiatric conditions and substance abuse. In the hypothetical situation of the employee with a crisis, a long wait for an appointment with a caregiver could mean the difference between outpatient resolution of the problem and the necessity for hospitalization or for employee termination.

Employee Assistance Programs

Employee assistance (or alcoholism) programs (EAPs) provide various mental health services that have been traditionally organized within the corporation itself. As the name implies, EAPs were originally focused on the treatment of alcohol and its related problems as reflected in the workplace. The identified alcoholic might be the employee or a family member.

EAPs proliferated in the 1970s. Later, some EAPs broadened their scope to include other drug problems, wellness programs, and mental health programs.

The Department of Health and Human Services (DHHS) says the goals of an EAP are "to restore valuable employees to full productivity." Specifics were delineated by DHHS:

1. Identify employees with alcohol, drug abuse, emotional or behavior problems resulting in a pattern of deficient work performance
2. Motivate such individuals to seek help
3. Provide short-term professional counseling assistance and referral
4. Direct employees toward the best assistance available
5. Provide continuing support and guidance throughout the problem-solving period

To carry out these goals, EAPs should provide clinical services and referrals. An EAP should offer consultation to corporate supervisors, as well as employee orientation to the program. EAPs should also offer preventive health education programs.

EAP staffs vary, determined to some extent by the goals of a particular program. Some EAPs employ treatment staff including psychiatrists, non-psychiatric physicians, psychologists, MSWs, nurses, family therapists, and marital therapists. Some use clinicians or administrators to triage employees into appropriate services.

Historically, EAPs have been organized within the corporation. Now, some programs are contracted out to providers in the community. In a further variation, some businesses are developing joint EAP programs. Some employees receive mental health or substance abuse treatment on a contract basis within the community after referral from the EAP. In some corporations the EAP staff act as gatekeepers (see below)—liaisons between employees and community-based providers.

Employees can refer themselves to the EAP or can be referred by management. The treatment process varies slightly depending on the referral source. If the employee is self-referred, the entire process takes place without feedback to supervisors, but if the employee is referred by management, treatment progress reports (leaving out personal details) can be given to management (see Chapter 3).

There are advantages to EAPs, including the flexibility to offer specific services and the potential for greater control over mental health care resources. Programs can be customized to fit employees' needs. They have been found cost-effective not only by reducing absenteeism, accidents, and improving productivity but because services are often provided more economically than they are when the company offers traditional mental health benefits as part of an insurance policy. The location of an EAP within the corporation is more convenient for the employee and facilitates follow-up care.

Potential disadvantages of an EAP include use of gatekeepers and clinicians with limited training and with a financial bias not to refer employees for psychiatric care. As a result, EAP gatekeepers are often reluctant to refer employees for more sophisticated psychotherapy or for medication treatment (and in about half of all patients, medications are indicated for specific symptoms or syndromes). Gatekeepers tend instead to refer to low-cost providers. Such providers may have limited training and often have less experience than other providers in the community, resulting in potentially suboptimal care.

Other disadvantages of EAPs include their inherently greater possibility for breech of confidentiality (although EAPs must follow strict confidentiality procedures) and the heightened stigma that employees may feel in seeking, being sent for, or obtaining treatment at their place of work. The employee may feel that the company has a vested interest in his or her productivity that is of greater importance than the employee's health itself. The appearance of a potential conflict of interest or goals could lead to resentment.

The Public Sector

Those employees who have no mental health benefits and who cannot afford to pay for care out-of-pocket in the FFS system have another option: to seek care within the state or local mental health system. Due to a number of factors, psychiatric care has been funded by the public sector to a much greater extent than other types of medical care. A state hospital system for inpatient care is available to those without insurance or who run out of benefits. A system of local community mental health centers (CMHCs) provides a continuum of mental health care, including 24-hour emergency services, inpatient care, partial hospitalization, rehabilitation, and other outpatient services. State-funded clinics also exist, with similar structure.

CMHCs charge lower fees than the private sector and readily use sliding scales for reducing fees. They have the funding flexibility to care for those in lower socioeconomic classes, whom it is their mission to serve. They bill uninsured patients directly and bill third-party payers for clients with coverage.

Providers in CMHCs include psychiatrists, psychologists, MSWs, and mental health counselors. The psychiatrist is usually in the position of supervising the rest of the team and prescribing medications as necessary. Psychotherapy is almost always provided by the nonphysician staff.

The overriding advantage of the public sector is its lower cost and its ability to provide care for the uninsured or underinsured population. The potential disadvantage of care in the public sector is that due to government budget limitations, services may be inadequate in breadth or duration. However, this is highly variable, depending on geographic area and the particular problem facing the patient. For the troubled employee without private-sector coverage, the public sector provides a viable option.

The public mental health care sector includes a network of state hospitals for inpatient care. State and local clinics provide income-adjusted outpatient care to the population. In large cities such as New York, city hospital clinics provide low-fee care to the poor. Private agencies, often run by religious groups, are another low-fee alternative found in most urban areas. Additional sources of reduced-fee care include teaching clinics staffed by physicians in training, research clinics for people with designated conditions, and psychoanalytic training institutes.

COST CONTAINMENT

Causes of Rising Costs

U.S. health care costs began to skyrocket in the 1960s. The reasons for severe cost inflation are complex and numerous, but several factors predominate. General inflation was a major factor, as the cost of most goods and services in the economy increased. However, health care costs increased in excess of the general inflation rate. In addition, the U.S. population grew during these years. FFS reimbursement pushed costs higher as well, because this payment method does not reward cost-conscious decisions about resource use (see Starr 1982; Stoline and Weiner 1988).

Specific to the mental health care sector, inpatient adolescent units and substance abuse care are the main additional causes of rising expenditures. Greater use of these services reflects increases in societal stress from a relative breakdown in family structure, as well as a weakening of church and work relationships that formerly provided channels for handling personal problems. It also reflects a controversial and dramatic growth of for-profit hospitals, many of which specialize in these services.

The growth in number of mental health care providers has also contributed to increased costs. Decreased stigma in seeking psychiatric treatment has increased the pool of potential patients. In addition, studies have revealed an increasing prevalence of major depression in the U.S. population, as well as a high incidence of people in the general population with undiagnosed and untreated psychiatric conditions. If all of these people were to obtain care, expenditures would be even higher.

U.S. health care expenditures reflect the magnitude of these factors. Federal analysts estimate that all health care costs totaled more than $600 billion in 1990, consuming more than 12 percent of the GNP (gross national product). Approximately 13 percent of these total expenditures paid for treatment of mental disorders and substance abuse. In 1990 this component would have totaled more than $72 billion. Although individuals are affected by costs, this cost crisis primarily affects the third-party payers of care: government, private insurers, and U.S. corporations.

The cost problem affects different payers in distinct ways. For example, government derives its revenue from taxes or from creating a budget deficit. Policymakers may choose either approach to fund health care.

For employers, fringe benefits were instituted in the United States through union negotiations during World War II. Since then, they have been a staple of worker employment packages in most (e.g., 98% of manufacturing firms) large U.S. corporations. Corporate sponsors of health insurance have been hit hard by the health care cost crisis, and surveys reveal that they believe rising health care costs are more threatening to companies' international competitiveness than higher interest rates or the federal budget deficit. For mental health and substance abuse benefits, a 1989 survey revealed that companies with more than 5,000 employees paid an average of almost $300 per employee annually. The American Medical Association (AMA) estimates national averages for corporately purchased medical premiums at $2,400–$2,600 per person annually. Such expenditures, coming as they do at a time of strong foreign competition, have motivated employers to join the search for ways to reduce costs.

Insurance companies are theoretically not affected financially by increased health care costs, because they pass on increased costs to their customers in the form of higher premiums. However, insurance companies became involved when their corporate customers revealed concerns about higher health care costs by switching to self-insurance rather than paying increased premiums. Once faced with reduced revenue, private health insurance companies also mobilized to fight the cost crisis.

Concerns About Quality

As payers became more concerned about costs, it was perhaps natural that they wondered what they were paying for. As a result, concerns developed about quality of care. Payers looked at data such as those comparing U.S. health with health in other countries and they wondered why we fare poorly despite the largest expenditures. They looked at the inflationary incentives of the reimbursement system and they wondered how much care was superfluous: a padding of hospitals' and clinicians' income. Payers used these concerns to justify benefit cuts, managed care, utilization review, and other cost-control measures.

The partial validity in their argument has complicated the often heated arguments between payers and providers. Payers feel their actions are justified by the evidence and that health care cost reductions are a positive, but incidental, side effect. For their part, providers insist that payers' stated concerns about quality are disguised concerns about expenditures. There is some truth to both arguments.

Providers were initially fairly passive in their response to cost-containment initiatives. However, as the health care cost crisis has progressed, providers experience increasing constraints on their latitude to make clinical decisions and to use the resources they feel are necessary to adequately care for patients. (Effects on income no doubt also play their part in providers' concerns about third-party interference in the health care process.) Mobilized in response to these various factors, U.S. health care providers are now working with government and private researchers to critically examine the health care delivery process, with the goals of maximizing resource use and optimizing outcomes of care. As a result, guidelines, protocols, and other treatment tools are being developed. Ultimately, these changes will be good for the U.S. health care system. Nevertheless, this system is in flux, and most providers do not base their clinical decisions on protocols. Thus, payers still perceive a need for the cost-quality control interventions described below.

Large third-party payers are best able to influence the health care system by changing regulations and payment approaches, and all of the third-party payers have instituted various cost-containment approaches. Many of these approaches started in the public-sector programs, Medicare and Medicaid, and were then adopted by private-sector payers.

Mental health care providers and their patients have not been spared the effects of this process. Many payers feel that the care is ill-defined, that it is either for the worried well or the hopelessly ill, justifying lack of benefit parity with other conditions. In addition, the stigma surrounding mental illness and its treatment diminishes potential voices of protest. Thus, the mental health component of health care has taken harder hits than most other sectors.

Benefit Design

Common sense dictates that benefit design would be a very important method to control corporate health care costs. After all, a decision not to cover a particular service translates into dollars the business does not spend on health care coverage.

The scope of insurance policy benefits greatly affects the costs a company can expect to incur; reducing benefits reduces costs. Corporate management can use predictions of both corporate revenue and health care expenditures to determine how much coverage is reasonable and affordable. Unfortunately for employees, mental health care is often felt to be more discretionary and thus is first to be cut out of the budget.

Many traditional insurance policies do not include mental health care. For policies that do include psychiatric care, it is usually subjected to more stringent benefits, known as inside limits, compared to other medical-surgical benefits. The majority of policies have inside limits for mental health care, including higher copayments and limits on the number of visits or in-hospital days. As a result, many insured persons are underinsured for mental health care, putting them at risk for exhausting their mental health coverage.

Cost sharing, in which the policyholder is required to pay a portion of the costs of care when such costs are incurred, is another way to save on health care costs. The advantages to the insurance company of cost sharing include reduction in payouts, as well as the employees' tendency to seek less care when they bear some financial liability for it. Both cost sharing and providing fewer benefits at the same premium reduce the insulation between patients and their medical bills. An increasing number of employers are incorporating cost sharing into their benefit plans.

Cost sharing provisions take a variety of forms. With coinsurance, the policyholder pays a predetermined percentage of the medical bill, typically 50 percent for psychotherapy and other mental health services, and 20 percent for all other services and conditions. (Although Medicare has begun differentiating between mental health services, such that medical management is covered with 20% copayment, whereas psychotherapy remains at 50%. This trend may spread to other payers.) With copayment, a fixed dollar amount per unit of service is required, such as $5 per prescription or office visit. (This arrangement is common in HMOs.) With a deductible, a set sum must be paid by the employee before benefits are activated. The amount is frequently $100 or so, although in some basic benefit policies it may be as high as $500 or $1,000.

Flexible benefits are used by some companies and in the era of cost containment some innovative approaches have been tried. For example, one company provides a basic benefit to all employees and concurrently creates an account for each employee, from which medical bills are paid. At the end of the year, a portion of the unused funds is returned to the employee as a bonus. Thus, the employees' incentive is not to use medical care and presumably they consider absolutely necessary those services they do seek. Some businesses offer employees more expensive and less expensive options, but if the more costly policy is chosen, the employee must pay the difference out-of-pocket.

A combination of these cost-sharing methods may be used. Cost sharing becomes a cost-containment method as the provisions are made more stringent: Company payouts are reduced further and policyholders become more critical of their need for care because of the consequent out-of-pocket payment. However, not all corporations will want to use cost sharing and limited benefits to control costs. Such approaches might be opposed by unions. They may appear too harsh to employees.

Case Managers and Gatekeepers

Under case management and utilization review, benefits are included in the policy, but the use of the benefits is monitored for necessity. It is estimated that 80 percent of traditional FFS insurance policies currently include some type of resource management. These approaches become operative when benefits are actually used.

One approach developed in the era of cost control is to manage resources at the level of the individual through the use of administrators who oversee the care process. A high-cost case management approach within the mental health care sector focuses on those few individuals in any insured group who have generated or are likely to generate very high expenditures. These individuals are assigned to a case manager. Case managers are known in some systems as gatekeepers, but that term generally has a different connotation (see below). The technique of high-cost case management determines whether extra assistance in the planning, arranging, or coordination of a specialized treatment plan will appropriately permit less costly and possibly higher-quality care.

Thus, the case manager's role is to coordinate the care of the identified individual. The case manager will get to know the details of the employee's case and help in the determination of the need for hospitalization, specialized diagnostic tests, or services. The case manager will work with the employee and the provider to streamline use of services, such as eliminating unnecessary or duplicated tests and treatment.

In certain instances, the case manager may arrange for an extra contractual benefit to cover services not otherwise included in the policy. This can be quite important for the quality of care of patients who need more extended alternatives to hospital care such as residential services, day treatment, and outpatient visits. Provision of such extra benefits can also be cost-effective for the payer. For example, many policies do not include a partial hospitalization (also known as day hospital) benefit, which costs less per day than inpatient care. For the hospitalized enrollee with major mental illness who has improved enough clinically to allow release to a day hospital program, it would be in the company's interest to provide day hospital services rather than pay for continued hospitalization. A case manager is in an optimal position to coordinate and oversee this process.

Case managers may be employed by a corporation, an insurance company, or a care provider. EAP staff often serve the role of case manager. They are in a position to work as liaisons between the employee and the caregiver, and can be perceived as working in the employee's best interest. Employees are generally targeted for case management if they have above average medical care costs, if they have a condition likely to be costly or complicated to treat, or if they have a condition likely to need coordination among different providers. Case management may be for an employee or family member who develops major mental illness, as this situation usually necessitates frequent hospitalization as well as regular outpatient visits. The employee in long-term psychotherapy may also be referred for case management.

Some payers, particularly HMOs, have gatekeeper programs. Under this arrangement, the enrollee is informed up front that he or she must seek permission from the gatekeeper to seek certain types of care, on penalty of nonpayment. Typical limitations include a requirement that the enrollee call the gatekeeper to obtain permission for hospitalization or before consulting with a specialist. This arrangement differs from case management in that the gatekeeper rarely has personal knowledge of the particular employee and the employee may not have been previously identified as a high user of services. However, this is a way for the payer to manage the use of resources: By interposing a check in the decision-making process, the clinician and/or the patient are forced to consider whether the treatment plan is warranted and to successfully justify the necessity of resource use.

Gatekeepers and case managers are often not credentialed and people with a wide variety of backgrounds are hired to fill these positions. They might be administrators without clinical training. Their objective may be to save money for their employer, rather than to assure quality of care for the employee. The effect of case management and gatekeeping on quality of care is currently unknown, but they are unlikely to improve quality and are instead a likely cause of deterioration in quality of care. In the mental health arena, patients are less likely to recognize poor care and are not likely to complain because of the stigma attached to mental health treatment. This combination of circumstances currently protects substandard provider organizations. However, given the proliferation of the managed care phenomenon, some states have developed mandatory guidelines for the case management and gatekeeping processes, and implementation of legal standards is under consideration in some states.

Utilization Review

Utilization review is another oversight process designed to reduce unnecessary use of services. There are several types of utilization review: prospective, concurrent, and retrospective. Each arrangement has advantages and disadvantages to the employee, clinician, and payer. The goal of utilization review is to restrain health care expenditures through case-by-case assessment of the appropriateness of services and resources used, selectively reimbursing those services determined to be medically necessary and appropriate.

In prospective utilization review, the reviewer confers with the employee and/or with the care provider before treatment is given or received. Reviewers usually expect a short summary of the case, which they will (or should) compare to predetermined criteria of necessity. In mental health care, expensive services such as elective hospitalization commonly require prospective review and approval. If the case does not appear to meet the criteria for severity or necessity, the reviewer may ask the provider or employee if there are extenuating circumstances that would justify the service; however, as cost containment has become more stringent, granting of exceptions has become rare.

With concurrent review, the review is done while treatment is in progress. Reviewers seek information about the case to determine whether continued care is justified, given the patient's current condition. Again, the case may be compared with standards and exceptions can be made. Services commonly subjected to such review include inpatient care and long-term psychotherapy. At the conclusion of the exchange, if the reviewer is convinced that continued treatment is warranted, he or she usually approves a given number of days of further hospitalization or a given number of additional psychotherapy sessions.

In retrospective utilization review, the services are reviewed after the care is provided. In such cases, the provider may be at financial risk, because if the care is determined not to be medically necessary, the patient is often held harmless for responsibility for the bill. Hospitalizations are commonly subjected to this type of review, with the result that some portion of the hospitalization or in some cases the entire admission may be determined unnecessary. In the era of cost containment such unnecessary care is not reimbursed.

Retrospective reviewers usually have access to the medical record, which is often more accessible than the care provider. This highlights the need for careful documentation on the part of the provider, such that the medical record indicates why continued hospitalization was necessary, how closely established goals were met, and so on.

With regard to all types of review, disagreements between provider and reviewer go through a prearranged appeal process that may involve the reviewer's superior. In many cases, this is the first time that a physician in the same specialty (such as a psychiatrist) may be involved in the review.

The limitations in training and qualifications for utilization reviewers are similar to those described above for case managers and gatekeepers. As with case management and gatekeeping, legislative initiatives are underway in many states to regulate this new industry, with the potential for providing uniform guidelines for the utilization review process.

Coping with Case Management and Utilization Review

As the previous discussion makes clear, there are pros and cons to both case management and utilization review. These processes work to minimize the unnecessary use of resources. They are also theoretically a way to begin optimizing quality. A case manager may be quite helpful to patients and providers in organizing and streamlining a complicated case, and may be perceived as the employee's advocate.

However, reviewers, gatekeepers, and case managers are often perceived by both employee and provider as intrusive and at times even destructive to the goals of therapy or hospitalization. This situation can be anxiety-provoking and even threatening, particularly when benefits or reimbursement are withheld.

For example, in concurrent review the care provider usually interacts with the reviewer, although in the case of concurrent in-hospital review it is not unheard of for a reviewer to request an interview with the employee while he or she is on a psychiatric ward. Providers and their patients are uneasy with these contacts as they sense an invasion of the patient's privacy. It is important for the employee that confidentiality be maximized in each of these oversight programs.

As might be expected, most providers are uneasy with the oversight process, feeling that it intrudes on clinical practice. Providers are also disturbed to find themselves in the position of justifying clinical decisions to nonclinical reviewers, or to people with less knowledge and skill than themselves. The process can be made easier by using peer reviewers when possible, which becomes mandatory in appealing disagreements between gatekeeper and provider. Availability of gatekeepers and case managers (24 hours per day, 7 days per week) is also necessary.

Contacts between case managers, gatekeepers, utilization reviewers, and provider can be made less onerous through flexibility and a positive attitude by both care provider and care reviewer. A prearranged time for telephone consultation can help. Letter writing is preferred by some providers. Spacing reviews to reasonable intervals is also helpful, whereas daily updates during a patient's hospitalization often feels like harassment.

Thus, it is important that reviewers be aware of their potential impact on care and, particularly in mental health cases, make themselves as unobtrusive and positive as possible. Similarly, mental health professionals must recognize that managed care and cost containment are current realities. Adaptation is necessary while the mental health sector works toward defining and studying its treatment methods and thereby earns the right to continued decision-making autonomy.

SUMMARY

This chapter reviews the major components of mental health care in the U.S. health care system. The variety of professionals available within the mental health care system are described. Advantages and disadvantages in choice of health care provider are explored; in most cases, psychiatric evaluation is the optimal initial evaluation for a troubled employee.

Employees may be treated in a number of different types of health care systems, including traditional fee-for-service care, discounted fee-for-service such as preferred provider organizations, or managed care systems such as health maintenance organizations. Many corporations have established employee assistance programs within their businesses to provide referral, and in some cases treatment, to employees who need psychiatric care or treatment for substance abuse. The public sector and a variety of reduced-fee private agencies are available for those who are underinsured or have no coverage for mental health care.

Rising health care expenditures motivated third-party payers to implement cost-containment approaches. Benefit design including cost sharing is now often considered a method of cost control. Gatekeepers and case managers are used in many organizations to regulate use of mental health care resources. There are potential disadvantages to these cost-control systems, including uncertain effects on quality of care. The rationale for choosing a particular managed-care program is explored and strategies for coping with the negative effects of managed care are described.

Bibliography

Association of Labor-Management Administrators and Consultants on Alcoholism, Inc. (n.d.) *Standards for Employee Alcoholism and/or Assistance Programs.* Arlington, Va.

Frank, R., and T. McGuire. 1990. Mandating employer coverage of mental health care. *Health Affairs* **9**(1):31-42.

Frank, R., D. Salkever, and S. Sharfstein. 1991. A new look at rising mental health insurance costs. *Health Affairs* **10**(2):116-123.

Gabel, J., S. DiCarlo, C. Sullivan, and T. Rice. 1990. Employer-sponsored health insurance, 1989. *Health Affairs* **9**(2):161-175.

GAP/HRD-91-102. 1991. *U.S. Health Care Spending.* Washington, D.C.

Manderscheid, R., and M. Sonnenschein (eds). 1990. *Mental Health, United States, 1990.* DHHS Pub. No. (ADM)90-1708. Washington, D.C.: National Institute of Mental Health.

Scheidemandel, P. (compiler). 1989. *The Coverage Catalog,* 2d ed. Washington, D.C.: American Psychiatric Association Press.

Sharfstein, S., and L. Koran. 1990. Mental health services. In *Health Care Delivery in the United States,* 4th ed., A. Kovner and contributors, pp. 209-239. New York: Springer-Verlag.

Standards and Criteria for the Development and Evaluation of a Comprehensive Employee Assistance Program. U.S. Department of Health and Human Services. December 1986.

Starr, P. 1982. *The Social Transformation of American Medicine.* New York: Basic Books.

Stoline, A., and J. Weiner. 1988. *The New Medical Marketplace.* Baltimore: Johns Hopkins University Press.

Yager, J. 1989. *The Future of Psychiatry as a Medical Specialty.* Washington, D.C.: American Psychiatric Association Press.

3

Ethics and Confidentiality: Mental Health in the Organization

Robert C. Larsen, M.D., M.P.H.

ABSTRACT

In conducting an occupational psychiatry consultation, it is always important to emphasize the importance of proper communication and adherence to ethical standards. Referral source, patient, and clinician all must be fully informed about the nature and method of the consultation, reporting requirements, and any limits on confidentiality. When communication will take place between company and clinician, the patient/employee must be informed beforehand. Inattention to ethical standards or to proper communication can result in breaches of confidentiality, lack of informed consent, conflict of interest, perceived conflict of interest, undue administrative influence, and concerns about access to medical records. Appropriate attention to these issues increases the chance of an effective consultation process.

INTRODUCTION

Whether consulting with an attorney, accountant, or physician, people expect to be treated with respect and professional concern. They do not want confidential information disclosed. Material contained within their file is considered privileged and can only be released under certain circumstances. In mental health, public expectations and the restraints of privilege are especially subtle and complex.

Ethical conduct and respectful behavior are not easily taught. Formal seminars and individual supervision guide clinicians in training. They learn the proper steps in conducting an interview, maintaining a relationship with the patient, and disclosing information to third parties where appropriate. Supervised clinical hours are part of training before and after receiving one's clinical degree. This is an attempt to assure proper attention to the role that one assumes in dealing with the emotional well-being of people. This chapter focuses on additional professional responsibilities in communications of which both the doctor and the referral source must be mindful.

CONFIDENTIALITY AND ITS LIMITATIONS

The principles of medical ethics derive from the physician's duties and responsibility for the patient's well-being. The American College of Occupational and Environmental Medicine has a code of ethical conduct to which its members subscribe (see the appendix). Physicians and other clinicians are not always in the role of providing treatment and their responsibilities can be different when they are in other medical roles. It is thus crucial to the referral source, to the physician, and to the referred employee that the purpose of the meeting be completely clear to all parties.

Often a company will refer an employee into a traditional doctor-patient treatment relationship. Even a helpful confirmation that the employee has come for consultation or entered treatment is a break in absolute confidentiality. There are exceptions, though, as long as the employee-patient gives his or her consent.

In order to provide information about diagnosis, recommended treatment, fitness for duty, or the need for job modification, the individual employee must first give consent. This consent should not be obtained after the employee has already disclosed the information. Early in the consultation the person should be made aware that such disclosure will take place. This practice follows ethical guidelines and avoids legal issues that might be raised if the employee is not aware of possible third-party disclosure from the onset. Furthermore, the individual should be aware of what type of information will be disclosed and in what format. An employee's job might be affected if the employer learns that drug abuse is an active clinical issue. Candidacy for a managerial position might be affected if others learn of a personality disorder diagnosis. Having access to psychological test results does not give a practitioner the right to share that information with others. The person evaluated must agree to a release of the data. If an employer, or other party, hold privilege to the data, then their consent must also be obtained. Dr. Jonas Rappeport, a prominent forensic psychiatrist, emphasizes the critical importance in obtaining fully informed consent (Rappeport 1981). When employees present for evaluation purposes, any limitations on confidentiality between the physician and employee must be clarified. Keeping that principle in mind, there are three different settings where the role of the physician alters the doctor-patient relationship.

The Traditional Doctor–Patient Relationship

Most people expect that a physician's intention, whether internist or psychiatrist, is to diagnose illness and institute treatment to improve one's health. An employee referred for mental health services expects that the clinician will not disclose matters discussed in the clinical setting. Yet, in today's world, limited reporting outside the office frequently takes place. The use of health insurance usually requires the physician to submit insurance forms with information about diagnosis, dates of visits, and fees. Alternative delivery systems (i.e., health maintenance organizations, preferred provider organizations) and managed care organizations often request even more information from the treating physician. The physician may be asked to give a summary of his or her patient's history, clinical course, prognosis, and diagnosis. A treatment plan in writing may be required by a third party to authorize payment for services. Based on the diagnosis, treatment plan, or prognosis, a third-party reviewer may authorize treatment for the period requested or not. It is important to recognize the impact on treatment that this release of information can have. This recognition must be shared with the patient beforehand for there to be informed consent.

Commonly, patients looking for mental health treatment worry that others might learn that they are in therapy. Some people are so wary of this that they may choose to forego insurance benefits or to delay entering treatment. In companies where a fellow employee may be monitoring health claims, this concern becomes primary. Such employers might be better off with an independent party monitoring mental health claims. Psychiatrists are sensitive to their responsibility to maintain confidentiality. A patient's identity will be disguised when a psychiatrist receives professional consultation from a colleague. Commonly, patients in group psychotherapy are instructed not to discuss the disclosures of fellow group members outside the therapy setting.

To summarize, when an employee enters a doctor-patient relationship, treatment is largely confidential. Physicians must tell their patients about any third party who will obtain clinical information. Human resource professionals should not expect feedback from the psychiatrist of an employee who is given a list of recommended clinicians. Patients can be comfortable discussing intimate details of their lives only when they have no concern about public disclosure.

The Occupational Psychiatric Consultation

When asked to assume the role of an evaluator, the psychiatrist's duties to the employee are quite different. Taking a history, making a diagnosis, and recommending treatment may seem very similar to traditional doctor-patient relationships. However, in circumstances of an occupational evaluation the employee is not a patient. Treatment is not started. Instead, an employer representative (e.g., an internal employee assistance program or the company's medical department) is requesting an employee evaluation to assess certain issues. The employee should be aware before walking through the psychiatrist's door that the employer expects feedback on the issues of concern. If this point is not clear, problems can arise.

Typically, the evaluator issues a formal report. The report comments on reported signs and symptoms, observed behavior in the interview, a review of medical and other records, psychological testing, and occasionally investigative reports. The examiner strives to be independent, neutral, and unbiased in the assessment of the employee.

Occasionally, concern by the employer for the employee's well-being prompts a request for evaluation. Usually the issues in this situation involve more than a benign concern of the employer for the employee. A long-term employee may begin using undue amounts of sick leave and demonstrating erratic behavior at the workplace This behavior comes to the attention of management because it disrupts an important work group. A mental health consultation may be demanded of the individual. Forensic reports can also be required for cases of long-term disability or work-related injury (see Chapter 5).

Case Example 1

John Smith, a manager in his mid-forties, has had lengthy work absences because of gastrointestinal symptoms. His supervisor referred him for a psychiatric evaluation. John suggests that his symptoms, by his assessment, began after a major company reorganization. He describes a marked increase in work volume accompanied by a reduction in staff support. He does not complain of feelings of depression or anxiety. He focuses on abdominal pain and the need for antacids. During the interview John refers to misrepresented aspects of his work history on his employment application when hired 15 years earlier. Only after the interview ends does John learn that a report will be issued to his company's medical department, including his prior work history. He pleads with the examining physician to alter the record so that it will be consistent with his initial application. Fearing the loss of his long-term job position, John contacts his company's personnel department and informs them that he will be returning to his position. With that decision, further assessment of disability is not necessary. The company then cancels the reporting requirement without learning of John's misrepresentation. Had he known the examination's purpose and reporting arrangements ahead of time, he might have dealt with this sensitive topic in a different fashion. Both he and the company would then have been able to make the best use of the evaluation.

Most people are not familiar with physicians in administrative roles and with making administrative decisions. Many employees referred for occupational psychiatric consultation expect the psychiatrist to be their advocate or at least a source of benevolent concern. Evaluating psychiatrists must make clear the purpose of the evaluation, and that no treatment will be initiated.

Usually, what is good for the employee is in turn good for the employer. For example, an employee who is appropriately placed on a leave of absence for chemical dependency treatment can return to the work site as a productive contributor. The leave may have resulted from an employee-mandated psychiatric evaluation. The resulting information was needed to make an administrative decision. However, the employee was required to cooperate with the evaluation process knowing that information would be released to specific people in the company. There are other instances in which employee and employer needs and desires may be at odds. For instance, when disability determinations are influenced by ongoing litigation, the clinical evaluation often becomes an adversarial process. The physician reports to the insurer, the company representative, attorneys, or a judge. The physician is asked to assess clinical issues associated with the employee's state of mind and disability. An employee's benefits might be curtailed or the employer might be obligated to provide assistance where it did not feel benefits were due.

The Limited Clinical Consultation

Employees are sometimes referred for a brief clinical assessment to a physician outside the company structure. One to four visits may take place, with the goal of helping the employee resolve certain personal issues. Here the physician is providing treatment. However, referral was made because personal problems were suspected as a cause of deficient work performance. In this scenario, a human resources officer or the employee's manager expects to receive confirmation that the consultation has been completed and that the problem is being treated. For example, suggestions to the employee may include couples therapy, medication, or substance abuse treatment. The physician is acting solely in the patient's interest here, but the employer may want at least an informal telephone report from the physician. Here, too, the employee must give consent to any breach of confidentiality. If a written report is needed, it is often prudent to give the employee a copy. The limited clinical consultation is generally less comprehensive and more confidential than the occupational psychiatry consultation.

MENTAL HEALTH REFERRAL SITUATIONS WITH POTENTIAL FOR MORAL CONFLICT
Lack of Informed Consent

This chapter emphasizes the necessity of employees' prior knowledge of any consultation's purpose and prior consent to any release of clinical information. In practical terms, the employee often has little choice about going for evaluation. In actuality, the employee does not have to comply and disciplinary or legal actions can be pursued instead. Problems arise when the purpose of the evaluation process is misrepresented to the individual.

Case Example 2

Burt Jones, a company salesperson, was referred by his employer for evaluation of his erratic behavior with clients. The company suspected drug abuse and Burt had attended company sales meetings while intoxicated with alcohol. Burt went to the psychiatric consultation. He disclosed that he had been drinking, taking cocaine daily, and sometimes using amphetamines. He has a family history of substance abuse. He had never sought out treatment before and he was not certain that he wanted treatment. The psychiatrist recommended inpatient treatment, but Burt did not want to take a leave from work. Only late in the interview did he learn that his employer would be sent a report describing his substance abuse problem and his resistance to treatment. Burt responded by threatening the psychiatrist with legal action if confidentiality was violated. Neither the employer nor the psychiatrist had told Burt to expect anything other than a confidential clinical consultation, solely for his own purposes.

This case emphasizes the importance of obtaining prior informed consent from employees. An even worse scenario can occur if the employee follows through on a recommended consultation and only later learns about telephone discussions between the consultant and company representatives. This kind of episode creates problems for that particular consultation and makes it less likely that the employee will obtain needed treatment. In addition, it can lead to widespread mistrust of management. Compliance with psychiatric referral is directly related to employee expectation of a professional and trustworthy referral and consultation process.

Conflict of Interest

It is also important that the clinician and referral source keep in mind any real or potential conflicts of interest. This is particularly important when administrative or legal decisions are at issue. Here, medical evidence and opinion are used to determine if an employee is entitled to certain company benefits. A psychiatrist in this role has a potential conflict of interest if he or she is an employee or shareholder of the company.

Case Example 3

Dr. Cindy James is the salaried psychiatric consultant to a large microelectronics firm. Through a program provided for management, Sam Green, an accountant with the firm, has come for short-term counseling. Sam reveals a planned corporate takeover and expectations of significant corporate change. Sam says that the information was revealed as a courtesy and asks that it not be revealed to others. Sam thinks that his position with the company would be jeopardized if his role in the planned takeover were known. Dr. James finds herself in a quandary. On the one hand, she feels she must protect confidentiality and the doctor–patient relationship. On the other hand, she is a member of management who has signed a sworn statement to reveal any evidence of fraud, embezzlement, and deleterious acts directed toward the company. Her assessment is that the takeover would constitute such a deleterious act. The company's top management had taken great pains to fend off a similar hostile takeover attempt the previous year. A further complication involves the possibility that Dr. James would lose her salaried consulting position in the aftermath of a takeover.

In this case, Dr. James is not only a treating physician but she is also an employee, administrator, and member of the management team. As a result, she has conflicting obligations. She is faced with seemingly incompatible obligations to patient confidentiality and to managerial needs to protect the company against threats against its well-being. If the doctor was not a member of management, it would be clear that confidentiality would be owed to her patient. On the other hand, if she were an evaluating physician functioning solely in an administrative role she would have indicated to the employee that the consultation was not confidential. She could then disclose the information to the company.

Perceived Conflict of Interest

Conflict of interest problems are not always easy to anticipate. Even the appearance of a conflict can pose substantial practical, administrative, and clinical problems.

Case Example 4

Joyce Black, a laboratory technician at a local university hospital, was referred for disability consultation to a member of the medical center's faculty, Dr. John Wright. The employee had been on a leave of absence for 3 months. Her treating psychiatrist for the past 3 months reported that she suffered from symptoms of depression and anxiety that stemmed from interpersonal conflict between Joyce and her immediate supervisor. The company wanted to know if her leave, symptoms, and need for treatment were from a work-related condition. Joyce went to the consultation and learned of Dr. Wright's faculty appointment. As it happened, she was working in the same medical school department. She then said that she felt he could not be unbiased and that she was uncomfortable revealing information to him. Joyce ended the interview convinced that she had been set up by management. She later contacted her union and was directed to legal counsel.

This case illustrates how referral sources and consultants must be sensitive to even the appearance or perception of a conflict of interest. Other clinicians in the community could have been used for the needed consultation, in which case the employee may have cooperated and an adversarial process might not have followed.

Criminal Conduct

Analogous to the case of Mr. Green, criminal activities are sometimes disclosed in a confidential clinical setting. This information may threaten the continued viability of the treatment process. In such circumstances the clinician might sometimes encourage the patient to confess to authorities if treatment is to continue. State laws generally require clinicians to breach confidentiality when there is a real and present danger to the patient or to others. At other times, the clinician will feel torn between duty to the patient and other social obligations.

Case Example 5

Officer Peter Jones was a 10-year veteran of the municipal police department's narcotics unit. He was referred to the department's psychiatrist, Dr. Forrest Evans, after a shooting incident. This was standard departmental procedure and Peter's conduct was not under investigation. However, during short-term psychotherapy for posttraumatic symptoms, Dr. Evans learned that Peter was involved in drug sales. Dr. Evans felt he had a confidential relationship with Peter and so he could not reveal the drug sales to the commanding officer who made the referral. Dr. Evans instead worked therapeutically to have Peter come to terms with his illegal actions. Dr. Evans did not think the criminal behavior posed any imminent dangers. Peter did not turn himself in. Months later, evidence surfaced from an unrelated source and Peter was arrested. He resigned his position and served a brief jail term.

Administrative Influence

Situations also arise where clinicians are in salaried or contracted employment and companies attempt to influence the outcome of the clinical evaluation. There are times at which a company does not wish an employee to reenter the workplace. There are other instances in which the company does not feel that disability benefits should be granted. When these matters arise, there is danger that the clinician administrator may act in a way that is anything but unbiased.

Case Example 6

Dr. Kevin Harsch is a psychiatrist in charge of employee assistance services for a Fortune 500 corporation. Dr. Harsch decided to set up an outside evaluation of a middle-level manager. During a telephone conversation with the potential consultant, Dr. Harsch said that the manager had been on leave for major depression. He made it clear that the manager was not wanted back by senior management. However, the treating psychiatrist had released his patient for unrestricted return to his normal managerial duties. Dr. Harsch made it clear to the potential consultant that a report was expected that would preclude the manager from ever returning to work with the company.

This case reflects the power and potential for abuse that can come from a disregard for ethical issues in the mental health referral process.

Political maneuverings may be commonplace in any organization and often include improper actions. In clinical practice, professional ethics and the need to maintain public confidence require a scrupulous avoidance of improper actions.

Access to Professional Opinions and Records

Where a consultative report about an employee's condition and capacity to perform normal work duties is issued to a company, the employee will often want his or her own copy. Employees commonly assume that they have the ordinary rights to their medical records. The records here include all reports, doctor's notes, correspondence, and testing. In these administrative consultations, the employee must be told that resulting records are not generally covered under the same rights. The employee might obtain a copy of the formal report either with the consent of the company or through legal channels.

SUMMARY

Psychiatrists and other mental health clinicians have traditional responsibilities to patients and to confidentiality. When they are acting in administrative, legal, or consultative roles, they may have competing obligations as well. It is essential to make sure that referring sources, clinicians, and patients are all fully aware of the nature and obligations of every consultation. Confidentiality and its limits must be carefully discussed with referred employees. The purpose of the employee's meeting with a mental health practitioner should not be vague or misleading. Inattention to ethical guidelines or to proper communication can result in breaches of confidentiality, lack of informed consent, conflict of interest, perceived conflict of interest, undue administrative influence, and concerns about access to medical records. Appropriate attention to these issues increases the chance of beneficial results of the consultation process.

Bibliography
Committee on Medical Education, Group for the Advancement of Psychiatry. 1990. *A Casebook in Psychiatric Ethics.* New York: Brunner/Mazel.
Larsen, R. C. 1988. Ethical issues in psychiatry and occupational medicine. In *Psychiatric Injury in the Workplace,* R. Larsen and J. Felton (eds.), pp. 719-726. Philadelphia: Hanley and Belfus.
Rappeport, J. R. 1981. Ethics and forensic psychiatry. In *Psychiatric Ethics,* S. Black and P. Chodoff (eds.), pp. 255-276. New York: Oxford University Press.
Stone, A. A. 1987. *Law, Psychiatry and Morality.* Washington, D.C.: American Psychiatric Press.

APPENDIX

American College of Occupational and Environmental Medicine: Code of Ethical Conduct for Physicians Providing Occupational Medical Services

These principles are intended to aid physicians in maintaining ethical conduct in providing occupational medical service. They are standards to guide physicians in their relationship with the individuals they serve, with employers and workers' representatives, with colleagues in the health professions, and with the public.

Physicians should:

1. accord highest priority to the health and safety of the individual in the workplace;
2. practice on a scientific basis with objectivity and integrity;
3. make or endorse only statements which reflect their observations or honest opinion;
4. actively oppose and strive to correct unethical conduct in relation to occupational health service;
5. avoid allowing their medical judgment to be influenced by any conflict of interest;
6. strive conscientiously to become familiar with the medical fitness requirements, the environment and the hazards of the work done by those they serve, and with the health and safety aspects of the products and operations involved;
7. treat as confidential whatever is learned about individuals served, releasing information only when required by law or by over-riding public health considerations, or to other physicians at the request of the individual according to traditional medical ethical practice; and should recognize that employers are entitled to counsel about the medical fitness of individuals in relation to work, but are not entitled to diagnoses or details of a specific nature;
8. strive continually to improve medical knowledge, and should communicate information about health hazards in timely and effective fashion to individuals or groups potentially affected, and make appropriate reports to the scientific community;
9. communicate understandably to those they serve any significant observations about their health, recommending further study, counsel or treatment when indicated;
10. seek consultation concerning the individual or the workplace whenever indicated;
11. cooperate with governmental health personnel and agencies, and foster and maintain sound ethical relationships with other members of the health professions; and
12. avoid solicitation of the use of their services by making claims, offering testimonials, or implying results which may not be achieved, but they may appropriately advise colleagues and others of services available.

Reproduced with permission from the American College of Occupational and Environmental Medicine.

4

Psychiatry and the Organization: A Brief History of Occupational Psychiatry

Alan A. McLean, M.D.

ABSTRACT

From the time of Elmer Southard, chief of psychiatry for the U.S. Army during World War I (and later chief psychiatrist at Harvard and consultant to the Engineering Foundation), to the early 1980s, psychiatrists were the dominant force in work organizations concerned about employee mental health. This chapter outlines the development of the role of the occupational psychiatrist by summarizing the work of dozens of leaders in the field. Their early contributions focused on the emotionally disturbed employee. More recently the field has grown to encompass the impact of the organization on the individual and the health of the organization itself. Specific activities included clinical work consulting with employee-patients, applied research, management and employee education, and consultation on organizational policy. As more nonmedical professionals have become involved with employee mental health problems, occupational psychiatrists have broadened their role to include concern with mental health benefits and many of the more sophisticated issues considered in other chapters of this book.

Industrial medicine exists, industrial psychiatry ought to exist. . . . I think that we will have a place in the routine of industrial management not as a permanent staff member (except in very large firms and business systems) but as consultants. The function of this occasional consultant would be preventative rather than curative of the general condition of unrest.

Elmer Southard (1920)

INTRODUCTION

Historically, concern for the mental health of people at work has been the province of psychiatrists to a greater extent than any other discipline. In the same way that the occupational physician over the years has been mainly responsible for the physical well-being of workers, so too, the medical arm of the mental health disciplines pioneered and maintains the leadership role when it comes to clinical concerns for psychiatric aspects of health.

To be sure, "basic" sciences, from early on, have also made significant contributions to the understanding of physical and emotional aspects of individuals reacting to their work environments Toxicologists, ergonomists, and industrial hygienists have provided specialized understanding of the potential threats of the physical work setting. Social psychologists and other behavioral scientists have given us tremendous knowledge of behavior in the work force. But the prime responsibility for both dealing with the impact of mental and physical disorders in the world of work and promoting healthy behavior has fallen to the physician.

Illustrative of one aspect of the practice of occupational psychiatry from its early days to date are situations that involve individual psychopathology and its interaction with the work organization. The clinical side of practice often involves evaluation of patients referred by medical department staff, by management, and, of course, by employees themselves. In one sense this is the traditional role of the medical consultant in any setting. In the occupational setting, the focus of complaints is more often apt to be work-related; intervention strategies frequently enlist some aspect of the job.

Clinical Case

Some years ago in a large manufacturing plant, fifteen women worked in the secretarial pool, a staff that provided support for most of the supervisors and managers in the 5,000-employee organization. Many considered their jobs stressful. The work flow entailed the transcription of dictation with little face-to-face contact with those whose work they processed. In fact, they often could not associate a face with the nameless voices, sometimes garbled, whose documents they transcribed. The main feedback to the transcribers was usually in the form of criticism of the final reports or letters that were sent anonymously back to the dictators. There was time pressure in the form of different voices asking why a document was not yet transcribed. The department was managed by a supervisor and two assistant supervisors who were also women.

There was an excellent medical department at the location with two full-time physicians and several part-time consultants including a half-time psychiatrist. Over the course of several weeks, twelve of the secretarial staff reported to "Medical" with a variety of stress-related complaints. There were psychophysiological reactions, and significant symptoms of anxiety and depression. A number of cases were referred to the psychiatric consultant who, in addition to evaluating and often referring the patient, made a detailed inquiry into the current work situation.

The secretarial pool was known to be a trying place to work. In the past, only an occasional employee felt the need to seek medical department help. "What might have changed?" wondered the consultant. This was the question he put to each secretary he saw.

The replies were invariably the same. The department supervisor had become increasingly short-tempered and demanding. She did not seem to be as much on top of the work load as she had been previously. Rather than serving as a buffer between secretaries and the "client" dictators, she simply relayed their frustrations and complaints, often siding with them and demanding that all their needs be met. (As one of the patients said, "I can't satisfy thirty people every day in every way. I can't have thirty bosses!")

The supervisor had also been a recent visitor to the medical department. There were entries over the past few months in her medical file about serious personal problems (potential marital breakup), menopausal symptoms, and mild depression. She had not been referred to the psychiatric consultant. Nor did it appear necessary to do so. She was apparently receiving good care from her own physician with whom the local medical director had been in touch.

In a meeting between the consultant and the medical director, the psychiatrist's observations were reviewed. Clearly, he thought, the symptoms of the employees were related to those of the supervisor. The medical director, without breaching confidence, sought a meeting with the supervisor's manager. He suggested that there were an unusually large number of medical cases coming from the department and suggested that the manager look into the situation. Being a competent executive, the manager launched his own low-key investigation, visiting the department more often and talking with the employees and supervisor. He rapidly came to the same conclusion as the consultant.

In a matter of days, he arranged for the supervisor to receive a new temporary assignment: a staff project that was recognized as requiring her skills and that resulted in no loss of face for her. One of the assistant supervisors was appointed the new supervisor of the department. Within a short time, employees' symptoms vanished, morale improved sharply, and productivity rose.

This rather classic combination of the application of clinical and managerial skills demonstrates the kind of effect an occupational psychiatric consultant can have on both individuals and organizations. Rather than suggesting treatment for the employees who presented with significant symptoms, he explored their work environment indirectly and effected the best health interests not only of the employee-patients but also those of their supervisor.

During recent years, there has been a sharp increase in practitioners of nonmedical disciplines who have become concerned with the mental health of employees and their dependents. For a while in the 1950s in the southeastern United States, pastoral counselors outnumbered psychiatrists as consultants to employers and employees. The R. J. Reynolds Tobacco Company built a chapel in which employees were counseled by a minister. Of considerably greater significance, the employee assistance movement, originally staffed mainly by recovering alcoholics in the 1950s (starting at DuPont and Mobil), burgeoned during the 1980s into a much more sophisticated group of employee counselors who are often psychologists and psychiatric social workers. There are now more than 6,000 such professionals providing counseling and referral services to employees and their dependents. Although some see this movement as a professional threat to occupational psychiatry, the employee counselors' role is much more limited than that of the psychiatrists; their skills are largely confined to short-term clinical evaluation and referral of workers and their families, only sometimes with psychiatric supervision. The scope of employee assistance program (EAP) activities is also expanding to encompass mental health case management, although that activity remains largely the province of firms specializing in such services (see Chapter 2).

At the same time, the role of the psychiatrist has assumed a breadth unforeseen by Dr. Southard, even though the preventive, consultative responsibilities he suggested in 1920 remain the principal work in the field. The readings in this book clearly testify to that fact.

EARLY HISTORY

In the first issue of the journal *Mental Hygiene,* Herman Adler, chief of staff of the Boston Psychopathic Hospital, reported on the psychiatric symptoms of patients for whom the lack of a job had been a serious problem (Adler 1917). These males, between the ages of 25 and 55, were grouped into three classifications: paranoid personalities, inadequate personalities, and the emotionally unstable. Three years later Mary Jarrett followed up this same group of patients, and observed that 75 percent had become successfully adjusted from an occupational point of view (Jarrett 1920). These were among the first articles appearing in the literature that could properly be included in an emerging field of occupational or industrial psychiatry.

Meanwhile, in England, starting at the time of World War I, the Industrial Fatigue Research Board began to focus attention on the psychological components of industrial accidents (Greenwood 1918), on fatigue, and on psychiatric illness in the work setting (Culpin and Smith 1930). Basic concepts of accident proneness and our first indications of the prevalence of psychiatric disorder in an industrial population came from this work.

1920S AND 1930S: PSYCHIATRISTS IN THE WORKPLACE

The first "Review of Industrial Psychiatry" in the *American Journal of Psychiatry* in April 1927 summarized the literature to date, defined the field, and traced its development. Mandel Sherman, the author, considered the psychiatrist's proper area of concern to be the "individual's adjustment to the situation as a whole." The psychiatrist, working in industry, was also portrayed as one who "attempts to forestall maladjustments by aiding in developing interests and incentives" (Sherman 1927).

At the conclusion of his review of the field, Sherman said that, among the various methods of industrial psychiatry, the most successful procedure used to aid the individual in adjusting to industry had been the analysis of the total situation: the patient's early life history, social situation, and his or her motives and incentives, in addition to the immediate difficulties at work. His major appeal was for increased vocational guidance during the formative years to obviate many later industrial maladaptations.

While the language may seem archaic, the meanings of Sherman's words seem remarkably contemporary some 65 years later: Consider all aspects of the patient's situation and focus preventive work on early exposure to work-related activities.

In 1922 the first full-time psychiatrist (of which we have a full description) was employed by an American business organization. Lydia Giberson joined the Metropolitan Life Insurance Company in New York. At first she apparently focused on clinical work in the medical department, later moving to the personnel area with broader responsibilities including involvement with organizational policy and practice (Giberson 1936). It may be of some interest that 65 years later The Metropolitan hosted one of a series of dinner meetings of the New York Occupational Psychiatry Group in the same building in which she had worked.

In 1924 a mental health service was introduced at the R. H. Macy department store. V. V. Anderson (1929) summarized this program in the first book on industrial psychiatry. He described modeling his activity after the child guidance clinics of the time: that is, with a psychiatrist, psychologist, and psychiatric social worker serving as staff.

In addition to clinical counseling of employees and consulting to management on "problem" behavior of employees, Anderson became interested in several organizational problems such as the high accident rate among delivery truck drivers. In the space of some 2 years he implemented programs that reduced that rate by two thirds. With the onset of the economic depression in 1930, Anderson's program was discontinued. In the late 1930s, Macy's again sought a psychiatrist to serve as a full-time organizational consultant. Temple Burling focused on morale issues, among others. In the process, he found the "executive elevator" and other status symbols to be disruptive and his suggestions led to a less hierarchical administration (Burling 1942).

1940S: WAR STRESS AND INITIAL ACADEMIC EFFORTS

After World War II, Burling went to Cornell University's School of Industrial and Labor Relations in Ithaca, New York, where he headed the program of 2-year Carnegie Fellowships in Industrial Psychiatry for psychiatrists who had completed their formal clinical training. (Some twelve fellows completed that training; Burling and Longaker 1955). His distinguished academic career at Cornell provided leadership for nonpsychiatric graduate students, impressive behavioral research (Burling, Lentz, and Wilson 1956), and active participation in the distinguished research and teaching of the human relations group on that campus. The group included psychiatrists Alexander and Dorothea Leighton, sociologist William Foote Whyte, and so many other brilliant academicians that the rest of this chapter could easily be consumed with a litany of their works.

Although Alexander Leighton would consider himself a social psychiatrist rather than an occupational psychiatrist, his research teams at Cornell often included industrial psychiatry fellows. His exhaustive studies of behavior, mental health, and mental disorder in defined populations established methodologies equally applicable to the assessment of work populations. His students subsequently did apply many of his concepts in understanding both healthy and disordered behavior in industry (for instance, see Leighton 1959.)

To keep this condensed version of the history of occupational psychiatry within the bounds of allotted space, readers are referred to an excellent summary of developments during the 1930s (Rennie, Swackhamer, and

Woodward 1947). Actually, the depression years were characterized by quiescence in the field; even the annual review of industrial psychiatry that had appeared regularly in the *American Journal of Psychiatry* for several years was dropped.

The Second World War exerted a remarkable impact on the clinical applications of psychiatry in the industrial setting. The expectations on the part of employers were high, perhaps unrealistically so, and to a certain extent psychiatry was oversold. Yet during the war years greater and more sophisticated applications could be seen (Brody 1945; Ling 1945; Lott 1946; McLean and Taylor 1958).

Among the many mental health programs in wartime industry, those at the Oak Ridge, Tennessee, Industrial Community subsequently received much attention (Burlingame 1946, 1947, 1948, 1949). With available psychiatric assistance, primarily through "emotional first aid stations," a minimum of on-the-job treatment led to conspicuous performance improvements among employees. As with the writings of psychiatrists before the war, those reporting their wartime experiences in civilian industry noted that stressors associated with psychiatric disabilities lay primarily in individual vulnerability or in the home or nonwork social surroundings, rather than in the job situation.

Meanwhile, in the Armed Forces, psychiatrists were called on to make significant clinical and research contributions that in many ways paralleled their prewar and postwar activities. Roy Grinker and John Spiegel, two psychiatrists in the Army Air Force, observed a large number of combat fliers in the European theater. Their careful observations of these men under stress included background details, personality characteristics, types of breakdown, and a description of the day-to-day existence of hundreds of fliers. This work provided valuable insight into reactions to major environmental stressors (Grinker and Spiegel 1945, iv). They concluded

> The stress of wars tries men as no other test that they may have encountered in civilized life. Like a crucial experiment it exposes the underlying physiological and psychological mechanisms of the human being. Cruel, destructive and wasteful though such an experiment may be, exceedingly valuable lessons can be learned from it regarding the methods by which men adapt themselves to all forms of stress, either in war or in peace.

They went on to say, "If the stress is severe enough, if it strikes an exposed 'Achilles heel' and if the exposure is sufficiently prolonged, adverse psychological symptoms may develop in anyone."

Their work helped to establish a baseline for our subsequent understanding of major stress reactions and such entities as posttraumatic stress disorders. In many ways, Grinker and Spiegel laid the groundwork for clinical methods of studying occupational stressors and psychosomatic reactions to them.

Following the war, with the sharp cutback in defense industries that had employed psychiatrists, many industrial mental health programs came to a halt. It is noteworthy that almost all occupational and military mental health activities before, during, and for some time after the war were headed by psychiatrists and were firmly embedded in occupational health units.

A number of new postwar psychiatric programs, such as those at Eastman Kodak Company (Dr. Ralph Collins) and American Cyanamid (Dr. Walter Woodward), grew out of a corporate desire to help returning veterans adapt successfully to their peacetime work. The federal government initiated the Vocational Rehabilitation Act Amendments of 1943 and established the Office of Vocational Rehabilitation. Stimulus was given to the training of clinical psychologists in greater numbers, primarily in programs of the Veterans Administration. Many were subsequently to work in industry.

1950S AND 1960S: INCREASING CLINICAL INVOLVEMENT

The decade following the war saw a rapidly growing interest in the field among psychiatrists and employers. The activities of Collins and Woodward may serve as examples of private-sector programs. Ralph Collins was both a neurologist and psychiatrist who devoted half time to the medical department at Eastman Kodak in Rochester, New York. His efforts also included private practice. His concerns were, for the most part, clinical. He evaluated patients referred to him by other physicians in the medical department and made recommendations about their psychiatric treatment and ability to work. Perhaps more important than his daily efforts at Kodak was his role as a spokesperson for industrial psychiatry. During the 1950s and 1960s he served as chairperson of the American Psychiatric Association's (APA) Committee on Industrial (later Occupational) Psychiatry for more than a decade. In the same capacity at the Group for the Advancement of Psychiatry, Collins made these bodies the centers of professional interaction in the field. He was also influential in ensuring a place on the annual APA program for speakers on topics relating to occupational psychiatry.

Worker compensation for disability "arising out of the course of employment" received increasing attention. By the 1950s the courts had ruled a wide variety of illness and injury, including psychiatric, to be compensable. Coronary infarcts occurring on the job following occupational stress, hypertension, cancer, and tuberculosis activated by employment, suicide caused by job-related depression, and "paralysis by fright" had all been ruled compensable (Lesser 1967). This trend continues to receive close attention as awards for "work stress" and psychiatric disability increase annually. Indeed, for several years during the late 1970s and early 1980s in the state of

Michigan, following a State Supreme Court case, a worker had only to "honestly believe" that his work was responsible for psychiatric disability to be eligible for worker compensation benefits. As we move into the last decade of this century, in California at least, awards for "cumulative psychiatric injury" are among the most common of worker compensation cases. Psychiatric evaluation and worker compensation court testimony, which started in the late 1940s, remains an increasingly important segment of occupational psychiatry (McLean 1979).

Work in occupational psychiatry was not limited to the United States. From the Tavistock Clinic in London came the first volume of the seminal Glacier Metal Company studies, led by Elliott Jaques (1951). Both the methodology and the research results of this pioneering application of psychoanalytic concepts to the study of organizational behavior had considerable influence on the development of subsequent programs. Jaques's volume is a highly recommended landmark for psychiatrists interested in work organizations. Jaques's later concepts of equitable wage payment based on the time span of job responsibility were published in the 1960s but had their roots in earlier work (1956).

During the 1950s, Erland Mindus from Stockholm conducted a 6-month study of industrial psychiatry in Great Britain, the United States, and Canada for the World Health Organization. He later developed his own concept of industrial psychiatry (Mindus 1955). The survey resulted in an extensive report on occupational psychiatric programs in English-speaking countries. Mindus visited plants, universities, institutions, agencies, and union facilities, summarizing his observations and relating them to earlier experiences in the Scandinavian countries (Mindus 1952).

Formal interest in, and acceptance of, the role of the psychiatrist in work organizations in Western Europe and North America was made clear at the Fourteenth International Congress of Occupational Health held in Madrid in 1963. More than forty presentations were concerned with the psychological problems of the work environment. The 1964 annual meeting of the World Federation for Mental Health (at the time a fairly powerful international force whose annual meetings brought together well over a thousand attendees) held in Berne, Switzerland, had its entire program devoted to mental health in industry. During that meeting some twenty mental health professionals (mainly psychiatrists) formed the International Committee on Occupational Mental Health. This group is still active in the 1990s, with some four hundred members mostly in Western Europe. The First International Congress on Social Psychiatry in London, also held in 1964, included many formal presentations on occupational psychiatry.

In the United States, APA surveys indicated that more than two hundred psychiatrists were active in work organizations. New professional organizations were created, including the Occupational Psychiatry Group in New

York City (still active as a part of the New York State Occupational Medical Association) and the Center for Occupational Mental Health that sponsored seminars and published their proceedings, trained psychiatric fellows, produced *Occupational Mental Health Notes,* and published the journal *Occupational Mental Health* from 1970 to 1973. The center was started by me in 1963, became a part of the Department of Psychiatry at Cornell University Medical College in 1966, and remained an interdisciplinary communications center until the early 1980s. Some of the center's conference publications are listed among the references (McLean 1967, 1970, 1974, 1978).

Under the leadership of clinical psychologist Harry Levinson, the Division of Industrial Mental Health of the Menninger Foundation conducted research on the psychological meaning of work to employees and operated a fellowship program in industrial psychiatry and educational programs for management personnel and occupational physicians. A variety of seminars and other mental health programs for managers and others continue to be made available at Menninger's. Levinson moved to the Harvard Business School and later started the Levinson Institute in Cambridge, Massachusetts, which remains an active, psychoanalytically oriented center for consultation and education in the occupational mental health arena.

During these two decades many new programs of psychiatric consultation got underway. The majority were staffed by part-time consultants, although some full-time psychiatrists were also employed. Most were based in occupational medical departments, although a few reported to personnel and other management staffs. Their work might consist of straightforward clinical evaluation or treatment with varying regard to the circumstances of the work setting, of clinical consultation, education, training, policy consultation, research, or a combination of these; the last arrangement was most common for those spending a major part of their time in the work setting.

Publications of the 1950s and 1960s varied in their content from psychodynamic speculations to descriptions of occupational mental health programs. Many writers continued an earlier trend of exhorting and directing others to develop better mental health programs or to become interested in psychiatric problems in the world of work. Carefully executed clinical research was not often seen in the literature. Many clinical programs of fair sophistication did not see the light of the printed page, the feeling of some employers being that the conduct of mental health programs and the results of related research within organizations are properly proprietary.

Annual reviews of publications and activities in industrial psychiatry, reinstated by Burlingame (1946), continued in the *American Journal of Psychiatry* written by Collins and others (for instance, see Collins 1956). Business publications of the time contained fairly regular articles on occupational mental health issues as well as quotations from psychiatric consultants to industry. These publications, such as the *Wall Street Journal,* provided sound, objective reporting. Others made light of programs and psychiatric commentary. One example of the latter will serve to illustrate. The publication of *Mental Health in Industry* received considerable publicity and led to invitations to both Graham Taylor and the author to provide interviews and make various presentations (McLean and Taylor 1958). At a one-day seminar at the University of Santa Clara, one of the topics discussed (which had been covered extensively in the book) had to do with the way in which various personality characteristics determine career choices. It was pointed out that an individual with fairly deviant behaviors could be quite productive if properly placed in a work organization. Although the author had been told the press would not attend the program, the *San Francisco Examiner* the next morning carried a headline, "IBM Hires Nuts!" (At the time the author was chief psychiatric consultant for the company.) The story was picked up by more than two hundred papers around the country.

1970S, 1980S, AND 1990S: EXPANDING PSYCHIATRIC HORIZONS

In addition to the kinds of ongoing activities previously described, the practice of occupational psychiatry during the past two decades became increasingly concerned with five important areas of interest: (1) work stress, (2) drug abuse among employees, (3) employee assistance programs, (4) mental health benefits utilization, and (5) the study and enhancement of organizational culture. Advances in these areas are discussed in other chapters of this book. In particular, advances in occupational psychiatry have paralled the advances in psychiatric diagnosis and treatment.

THE ORGANIZATION AS THE PATIENT

Today some psychiatrists speak of the organizational climate. Others write of concern with a corporate culture. Still others talk of their work in organizational development. Each has moved away from clinical concerns with individual patients in the work setting and with their psychopathology to the development of techniques to enhance the positive health-promoting aspects of the organization itself. Although the roots of this concern for stimulating a healthy work environment have been evident in the historical outline presented earlier, psychiatric activities in pursuit of this goal have trended upward in the past several years.

Some psychiatrists have dealt with specific problems, such as those inherent in the stress felt by the employees remaining in an organization that has been downsized. Others have worked with organizational members (not always management) when there is an executive effort to realign and reorganize to become a more effective enterprise. Some have identified a problem, such as that referred to at the beginning of this chapter where an entire department was turned around by psychiatric intervention as a result of an excessive number of employees reporting with specific psychosomatic or emotional complaints. The study described as follows falls somewhere in between.

Applied Occupational Psychiatric Research

Applied occupational psychiatric research was a part of the IBM mental health program from its inception in 1957. Each major location with a medical department had a local psychiatric consultant. Until the organization decentralized in the late 1960s, Corporate Headquarters used a full-time psychiatrist (at times with a small research staff) who coordinated all IBM mental health services. This person, as part of his subsequent duties managing various aspects of IBM medical programs, continued to be viewed by the company as its chief psychiatrist and organized studies of various applied mental health research projects.

In the course of the consulting work, much of the psychiatrists' time was spent meeting with groups of managers in both formal executive development programs and in less formal visits to various departments in development laboratories and factories. Over the course of several months during the early 1960s there was a sharp rise in the number of complaints and concerns about an increase in stress perceived by some managers. They gave personal examples of the increased pressures to produce "impossible" results: to push their people beyond reasonable productivity. They reported personal symptoms of both physical and emotional reactions to this increasing work stress in the work environment. This was in contrast to a firm but understanding emotional climate that had existed in prior years. Many managers perceived this change as coming from the top of the company.

The chief psychiatric consultant did not want to go "up the ladder" with such anecdotal reports and to be seen as an alarmist. The entire top management was aware that the heat was on to develop and manufacture a new, extremely sophisticated, product line. The consultants were all sure that top management would not want to hear that the process was so stressful to those involved as they had been hearing. Nor were they convinced that they had hard data.

As with the introduction of any new process or product, adaptation to the challenges and problems associated with its introduction are first felt in the development laboratories, then in the manufacturing facilities, then in the marketplace, and then in customer locations. The need to adapt moves across the organizational units of a company and many work units is affected by the force of the results. So also are the many individuals within those units, in this case, most particularly those in management. The decision was therefore made to try to understand more clearly some of the stressors acting on the organizational system and the individuals who were a part of it. The idea was to identify the specific pressures faced by these individuals with a view toward moderating them if possible. The goal was also to be able to present quantified data to top management to help them "size" the problem and be able to act on the most pressing issues that had been identified by an intense, but careful, study.

Applied Research Example

With the help of academic consultants and company personnel research professionals, a questionnaire was prepared and rapidly pretested. It examined satisfaction with work, perceived stress of the organization and specific tasks, and the extent of specific physical and emotional problems. Twelve questions also centered on anxiety levels. All questions were structured to compare the participants' current feelings with their feelings on the same issues 3 years before, which was a time of relative organizational calm. Questionnaires were returned to the chief consultant anonymously.

Armed with the results of the first few hundred questionnaires, the chief consultant was able to persuade key management personnel to allow him to present the data to top management. (By this time, he had learned that in such consulting one does not "blindside" those key people in subordinate positions by going directly to the top brass. A consultant generally needs the cooperation of as many players in the game as possible before dropping a potential bombshell in the lap of the chief executive officer and his or her immediate staff.)

Significant issues were indeed identified by the data. For example, it was clear that those who reported the highest job and perceived organizational stress were also those that reported the highest anxiety and the lowest morale. Specific stressors were identified for each of the development, manufacturing, marketing, and service divisions involved with the new products. Some trouble spots were able to be "fixed" by executive order. But the two most significant results of bringing the data to the attention of top management were (1) to promote dialogue about stressful situations between corporate and division officials, which led to greater corporate support for divisional efforts, and (2) to request additional studies on management stress over the next few years.

The corporate psychiatrist and his staff were encouraged to break out data by divisions and meet with divisional staff to discuss the ramifications and meaning of the data and to assist in utilizing the material to improve the situation for those divisional managers. A few departments in some divisions, for instance, had high morale and relatively low levels of perceived stress and anxiety. Calling attention to those productive groups allowed division management to study their department managers' leadership styles for possible lessons to apply elsewhere. In contrast, specific groups were identified with very high levels of perceived stress. They were the focus of intense divisional efforts to understand the unique problems present that led to the stress and to attempt to modify stressors.

Both the baseline studies and those carried out over the next 3 years allowed the researchers to trace the responses over time for the manufacturing, marketing, and service divisions involved with the new product. (The development people had, soon after the baseline study, returned to business as usual.)

The first two questions had to do with a manager's perception of the stress in the company. In each case the manager was asked to give a rating on a 5-point scale from "much more stressful" to "much less stressful." The top two classifications of "much more stressful" and "somewhat more stressful" were combined to give the percentages shown in Table 4-1.

In this table the baseline population was, unfortunately, not sufficiently differentiated to give separate figures for the three groups. Note that those responsible for manufacturing felt the company was less stressful after 36 months than at 18 months. At 18 months, 81 percent felt the company was much more or somewhat more stressful than 3 years prior, and at 36 months, only 60 percent did. The marketing group's perception of stress rose considerably at 18 months to 89 percent and dropped at 36 months to a still relatively high level of 77 percent. The service managers' perception of stress also rose dramatically as they became enmeshed in learning about and installing the first pieces of equipment, and it remained very high at 36 months. Service people, of course, are the last to feel the impact of new processes.

One of the questions that was used to get some feeling for anxiety level led to important information. It suggested one reason that a high correlation was

TABLE 4-1   **Manager's Perceived Stress During New Product Development and Introduction**

	Manufacturing	Marketing	Service
Baseline	82%	82%	82%
Plus 18 months	81%	89%	96%
Plus 36 months	60%	77%	88%

found between anxiety level, perception of increased stress of work, and job dissatisfaction. The question was, "How often do you feel tense or nervous on the job?" The question correlated highly with the total anxiety scores. The responses demonstrated a slight rise from baseline for manufacturing and service managers at 18 months, and a moderate rise for marketing personnel. At 36 months, however, the curves even more closely mirrored those for perceived job stress and morale. (Today it is generally accepted that a fairly high correlation exists between anxiety, job stress, and low morale — indeed most researchers would be surprised if it were not the case in studies such as this one. At the time of the work described, however, this information was new.)

What was seen in this study was a wave of perceived stress, anxiety, and low morale sweeping across parts of an organization, catching up those whose work was most affected at the time. First, the development and manufacturing people struggling with a technology that was totally new to them. Next, the involvement of those who had to present the new equipment and its applications to the outside world before they were comfortable with it, and finally, those whose work was to install and maintain machinery that represented a new and much higher level of technology than they had ever known. By building into the system ongoing monitoring and feedback to top management, the psychiatric consultation process both allowed sophisticated input and dialogue, and probably reduced the reactions reported above.

This study suggests that psychiatric consultation can successfully use many methods in assessing and working on dynamic organizational issues. A common theme, however, of much of the material presented in this chapter is that the occupational psychiatrist needs to have in sight the fact that the patient is not only the individual in the organization but the organization itself!

SUMMARY

The long history of occupational psychiatry dates back at least as far as World War I. In that time, psychiatrists have played an increasing role in addressing workplace issues of individual and organizational mental health. Increasing knowledge and workplace contributions have resulted from the efforts of many psychiatrists. While the earliest activities focused on emotionally distressed employees, the field has grown to encompass the impact of the organization on the individual and the health of the organization itself. These pioneering efforts have broadened to reflect concern with mental health benefits, the recent contributions of nonmedical professionals, and the more sophisticated issues that are considered elsewhere in this volume.

Bibliography

Adler, H. 1917. Unemployment and personality. *Mental Hygiene* **1**:16-24.

Anderson, V. V. 1929. *Psychiatry in Industry.* New York: Harper & Brothers.

Brody, M. 1945. Dynamics of mental hygiene in industry. *Industrial Medicine and Surgery* **14**:760.

Burling, T. 1942. The role of the professionally trained mental hygienist in business. *American Journal of Orthopsychiatry* **11**:48.

Burling, T., E. M. Lentz, and R. N. Wilson. 1956. *The Give and Take in Hospitals.* New York: G. P. Putnam's Sons.

Burling, T., and W. Longaker. 1955. Training for industrial psychiatry. *American Journal of Psychiatry* **111**:493.

Burlingame, C. C. 1946. Psychiatry in industry. *American Journal of Psychiatry* **103**:549.

Burlingame, C. C. 1947. Psychiatry in industry. *American Journal of Psychiatry* **104**:493.

Burlingame, C. C. 1948. Psychiatry in industry. *American Journal of Psychiatry* **105**:538.

Burlingame, C. C. 1949. Psychiatry in industry. *American Journal of Psychiatry* **106**:520.

Collins, R. T. 1956. Industrial psychiatry. *American Journal of Psychiatry* **112**:546.

Culpin, M., and M. Smith. 1930. *The Nervous Temperament.* Medical Research Council, Industrial Health Research Board, Report Number 61. London: His Majesty's Stationery Office.

Dickerson, O. B., and A. J. Kaminer (eds.). 1986. *Occupational Medicine: State of the Art Reviews,* vol. 1 (no. 4), *The Troubled Employee.* Philadelphia: Hanley & Belfus.

Giberson, L. G. 1936. Psychiatry in industry. *Personnel Journal* **15**:91.

Greenwood, L. G. 1918. *A Report on the Cause of Wastage of Labour in Munitions Factories.* London: Government Publications, Medical Research Council. His Majesty's Stationery Office.

Grinker, R. R., and J. P. Spiegel. 1945. *Men Under Stress.* Philadelphia: Blakiston.

Group for the Advancement of Psychiatry, Committee of Governmental Agencies. 1973. *The VIP with Psychiatric Impairment.* Report No. 83. New York: Group for the Advancement of Psychiatry.

Group for the Advancement of Psychiatry, Committee of Psychiatry in Industry. 1982. *Job Loss—A Psychiatric Perspective.* Report No. 109. New York: Mental Health Materials Center.

Group for the Advancement of Psychiatry, Committee on Research. 1966. *Psychiatric Research and the Assessment of Change.* Report No. 63. New York: Group for the Advancement of Psychiatry.

Jaques, E. 1951. *The Changing Culture of a Factory.* New York: Dryden Press.

Jaques, E. 1956. *Measurement of Responsibility.* Cambridge, Mass.: Harvard University Press.

Jarrett, M. C. 1920. The mental hygiene of industry. Report of progress on work undertaken under the Engineering Foundation of New York City. *Mental Hygiene* **4**:867.

Kahn, R., K. Hein, J. House, S. Kasl, and A. McLean. 1982. Report of stress in organizational settings. In *Stress and Human Health* (A study by the Institute of Medicine/National Academy of Sciences), G. R. Elliott and C. Eisdorfer (eds.), pp. 81–118. New York: Springer.

Leighton, A. 1959. *My Name Is Legion.* New York: Basic Books.

Lesser, P. J. 1967. The legal viewpoint. In *To Work Is Human,* A. McLean (ed.), pp. 103–122. New York: Harper.

Ling, T. M. 1945. Roffey Park Rehabilitation Centre. *Lancet* i:283.

Lott, G. M. 1946. Emotional first-aid stations in industry. *Industrial Medicine and Surgery* 15:419.

McLean, A. A. 1967. *To Work Is Human: Mental Health and the Business Community.* New York: Macmillan.

McLean, A. A. 1970. *Mental Health and Work Organizations.* Chicago: Rand McNally.

McLean, A. A. 1974. *Occupational Stress.* Springfield, Ill.: Charles C Thomas.

McLean, A. A. (ed.). 1978. *Reducing Occupational Stress.* DHEW (NIOSH) Publication No. 78-140. Washington, D.C.: National Institute for Occupational Safety and Health.

McLean, A. A. 1979. *Work Stress.* Reading, Mass.: Addison Wesley.

McLean, A. A., and G. Taylor. 1958. *Mental Health in Industry.* New York: McGraw Hill.

Matteson, M. T., and J. M. Ivancevich. 1987. *Controlling Work Stress.* San Francisco: Jossey-Bass.

Mindus, E. 1952. *Industrial Psychiatry in Great Britain, the United States, and Canada. A Report to the World Health Organization.* Geneva: World Health Organization.

Mindus, E. 1955. Outlines of a concept of industrial psychiatry. *Bulletin of the World Health Organization* 13:561.

Quick, J. C., R. S. Bhagat, J. E. Dalton, and J. D. Quick. 1987. *Work Stress.* New York: Praeger.

Rennie, T. A. C., G. Swackhamer, and L. E. Woodward. 1947. Toward industrial mental health: An historical review. *Mental Hygiene* 31:66.

Sherman, M. 1927. A review of industrial psychiatry. *American Journal of Psychiatry* 83:701.

Southard, E. E. 1920. The modern specialist in unrest: A place for the psychiatrist in industry. *Mental Hygiene* 4:550.

II

Common Organizational Problems

5

Disability, Worker's Compensation, and Fitness for Duty

Brian L. Grant, M.D., and David B. Robbins, M.D., M.P.H.

Work-Induced Psychiatric Injury
Fitness for Duty and Risk Assessment
Summary

ABSTRACT

Handicap and disability are defined as legal concepts and are distinguished from the medical concept of impairment. Several components of a detailed consultative impairment examination are outlined. There are important differences between treating physician and evaluating physician roles. Various types of disabling psychiatric injuries are found in the workplace and assessment is complicated by barriers to accurate data collection. Therefore, causal disability determination is a complex task with special challenges, somewhat unique among medical evaluation roles. A related evaluation task is psychiatric fitness for duty determination. Prevention of disability includes attention to factors both internal and external to the worker.

INTRODUCTION

The social, human, and economic costs of disability are enormous. Determination of disability for administrative and legal bodies is a complex and unique task that differs from the usual practice of medicine. The legal determination of disability differs significantly from the appraisal of medical needs. The evaluation is typically done at the request of a third party rather than the patient and the usual doctor-patient relationship is often absent. The disability determination evaluation includes usual clinical data. Special attention to causality determination, including attribution of injury or condition to a particular event, requires specific techniques. Complicating factors make such determinations especially challenging.

Psychiatric injury in the workplace has many causes and manifestations. The psychiatric assessment requires specific attention to the disability process, disability prevention, worker's compensation systems, and fitness for duty determination. There is a special role for such screening techniques as drug and psychometric testing. Predictive value is enhanced by a careful history of actual past functioning in comparable or parallel settings.

WORKPLACE DISABILITY PROBLEMS AND DEFINITIONS

Medical and psychiatric conditions contribute significantly to disability, lost work, and productivity. An estimated 9 million person years of restricted activity and 2 million person years of full disability due to illness occurred in 1980 (Parsons et al. 1986), and have dramatically increased since then. The cost of lost employment productivity during that year was more than $226 billion. The cost for diagnosis, treatment, and medical management was $154 billion. The total cost of disability illness and injury exceeded $380 billion in 1980. While physical injuries and poisoning account for only 8.8 percent, mental disorders represented a larger 9.4 percent of the total direct costs. The numbers are understated, since they do not account for the real value to society of volunteer and homemaker labor. Nor do the numbers include such nonquantifiable factors as psychological distress. In 1984, disability absence from chronic pain exceeded 700 million workdays. In 1985, 50 million people were partially or totally disabled. In many jurisdictions, claims and costs of psychiatric injury and stress are increasing at dramatic rates.

The costs to the affected employees are pain and suffering, lost wages, and social disruption. Also affected are the family of a disabled wage earner; productivity losses to industry and society; and costs borne by employers and government for wages, health care, and disability benefits. Since most workers spend much of their waking hours at work, and since work demands can be stressful, it is common for an impairment to first make itself evident in the workplace. This occurs whether the impairment is caused by work, aggravated by work, or even incidental to work.

Although this book concerns itself primarily with psychiatric issues, it is important to remember that many physical impairments have prominent emotional components that can result from disability, exacerbate disability, or even cause disability. An employer should be concerned about conditions that impair employee ability to function in the workplace. Enhanced awareness makes possible appropriate screening of workers and applicants, workplace prevention, and treatment of affected employees, which may help decrease the incidence and morbidity of these conditions.

The Legal Meaning of Disability

Disability is a multifaceted concept, with diverse connotations for both employee and society. It includes the legal meaning and definition, the individually experienced disability process, and the social implications. As a legal and administrative condition, disability is determined by a process that considers medical evidence and other criteria. According to the U.S. Social Security Administration definition, disability is "the inability to engage in any gainful activity, by reason of any medically determinable physical or mental impairment, which can be expected to result in death, or has lasted or can be expected to last for a continuous period of not less than 12 months." This description of disability essentially precludes any worker who can perform alternate work. Some other definitions have less stringent requirements.

Impairment

Disability occurs when medical impairment impedes ability to respond to external demands. Changes of either impairment or demand levels can initiate or eliminate disability. Physicians contribute to disability determination by establishing medical impairment.

Medical impairments are alterations in health status, medically measured as specific signs, symptoms, and laboratory findings that are attributable to bodily organ systems. Quantification efforts have resulted in impairment schedules that have been adapted by administrative bodies responsible for disability compensation determination. In addition to Social Security guidelines, the American Medical Association has offered its *Guides to the Evaluation of Permanent Impairment.* Also, some states have enacted their own specific guidelines for their worker's compensation systems. Each of these schedules attempts to rate impairment on a graded scale of severity. The correlation of medical status to a corresponding impairment rating is a complex task. It requires specific physician efforts that extend beyond the usual medical evaluation.

It is important to note that an impairment does not automatically constitute a disability. Even an impairment that would constitute a disability at one particular job might not be significant elsewhere. For example, an employee unable to remain standing for prolonged periods might be disabled for a job as a clothing salesperson but could still be a seated cashier. An employee's failure to function at work may be the result of many factors, including motivation and other voluntary elements. Impairment determination, though, should be based on objective medical and psychiatric data.

Handicaps

An individual is called handicapped if he or she has an impairment or record of an impairment that substantially limits one or more life activities, including work. In some settings people can be considered handicapped if they are merely regarded as having such an impairment. This definition is broad and is subject to legal interpretation. Operationally, handicap status is assigned when a barrier to functional activity exists. Accommodation to such barriers can often be accomplished with assisting devices, or modification of work or life environment and activities. If a handicapped employee still cannot perform employment tasks, he or she is considered disabled.

THE TREATING PHYSICIAN'S ROLE

The treating physician's role in impairment determination is complex. A patient may first present to a treating physician for clinical treatment with no expectation that impairment and disability might be at issue. Other patients, already pursuing a disability claim, may seek a treating physician with implicit or explicit expectations of medical evidence to support their claim. In both cases, the role of the treating physician should remain the same: to provide and record diagnosis and treatment. Not infrequently, the treating physician is placed in the untenable role of being asked to meet the perceived needs of patient, attorney, government, and employer. These several interests often have incompatible, or even antagonistic, needs.

In interaction with the patient, the treating physician has a special responsibility regarding diagnosis and treatment within accepted medical standards, and adherence to the requirements of the doctor-patient relationship. The doctor-patient dyad is fragile and is frequently challenged where disability is at issue. Tenets of this relationship include placing the interests of the patient first. Confidentiality can be broken only when waived by the patient, revoked by a court of law, or modified by predetermined administrative realities.

Legal revocation of confidentiality may occur when a patient makes a legal claim on a medical basis, declines to voluntarily waive confidentiality, and medical records are sought for a legal defense of the claim. For example, proper assessment of an employee who claims work-related psychiatric injury should include all past psychiatric history. The employee might be required to waive confidentiality of prior psychiatric evaluation and treatment. Legal revocation may also occur in criminal matters when medical history is felt to be relevant but the court has been denied access to medical records by the defendant. Confidentiality is regularly compromised in the normal course of medical practice by the requirements of financially responsible third parties. Medical records are obtained to process claims and determine medical necessity. Participation in insurance, reimbursement, and worker's compensation plans may imply a limited waiver of confidentiality as a condition of enrollment. Maintenance of an effective doctor-patient dyad requires careful attention to the therapeutic relationship and to breaches of confidentiality for third-party needs (see Chapter 3).

The treating physician is not necessarily concerned with determination of illness causality, unless causality affects treatment. For example, when treating a patient with back pain, it is important to learn if there is a vertebral fracture and how it occurred. However, a treating physician would be little concerned whether the fracture took place at work or in a backyard. That causal distinction is of utmost importance to an employer asked to accept legal or financial responsibility.

A treating physician must not become a patient advocate. It is essential to focus on proper diagnosis and treatment, while leaving advocacy to others. For example, physicians may be asked for statements of degree and cause of impairment. Reports should be limited to opinions of medical probability or certainty, regardless of the resulting legal or social effects on the patient.

Patients may become angry or seek care elsewhere when the physician's opinion is not consistent with their beliefs or wishes. Even so, the treating physician's obligation is clinical objectivity, despite his or her own emotional or financial concerns. To protect medical objectivity and the doctor-patient relationship, the physician may suggest an independent consultative examination.

THE PSYCHIATRIC DISABILITY CONSULTATIVE EXAMINATION

A disability claimant may be asked to attend a consultative examination separate from treatment. The examination may be mandated by an administrative body before considering or authorizing benefits or entitlements. Consultative examinations are most often conducted to resolve a medical question of concern to a third party. Interested third parties may include employers, insurance companies, courts of law, and attorneys for claimants or defendants in injury claims.

Reasons for consultative examination include assessments of impairment, cause of injury, and appropriateness of treatment. Examination results help determine eligibility for Social Security and private disability coverage, worker's compensation, benefits for work-related occupational disease (such as asbestosis claims), and they help determine outcome of civil litigation of tort claims. Consultative examinations are also used to assess treatment for the treating physician or a third party (such as the surgical second opinion required by many insurance carriers).

Both consultative examinations and clinical treatment include a careful and comprehensive medical history, review of pertinent records, and examination of the patient before reaching a medical opinion. Consultative examinations should only be conducted by qualified physicians and should abide by the same professional standards expected for clinical treatment. The consultation examination is solely for medical opinion and should not include treatment. However, the resulting medical report can offer useful information to the treating physician. Confidentiality must be explicitly waived in advance, since a medical report will be provided to a third party (see Chapter 3). Since competing interests may result in an apparently adversarial situation, the doctor-patient relationship is not usually maintained after the examination.

Subsequent clinical treatment by the consulting physician should be undertaken only with full awareness of competing obligations, associated emotions, potential problems, and alternate sources of medical care. Many consulting physicians will never treat anyone they have evaluated. Conflicts can arise between consulting physician and referral source, or current treating physician. In particular, questions can arise about the consulting physician's objectivity, if he or she provides treatment during continuing litigation or dispute resolution. Treatment under these circumstances might also be construed as a conflict of interest, potentially damaging the physician's reputation. In referrals for legal matters, the physician is sometimes expected to be explicitly unavailable to the patient (or representative) outside of a formal legal setting.

Regardless of purpose, any doctor-patient relationship must be compassionate, courteous, and respectful. The patient must be reminded at the outset that the examination is not for final diagnosis, not for medical treatment, not confidential, and that a written report will be provided to a third party. While it is not uncommon for an examination to uncover new medical problems or details, the patient must not rely on the consultative examination for comprehensive diagnosis or for medical care. A psychiatric examination, for instance, will not directly assess cardiac or neurological problems. Nevertheless, resulting medical information and opinion is of potential value to both the referring third party and to the patient.

EXAM CONDUCT

The following evaluation information should not be used as a beginner's guide to a psychiatric interview. Effective interviewing requires specific prior knowledge, training, and experience. Moreover, while this discussion assumes a careful and comprehensive standard psychiatric approach, it emphasizes only the more specialized aspects of disability examinations. Although technique will vary with every clinician, it is vital that examinations be careful and comprehensive, and that reports include all necessary medical data and resulting conclusions. Reports should be easy to read and should avoid esoteric technical jargon. Many parties without medical training may need to understand the findings, logic, and conclusions of the report.

Who Should Be Present

Since a psychiatric disability examination is a medical procedure, the physician should determine the process. Psychiatric interviews deal with personal experiences and feelings, and are always potentially sensitive or uncomfortable.

While patients should be protected from undue discomfort, full and honest responses are necessary for accurate assessment. Patients will sometimes request, or even demand, that they be accompanied during examination. Since refusal to allow an observer may lead to refusal of the examination, this issue is best discussed in advance.

Depending on local laws and the type of evaluation process, some patients may have a legal right to representation during examination. In these cases, the representative should not interfere either by offering unrequested information or by advising the patient not to respond to certain areas of inquiry. Any objections to particular questions should be saved for the subsequent administrative process.

There are also circumstances where the physician may request the presence of an assistant to help with a severely impaired or potentially violent patient. When physician and patient do not share a common language, a professional interpreter should translate rather than family or friends. Language interpretation requires training, experience, and sometimes special certification. Family or friends may have personal interests in the examination outcome and could inadvertently alter clinical data presented by the patient. Frequently, the patient will be unwilling to discuss intimate material in the presence of close companions.

Audiotape or videotape recording by patients is beyond the scope of normal procedures and should be discouraged. It intrudes on the privacy and comfort of the physician, especially if there is no control over disposition of the recording. Exceptions should be made by prior agreement and where the recording will be kept safely in administrative hands.

Medical Record and Collateral Information Review

The evaluating physician should review pertinent records for additional and independent information about the patient. In complex or prolonged cases, there may be many volumes of material. Record review should include past medical and psychiatric evaluation and treatment. Assessment of impairment can also utilize vocational reports, school records, employment records, and performance evaluations. These records can provide data about level of functioning over time, especially before the onset of the claimed disability. The written report should concisely summarize the records reviewed and allow the reader to easily retrieve relevant material.

Presenting Problem

One way to start the interview is with a nontechnical and nonspecific question about the patient's view of his or her disability or problem. For example, where a psychiatric condition is claimed, it is better to ask, "How are your spirits?" rather than "Do you have posttraumatic stress disorder?" Psychiatric terms often have varied meanings and a common definition should never be assumed. When patients have physical complaints that others feel have a significant emotional component, the physician might choose to avoid any initial reference to emotions. For example, a repeatedly disabled patient undergoing an evaluation for worker's compensation benefits might first be asked, "What situation keeps you from being able to work?"

Current, Past, and Family Psychiatric History

The next phase of the interview is commonly a psychiatric review of systems for potentially relevant psychiatric syndromes. Disability cases often involve affective (depressive) and anxiety disorders, psychosis, drug and alcohol abuse, organic mental disease, and personality disorders. Detailed past psychiatric history includes a careful review of past symptoms, syndromes, diagnoses, and treatment. Counseling and psychotherapy for emotional distress can come from a wide variety of sources. Substance abuse and other emotional problems often lead to encounters with police, court, and prison. A careful history of legal problems and litigation is also needed. Family history of psychiatric illness and treatment helps in diagnosis, and can be facilitated by drawing of a simple pedigree chart. The assessment should include requested impairment ratings according to a standard scale, such as the *American Medical Association Guide*. Never assume that level of functioning has necessarily declined as much as patients believe. For example, a young parent might leave clerical employment, yet continue to function well as primary caretaker of several children and a home. An administrator might feel unable to sit at an office desk, yet spend many hours reading at home.

Developmental, Social, and Employment History

Family and culture of origin are the primary sources of emotional outlook and define the framework of later interpersonal relationships. Early childhood experiences help mold adult personality and are important contributors to later problems, including psychiatric and medical disability. Adult experiences are more likely to shape existing structures than they are to induce entirely new problems. Knowledge of a patient's early life is essential for understanding present circumstances. One approach is to ask about early relationships with family and friends. Recent interest in childhood emotional, physical, psychological, and sexual abuse and neglect has focused attention on later development of adult depression, anxiety, dependence, and somatization. It is also important to understand religious and socioeconomic background, early home environment (including nontraditional arrangements), and family occupations. Early family losses and separations can have lasting effects, especially if there is limited contact with parents living elsewhere. The developmental social history leads to the current social history. Educational achievement reflects past functioning and occupational coping mechanisms. Not surprisingly, high school dropouts are at increased risk for future disability. This may reflect a decreased ability to cope with external academic and occupational demands, decreased social skills, a disruptive social environment, or diminished capacity for delay of gratification. High school dropouts also have fewer academic skills to compensate for changing work requirements or impaired physical abilities.

Complete employment history is a primary goal. The job types, performance levels, lengths of employment, reasons for leaving positions, history of related injuries, and job satisfaction are all important. Similarly, military history includes rejection for service, level of performance, highest rank, discharge type and reasons (i.e., honorable, general, or dishonorable; end of enlistment term or earlier), and service-connected disability. Special attention should be given to the most recent employment.

In the context of a worker's compensation claim, critical issues include duration of the implicated employment, work environment, job satisfaction, and quality of relationships with management, supervisors, and co-workers. Income from current employment, family employment, investments, time-loss compensation, and welfare or other public funds helps to clarify financial status and potential economic motivations. Future employment or training plans are similarly useful.

All past, present, and contemplated litigation should be explored. Claimants are routinely represented by counsel in some circumstances and may elect legal assistance in others. The use of legal assistance by a patient should not prejudice the examiner. As clinical data, legal assistance may reflect a thoughtful and adaptive response to a complex process, or an adversarial stance. Legal strategies and clearly irrelevant factors (if any) may be considered privileged information. The patient's attorney should ideally facilitate the evaluation process and patient comfort by providing information about the administrative process.

Personal relationships frequently contribute to and are affected by disability status. History should include important relationships, living arrangements, and changes over time. Past and present relationships with family and friends will parallel workplace relationships. Marital and other intimate relationships can profoundly interact with a disability claim. For example, occupational disability can be a powerful form of family communication and conflict resolution, or a major cause of family discord. Current relationships and adaptation are also reflected by quality and number of friends, club or organizational involvement, and religious activities.

These psychosocial factors are only a partial list. All data that help to understand the character and adaptation of the employee are relevant, although potential relevance may not always be apparent to the patient or attorney. Such concerns can be answered with the explanation that it is important to understand the whole person, and that emotional factors can both influence and be affected by a disability.

Past Medical History

When only psychiatric disability is claimed, the psychiatrist will usually perform the examination without other medical specialists. It is essential to obtain a complete standard medical history from the patient, questionnaires, other physicians, and medical records. Current medical problems, medications, and attending physician names should be included. Prior specialty consultation, or a preprinted general health questionnaire, is not an outright substitute for a careful integrated evaluation. But it will reduce the time needed for medical review of systems and will allow the psychiatrist to further explore pertinent details. The data can show other medical conditions of diagnostic importance and critical information about health beliefs and patterns.

Obtaining the past medical history is also a second opportunity for psychiatric review of systems. For example, an unexplained neurological problem might represent a conversion disorder; chest pain or shortness of breath can be caused by panic disorder. Past and present medical conditions and diagnoses are often mistaken diagnoses, and they may represent masked psychiatric syndromes (see Chapter 18).

Mental Status Examination

The mental status examination (MSE) is the psychiatric equivalent of a physical examination. It includes both structured and unstructured observations during the interview. The MSE addresses appearance, behavior, affect (outward emotions), mood (reported emotions), speech, thought content, preoccupations, and suicidal or homicidal thoughts. Cognitive and intellectual functioning is assessed through fund of knowledge, tests of short, medium, and long-term memory, capacity for abstract thinking, and orientation. The MSE is formally recorded, to allow for assessment of changes over time.

Psychological Testing

Psychological tests are never an appropriate substitute for clinical evaluation. Even in qualified hands, they are incomplete or inaccurate measures of psychiatric diagnosis and clinical status. Although often useful, and sometimes seductively elegant, standardized tests must be used with caution. Results are subject to influence by conscious and unwitting patient concerns; by social, testing, and legal environments; and by improper administration or interpretation. Certain kinds of tests can systematize such patient data as intelligence (IQ), personality traits, and organic impairment (neuropsychological testing).

Summary, Assessment, and Recommendations

A typical medical consultation concludes with diagnostic information and treatment recommendations. The consultative examination instead concludes with responses to specific third-party questions. The *Diagnostic and Statistical Manual,* third edition, revised (DSM-III-R), of the American Psychiatric Association represents the current standard for psychiatric diagnosis. DSM-III-R provides a five-axis format that includes current psychiatric diagnoses, developmental and personality disorders, concurrent physical diagnoses, level of psychosocial stressors, and overall level of functioning. The five-axis model offers a concise summary of health and social functioning. DSM-III-R diagnoses reflect only observable signs and symptoms, and do not reflect etiology for either particular syndromes or individual patients.

Therefore, the summary must include a psychodynamic or phenomenologic explanation of symptom development and pathogenesis. Common themes are early developmental issues, with their potential reenactment in current relationships and workplace; temporal relationships between significant personal events and symptom onset; and natural history of possible psychiatric diagnoses. It is critical to logically justify conclusions with documented clinical data. Avoid esoteric jargon and unnecessary complexity. A nontechnical reader should not have difficulty reading and understanding the report.

Opinions as to level of stability, need for specific treatment, further evaluation, and prognosis may be required. Sometimes the opinion may need to be incomplete pending additional information, such as a need for more records or further testing. When this occurs, arrangements should be made to obtain the information as soon as possible to complete the evaluation.

When a psychiatric condition is suspected, treatment suggestions should include type of treatment (such as specific psychotherapies or medications); anticipated treatment intensity and duration; and selection of an optimal treating clinician. Depending on the circumstances of the evaluation, the consultant might suggest several qualified local practitioners with specific expertise.

DETERMINATION OF CAUSALITY

Case Example 1

Jane Wylie, a 35-year-old single accountant, sought disability leave for anxiety that kept her from working. Jane reported she had gotten along well with her male supervisor for 7 years, but that he had been increasingly critical and overbearing during the last "3 months." She started to have panic attacks and severe anxiety. Since she was too nervous to work, she sought a disability leave. A human resources memo said that co-workers had not noticed any change in the supervisor's behavior or management style. The psychiatric consultation elicited a 10-year history of panic disorder, exacerbated for 3 months. Jane and her boyfriend had been growing closer lately. At the boyfriend's insistence, they had moved in together last year, and he had proposed marriage 3 months ("12 weeks") ago. As a result of her panic disorder, he was taking time off from his job to take care of her. Jane was referred to a psychiatrist for brief psychoanalytic psychotherapy and desipramine (an antipanic medication). After 4 weeks of treatment, she was back at work. After 10 weeks, she was able to recognize that she had fears of intimacy and that the marriage proposal had worsened her existing panic disorder. She did not yet know what all of those fears were, but she did make amends with her supervisor, and she returned to her usual high level of professional performance and interpersonal skill.

Clinical medicine is concerned with pathogenesis of disease whenever it affects diagnosis and treatment. Causality is also important for benefit determination, but may not be important for Social Security or other disability insurance benefits. The legal standard for opinions of cause in civil proceedings is "on a more probable than not basis." This is equivalent to a 51 percent or greater chance that a particular circumstance has caused the reported medical condition or disorder.

The determination should consider whether the disorder would likely have occurred in the absence of the particular circumstance. Since most psychiatric disorders are multiply determined, they cannot easily be attributed to a single circumstance. Even a traumatic triggering event will generally require other concurrent circumstances, as well as social or genetic vulnerability, for emergence of overt psychiatric symptoms (see Chapter 10). Unequivocal determination of cause is frequently not possible.

BARRIERS TO PROPER ATTRIBUTION OF CAUSE

Case Example 2

Marshall Frampton, a 20-year-old single man, was employed as a countertop installer for 5 months and claimed that he was poisoned by chemical solvents used for plastic laminate installation. Both he and his family internist said that the solvents had caused auditory hallucinations. The solvents were always used with industry ventilation standards, there was no scientific literature describing psychiatric effects, and no co-workers reported any problems. The evaluating psychiatrist noted a young man with flat affect (no emotional depth) and a fearful expression. Marshall's marked deterioration in function had clearly started after his mother's death 10 months earlier. Always a loner, he had become even more socially withdrawn, no longer attended church, and had stopped cleaning his apartment. Marshall knew that his older sister had been chronically hospitalized for agitated behavior in another state. But since the thought made him nervous, he had never told his internist. The medical data strongly suggested a diagnosis of schizophrenia and the work-related disability claim was denied. Marshall disagreed and he declined a referral for treatment until emergency hospitalization a year later.

Causality determination always involves understanding the diagnostic basis and emotional meaning of symptoms. Patients, lawyers, and treating physicians will often misattribute cause to recent external events, while not considering developmental, personality, and genetic factors. Misattribution is often due to

Primary gain: The symptom creates relief from unconscious internal emotional conflict. The symptom is useful in reducing the interpersonal conflicts or other external threats that triggered the internal conflict.

Secondary gain: The symptom improves relationships or life circumstances through real or symbolic emotional support evoked from others. These advantages might not have been sought or foreseen when symptoms first occurred.

Denial of psychiatric illness: The employee is emotionally unable to accept the existence of psychiatric illness (for instance, to preserve an image of self-reliance) and therefore seeks an alternative explanation of symptoms.

Ignorance or confusion: Misattribution is inadvertent, without any obvious psychological intent.

Malingering: Conscious goal-directed behavior is designed to derive inappropriate financial or other advantage through false representation of symptoms.

By their very nature, psychiatric symptoms are defenses that protect patients from underlying emotional discomfort. Patients will thus usually be unable to provide full and correct explanations of true emotional causality. They will usually be unaware that they are misattributing personal concerns or psychiatric symptoms to the workplace setting. Until they benefit from appropriate treatment, the underlying emotional discomfort will prevent them from recognizing misattribution of cause.

Superficial assessment will often mistakenly assume a causal role for prior apparent stressors (*post-hoc, ergo propter hoc:* it preceded, therefore it caused). Complex psychiatric conditions are typically caused by many factors that usually include inapparent emotional issues, but sometimes do not include seemingly obvious external circumstances. Depression is one such complex disorder. One employee might experience a major depression after a traumatic workplace event, whereas the employee's co-workers do not. That same employee might have a later recurrence with no obvious workplace stressor. Differing risk for depression could be due to increased family susceptibility, early childhood neglect, recent marital stress, undetected onset of thyroid disease, and many other factors.

There are also many barriers to correct causal attribution by the consulting psychiatrist. Objective physicians offer medical opinion without bias toward the referral source or patient desires. But when subtly influenced by conscious or unconscious feelings, evaluating physicians can deviate from intended medical objectivity. This response is known as countertransference (see Chapter 1). Broadly defined, countertransference includes patient-induced physician emotions such as anger, boredom, sexual attraction, or nurturing. The more narrow definition of countertransference refers only to unresolved internal conflicts of the clinician, nonspecifically evoked by patient attributes. For example, a patient who resembles a physician's intrusive parent may evoke feelings of hostility that color clinical judgment. Psychiatrists in all settings must recognize and understand these feelings to preserve their objectivity. Countertransference feelings can also provide clinical data. If a patient engenders certain feelings in the psychiatrist, he or she may have similar effects on other people.

Confusing differences of opinion can occur when clinicians selectively focus on limited aspects of the medical data and fail to comprehensively integrate symptoms, recent events, and developmental factors. The assessment and formulation in the disability report should reflect an integrated view and indicate which factors are emphasized in reaching an opinion. Failure to do so may reflect countertransference, deficient or ideological training, inadequate medical data collection, or patient misrepresentation.

Unfortunately, health care costs can also impede honest assessment. Despite clinical detachment, the physician will feel some responsibility for consultation patients. Financial coverage for treatment is sometimes only available through litigation or administrative process. Worker's compensation insurance usually covers treatment cost only for work-related conditions. A depressed patient without medical insurance may want to falsely claim employment injury in order to afford treatment. When a treating physician is involved in the process, he or she is faced with the difficult dilemma of either leaving the patient untreated (or not charging, with consequent transference and countertransference problems) or of misrepresenting his or her opinion (also with serious transference and countertransference implications).

The most disturbing barrier to objectivity can be physician concern for maintaining friendly relations with patients, families, and referral sources. Physicians may be reluctant to alienate those who do not share their assessment of impairment level or causation. Patients and referral sources gravitate toward physicians with similar views of illness and health. Professional, ethical, and societal considerations mandate unbiased opinions. Referral sources should seek proper evaluation, but must respect adverse determinations. Patients should try to benefit from a comprehensive review of their condition and treatment. Evaluating physicians should insist on their right to integrity. Mutual respect for the truth is essential for maintaining integrity of the disability determination and impairment rating process, and of medical consultation and treatment in general.

Malingering

Malingering is the intentional representation of false or exaggerated symptoms. Although malingering is seen in medical treatment settings, it is especially common in settings where apparent illness can produce economic or social benefit. Malingering is always difficult to determine, since there may be skillful efforts at falsifying symptoms. Physicians are often reluctant to believe that a patient might deliberately mislead them. Evidence will often surface through markedly inconsistent data from the patient, or contradictory information from collateral sources and medical records. Malingering can also be confused with factitious disorder, where intentional falsification of symptoms meets a psychological need to assume the sick role, and where external incentives appear to be absent. Somatization differs from malingering and factitious disorder because reported symptoms are produced by unconscious mechanisms rather than by conscious intent (see Chapter 18).

ADMINISTRATIVE MEDICAL REVIEW

In certain administrative proceedings, a medical reviewer is an additional physician in the evaluation process. The reviewer will examine the medical evidence and then interpret the findings according to administrative rules. The reviewer will not usually meet the patient directly, but may issue the actual disability determination. Further administrative, adjudicative, or appellate processes are often available when involved parties want a determination modified.

ADOPTING THE DISABILITY ROLE:
A PSYCHOLOGICAL PROCESS

Case Example 3

June McGraw, a 37-year-old divorced aircraft manufacturing employee, sought compensation for posttraumatic stress disorder. Four months after she started work, she hit her thumb with a hammer. She did not seek medical treatment until several weeks later, when she also started having arguments with her supervisor and co-workers. She described her workplace as psychologically intolerable. June entered treatment with a mental health professional who sympathized with her unhappiness, and concluded that she suffered a disabling posttraumatic stress disorder as a result of her thumb injury. However, DSM-III-R posttraumatic stress disorder symptoms were not present. Psychiatric consultation, requested by the employer, revealed that June had suffered from sexual molestation in childhood. She subsequently developed a chaotic school, employment, and marital history. She had never held any job for more than 6 months and had been relying on her parents for financial support. Her father, a long-term company employee, arranged the job for her and told her that she was now old enough to fend for herself. Previous brief attempts at emotional independence had always led to transitory extreme dependence on nonfamily members, followed by an angry return to family dependence. June complained that her supervisor, like her father, was argumentative and unsupportive. She also complained that her male therapist would not accept more than one phone call per day and asked the psychiatrist to offer her a more supportive treatment.

When an employee suffers actual physical injury and impairment, the level of disability will very much depend on personality and circumstances. Adoption of the disability role is a psychological process that can transform vulnerable employees. The process can occur before or after an illness or disability claim. The employee will perceive and present himself or herself as helpless and dependent. The illness may, in turn, allow unacceptable preexisting distress to be converted into a conscious physical condition. Psychological distress is often not consciously acceptable, if it is felt to suggest weakness in the face of a hostile world, or if it triggers unconscious fears of overwhelming emotion. Somatic symptoms, on the other hand, are used to protect self-esteem. This process is further supported by cultural influences, disability programs, and sometimes by legal, medical, and mental health professionals. There are strong social, psychological, and financial pressures to deny personal responsibility, affix blame elsewhere, and exact compensation.

Similarly, it is not uncommon for an employee to pursue a disability claim out of a psychological need to misattribute an actual psychiatric disorder. For example, an employee with panic disorder might be unable to see his or her anxiety and social avoidance as internally derived. Instead, that person might be more comfortable seeing an external cause of impairment and resulting disability. That kind of emotional solution allows for a more comfortable conscious adaptation to symptoms, but makes acceptance of effective treatment difficult. As the employee adapts to a life-style dependent on the sick role, he or she becomes still more resistant to insight and treatment.

PREVENTION OF DISABILITY

Causes of workplace disability may be broadly divided into factors external and internal to the employee. External factors include psychological and physical demands of the workplace. Of prime importance are organizational culture and management style. Employees who feel supported and in control of their work will be more satisfied and less disability prone. Rigid and authoritarian environments may promote feelings of powerlessness, and may contribute to illness and disability. Employment uncertainty and unwillingness to accommodate individual needs will also increase disability risk. The physical work environment can also play a small role. Areas of concern include such details as lighting, noise level, ergonomic design of workstations, and physical arrangement of desks and personnel.

When an injury has taken place or an impairment is present, efforts should be made to prevent disability. Genuine concern and a firm but supportive approach will encourage employees to readapt to the workplace. A modified or light-duty position will maintain function and is preferable to sending an employee home.

Internal determinants of disability include both longstanding personality factors and acutely stressful personal events. A worker with a troubled past, adversarial relationships, and difficulty with everyday demands may have reduced intellectual and psychological resources, as well as increased risk for disability. Careful and attentive management and training can partially address the issues, but there may be little that an organization can do to resolve an employee's internal deficits. Psychosocial support and psychotherapy can help more, but are not always sufficiently competent and intensive to make a real difference. Employees with chronic problems may be especially resistant to intervention. Since anxiety disorders, depressive disorders, and substance abuse problems are commonplace, prevention and intervention are also enhanced by ensuring the availability of optimal psychiatric diagnosis and treatment.

WORK-RELATED IMPAIRMENTS AND
WORKER'S COMPENSATION

Worker's compensation includes an evolving system of laws, health care, and vocational training designed to assist workers injured on the job. Worker benefits are available on a no-fault basis, without regard to injury cause, as long as the injury is considered work-related. An injured worker usually cannot sue his or her employer for financial compensation. However, the worker can still seek recourse through civil litigation against an involved third party. For example, an employee who becomes depressed after injury by faulty equipment could benefit through worker's compensation and also bring tort action against the equipment manufacturer. When third-party recovery does occur, some of the recovered funds will be used to reimburse worker's compensation costs.

Most U.S. employers are part of a worker's compensation system. Exceptions include railroad workers, longshoremen, and the merchant marine. Prior to the creation of worker's compensation benefits, workers disabled on the job often had little recourse or economic means. Basic benefits include:

Income replacement while unable to work
Medical benefits for work-related injuries
Disability payments or pensions for work-related impairments
Death benefits to survivors of a worker killed on the job
Rehabilitation benefits to restore stable physical functioning
Vocational rehabilitation to permit new employment with added skills
Compensation for certain job-specific occupational diseases

Worker's compensation benefits are typically provided by employers through commercial or government-related insurance policies. Some large employers will self-insure. Premium costs are based on factors including type of employment, work force incomes, and loss experience over time. Per worker hourly premiums can range from a few cents in sedentary low-risk jobs to many dollars in such high-risk industries as logging and construction.

WORK-INDUCED PSYCHIATRIC INJURY

Case Example 4: Physical/Emotional

James Watkins, a 22-year-old married construction laborer, was injured when a scaffolding collapsed underneath him. He fell 25 feet on his back, causing the rupture of a congenital arachnoid cyst. There was subsequent damage to the sacral nerves, causing impotence and incontinence. These impairments caused a marked reduction of his self-confidence and functional capacity. When evaluated, he had a major depression, with depressed mood, anhedonia, insomnia, anorexia, and impaired concentration. He had been previously happy and well adapted, and there had been little change in his personal life before the injury. He and his wife of 3 years had planned to have children in a few years. His depression was apparently induced by his reaction to injury-induced physical impairment.

Case Example 5: Emotional/Emotional

Franklin Cowlitz, a 32-year-old married police officer, shot and killed a robbery suspect who had drawn a gun and threatened bystanders and himself. Frank was cleared by routine police inquest and was quickly returned to the field without psychiatric intervention. Over the next 3 years, he gradually became distant from others, avoided entering stores that reminded him of the shooting, and became anxious around people who looked like the robbery suspect. He was jittery and couldn't sleep. When his captain finally referred Frank for psychiatric evaluation, posttraumatic stress disorder was identified. Several months of intensive psychotherapy allowed him to discuss feelings about the shooting and other issues, with a gradual remission of symptoms and return to his usual self.

Most employees with psychiatric conditions are fully functioning and unimpaired workers. Others, usually with more severe illness, are able to function well with careful accommodation to their psychiatric impairment. A few psychiatric disorders are fully disabling in all settings.

Prediction of disability from psychiatric impairment is difficult and imprecise. The best predictor of future functioning is past functioning in similar settings. Even so, people often do change for both better and worse, and psychiatric illness can both improve or deteriorate. Never assume that psychiatric impairment is necessarily caused by the workplace.

As reflected in cases 4 and 5, work-related psychiatric injuries can be broadly placed in two categories: physical injury causing emotional impairment (physical-emotional), and emotional injury causing emotional impairment (emotional-emotional). Less often encountered is emotional injury causing physical impairment (emotional-physical). An example might be a bank teller's myocardial infarction, reportedly triggered by the stress of a bank robbery (see Chapter 10). Table 5-1 lists disability types.

Optimal management of any emotional injury includes competent psychiatric evaluation and treatment. Most true psychiatric disabilities will respond promptly to appropriate psychotherapy and/or medication. Chronic personality disorders and other psychiatric conditions might be worsened under stress, but they are usually well ingrained. They are less likely to show prompt response to treatment. As detailed earlier, careful attention to preinjury functioning will usually help identify these patients.

TABLE 5-1   Proper Attribution of Disability to Workplace Factors

---

Physical/physical: Workplace physical trauma or occupational exposure leading to demonstrable physical impairment.

Physical/emotional: Physical workplace trauma leading to new or clearly worsened psychiatric condition.

Emotional/physical: Workplace psychological trauma* leading to new or clearly worsened physical illness.

Emotional/emotional: Workplace psychological trauma leading to new or clearly worsened psychiatric condition.

---

*Workplace psychological trauma might exclude stressful relationships and personnel actions ordinarily encountered in the workplace.

Worker's compensation standards hold that impairments are work-related whenever they are caused or worsened by work-related injury, even if the employee is predisposed to the impairment. This reductionistic legal construct is often at odds with the multidetermined psychiatric model of causality. Nonetheless, the compensation system mandates assignment of responsibility for work-related conditions.

Employees who experience work-related impairment or economic displacement may suffer emotional and financial consequences. Normal emotional response and social tragedy must not be confused with psychiatric illness. Most people will emotionally adjust to adverse circumstances, although some will develop significant psychiatric symptoms.

Work-related psychiatric illness will not always respond fully to treatment. Residual psychiatric impairment may then be assessed by a standardized rating scale, to determine financial compensation. If impairment is sufficiently severe to preclude employment, a permanent pension may be awarded through worker's compensation, Social Security, or private disability insurance.

FITNESS FOR DUTY AND RISK ASSESSMENT

Fitness for particular employment is a management decision that considers experience, aptitude, and attitude. Medical and psychiatric evaluations are frequently requested to assess continued fitness for duty of impaired employees. Clinical evaluations are also sometimes used for prospective employees in certain industries. Screening questionnaires can be useful for rough measures of physical health, personality style, and mental health. Although they are less expensive, less intrusive, and more convenient, they should never be considered equivalent to expert clinical evaluation. Drug testing is a common and controversial screening method, but with concrete results that imperfectly predict performance (see Chapter 15). Positive drug tests may sometimes indicate adverse personality traits, but such results also occur in highly productive individuals.

Regardless of evaluation method, employment decisions should ultimately be based on predicted performance. Past performance is the best single predictor of future performance. Exclusion by psychiatric diagnosis alone is unfair, illegal, and counterproductive. Psychiatric illness is commonplace, but usually it is not disclosed to employers by their workers. An absence of reported history can sometimes reflect dishonesty or avoidance of needed care. Discrimination on the basis of psychiatric diagnosis discourages employees from seeking effective treatment and thus perpetuates any impairment. Employees are more likely to fail at a job from adverse personality traits than they are from such past problems as depression and anxiety. Good management will always improve the odds.

Psychiatric risk assessment or fitness for duty should always be performed by a trained psychiatrist. The report should focus on data and opinion relevant to legitimate employer concerns, with appropriate respect for confidentiality (see Chapter 3).

When an employee demonstrates substantial emotional dysfunction on the job, a psychiatric fitness for duty evaluation may be required as a condition of continuing employment and again before returning to work from treatment. Examples include employees with severe interpersonal conflict, depression, or apparent drug or alcohol abuse. Fitness to remain at work is determined by issues of physical safety, psychological well-being, and adequate functioning for the employee's particular duties. Evaluation can also be requested for declines in performance when emotional factors are suspected. The evaluator may also provide needed treatment or refer the worker elsewhere for treatment when indicated. Early recognition, evaluation, and treatment will reduce the risk of crisis and of psychiatric disability. The psychiatrist can also help dispel misconceptions about mental illness and help management promote productive return to work.

SUMMARY

Impairment assessment and disability determination are challenging clinical tasks that differ from psychiatric treatment. Disability is multidetermined, with contributions from the employee, society, and workplace. Since employers, employees, and their representatives are often reluctant to consider complex causal models and interventions, understanding and reducing disability is an enormous challenge. Disability costs affect everyone: employees, co-workers, families, employers, and society. Ongoing efforts at disability management should emphasize accurate diagnosis, prevention, and early intervention.

Bibliography
American Psychiatric Association. 1987. *Diagnostic and Statistical Manual of Mental Disorders,* 3d ed., revised. Washington, D.C.
Diorio, P. G., and L. F. Fallon, Jr. 1989. Workers' compensation, impairment and disability. In *The Management Perspective: Occupational Medicine,* L. Fleming, L. F. Fallon, Jr., O. Bruce Dickerson, and Paul W. Brandt-Rauf (eds.), pp. 145–152. Philadelphia: Hanley & Belfus.
Egdell, F. A., et al. 1988. Psychiatric disorders, alcohol, and drug abuse. In *Fitness for Work: The Medical Aspects,* F. C. Edwards, R. I. McCallum, and P. J. Taylor (eds.), pp. 382–423. Oxford, Mass.: Oxford University Press.
Engelberg, A. L. (ed.). 1988. *Guides to the Evaluation of Permanent Impairment,* 3d ed. Chicago: American Medical Association.
Harlan, L. C., et al. 1990. The economic impart of injuries: A major source of medical costs. *American Journal of Public Health* **80**(4):453–459.
Pannzarella, J. P. 1991. The nature of work, job loss, and the diagnostic complexities of the psychologically injured worker. *Psychosomatics* **21**(1):10–15.
Parsons, P. E., et al. April 1986. Costs of illness, United States, 1980. In *National Medical Care Utilization and Expenditure Survey,* National Center for Health Statistics, Public Health Service. Series C, Analytical Report Number 3. Department of Health and Human Services Publication Number 86-20403. Washington, D.C.: U.S. Government Printing Office.
Robbins, D. B. 1988. Psychiatric conditions in worker fitness and risk evaluation. In *Worker Fitness and Risk Evaluations,* Jay S. Hillelstein and Glenn S. Pransky (eds.), pp. 309–321. Philadelphia: Hanley & Belfus.
United States Department of Health and Human Services. 1986. *Disability Evaluation Under Social Security.* SSA Publication Number 05-10089. Washington, D.C.: U.S. Government Printing Office.
Weinstein, M. R. 1978. The concept of the disability process. *Psychosomatics* **19** (2):94–97.

6

Executive Distress: Organizational Consequences

Jeffrey P. Kahn, M.D., and Mark P. Unterberg, M.D.

ABSTRACT

Leadership strengths and failings are central to organizational structure and function. Recent years have seen continued attention focused on such problems as productivity, dishonesty, fostering creativity, and succession planning. Under the pressure of emotional distress, there is an increased potential for executive behavior with problematic organizational consequences. Problems arise for specific reasons, have specific solutions, and are always more complex than they seem. The underlying work, family, or intrapsychic causes are usually complex and are often hidden or subtle. Narcissistic-level personality problems, re-created family dynamics, personality styles under stress, and psychological defenses are all important constructs for understanding the mechanisms and organizational effects of distressed executives. Treatment must consider not only job issues themselves but also family concerns, specific psychodynamic and psychiatric diagnoses, and the possibility of medical illness. Careful consideration of underlying causes allows potential problems to be recognized, addressed, and ultimately avoided.

INTRODUCTION

Executive leadership is the lifeblood of any organization. Leadership decisions, vision, and behavior set the tone for organizational structure, function, and culture. No organization can be better than the model that its leaders see or that they themselves demonstrate. The problem, of course, is that leaders are human beings. They have strengths and weaknesses, and they are prone to the same emotional vagaries as everyone else. A public persona may be designed to hide away whatever emotional mechanisms lurk within, but under the pressure of emotional distress, the potential for organizational problems increases. The underlying work, family, or intrapsychic causes are usually complex and subtle. The solution is to understand the problems as well as possible, in order to address and resolve them as they arise, and in order that organizational structures can be designed to counterbalance the vagaries of human emotion.

This chapter gives examples of some common organizational problems and corresponding psychodynamic concepts. The cases fall into four general categories. The first two cases are about narcissistic-level personality problems (only under stress in the second case). The next two are about re-created family dynamics (both cases are about aspects of intergenerational oedipal competition). The third pair describes two personality styles under stress (paranoid and obsessional). Finally, the last pair of cases is about psychological defenses against the experience of painful emotions (displacement and suppression). Notably, there are always overlapping mechanisms, and no one case is ever a simple and discrete problem. The cases are written to emphasize the particular concept in question.

Organizations and managers should not feel obliged to personally address these issues with an employee. Rather, there should be an awareness that these problems arise for specific reasons, that they have specific solutions, and that they are always more complex than they seem. Psychotherapy pursues identification of the underlying causes, relief of distress, and future avoidance of problematic behavior. As the cases show, treatment must not focus on job issues alone. Superficial efforts yield superficial results. Ignoring family concerns, specific psychodynamic and psychiatric diagnoses, and potential medical problems can severely limit psychotherapeutic value and may allow problems to worsen.

PATCHING OVER THE UNCARING WORLD: NARCISSISTIC PROCESS

Organizational leaders need to have a healthy and realistic appreciation of their own abilities. Such healthy narcissism contributes to effective leadership style and productive team efforts. However, excessive narcissistic traits may reflect a relative incapacity for emotional intimacy. Under the pressure of intrapsychic, family, or organizational changes (often subtle or hidden), narcissistic individuals are vulnerable to episodes of heightened mental distress. Thus, with an intensified or altered emotional frame of reference, it becomes more difficult than usual to realistically perceive and address organizational circumstances. Notably, there can be an intrapsychically determined assumption that the organization or its members are not supportive and a consequent increased likelihood of depression, substance abuse, and other behaviors with adverse effects on the organization. Two adverse behaviors of particular concern these days are self-serving grandiosity and dishonesty.

Empire Building and Masters of the Universe: Grandiosity

Successful managers like to feel that they are good at what they do, and that they are wanted and needed by those around them. "Doing well by doing good" is the motto of healthy adult narcissism and the manager with that approach is a benefit to subordinates, superiors, clients, shareholders, and the organization itself. In whole or in part, though, ambition can be a grandiose attempt to cover inner distress. Excessive grandiosity can lead to unfeeling and self-destructive behavior. Grandiose plans are designed for their immediate emotional reassurance, not for the pleasures of success, and they are implemented without real concern for others. And what looks on the outside like infantile behavior can make some people see only a desire to "have their cake and eat it too," rather than the hidden inner loneliness. Unfortunately, further feelings of rejection from the group are a common result.

Case Study 1

John Boynton had been on the fast track since his first day in Selco Corporation's executive training program. From the start, people knew that he was someone who would rise to the very top. It was only a question of how fast. John developed many ambitious and exciting projects. Many fell apart, but there were a few that he turned into big successes. He moved up the corporate ladder, took on increasing responsibility, and managed to build a bit of an empire for himself. His department expanded in size and scope, and it appropriated some tasks from other departments. Even so, he traded favors with other executives and became known as a consummate corporate politician.

Recently, though, his career had run into some difficulty. His superiors still seemed pleased, but there were increasing complaints from colleagues and from within his own department. Fellow department heads noted that John had become more intense and disagreeable at their weekly meetings. He continued to accept their help, but he now often refused to help in return. In one notable case, another department head needed to borrow five engineers. John asked that his department be paid in advance for their time, but then assigned only three engineers for the project. Before, his good-natured style had made him the center of attention at business meetings and social gatherings. Now, though, there were frequent outbursts at employees who did not do their work precisely as he asked. Colleagues and subordinates felt increasingly estranged, and some even tried to talk with John. He didn't take all this criticism too seriously. He figured that his special talents entitled him to rise above ordinary rules and that his actions were really for the company's good anyway.

Curiously, John's personality change seemed to coincide with the continuing financial success of his department. John had always kept an inner loneliness carefully hidden from himself and others, all the while searching for compensatory recognition. But despite his current success, John was actually less happy than usual. He now spent hour upon hour in his office, writing detailed memos to the CEO (chief executive officer) about his ideas for the company's future. Not a few of these ideas were taken, without credit, from eager subordinates. John envisioned one or two of the ideas catapulting him up the corporate ladder, perhaps soon becoming special assistant to the CEO. Secretly, he thought of replacing the current CEO, who John felt sure was not as competent as himself. He was aware of the danger of talking openly about such matters, so he only discussed them with his wife. She certainly seemed to agree with him, although she pretty much agreed with all of his thoughts, comments, and demands. Her passive adulation and praise had won her stability in their 15-year marriage. Even so, she and their three children had always felt that he was emotionally detached and she now worried about his increasing tirades at home.

John also became increasingly isolated from his colleagues and departmental subordinates, and he eventually was called to discuss "a matter of importance" with the CEO. John was convinced that the CEO would ask him to leave his current post for the special assistant position. No doubt the CEO had recognized the importance of his ideas for the future of the company, and would want him in charge of their implementation. Anticipating the good news, John arrived early for the meeting.

In his office, the usually lighthearted CEO looked worried. Concerned at first, John quickly figured that the CEO was worried about the implications of selecting him for promotion over more experienced senior managers. The CEO, however, had a frank discussion with John concerning the many complaints about his leadership and behavior. There were several written statements from other department heads, who had been approached by employees afraid to talk directly to John. The complaints focused primarily around his need for absolute control over everything within the department. People were feeling browbeaten and under the "dictator-ship" of a "tyrant." There were many specific examples of angry outbursts, unavailability, lack of rewards, and perceived dishonesty. The CEO thought that John was acting more like an enfant terrible than a mature leader. He pointed out that John's department would never continue its success with ever-sinking morale and that someday one of John's grandiose business plans would go badly wrong. He strongly advised John to seek psychiatric help before he found his career in the company more seriously jeopardized.

The therapy did not start easily. John at first saw himself undergoing an unwelcome and unnecessary business assignment. Eventually, though, he became more aware of his painful lack of emotional intimacy and of his consequent need for compensatory accomplishment and adulation. He understood, too, that each success had brought with it fears of envy and thus greater loneliness. Instead of increasing his distress as in the past, John's new accomplishments could now bring him greater feelings of security, respect, and well-being.

Causes
There is always a tension between the emotionally self-protective need to seek accomplishment and attention, and the interpersonal demands of the real world. In the process of growing up, two environmental factors can impede the ability to develop an adaptive balance. In some families, affection or material needs are withheld or withdrawn. As a result, it is harder to see other people as a source of joy and security, and there is an increasing need for self-reliance. Such early deprivation leads to insulation against the vulnerability of relationships. More importantly, it also leads to a need for ultimate control and mastery of the universe, in order to make the world right at last. Surprisingly similar are families where the child is given too much superficial affection and material things. The child becomes an adult with an inflated narcissism, a sense of entitlement, but still an underlying failure of interpersonal security. Anger and "righteous" indignation result when others fail to go along with their perceived entitlement.

Effects
These individuals, however likeable, effective, and bright they are, can have devastating effects on an organization. Their self-protective "master of the universe" position ultimately goes against reality and causes difficulty among the other members of the group. Dissension within the group results from the ability of these individuals to seduce some members into supporting them against the attacking forces of the others. Playing people off against each other might seem useful in business, but it will usually lead to serious morale problems. And judgment can be an issue of real concern. When grandiose plans take precedence over realistic ambition, failure is a common result. Even when the grandiose plans unexpectedly succeed, they can result in seemingly paradoxical despair, a heightening of interpersonal conflict, and subsequent detrimental actions that negate the success. Importantly, their behavior can set a bad example for some, leave others feeling cheated, usurped or ignored, and can generally lead morale downhill.

Intervention and Prevention
Ideally, it would be nice to harness the energy and creativity of narcissistic grandiosity while still protecting against its adverse effects. This is not easy to do. A generally supportive and secure work environment is less likely to provoke needs for grandiose efforts. Specifically, care must be taken to recognize individuals and their contributions, and to maintain an atmosphere of honesty and common cause. Problems will always arise anyway and it is then important to remember the underlying distress. That distress can't be solved in the workplace, but it can be substantially helped in a sophisticated psychoanalytic psychotherapy.

Understanding and resolving the problem ultimately involves recognition of the deep-seated lack of emotional trust, and of the compensatory needs for self-protection and dramatic accomplishment. As with any patient in therapy, careful attention should be given to the possible specific benefits of medication for identifiable mild anxiety or depressive disorders (see Chapter 1). Even the most effective treatment is gradual, and it does help a subordinate to feel the continued support of a supervisor and others, particularly in assessing his or her positive assets. Prevention is more difficult. Grandiose job applicants are often desirable candidates, with very substantial accomplishments that speak well for their future efforts. However, it is always important to carefully assess both productivity and people skills, as well as watching helpfully for signs of emotional distress. Evident support, unambiguous rules, clear feedback, and opportunity for self-reflection all promote the idea of doing well by doing good.

Dishonesty: Perceived Infantilization, Hidden Rage, and Rationalized Entitlement

Every week seems to bring new revelations about scandal and unethical conduct in business and government. The more obviously sociopathic or criminal employees may be easier to spot in advance and are thus less likely to catch an organization by surprise. The stories that get the most media attention are those that involve seemingly happy and successful individuals, apparently involved in dishonesty for the first time. Less dramatic examples are commonplace and are a continuing concern for organizations.

Case Study 2

Tom Hardy was in charge of government sales at the Chicago Motor Company. His salesmanship had been instrumental in the fivefold growth of this market for the company in only 5 years. Senior management showed its appreciation with friendly approval, public awards, and ever increasing financial compensation. Tom had unsuccessfully sought broader management responsibilities, but was absorbed by his sales position, lived quite well, and had a stable family life.

As Tom approached his fiftieth birthday, his eldest son was accepted at a prestigious college and Tom began to feel more stressed at work. While he had never before been preoccupied with sales quotas (nor had he needed to be), he now became obsessed with finally selling 50,000 cars in the sales year. He spent his weekends working ever harder on sales proposals. Family fishing trips became fewer and fewer, and an emotional distance grew in his family. As the end of the sales year drew near, Tom was in final negotiations for a 3,000-car state government sale that would put him over the top.

To be certain that he would win the contract for Chicago Motors, Tom called an old friend at the state purchasing office. Reminding his friend of past favors, Tom was able to learn his competitor's bid and he set his own prices just a fraction lower. He reasoned that Chicago Motors was entitled to the contract, since they did good work and were established state suppliers. He also figured that ensuring the sale would help Chicago Motors by boosting yearly sales numbers and would help stockholders by increasing the share price. He knew that management would be concerned mostly with whether he could get away with it and he thought that no one outside the company would notice. While all this was going on, he started a pattern of slipping one morning paper (the one with the funnies) inside another, thus saving 50 cents a day.

He boasted to friends about how closely he had underpriced the competition, but then he began to worry that he would be found out and disgraced. Soon, Tom was unable to sleep, began to have daily episodes of shortness of breath, and started to dread going to work. One day, he went by the medical department to ask for sleeping pills. The doctor there saw how troubled he was and referred him to the consulting psychiatrist. Tom was secretly pleased at this opportunity to talk about his plight.

The psychiatrist recognized Tom's shortness of breath as panic disorder and prescribed clonazepam 0.5 mg twice a day. With relief of his panic attacks and insomnia, Tom could now start talking through his situation. Over the course of many psychotherapy sessions, he came to recognize that he had long felt kept down by authority figures. As a child, he felt obliged to underachieve in school in order to seek his parents' affection. Since he did not see his childhood money-making schemes as mature behavior, he felt free to excel there. Similarly, he felt free to succeed at sales as an adult, and his success was also an expression of defiance to those who would keep him down.

Management's failure to give him broader management responsibilities was their unwitting recognition of his uneasiness at a more authoritative role, as well as their reluctance to lose their best salesperson. But Tom reexperienced the hurt he had felt since childhood at being denied grown-up authority. His anger and frustration intensified as he approached his fiftieth birthday milestone, and at the same time he felt an unconscious envy of his son's acceptance into a prestigious college. Tom's intensified sales efforts had been his characteristic method of covering unpleasant feelings, while also seeking the company's approval. This time, though, he felt angrily entitled to succeed and his anger had colored his actions. The result was that he had set up an illegal government contract, at some risk to both himself and his company. While at first Tom rationalized his behavior on business grounds, discussion of his indefensible newspaper thefts helped him to see his angry entitlement more clearly.

Causes

It is not always easy to see the causes of dishonest behavior among successful, and often generally honest, individuals. From one perspective, dishonesty is a form of narcissistic entitlement. In other words, the individual has a hidden basic mistrust of others and does not expect them to be on his side. Under certain emotional stresses, the underlying mistrust is heightened, along with fear and anger. Consciously, the individual comes to defiantly believe that he is entitled to break the rules, because he cannot count on the system to reward or remember him. Often, this will progress to the notion of a competition with the system and thus an interest in breaking the rules just to "get away with it."

These kinds of behaviors are encouraged by organizations that foster a culture of maximum income or power, without a corresponding focus on principles, rules, and the inherent value of the work at hand. Employees who see no real value in their company, colleagues, products, family, or self may look to income or power alone for gratification. Further encouragement is provided by organizational cultures that tolerate or lionize dishonesty of any kind. The well-publicized Wall Street and savings and loan scandals were not a complete surprise to everyone at the companies involved. In many cases, knowing management gave implicit or active support to the dishonest conduct. In other cases, dishonest employees felt that dishonest behavior had been accepted in the past and would be in the future. Moreover, individuals who see others "getting away with it" may feel angry and may be afraid of being left out of the benefits. They do not want to be chumps.

Effects

Dishonest behavior has some obvious ill effects, even when it is supposedly in the organization's interest. It can lead to criminal and civil legal actions, alienate customers and employees, and encourage other dishonesty within the organization. By its demoralizing effects, it can also detract from accomplishment and productivity.

Intervention and Prevention

The most important preventative is to establish an environment of respect for rules, principles, and the value of a company's employees and products. Employees must feel rewarded for their work and must be treated fairly within the organization. Without jeopardizing the organization, there should be a way that they can let their needs (financial and emotional) be known and can seek to effect remedies for others' dishonesty. Rigid or unprincipled systems do not lend themselves to these purposes. Rule breaking and dishonesty must be dealt with fairly, clearly, and firmly when it does occur. In the extreme, remorseless sociopaths have no place in a healthy organization (see Chapter 14). There are many consultants on ethical conduct who can offer helpful courses and advice, but who by themselves are no cure for either a disaffected organizational culture, or for the dishonest employees themselves. More definitive solutions lie in thoughtful and deliberate attention to organizational culture, and to the emotional outlook of employees involved.

COMPETITION GONE AWRY:
INTERGENERATIONAL OEDIPAL CONFLICT

Organizations thrive on competition. Corporations compete with each other for customers, skilled employees, technological advances, and investment capital. Individuals within the organization compete for accomplishment, advancement, income, and status. By and large, healthy competition has healthy results. But problems arise when competition is tainted by hidden agendas or unrecognized fears, and when competitive strivings are muffled instead of encouraged. Organizations are always concerned with the development of new leaders and ideas, and with succession planning.

Promotion and Suppression of Creativity:
Oedipus and Laius Go at It Again

Every organization looks to the development of new ideas and leaders for improving and maintaining its activities. The need for new ideas is particularly strong among companies where products, processes, or marketing change rapidly. Inevitably, though, any new idea comes into conflict with established ideas, and interpersonal conflict can result. These conflicts are heightened when competitive individuals are involved, and they escalate even more when existing power structures let emotionally threatened managers maintain a rigid or unprincipled organization. The organization's purposes can suffer most of all. This age-old conflict is represented in Greek literature and psychoanalytic thought through the story of young Oedipus and his father Laius.

Case Study 3

Ed Taylor was fresh out of business school when he started to work at Oceanblue Entertainment. He had been very successful in graduate school, and had impressed those who knew him with his hard work, intelligence, and creativity. He had been heavily recruited by many companies. He chose to work for Oceanblue because he saw there an opportunity to help renew an inactive section of a company that promoted creative accomplishment. With the encouragement of management, the section leader had specifically sought new creative input and there seemed to be a creative vacuum for Ed to fill. It looked like a perfect fit.

Lee Kellogg was his section leader at Oceanblue. Lee had been with Oceanblue for 30 years. Early in his career he had risen rapidly in the company. He had made few innovative contributions, but had run his small section effectively, had not sought strong subordinates, and had maintained his position through company politics. For many years, though, he had felt stuck in that position, and had remained preoccupied with protecting his organizational turf. He would often sacrifice apparent business advantages (such as obtaining new computers with discretionary section funds) if they had a perceived political disadvantage (appearing weak in Oceanblue if his computers were not specifically funded by the company).

Ed started the new job full of plans and ideas. At first, he seemed to have Lee's support and encouragement. Soon, however, Ed realized that Lee's verbal support was not matched by actions. In fact, Lee was withholding managerial, secretarial, and material support, thus passively weakening Ed's efforts. Ed tried to talk with Lee, but it didn't get anywhere. Rather, Lee responded to these attempts at dialog with avoidance and poorly hidden rage. He made it implicitly clear that Ed was not to succeed in his projects and explicitly clear that neither was he to seek employment elsewhere. Ed was confused. He did not realize how desperately Lee wanted to demonstrate his section's achievements to the company, all the while feeling hopelessly threatened by Ed's plans and accomplishments. Ed also did not know that Lee was yet again seeking a promotion, after many years of frustrated efforts.

After many months, Ed was finally given approval for some projects. But to Ed's dismay, each time a project was started, Lee actively removed it from Ed's purview, and the project soon faded. One of Ed's projects was a collaborative effort with the Oceanblue film restoration section. When Lee tried to intervene there, the other section would not let the project be dropped. As Lee felt more endangered and enraged, he threatened the other section leader and he accused Ed of trying to undermine him. Ed felt increasingly frustrated, trapped, and demoralized. Although management seemed sympathetic to Ed, they also wanted to preserve the organizational status quo, especially since Lee might finally achieve his long-sought promotion. Lee did win his promotion, but his section continued as a small and low-performing unit of Oceanblue. Ed was unable to find a suitable job elsewhere, but he ultimately found a similar position, with diminished career potential, in another Oceanblue section. Much later, he found a position at a competing firm.

Causes

Almost by definition, creativity and leadership development involve the development and advancement of novel ideas. These ideas will necessarily be at odds with established wisdom. As if this were not enough potential for discord within an organization, there is commonly a rather pronounced conflict of personalities as well. Established and senior members of the organization will feel an emotional and also practical investment in the status quo. They may feel that their positions are dependent on current methods, and on their past development of those methods and ideas. This applies to issues as diverse as organizational structure, technological and scientific knowledge, and marketing strategies. Although an organization will look to members for novel approaches, often newer members, it will always have mixed feelings about accepting and incorporating those ideas. Aggressively creative members may have more novel ideas, and greater success at developing and implementing those ideas, but will also find that they meet greater resistance. Their approach will be seen in a more threatening way from above. This sort of problem has many causes that can be attributed to the individuals involved, as well as to the organizational structure.

Effects

Many of the effects of these problems are obvious: retarded creative development, weak leadership, discord and strife, loss of good workers, failure to adapt to changing markets, failure to rectify rigid and corrupt organizations, and substantial effort wasted on emotional interpersonal conflicts instead of smoother cooperative ventures.

Intervention and Prevention

Though there will always be tensions surrounding the promotion and acceptance of new ideas and leaders, efforts can be made to keep the process from self-destruction. Promotion of a work environment that allows and encourages creativity and accomplishment and that rewards managers for the success of their subordinates and colleagues is essential, but it is often difficult to accomplish. When a system is awry, a consultant can play an essential role. As in this intensified case, effective interventions may require group seminars and brief psychotherapeutic interventions for the key individuals. Adapting management styles to prevent such problems requires the active attention of senior management and of human resources. Creativity must be both sponsored and protected from above, with considerable attention to the concerns and fears of employees and managers at all levels.

Problematic Succession Planning: Fear of Subordinates

Organizational success and growth depends on leadership strength, depth, and continuity. This is not always easy to accomplish. For example, leaders at the top may have risen there because of inner needs to control their circumstances and to minimize their competition. As a result, they may feel threatened by subordinates with real leadership potential and they may prefer weak or deferential subordinates. Such self-protective behavior can weaken leadership strength and can be a particular impediment when leaders find themselves in the awkward position of developing or selecting their own successor.

Case Study 4

Jack Widener had worked long and hard to become president of Alderwood Air Charter. The company was his life and he thought of himself as the very soul of Alderwood. That didn't make it easy to develop the executive ranks. Talented junior executives would arrive at Alderwood with freshly minted credentials and eager career plans. Sometimes Jack thought they weren't really so good and he would push them toward the door. Other times, they just seemed to stay in the background until one day they were gone. Jack figured that they didn't have what it takes for the rough and tumble of the air charter business. Every once in a while, though, he'd be surprised when one of them made vice-president at some competitor.

Then there were the ones Jack called "troublemakers." They'd arrive on the scene, and after only a few months or a few years, they'd be coming up with all sorts of ideas for how things should be different. But Jack always liked things his way and the troublemakers didn't last too long. So, the Alderwood executive ranks were filled mostly with loyal and steadfast plodders. They admired Jack's vision and approach, gladly followed his unchallenged leadership, and never took much initiative themselves. Alderwood was a stable company with a protected market niche, few big mistakes, and little significant growth.

Now that Jack was 4 years from mandatory retirement, he recognized that he should plan for his succession and that the future would bring increasing competition to Alderwood's market niche. He knew that Tom Nabish, his right-hand man, expected to succeed him, and that others wouldn't mind the job either. But when Jack looked around the company, he didn't see anyone he respected enough for the top job. Instead, he decided to mentor two talented new executives. One was president of a newly acquired fuel supplier and the other was hired away from a major airline. Despite Jack's conscious intentions, they fared no better than the junior executives of years past. As Jack took control, confrontations over strategy escalated with the fuel executive and the fuel business started to lose money. Finally, Jack asked him to move on. For the airline veteran, the lack of increasing recognition led to demoralization and declining ambition. Jack seemed to oppose every attempt at increasing market share, or even improving efficiency. He felt grateful when the airline veteran left without confrontation and he reassured himself that neither of the two were really any good after all. Then Jack again realized that he could not stay on forever.

This conflict also showed itself at home, where Jack's need to be "number one" had always interfered in his relationship with his wife and children. There were particular strains between him and a son who had recently become the college football star that Jack never was. When the son refused to stop playing football to concentrate on his studies, Jack wouldn't talk to him for 7 months.

When retirement finally arrived, Jack reluctantly turned over the president's title to Tom Nabish. Tom found the company in surprising disarray. Productivity had actually fallen in the last 3 years, fledgling competition had eaten into Alderwood's traditional niche, and the fuel supply losses were mounting rapidly. He couldn't understand how Jack had let the company go to seed in his final years. But with Jack still watching over him, Tom was afraid to make strategic plans, and he was viewed as passive and ineffective by the employees. He did not know what to do. Jack, on the other hand, saw Alderwood's regrettable decline as the natural consequence of his own retirement. On a deeper level, he also felt reassured that he was indeed irreplaceable and that no one would ever overshadow his accomplishments.

Eventually, Jack's wife became quite concerned about the standoff between Jack and their son. She also saw the parallel to Jack's standoff with Tom at

Alderwood. Despite Jack's anger and denial, she convinced him to see a psychiatrist for help. In therapy, Jack realized that he was keeping things paralyzed at home and at the company. And he fondly remembered that he had once been considered a bit of a "troublemaker" himself. With that recognition, he spent more time at his Palm Springs retirement home, and he was able to allow more freedom for both Tom and his son. Tom then hired an outside consultant, who helped formulate a new plan for Alderwood's future. Jack felt less threatened by the outsider's plans. That way, the succession process did not make him feel like he had been defeated by his organizational son. Jack was ultimately pleased that Alderwood did well, but he never stayed long enough in therapy to really understand why the succession was so turbulent.

Causes

Competitive individuals often arrive in adulthood not only with drive and skill but also with an acute awareness of the opposition. Although this obviously has some competitive advantages, it can cause problems when it spills over into more cooperative relationships. Leaders who are unable to recognize or appreciate collaborative relationships may view them instead through a largely competitive focus. They are still fighting their incessant childhood battle for affection, respect, and recognition. Growing up in a family environment of emotional deprivation will increase the intensity of competition for what little affection or respect is available. And, the competitive drive will be tinged with fears of competitive loss, emotional abandonment, and retributive opponents. At the organizational level, these problems are encouraged by exaggerated focus on independent accomplishment, combined with inadequate attention to constraints on power and to the responsibilities of leadership.

Effects

When leadership talent is squelched by the fears of those in power, the effects are not always immediate. Rather, there may be a period of increased stability, but with a growing stagnation of ideas and growth. Ultimately, the absence of sufficient leadership strength, depth, and consistency will result in impaired competitiveness for the organization as a whole. Belated attempts at compensation might then include reliance on new leaders from outside, but with risks of unnecessary turmoil and demoralization. In extreme cases, there can be catastrophic effects on performance, especially when a succession is finally necessary.

Intervention and Prevention

The individual who has difficulty with unresolved issues of rivalry may be difficult to help, as his rationalizations effectively counter the criticism directed at him. A deeper understanding of maladaptive competitive behavior is needed and it can be addressed in psychoanalytic psychotherapy by understanding connections between present and past competitive circumstances. Ongoing treatment will bring increasing change, as the patient gradually gains greater understanding of personality traits that had seemed self-protective. Clear organizational policies about the use and abuse of authority should be disseminated and enforced. Those few individuals who continually impede the success of others need careful attention and might ultimately risk dismissal. Outside consultants, not entangled in organizational rivalries, can be valuable agents of change. Proper intervention can help bring about smooth and effective succession, and can counsel both overly threatened leaders and younger talent in difficult competitive environments.

WHEN IT LOOKS LIKE CHARACTER IS DESTINY: RIGID PERSONALITIES UNDER STRESS

Everyone has a personality style and uses that style in adapting to stressful and changing circumstances. Rigid personalities, though, can have a tough time of it. Unable to recognize the hidden emotions that guide their behavior, they have little room for flexible adaptation to new demands. Old habits become burdened with mounting distress and problematic consequences can keep growing until something gives way (see Chapters 9 and 14). Suspiciousness and compulsiveness can each have some advantages, but when exacerbated under stress they can cause serious problems.

Oversuspicion as Avoidance of Emotional Distress: Self-Reference and Paranoia

It is not uncommon to imagine what is going on in another person's mind. When a person's future depends on the undisclosed decisions or opinions of others, anxiety and speculation can run rampant. By projecting feelings, fears, and imagination onto another person, anxious uncertainty is replaced with seeming predictability. In effect, individuals will sometimes confidently believe that their own thoughts are what others have secretly in mind, all the while blissfully unaware of their projection. But there are problems for all involved when imagination merges with reality, and when unconfirmed fantasy is seen as fact. An especially confusing picture can emerge when good fortune develops for someone who has long avoided too much success.

Case Study 5

Joseph Toth is a 45-year-old vice-president for Yoshida Design Associates. Over 20 years, his cautious approach had earned him a respected but low-key role in the firm. He always played his cards close to the vest and he just never seemed comfortable with high-profile successes. Last year, though, the president asked Joe to assemble and manage a new team for computer equipment design. Apprehensively, Joe accepted. The president was pleased and surprised by the high quality of the resulting work, and he rewarded Joe with a raise, a promotion, and invitations to his private club.

Joe was pleased, too, but he began to feel increasingly uneasy about work. He thought that his current work was poorly received by his supervisors and he began to talk about possible early retirement. He saw their reassurances as meaningless praise, or even as an attempt to keep him off track. More significantly, he began interpreting conversations, memos, and other communications within the firm in a negative and peculiar manner. Eventually, Joe became convinced that he would be let go through the efforts of certain top-level people who were out to get him. At meetings he became more aware and attentive of who spoke to whom and how things were phrased, and he became increasingly angry at what he perceived as subtle but consistent rejection.

Joe was angry, bitter, confused, and increasingly concerned about his professional and personal life. He was spending more time talking to other employees about senior people than doing his work. He would frequently lash out at others and his comments about colleagues were a cause of concern within Yoshida Design. They seemed off the mark in regard to others' perceptions of the senior people. Joe's personal life was hurting too. He had been divorced for 5 years from a distant alcoholic wife and Joe had been dating a 24-year-old woman for a year now. Although she had been pressing for marriage, Joe lately suspected her of secret sexual affairs. He saw her reassurances as an attempt to keep him in the dark until she was ready to leave.

One day, Joe became enraged over a miscalculated medical bill. He stormed into his family doctor's office to complain. The doctor explained the bill to Joe and convinced him that there was no error. Joe apologized and sheepishly acknowledged his passing conviction that someone from Yoshida Design had manipulated the bill. The doctor did not challenge Joe's fears, but did get him to accept a discreet psychiatric referral. In treatment, Joe did not need any medication and he soon recognized that his fearfulness seemed to follow his successes at work and home. He had had milder such reactions to college graduation and to his marriage. Much later, continued analytic psychotherapy uncovered the internal criticisms that Joe had developed in childhood and that he was now projecting onto others. At Yoshida Design, the president gradually sensed the return of Joe's old style. Uncertain and a bit mystified, the president hesitated before giving Joe another challenging new assignment, but decided to ask him to the club again.

Causes

Paranoid personality traits have been a topic of much debate, particularly with regard to etiology. They are quite different from true psychotic illness. Some see them as exaggerated sensitivity to the emotions of others and as a particular concern for their hostility. At the same time, paranoia may well represent unacceptable aggressive feelings placed outside the self and into another person. The other person thus becomes the perceived source of feelings that an individual does not want to recognize in himself or herself. This dilemma reflects a childhood inability to express natural aggressive thoughts and feelings, and instead, a felt need to keep those thoughts secret to prevent some frightening consequence. Other possible contributors to self-referential and paranoid personality traits can include anxiety and depressive disorders and insufficient social supports. Notably, paranoid traits can be substantially heightened both by emotional loss and by emotional or material accomplishment. Although severe paranoid behavior may reflect a real or incipient psychotic process (see Chapter 17), it is also important not to mislabel more flexible personality traits. Organizational factors that can aggravate tendencies toward self-reference and projected aggressive feelings might include limited communication, limited availability of information essential for self-assessment, an unpredictable or changing work environment, and unethical or capricious management.

Effects
Sensitivity to the feelings and hostile intentions of others may offer some advantages, but oversensitivity helps no one. It is clearly detrimental to any organization when employees or managers are paranoid about co-workers, supervisors, or organizational intent. Left unaddressed, such situations often lead to emotional crisis or acrimonious departure. At the very least, it is less than productive for the organization to have employees who spend their energies pursuing figments of their imagination. On the level of the individual, there is also increased risk for serious depression, substance abuse, disruption of family relationships, performance impairment, and disgruntled employees. At the organizational level, there are substantial risks when management impairment has compounded effects on morale, ethics, communication, and leadership.

Intervention and Prevention
Since personality style colors the way people see the world and themselves, no one can fully understand how other people see them. And since paranoia lends itself to suspicion, paranoid people can be uncomfortable to approach. Nonetheless, intervention is quite important. Documentation of unusual behavior is often a prerequisite for successful evaluation and diagnosis, and it should be obtained before recommending referral for professional consultation. Initial treatment emphasizes the need to distinguish between thoughts from the imagination and objective reality. This task can be especially difficult when the organizational climate is one of bona fide hostility, intrigue, or uncertainty. Treatment works best in the company of a supportive organization and family.

Missing the Forest for the Trees:
Counterproductive Compulsiveness

Compulsive personality style is nearly always a career advantage. It allows individuals to focus much of their attention on work, thus leading to career accomplishments. On the other hand, compulsive traits may diminish interpersonal skills at home and on the job. And even the advantages of the compulsive work orientation can become impediments at times of emotional stress. Top heavy with successful compulsive individuals, the organizational consequences can be serious.

Case Study 6

Frank Kendall was a very hard worker. His job as director of marketing for Arden/Oak Data Services was always more important to him than everything else. He was known around marketing for his marathon project efforts, for his attention to organization and detail, for his ability to clearly define business problems and solutions, and for his dedication to Arden/Oak. Even so, many of his colleagues felt him to be perfectionistic, controlling, and emotionally distant. In particular, Frank was known for his procrastination.

Arden/Oak had been a successful regional company for many years, growing steadily during a period of economic expansion. Frank's contributions to company growth were legendary. Now, however, with a recession underway, the Arden/Oak CEO decided to market company services in four new midwestern states. Midwestern marketing was to be handled through a newly acquired midwestern competitor. Meanwhile, Frank was given a raise and a promotion, and he was asked to focus on the essential task of retaining existing business.

Frank understood the business considerations, readily consented to the division of marketing into two sections, and outwardly was grateful for the recognition of his past contributions. Inside, though, Frank was enraged by what felt like a personal rejection, a loss of respect, and an insufficient reward. Nor was he able to discuss these feelings with management, colleagues, family, or even with himself. Instead, he felt more driven than ever toward his work. Rather than just his assigned task, he also started trying to expand existing accounts to new products. He was going to prove himself to management. He wrote and rewrote a far-fetched business plan to sell high-priced on-line financial data services for high school economics classes. But no matter how much he reworked the details, he wasn't satisfied.

With all this effort, Frank found himself sleeping and eating less, and he enjoyed his family less than usual. Although he thought of himself as determined to succeed in this project, others found themselves feeling vaguely irritated by his plans. And he kept delaying the projected start date for the effort, making excuses and saying that he was making the plan better still. With all this exertion, his departmental subordinates felt ignored and his inattention to existing customers began to take a toll. A new enhancement of existing data services was inadequately marketed and some customers fell away.

Finally, management realized that something was wrong and asked a psychiatric consultant for help. The consultant interviewed Frank, his marketing colleagues, loyal customers, and the CEO. The consultant reviewed the events at Arden/Oak, and noted that Frank was also upset that his only daughter had just left for college. He suggested a psychiatric referral for the major depression that had recently aggravated Frank's compulsive personality traits. He also suggested a brief series of group seminars to refocus marketing on the task at hand. In therapy, and with the help of imipramine 100 mg twice a day (an antidepressant medication), Frank began to understand his reaction to the new assignment. Later, he also understood his pattern of working hard to seek emotional acceptance (originally from his distant and hardworking father, now also from management), but also as a reflection of his defiant and angry perception that relationships could only disappoint him (the more he sought father's or management's acceptance, the more disappointed he felt, yet the harder still he worked). He was soon able to improve the morale and new function of his department, despite working fewer hours. Similarly, he began to forge a closer relationship with his wife.

Causes

Compulsive personality traits are presumably developed in childhood, but they can be made worse under stressful circumstances. Faced with any change, but especially with the loss of work roles important for self-esteem, compulsive employees may feel rejected, angry, and unimportant. Consequently, they may attempt to repair their lot by even harder work, but with less benefit to themselves or the organization. As in this case, the situation is compounded further when a major depression develops. Though compulsive people are quite sensitive to rejection, they are less likely to realize that they are depressed and they are less likely to convey depression to others. They find it quite difficult, even in psychotherapy, to think or talk about feelings. This tendency is encouraged by social pressures to keep all feelings inside. Organizational cultures that are perceived as unsupportive will increase the risk of problematic functioning.

Effects

While compulsive personality traits can be a decided advantage, they can cause problems as well. Successful organizations tend to attract and retain compulsive individuals. They are often very dedicated workers and are able to focus on detailed analyses of organizational and business problems. These same employees, though, may have a detached emotional style that can make them appear distant, unconcerned, angry, or controlling. In addition, their attention to detail is counterproductive when too much effort is put into minor concerns and when essential matters are squeezed out as a result. Resulting inefficiencies and emotional stresses cause further problems at the workplace and also at home.

Intervention and Prevention

In general, organizations can try to head off this common problem by encouraging employees to maintain a balance between work and personal life. Specific attention should be given to those employees who are known to work especially hard, display rigid managerial styles, or show signs of stress, depression, or excessive preoccupation with work. A careful and empathic psychiatric evaluation can then prevent the problems from worsening. Often, though, ambitious organizations and individuals will see such an approach as an impediment rather than as a competitive advantage. Hours worked and reports completed are like trees in the forest. They can be easily mistaken for long-term accomplishment. The organizational culture should not mistake work hours or report pages for true effectiveness.

HIDING AWAY THOSE PESKY EMOTIONS: REPRESSION OF EMOTIONAL DISTRESS

Anxiety, fear, anger, and sadness are regrettably common emotions. They are not usually too severe and they eventually diminish in intensity. Sometimes, though, there are such threatening hidden fears that the feelings cannot be thought about. Instead, they are repressed from conscious awareness and yet they remain potent covert determinants of mood and behavior. In that covert role, they can be handled through such mechanisms as displacement onto a less threatening perceived source. Or, attempts at mere suppression of distress may just cause a further intensification.

Emotions from Home Get Carried to Work: Displacement

When it comes right down to it, people are more concerned about other people than anything else, and they are concerned most of all about their families. For that reason, family worries are often the most troubling and thus the hardest to think about openly. Any real or potential change in the family environment will have emotional effects. But if the thoughts are troubling enough, they may be attributed to some convenient focus other than their true source.

Case Study 7

Hank Smith had been with Pawlet Advertising for 10 years. His business achievements had helped him on a steady career track over that time. Although he worked very hard, he did not usually feel stressed by the job. Hank was known for his dedication and independent mind, but also for his finesse at handling potential interpersonal conflict, thus avoiding consequent embarrassments for all concerned. From time to time he had found himself in difficult political situations, but he was always able to recognize the problems, think them through, and find diplomatic solutions for himself, his colleagues, and the company. Once, for example, he found himself reporting to a new boss with a very authoritarian management style. After a few difficult months, Hank was able to show his boss that he was a talented subordinate with a different approach. They recognized their differences and Hank's boss was helpful in arranging a promotion to another department.

Some time later, Hank found himself working under Louise Riley. Louise could be abrasive, dictatorial, and unsympathetic, but not necessarily more than Hank's prior authoritarian boss. None of her employees were happy, but after many months, Hank was notably miserable. He began to feel trapped in a hopeless situation and was surprised to note that a particular animosity had developed between Louise and himself. He remained a first-rate team player, but he unsettled Louise with a newly defiant aspect of his demeanor, and the office politics just kept getting worse. He kept thinking about his situation and wondered whether he might have to leave Pawlet Advertising, but also whether he might be missing something.

In psychotherapy, Hank initially wanted to talk only about Louise, but he was intrigued to realize that his problems with Louise intensified at the same time that he had become engaged for marriage. Hank had always kept an emotional distance from women, but this time he thought it was time to settle down. As his thoughts evolved, he realized that he saw Louise, his mother, and his psychiatrist as stern, controlling, and cold; and that he particularly feared that his affectionate fiancée would ultimately leave him trapped in a cold and controlling marriage. This had been too frightening a thought for him to contemplate, so he had instead focused his fears and anger on Louise.

Once Hank understood that these new emotions had colored his usual style, he could more clearly assess his problems with Louise. He worked at defusing the situation with his usual diplomatic finesse. Though the office tensions were by now established, Louise eventually turned her attentions away from Hank and she later left the company. Hank continued his steady career path at Pawlet, as well as a successful new marriage.

Causes

In this case, Hank's usual interpersonal office style was changed by his feelings about his upcoming marriage. With the onset of intense and hidden fear about being trapped in an intimate relationship, he was not able to realize where those intensified feelings had come from. Louise became an obvious substitute target. Because of her own personality and management style, the result was an escalating feud.

Effects

Displacement of feelings from home to work is rarely obvious, since the protagonists are themselves unaware of the external emotional fuel for their workplace distress. The potential organizational consequences are many and varied. Since reactions to the work environment can become exaggerated or unrealistic, coping strategies thus become ineffective or counter-productive. Morale and productivity can be further impaired by resulting emotional tension, conflict, and discord. Good workers may leave, as they feel the emotional toll and see the indirect effects on their own families.

Intervention and Prevention
In the long run, management and human resource attention dedicated to observation of interpersonal dynamics can increase the likelihood of early detection, before problems get out of hand. This can be accomplished with ongoing group meetings, as well as with contact and assessment by unentangled human resource officers or outside consultants. Whenever workplace emotions do intensify beyond a usual or reasonable level, care should be given to understanding all of the contributing factors, even when an obvious factor is present. Recognition of personality conflicts can lead to improvement through workplace interventions, as well as referrals for more sophisticated psychotherapy.

Problem and Solution Avoidance: Psychological Resistance to Change

All human beings have an inherent resistance to change, because change evokes two fears that most human beings attempt to avoid. The first is that change always requires loss. Dislike and fear are a natural response, particularly if the loss involves something familiar or comfortable. A second major resistance to change is the fear of the unknown. It is easier to stay with the familiar than it is to abandon it for something new but unmastered. As a result, many people actively avoid dealing with problems that may require them to change. They are left in a frustrating dilemma and are quick to decrease the frustration and conflict that they feel. Drugs, alcohol, and self-destructive behaviors often become means to that end. They become harmful self-treatment to decrease the pain of threatened change and unresolved problems.

Case Study 8

Susan Gold was a lawyer at the firm of Parette, McGuffey, and Weldon. Three weeks after promotion to partnership, she married her longtime boyfriend. She returned from her honeymoon refreshed, relaxed, and sporting a tan. She was sure she could handle both marriage and partnership with ease. Despite her somewhat limited people skills, senior partners had long appreciated Susan's intelligence, dedication, and long hours. Unusual for a woman at her firm, she felt encouraged to think in terms of even further advancement. She understood that she would be expected to start developing new clients for the firm. However, it soon became clear that her tremendous efforts were not producing new business. A short course on client development skills made intellectual sense to her, but it had little real effect on her approach. Her new husband was a consulting mechanical engineer, whose work hours were shorter and more flexible than hers. He had hoped marriage would lead to more time together and he was more than eager to start having children. Their relationship started to fray at the edges.

Susan became jealous of others who balanced their work and personal lives with seeming ease. She saw her own problem as merely one of "stress" that needed to be suppressed. When practical changes were suggested by her friends or by her many self-help books, she dismissed them quickly. She found more than enough reasons to keep her patterns unchanged. Susan became increasingly short tempered and lost her happy, enthusiastic disposition. An exercise program offered temporary relaxation, but she soon gave it up. While away on business, she sought a brief sexual affair to renew her spirit, but she ended up feeling mostly guilty. Susan started to drink more at professional functions and colleagues often noticed alcohol on her breath at the office.

Finally, after weeks of working around the clock on a new project, Susan called in sick. Her speech was slurred and she said that she might need a leave of absence to take care of personal matters. At this point the firm's psychiatrist was notified and Susan was asked to attend a nonconfidential consultation. The consultation would help determine whether Susan should seek treatment or leave employment. She pointed out that she had no problems worth mentioning, but she did reluctantly agree to the evaluation and to subsequent referral. In treatment, Susan was able to stop drinking and she slowly started to unravel the tightly hidden fears that led her to her recent travail. She soon repaired some of the damage to her career and marriage. Changes in people skills on the job and at home came more gradually.

Causes

Innate fears of change become excessive when childhood experience does not leave expectations of ready parental approval and instead leaves fears of retribution for positive change. Safe and predictable environments at least allow familiar ground and accustomed techniques for repressing and hiding emotional distress. Fears that change for the better will cause retribution or other problems are similarly kept under tight wraps.

Effects

The individual who struggles to ignore change will not have an easy time. Heightened and suppressed distress will manifest itself in problems at work or at home, and it can easily lead to more serious depression. There can also be ineffective and self-destructive attempts at anxiety reduction, including substance abuse, unethical behavior, and extramarital affairs. Lower echelon employees struggling with significant resistance to change can significantly affect productivity and morale. Corporations are even more keenly aware of the effects of such resistance among those in positions of leadership.

Many corporations have failed to succeed when key people had unwittingly maladaptive reactions to changes in organizational mission, circumstance, or structure.

Intervention and Prevention
For individual employees, it is essential to maintain awareness of the concomitants of both personal and professional changes. Any employee would be stressed by simultaneous marriage and promotion. Prompt professional discussion of changing roles and recognition of the difficulties involved will improve the odds of successful adjustment. In psychotherapy, getting past emotional resistances to change is a gradual and continuing process.

Many individuals are affected when major organizational change occurs and it is important to ease their concerns. A real crisis can develop if appropriate interventions are not instituted promptly (see Chapter 7). It is important not to confuse the temporary and limited benefits of stress management programs with improvements in individual or organizational adaptability. Stress management programs are a cost-effective approach to large-scale reactions to change, but they are more useful for short-term crises than they are for lasting or substantial benefits.

SUMMARY

These cases reflect the complexity of motivational forces among leaders in distress. Executive and organizational problems are often the consequence of hidden work, family, or intrapsychic concerns. Problems arise for specific reasons, have specific solutions, and are always more complicated than they first appear. Awareness of such constructs as narcissistic-level personality problems, re-created family dynamics, personality styles under stress, and psychological defenses are essential for recognizing, addressing, and avoiding problems. Effective treatment considers not only job issues themselves but also family concerns, specific psychodynamic and psychiatric diagnoses, and the possibility of medical illness.

Bibliography
Kets de Vries, M. F. R., and Associates. 1991. *Organizations on the Couch: Clinical Perspectives on Organizational Behavior and Change.* San Francisco: Jossey-Bass.
MacKinnon, R. A., and R. Michels. 1971. *The Psychiatric Interview in Clinical Practice.* Philadelphia: Saunders.
Rohrlich, J. 1980. *Work and Love: The Crucial Balance.* New York: Harmony Books.
Schwartz, H. S. 1990. *Narcissistic Process and Organizational Decay: The Theory of the Organizational Ideal.* New York: New York University Press.
Speller, J. L. 1989. *Executives in Crisis: Recognizing and Managing the Alcoholic, Drug-Addicted, or Mentally Ill Executive.* San Francisco: Jossey-Bass.

7

Organizational Structure and Change

Charles W. Swearingen, M.D.

Offer Leadership Support and Guidance
Carefully Assess Effects of Change
Maintain Organizational and Individual Mental Health
Summary

ABSTRACT

The way people structure and change organizations derives from human nature
and from the experience of family socialization. No matter how technical the
design or purpose of the organization, the "human equation" is always present.
Employees' feelings and beliefs strongly influence their motivation and performance. Effective organizations replicate the best features of good families.
They are supportive, authoritative but not authoritarian, and can create an
organizational ideal that benefits from employees' highest aspirations. Change is
always difficult. Recognizing that change may seriously affect the mental health
of organizational members is a necessary insight for effective leaders.

INTRODUCTION

Humans are social animals whose very survival from the instant of birth
depends on others. From the womb to the tomb, humans are intertwined
with and dependent on each other in a variety of roles. During psychological
development, critical and formative interactions with other individuals and
groups help shape personality. As they mature and interact with the environment,
people move from their first relationship with a maternal figure, to other
family members, to groups of peers, and then to organizations. Most of adult
life has to do with interpersonal interactions in an organizational context,
and careers usually involve working with or for an organization. This chapter
explores the psychological dimensions of organizations, and focuses on the
nature and experience of organizational change and its impact on individuals.

1. *The psychology of the individual.* Just as organizations can shape
individuals, one cannot understand what happens in organizations without
considering how they are shaped themselves by individual psychodynamics.
At some point in the analysis of any organizational problem or opportunity,
the level of discourse must shift to a focus on the individual players and what
motivates or troubles them. Individuals found, develop, preserve, and destroy
organizations. Each member remains a unique entity no matter how much
he or she is an "organization man."

2. *Organizations.* Organizations are groups of people with some kind of
rationally defined function and purpose. But whatever the rational task or

mission of the group or organization, there is an irrational, emotional dimension to group life that can make or break the group's accomplishment of its stated goals. Thus, these forces at work in groups need to be understood. The prototype for any group is the family. It is the first group to which each of us belongs and from which we learn our first lessons about social functioning. Understanding the way family systems operate can shed light on the dynamics of groups and organizations, and can illuminate the quandaries and passions so often seen in groups of humans.

3. *Leadership.*   Certain individuals will assume the leadership role in any organization or group. The leader and the group shape each other, and leadership style will powerfully affect the success or failure of the group. Understanding the nature of leadership, even at a basic level, is useful for anyone struggling with organizational life and change.

4. *Change.*   All organizations today are confronted with great demands for change. In some cases, the changes required are cataclysmic, and in others they are more subtle and less disruptive. But all change is stressful, uncertain, and demands a lot from organizational members and especially from those who are implementing the change. At some level, all change entails loss, and this experience must be processed by people in any changed group.

THE INDIVIDUAL AND THE FAMILY

What must be known about individual psychodynamics to better understand interpersonal relations in organizations? First, most social relations reveal only the tip of the iceberg of others' psychological functioning. Much more is revealed when people are under stress, in pain, or in psychotherapy. But most of the time, what's going on with someone must be inferred, using a model of psychological functioning derived from self-awareness and understanding. People are always "psychologizing" about others in everyday life, and everyone has an implicit if not explicit model of human psychology. Empathy is the tool with which humans guess what is going on inside the skin of another. It is the capacity to think and feel a little like the other person, and it is an essential means for success in organizational life. To be deficient in empathy is something like flying blind.

The Psychodynamic Model

The psychodynamic model of the individual provides a dynamic conception of people and relationships. It posits certain psychic "structures" with which most people are now familiar: id (impulses), ego (reason), and superego (conscience). It also stresses object relations (interpersonal relationships) and narcissism (the relationship of each person with himself). All these psychic structures develop and take shape primarily in the family, and it could even be said that the family is the original organization. There is a natural connection between the fundamental psychoanalytic principles of individual psychology and the organizational world: Individual personalities are the building blocks of organizational groups. The following basic psychodynamic ideas are the building blocks for understanding what each individual brings to a group (see also Chapter 1).

Unconscious Processes
People do not always know why they think, feel, or do things. But at a later point in time, they may discover what the missing reasons were. Or, their explanation for an experience may be revised and understood anew using introspection and new insights. It is common in organizational settings that people do not always mean what they say or say what they really mean. People are often completely unaware of the meaning of an action or of intense feelings that are evident to others. Unconscious love, hate, and guilt are powerful determinants of normal and abnormal behaviors. People behave in ways that act out (enact) unconscious emotional relationships, as though responding to an invisible script. Similarly, people can listen with a "third ear" and, consciously or unconsciously, pick up the hidden emotional meaning of a communication.

Case Study 1

Bill Garcia, the founder of a small but successful high-technology firm, had always prided himself on rational attendance to the needs of his company. But as he entered his seventh decade, he had great difficulty thinking about the question of his succession, and he was unaware of his own intense need for complete control. Bill repeatedly told his core executives that he was working on a plan. The staff privately discounted Bill's intended succession program. When a successor was finally picked after 3 years, Bill quickly undercut and dismissed him. The staff had correctly intuited Bill's actual, if unconscious, intentions.

Psychological Defenses
Individuals defend themselves against perceived threats from within as well as from without. One generally fights or flees from an external assault that could be physical, or could be, for example, an aggressive attempt to protect oneself against the reprimand of a superior. Internal threats are the experience of dysphoric affects (painful feelings), primarily anxiety and guilt. Here, the individual uses psychological defense mechanisms to ward off the unpleasant emotional states, to keep them out of consciousness. In the case

study, Bill cannot accept his mortality and the need to relinquish the reins of his company. The underlying emotions are too troubling to be allowed into conscious thought, so Bill defends himself by sabotaging the future and trying to show that there can be no company without him. The following defense mechanisms occur frequently in members of groups and organizations.

Consciously and unconsciously, people take on the characteristics of others. Each person's self-identity is powerfully influenced and partly formed by identification with others. In adult life, individuals typically identify with authority figures, admired ideal figures, or sometimes with powerful and abusive figures. Identification is a kind of cement for group life. It entails a sense of shared purpose and a wish to emulate or follow a perceived leader. Politicians induce followers to identify with their vision of how society should be organized. Identification defends against the experience of being a separate and isolated group of one and it also mutes the urge to oppose the person who is the object of identification. Indeed, identification with the aggressor (trying to be like a persecuting authority figure) is one way to deny a reality of persecution.

Projection is a way of disavowing unpleasant internal thoughts, feelings, or intentions, only to then project them onto (discover them in) certain other people. In its extreme and psychotic form, it is the central psychological mechanism of paranoia. Scapegoats in a group are the target of projections of other members. Whole nations may use projection to inflate nationalistic pride, while locating evil in some adversary nation.

A related defense mechanism is projective identification. Some theorists (for instance, Shapiro and Carr 1991) feel that projective identification is the bridge, the linking mechanism par excellence, from the individual to the group. In this mode, a person again disavows intolerable thoughts or feelings. These are projected onto (discovered in) another person and then experienced as coming from that person. Projective identification uses subtle cues to induce the other person to behave in a way that expresses the projected thoughts and feelings. In addition, there is a continuing relationship between the person projecting and the person responding. For example, at an annual corporate meeting, a senior executive had problems in his division and much reason to be nervous. He said several times that he was in no way shaky or afraid. He only worried that everyone else might have the jitters. His thirty executive subordinates all began to notice increasing anxiety, which they soon started to voice. The boss began working to assuage their anxiety. He thus unconsciously reduced his own anxiety, without any conscious awareness.

To a greater or lesser extent, all of the emotional defense mechanisms of individuals are present in organizational life. Thus, someone may defensively deny (forget) that something patently obvious remains true. Intellectualization about charged issues can calm the passions of group interaction just as it calms an individual. The tensions and pressures of relationships, especially in groups, can induce defensiveness in people quite readily. Of particular importance, group members can psychologically regress to childish patterns. Irrational and emotional perceptions then compromise consciously planned methods and purposes. In organizations, threats of any sort may induce such epidemic defensiveness that there might be group hysteria or paranoia. When defenses fail on a widespread basis, the group as a whole can become depressed or anxious. Where there is a high level of organizational mental health, the pressures and defenses are sufficiently balanced so that no substantial distress or clinical symptoms are apparent.

Transference

Whenever people interact, some of their behavior is determined by the effects of significant past relationships. Transference is the unwitting projection of thoughts and feelings from emotionally significant childhood figures onto other present-day people. These thoughts and feelings can produce behavior that is unconsciously enacted from a childhood script. Transference can be capricious, ambivalent, extreme, and inconsistent with consensually validated reality. Transference is ubiquitous in social life, but it is especially evident in relationships with authority figures and in organizational life.

Two types of transference patterns are common among individuals in groups. An idealizing transference comes from a need to feel bonded to powerful, wonderful, or idealized figures who will offer protection and love. Charismatic leaders are experienced this way, just as a young child sees only good in its parents. Someone who has found such an idealized figure will also form a mirror transference (a positive identification with the idealized figure). In this transference, the lover, spouse, supervisor, or leader is idealized and is also seen as idealizing the self. The original model for this is the child who sees a perfect mother and feels itself the apple of her eye. Transferential modes of relatedness and projective identifications are the interpersonal cement of family, group, and organizational life. They are normal aspects of psychological development, dominant in childhood, but seen nevertheless in adult life. These reactions are elicited in particular by stress- and anxiety-induced regression (a return to earlier modes of psychic functioning).

The Family Template of Organizations

First loves, hates, and feelings about ourselves stem from family relationships. Defense mechanisms, transference reactions, and much of psychic structure itself reflects the amalgamation of inherited traits and family interactions.

There are normative ways that children relate to parents and siblings, and normative rivalries, loves, and conflicts in family life. Psychodynamic understanding posits that the outcome of the intergenerational rivalries of the oedipal complex (also called the family romance) is a critical determinant of superego (conscience), ego ideal (moral values), and self-identity (see Chapter 6). Early interactions with parents and siblings form the foundation for later relationships with authority and rival figures. Moreover, the rivalries, disappointments, victories, and defeats that are remembered from childhood will also contribute to an unwitting perception of those same childhood interactions in present-day organizational relationships. In summary, two important childhood residues are core elements of the unconscious experience of organizational life. Leaders can be experienced as parents, and co-workers as siblings. This reexperience can harmlessly take place outside of conscious awareness. Too often, though, the hidden residue of unresolved oedipal issues can turn organizational groups into troubled families. These ubiquitous interpersonal conflicts explain much of the irrational rivalries and love–hate feelings that can seriously interfere with organizational accomplishment.

Parents also have the job of ensuring that children feel safe and feel secure about their own worth. This parenting function helps reduce and manage anxiety, and provides a role model for adult behavior. The nascent self forms through empathic relationships with parents. Dysfunctional families are always troubled by parental failure of empathy, whatever other problems might also be present. Secure self-esteem grows out of a supportive and understanding family milieu. Empathic failures in that milieu lead to a lifelong quest for the developmentally missed nurturance. If early childhood neglect and hurt are bad enough, the resulting psychological deficit can lead to substantial impairment of self-esteem. The quest for emotional repair can become quixotic or substitutive. When organizational members use work as a substitute for unmet emotional needs, the results can be intense and disruptive. Character pathology (damaged personality) reflects early emotional scars and may also lead to conflict with acceptable organizational behavior. In these situations, professional consultation is more often than not advisable.

Aspirations and Goals

People are possessed of a range of aspirations and strive to accomplish their goals. Everyone has a vision of the ideal self. This ideal starts in childhood with parental identifications and later includes other authority figures. The ideal self may have a mature and realistic design, or it may embody grandiose and unrealistic requirements of superhuman perfection. For most people, the ego ideal comes to include some aspirations identified with organizational membership. For some, only a leadership role will do. Others aspire to the role of a helpful, dutiful, and appreciated follower. Whatever the ego ideal, if it cannot be realized there is a always a lowering of self-esteem.

The point of this highly condensed and selective review of individual psychodynamic theory is that people are, in the main, shaped by dealings with important figures in childhood. Those childhood relationships affect organizational roles and identifications that are enacted in organizational behavior. This is especially evident in the workplace, where relationships with authority figures are essential. Influencing and being influenced by others at all levels (rational and irrational, conscious and unconscious, mature and immature) is what work life is all about. The case study illustrates the complex interdigitation of individuals, working task groups, organizational priorities, and the threat of emotional derailment and sabotage of stated goals.

Case Study 2

It looked like a great deal—Newhall Financial would bankroll Lou Savarini's fabulous new mall and would realize 35 percent on its investment of $50 million. Tom Brent and Lou Savarini had spent hours together and had worked out the specifics. But over the year, the economy became problematic. Lou became more anxious and less confident, and Tom was deeply involved in many other deals. Tom assigned two of his vice-presidents to Lou's project. Within 3 months they complained bitterly that they couldn't work with Lou. When they called Lou paranoid and said that they needed help, Lou's attorney called in an organizational psychiatrist. The psychiatrist found that Lou was indeed afraid that Tom would withdraw Newhall Financial's backing. Lou also felt that the vice-presidents were brusque, rarely available, and unsupportive. In turn, these junior executives felt that Lou called them all the time, usually sounded completely frantic, and then didn't listen to what they said. With time, they stopped trying to hide their hostility. After the consultant met with all of the parties, it was clear that anxiety and suspicion abounded on all sides. The emotional pressures were tempting some players to act in ways potentially harmful to the financial interests of all. Only the relationship between Lou Savarini and Tom Brent seemed unscathed and curiously viable. In fact, these two men had quite similar aspirations and ideals. Each respected the other's prowess, and they came to share a sense of superiority over the scurrying and worrying of their separate subordinates. It soon became clear that the subordinates wanted Tom and Lou to resume primary responsibility for working out the deal. Tom and Lou had to make major time sacrifices to resume their original roles. Nonetheless, the relational problems dissipated and the transaction was completed.

This case shows the threat to organizational affairs that can be caused by intense emotional reactions of involved individuals. As in the case above, people experience each other in unproductive, anxious, and irrational ways. Conversation and objective analysis of problems grind to a halt. Lou and the vice-presidents angrily pointed their fingers, and they projected feelings of fear and failure onto each other. It was as though the sibling sandbox wars could only be halted by parental intervention. These junior executives were uncomfortable dealing directly with a senior authority while they felt guilty for their inability to handle him. Their plight resembled the frustrations of young children who try to parent their disturbed parents. As visionary parents, Tom and Lou understood each other, despite their divergent feelings, projections, and personalities. When they resumed their direct negotiations, the subordinates saw them as positive parental figures. The emotional force of their problem-solving efforts stabilized the others and reset the stage for rational problem solving.

THE ORGANIZATION AND THE GROUP

Groups can occur with many sizes and stated purposes. This section focuses on subgroups of larger organizations that have definite social or economic missions or goals. Just as the individual is the constituent of any group, for our purpose, groups are the constituent building blocks of organizations.

Organizations are defined by visions, goals, and strategies that are developed at their highest level of authority. Subunits within the organization set about implementing these goals through whatever tactics and organizational structures are deemed appropriate. This is equally true for hospitals serving community medical needs, industrial companies making manufactured goods, and banks offering financial services.

There is another level of organizational definition that underlies any rational statements of purpose. Group members have underlying shared fantasies about the group (the "Basic Assumptions" of British psychoanalyst Wilfred Bion). The three basic fantasies concern dependency, flight–fight, and pairing. These shared fantasies are particularly relevant to groups or organizations undergoing change. At stressful times, members can become increasingly dependent, searching for leaders like lost children looking for parents. There may also be a concerted tendency to flee from change, or, conversely, to search for and fight a common enemy. Finally, a wish can emerge for some idealized parental pair to unite and resolve all problems (as with Tom and Lou in the case study). These Basic Assumptions integrate individual psychodynamic reactions and provide detectable patterns within organizational groups. At the same time, they can often subvert the purposeful tasks of the group.

The Classic Organizational Structure

For centuries, the most common structural form for an organization has been the kind of pyramidal hierarchy that is seen in the military. Authority concentrates at the very top and spreads out toward the bottom. There is a correspondingly clear line of responsibility that flows from the top to the various levels of subordinates beneath. Most organization charts show variants of this form, and, on paper, look logical and efficient. Much of the time, this model works well. But in recent years, greater attention has been paid to variant organizational structures that are better suited to some tasks.

The classic hierarchical organization concentrates control in the hands of a chief, such as a CEO, general, or surgeon-in-chief. In this model, organizational culture, task, and performance are highly determined by the personality and vagaries of a few leaders. The more that power is concentrated in the hands of a single individual or a small oligarchic group, the more pronounced will be this effect. Extreme examples abound of how this situation can lead to the abuse and misuse of power, to the detriment of the organization. When structures allow for unquestioned decision making, powerful or charismatic leaders can bend an organization to their personal wants or emotional needs. Such authoritarian behavior is often first viewed optimistically as authoritative and productive. Even in everyday situations, arrogance, anger, impulsivity, and paranoia among top managers will often continue for an extended period before recognition and attempts at correction. Organizations that isolate and insulate their leaders leave themselves open to the unchecked effects of adverse personality traits and other psychiatric problems. In general, the more authoritarian the organization, the more the likelihood that its members will feel and behave like children ordered about by willful parents.

Most organizational members want to be led and at the same time they resent their dependence. Children, too, are ambivalent in nearly any dependent setting. However, a psychological basis for compliance forms from their desire to please their parents. In military settings unquestioning compliance is a necessity, but in some other organizations it can allow executive psychopathology to flourish unchallenged.

Case Study 3

Mike Holloway was the section chief of a large bureaucratic organization. He was tyrannical and abusive, and he gave open evidence of his alcohol problem. For over a year, his subordinates complained to each other. Each one hoped that someone else would complain to Mike's boss. When interviewed privately by a consultant, each subordinate acknowledged dreading the possibility of Mike's continuing behavior, but also dreading the inevitable stress of change. In an interregnum, they would all have more responsibility, longer hours, and an uncertain future. Mike ultimately changed his behavior, but only when severe budgetary problems led his superiors to recognize what the subordinates had long understood.

Fear of criticizing a superior is like fear of criticizing a parent. It holds employees hostage in rigid organizational structures that are exclusively controlled from the top down. Rigid bureaucratic hierarchies are difficult places for subordinates to feel safe when commenting on even obvious problems. They also promote establishment of a dependency culture as a Basic Assumption.

Top-Down Communication

Most of what organizations do, and perhaps all of what service organizations do, is some kind of communication. As is true elsewhere in interpersonal existence, there is a vast range of communication style and effectiveness. The typical style of an organization is part of the organizational culture and structure. Thus, the classical top-down company typically has a formal system of communication to filter and strain the flow of information. Top management tries to decide what information is acceptable and relevant for employees down the pecking order. Censorship, bowdlerization, and withholding too often leave employees without the information they need both for themselves and for the company. Access to information becomes a perquisite for insiders at the top. Deprived of the facts of organizational life, others can feel left out or infantilized. Remarkably, even when information is withheld from highly placed executives, such discretion is often unnecessary for organizational well-being. Acquisition details, merger timing, and struggles to keep a CEO from defecting to a competitor are examples of information quite properly kept in confidence at the very top. Not all major decisions, especially those with intense time constraints, can be democratically aired. But what is withheld is often practical, tactical, and unrelated to organizational strategy. In any case, there is always an informal grapevine through which an unofficial information flow is subject to massive distortion.

Case Study 4

There had been a long and intense rivalry between the comparable divisions of a large company and its newly acquired former competitor. The senior executives architecting the merger repeatedly rebuffed the many questions about office locations, reporting relationships, and other essential concerns. Important junior executives and many other subordinates became anxious, angry, and demoralized. They started to feel less loyal to their original companies, and they also viewed the nascent hybrid organization with increasing skepticism and disdain. One executive from the acquired company resentfully described what he called the mushroom treatment: "After the acquisition we were kept in the dark, covered with manure, and allowed to stew. Then we were canned."

Not all classically arranged organizations are distasteful or dysfunctional. But when the structure is low on mutual participation and shared decisions, there is a greater potential for abuse of power and for constriction of communication. Consequently, autocratic managers and authoritarian organizations run a high risk of breeding adverse employee regression, transference reactions, and defensiveness. When employees revert to behaviors that stem from primitive group fantasies, there is a corresponding decrease in imaginative problem solving, loyalty, and productivity.

Frank Lorenzo, CEO of the defunct Eastern Airlines, is a case in point. Postmortem analyses of the collapse suggested that his uncompromising, dictatorial style of management played a major role in the ultimate dissolution of his company. Employees locked in battle with him, saw him as a villain, and refused to do his will. In the end, everyone lost.

The Search for Better Organizational Structure

Although there are no panaceas, there are healthy models for organizational structure. Not surprisingly, capable management and effective organizations are much like good parents and functional families. As in healthy families, the parental leaders set the tone.

How does an organization become like a good family? Obviously, there is no single model for the ideal family or organization. But a fair consensus probably exists that a good family system has certain definable features. In such systems, everyone gets heard: not endlessly, not always to everyone's satisfaction, but to some important degree. People are not just bypassed. There is also some capacity to imagine the needs and requirements of unique individuals. This shows up in the definitions of required duties and in how those expectations are presented. Distinct and relevant behavior patterns convey a clear message that everyone is valued. Attempts are made to reduce destructive rivalries and factionalism. Penalties for default and transgression are clearly defined and consistently applied. Praise for accomplishment is appropriately and generously awarded.

To be sure, there are many cultural variants of these principles. Some families are outwardly more liberal, giving members ample autonomy and latitude. Others appear more conservative, holding a tighter rein, and they are less tolerant of experimentation or deviance. At the cultural level, an Italian family is not a Japanese family, is not an English family. At a deeper level, though, "Happy families are all alike," as Tolstoy said at the opening of

Anna Karenina. So although tactics, ideals, and aspirations may vary between organizations, the underlying strategic qualities of effective management are surprisingly similar. The current American quest for better organizational structures is largely a search for the realization of a happy family in organizational settings.

Family-Run Businesses

The overlap of family issues and organizational tasks is most evident in businesses that are owned or run by a particular family. It should be remembered that 80 percent of American businesses are family owned, including 35 percent of the Fortune 500 companies. While there is a definite appeal to blending family intimacies with the seemingly less personal requirements of work, the tensions between underlying emotion and organizational purpose are high. Despite the enormous gratifications of a true family business, the incidence of trouble, dissension, and even dissolution is high. Only 10 percent of family businesses survive their founders, and the length of the family business life cycle is only 24 years.

The initial structural model for the company is usually set by the founder and it is inevitably based on the model of his or her own family. If founder and family are still running the show, it may take extra effort to create organizational structures that differ substantially from their family model. These enterprises also risk a developmental lag, caused by family members unable to leave home or acquire independent outside experience. Founders are often unable to surrender the company to heirs or professional management. In some cases, business growth is stymied when the family is unable to relinquish much ownership or control in return for outside investment capital.

Those family businesses that succeed are able to transcend their origins and infightings. The founders must achieve a vision of the business similar to that of parents for their offspring. They must be willing to allow independence, to let growth occur on its own, and to let go of total control. The story of IBM is instructive. Founder Tom Watson, Senior, groomed Tom Watson, Junior, as his successor. Yet over many years, Watson Senior rode herd on his son, criticized him, and tried to control him. IBM expanded and became successful partly because both Watsons could see that they were a part of an enterprise with immense potential that required them to resolve their difficulties. And, from early on, the elder Watson recognized professional management as an essential remedy for the troubles inherent to a family enterprise. He listened, at times, to the advice of his trusted top managers, and he later came to respect and listen to his son. A strong corporation grew out of these family origins. The history of IBM reads quite differently from that of a company like Ford Motors, where Henry Ford's autocratic and arbitrary control over both company and sons worked to everyone's ultimate detriment.

The Structure for Success

In Search of Excellence (Peters and Waterman 1982) describes two elements exemplifying the structural properties of the highly effective organizations they studied. Their book considers various abuses of the hierarchical model, and then describes and advocates what they call "simultaneous loose-tight properties," which refers to the ability of successful ("excellent") companies to concurrently centralize and delegate decision-making and managerial power. The excellent organization should be able to foster entrepreneurial independence, while still maintaining the efficiencies of centralization. In this view, authority and responsibility should not be concentrated solely in the hands of the few at the very top. Subunits of a company should have some real autonomy, yet operate in harmony for the good of the whole organization. Individuals should be treated as important contributors. While recognizing the need to protect truly proprietary or strategic information, communication should be diffused as widely as possible.

The example of Japanese industry is another source for the reexamination of traditional organizational hierarchy. Ironically, Japanese society is often regarded as very formal, authoritarian, and hierarchical. Nonetheless, companies there have successfully included considerable democratic participation in corporate decisions. The Japanese have taken a largely American organizational strategy and have implemented it with a passion. In Japanese business, an intense search for relevant ideas is coupled with a commitment to hear everyone out. Intense and disseminated communication is enshrined in this Japanese model. The ideals and vision of the company are rendered explicit and made part of everyday life in the organization. The "corporation ideal" becomes a part of the individual employee's ego ideal. Many Japanese companies have a company song, sung daily by all employees. A marketing slogan such as "Delight the Customer" is pursued as a realistic, achievable goal. Meticulous and pervasive commitment to quality is a continuing theme.

Common sense appears to suggest that it is harder to get away from the military model in a larger organization. While this is an appealing generalization, *In Search of Excellence* points out that, relatively speaking, some of the most successful enterprises the authors looked at had "simple form and lean staff," which means avoiding the penchant of large and complex organizations to become top heavy, with multiple layers of managers running other multiple layers, all of them reporting to executives back at headquarters. This kind of arrangement is not required by the laws of logic or business.

One immensely productive international firm reduced by 90 percent the staffing of some regional branches, yet found improvements in efficiency and productivity. With fewer layers, important communications are more easily transmitted, with fewer chances for delay, distortion, and disappearance. Simple form and lean staff can be built in at the start of a new organization and may become the template for future growth. It is a more complicated task to bring such revisions to an ongoing and mature hierarchical organization. Such change requires enlisting acceptance, if not enthusiasm, from those who would operate the new structure. Even so, the 1990s have seen a dramatic shift toward these newer models at many American companies. IBM, in particular, has embarked on a program of reduced management and decentralized divisions.

Elliot Jaques (1989) points out that, in spite of all wishes for egalitarian social structures, there will always be hierarchies with some people more powerful than others. He stresses the "accountability hierarchy" of the "requisite organization." This portrays an organizational structure where position and power are determined by cognitive capacity to plan projects for ever longer time spans—that is, chairpeople and heads of groups are often required to imagine, plan, and carry out strategic tasks over 10- or 20-year periods. Those employees at an organization's lowest level might only need to focus on the work for that day. Considerable stress and emotional pain can ensue when employees' abilities are not matched to their job requirements, and to their compensation and stature in the organization.

The Hidden Meanings of Organizations

The Psychological Contract
People are consciously bound to organizations by financial rewards and other satisfactions that are often spelled out in job descriptions or formal contracts. Yet, it is more often the unconscious, emotional contract that provides the strongest bond between individual and organization. This psychological contract materially determines employee loyalty and productivity. Because this unconscious contract is viewed through the employee's existing emotional framework, unresolved issues about the family of origin are brought to the workplace. People often have unrealistic and powerfully emotional demands of organizations. These demands usually exist quietly and unobtrusively. Often enough, though, an employee idealizes a job and hopes for the support, affirmation, and special recognition possibly missed in childhood. When that support does not materialize, or when it is not perceived, the employee can become angry and disappointed. The aspirations of the employee's ego ideal must fit with the job at hand and with the needs of the organization.

Case Study 5

Anne Gunnar was an extremely talented investment banker. During childhood, she had tried hard to please her demanding and distant father, and to outshine her siblings. Like her college dean father, Anne was the family intellectual, and she started out on a university career. As the years went on, Anne published many important academic papers, but she did not find the emotional recognition she sought from students and from senior professors. So, at age 34 she switched to a career in investment banking. Her banking skills were impressive, she soon had many clients, and she substantially increased her firm's revenue. Anne received large bonuses but little in the way of direct praise or managerial authority. Anne had a vague notion of wanting to be "a manager" of people. She saw managerial duties as a reward for generating revenue, an opportunity for interpersonal fulfillment, and an affirmation from the company. She did not realize that her attempts at matching her father's successes were still an attempt to replace his missing attention in her childhood.

The company viewed banking skills as the primary desideratum for management and selected executives who were gregarious and socially at ease with clients and colleagues. Her superiors liked and respected her banking skills, but they viewed her as something of a loner, with limited "people skills." They felt she was unsuited for executive authority over subordinates and they were surprised by her dissatisfaction with monetary reward.

Repeatedly passed over for leadership positions, Anne began to withdraw from participation in meetings. Her boss became quite concerned, but only thought of increasing her bonus. Anne's ego ideal had pushed her aspirations in a direction where she lacked skill. Her hidden psychological contract with the company thus threatened to disrupt the conscious written contract. When Anne began to think of yet another career change, a friendly senior executive suggested therapy with the firm's consulting psychiatrist. After many months, Anne started to understand the connections between career aspirations and hidden emotional needs. As she became increasingly able to distinguish the two, she continued her banking success and found new satisfactions in her private social life. After a year, some of senior management had noticed a subtle change in her office relationships.

Just like everywhere else, people in organizations look for support, validation, respect, and any of the myriad forms of love. They bring their deepest emotional needs and desires to co-worker relationships, and these expectations are especially transferred onto authority figures. In quiet, stable times for the organization, evidence of transference and family-like dynamics may be minimal and well masked but present nonetheless. It is useful, and often imperative, to recognize the distinction between conscious organizational aspirations and hidden emotional needs and expectations. Managers must be sensitive to the fact that people do not become one dimensional as they cross the workplace threshold. Jobs and assigned tasks can raise or crush self-esteem. Managers should not practice psychotherapy on the job and they do not really need to be trained in psychoanalytic theory. But, optimal organizational management skills include the ability to conceptualize relevant psychological issues and how they affect productivity.

Effective functioning in any group milieu requires knowing at least something of what superiors, peers, and subordinates feel about work issues. That knowledge can be implicit or explicit, intuitive or rational. Knowing what makes peers irritable and subordinates content, and what ethical issues touch on a superior's ideals, is highly useful information. Hours of in-depth interviewing are not required. This kind of information comes from personal experience with people in general and at work, and from what people tell you about themselves by their everyday interactions. The most successful leaders (and followers) can gather such information easily and naturally, and then they may use it to inform their actions. Awareness of the psychological contract is as important as awareness of the job description.

Top people in organizations have to recognize the importance of clarity and timing in what they say. Perhaps more difficult is the task of learning how to listen effectively to what others are saying. Sometimes what does the trick for employees is just the sense of really being heard, understood, and taken seriously. A famous early study found that if top management called in consultants, convened special meetings, or did anything special at all, employees reported feeling better about work. This Hawthorne effect does not require extraordinary measures, but rather awareness of what is really important to people.

Organizational Culture

Organizational culture is a broad notion that encompasses the set of values, goals, norms, rituals, history, and traditions that provide the unique "feel" of an organization. Culture colors interpersonal relationships and methods of accomplishment. It is an important constituent of the fantasies people have about any given organization, and it is the repository of esprit de corps, mission, and the emotionally charged notion of belonging. Individual employees need to understand that culture sets the parameters for the organization's side of the psychological contract. It is sometimes hard on short acquaintance to gauge correctly the culture of a group. So, individuals who represent the organization to newcomers, clients, or the outside world must understand the role of leadership. It has been said that the main job of any organizational leader is development and management of the culture. Harry Levinson has written that leaders are great storytellers and have the capacity to interest others in the organizational story (Levinson and Rosenthal 1984).

LEADERSHIP

Organizations are abstractions. Groups of people set forth to accomplish defined goals, under the direction of selected members. This is called management. Management activities are generally concerned with tactics, logistics, and practical implementation of the defined tasks. Leadership, on the other hand, is that superordinate managerial activity that is concerned with strategy, vision, and the fundamental decisions about organizational form. Like the task of parenthood, leadership has a broad impact on mental health.

Leadership comes in all sizes and shapes. A shop foreman on an assembly line can be a leader to her crew. She may develop creative approaches, microstrategies, and she may encourage the expansion of the company's goals with the tools at her disposal. Yet, when we speak of leadership, we generally have in mind those individuals operating with a still wider purview of influence. Their decisions influence a range of organizational levels and influence the lives of many. They must exhibit a broad range of technical and interpersonal skills, and they must be impassioned, despite a cool surface demeanor. Successful leaders also have an intense desire to learn and to share useful information, and they show a willingness to think before acting.

Leaders show an outward self-confidence, especially when the organization faces critical choices, or needs new goals and missions. Although many leaders will sometimes share their inner anguish (Winston Churchill suffered from chronic depression), their leadership is reckoned by what they actually did despite moments of doubt. When self-confidence becomes arrogance, however, and when healthy narcissism is thus replaced with a more extreme egotism, leaders and organizations are set for a fall (see Chapters 6 and 14). Narcissistic pathology is the most common plague of leadership. The old adage that "power corrupts and absolute power corrupts absolutely" is not without foundation.

The temptation to exploit the power of the leadership role for immediate personal gain is ubiquitous. The press is filled with stories of political, business, and other leaders who have brought ruin to themselves and others. Lehman Brothers, one of the country's oldest financial houses, was destroyed in the early 1980s when a senior trading partner demanded the CEO spot, threatening to move the entire trading division out of the company if he did not get his way. After much internal struggle, the managing partners gave in to the financial clout of the trading division and its leader. Within a year, many other partners quit, profits declined, and Lehman Brothers was sold to American Express. In the aftermath, it was said that one would-be leader's greed and selfishness destroyed a firm that had survived the Civil War and the Great Depression.

Such debacles are not a necessary consequence of leadership, or even of narcissism. What matters is the leader's conscience, ego ideals, values, and the ability to detach immediate personal needs from the overarching concerns of the organization. Good leadership maintains the organization in the present and perpetuates it into the future (a fundamental goal of virtually all organizations). Good leadership understands how employees, culture, and organization function emotionally, and how subordinates identify with leaders. Of course, leaders cannot eke out and analyze every way that subordinates experience them, or readily separate transference from more realistic responses. But good leaders, like good parents, good teachers, and good psychotherapists, do create a climate where transference and identification fuel the tasks of accomplishment and growth. Their actions keep the group's underlying Basic Assumption emotions from getting out of hand.

They do this by "walking the talk"—that is, they avoid hypocrisy and exemplify what they ask of others. They are supportive and strive to be directly available to their immediate subordinates. Firmness and toughness are not at all incompatible with supportiveness. As with parenting, it is important that reprimands and penalties be clear, specifically directed at unwanted behaviors, and never used for ad hominem assaults. Authoritative leadership breeds respect, whereas authoritarian approaches breed resentment and defiance. Good leadership strives to avoid damaging the self-esteem of subordinates, particularly when offering correction or discipline.

All leaders make mistakes. Those who do not learn from them become dysfunctional leaders, and they eventually become former leaders. Leaders who ignore their own responsibility for failure, and instead assign all responsibility to those lower on the organizational chart, are courting trouble. In 1991, a furor was created when the chairperson and CEO of IBM said, "The fact that we're losing share makes me goddam mad. . . . The tension level is not high enough . . . the business is in crisis." Many IBM employees were quoted as saying they were offended by his profanity, which was uncharacteristic of the reserved and formal culture of the company. Others were angered at the vast and vague scope of the indictment, and they felt the chairperson should first and foremost have accepted responsibility for the downturn himself.

Making people feel bad can be altogether counterproductive. An executive who does this, even inadvertently, must deal with the wounds inflicted, create new camaraderie, and generate new strategies to address the gathering problems. In response to a deluge of commentary, the chairperson of IBM did soon hold himself and his management team responsible for the shortcomings. In the months thereafter, he also offered a visionary plan for massive strategic reorganization of IBM, designed to improve its competitive position in the rapidly changing computer industry. Despite layoff announcements, these midcourse corrections appeared to mark a return to effective leadership style. The many impending changes in the IBM workplace will pose many more tests of leadership skills.

ORGANIZATIONAL CHANGE

It has always been true that organizations are subject to changing circumstances, goals, and structures. With the flow of time, technology and communications have caused a faster rate of change. People must now race ever faster to keep up with the changes they must face. The past 40 years in particular have seen vast innovations in American business practice. For example, companies have embraced such creative improvements as the information revolution and such necessary responses as improved competitiveness for the global market. All change requires some forfeit of the familiar, and thus always entails some anxiety and sense of loss. As an old Chinese curse says, "May you live in interesting times."

Types of Change

Organizations must redefine their goals and missions over time. Fine-tuning happens all the time, as small adjustments are made to meet external demands. But periodically, there are also large redefinitions of organizational methods, goals, and prognosis. When this happens, there are inevitable changes in the structure as well.

Expansion and Growth

Successful enterprises tend to expand in size and grow economically. These changes are usually welcome, but even changes for the better are stressful. Leadership is complicated by increasing numbers of employees and by revisions in the authority structure. Familiar and secure routines are disrupted by new modes of operation. Comfortable interpersonal relationships may change and unfamiliar new employees join the organizational group. Increasing impersonality, temporary disruptions, and new aspects of the organizational culture often lead to a sense of loss. Most distressing for some is the potential loss of a sense of family. Others can be distressed if they feel left behind within the expanding enterprise. Both are especially evident when a founder of a growing business cedes authority to outside professional managers.

Mergers

Case Study 6

A major insurance company built a large modern complex to centralize all of its head office operations. This entailed the geographic relocation of one division from a suburb to the downtown business district. It also required formation of a new unit, encompassing two executives with a history of mutual dislike. In addition, these divisions had had strikingly different methods and procedures. The merger and centralization required the creation of a team with a unified approach. The ensuing process was extremely disruptive and led to the resignations of several important employees. Hundreds of hours of belated consultation were ultimately required.

As competitive pressures increase, mergers are an increasingly common approach to problems of organizational growth and development. They can be an effective competitive solution, but also a painful experience for all concerned. Mergers are typically dictated by perceived competitive or financial expedience. They are not designed for the direct emotional and personal needs of the employee. Mergers throw together divergent organizational cultures and operating methods. Unfamiliar groups of people are joined together into new units. Organizational mergers thus bear a strong resemblance to family mergers by remarriage and the "stepchildren" of the new organization often have problems analogous to those of the new marriage. The new circumstances amplify existing concerns about management support and concern, and intensify competitive striving for position in the newly expanded family. Decisions about new procedures and missions are colored by the intense feelings involved.

Downsizings and Restructurings

Downsizing (also known as widespread layoffs) and restructuring (massive reassignment of employees to new tasks, positions, or locations) are two other large-scale events that have become increasingly frequent visitors to the organizational world. This euphemistic nomenclature has not occurred by accident. The emotional pain after such events is usually enormous (see Chapter 8). Serious depression, anxiety, substance abuse, and sometimes even posttraumatic stress disorder are common diagnostic sequelae of these sweeping changes. On a more readily observed level, affected employees may show irritability, family conflict, and greater reliance on such primitive defense mechanisms as denial ("It isn't really going to happen") and projection ("They have it in for me; they think I'm no good"). There is no getting around the central problem: Organizational layoffs and restructurings directly entail loss and major change. For some there is loss of job and livelihood. For others, there is loss of usual job description, level of responsibility, and network of co-workers and colleagues. Financial survival may require an employee's geographic relocation and consequent surrender of such familiar touchstones of life as neighborhood, friends, and schools.

The pain of change almost invariably makes people feel more dependent and leads to a search for someone to make things better. Under the pressure of radical change, an organization may revert wholly or in part to unhelpful expression of underlying emotional needs (Bion's Basic Assumption behavior). Irrational or pathological behavior then subverts the organizational task. Symptoms of stress and burnout appear, and not a few individuals will develop a major psychiatric illness (see especially Chapters 12, 13, 15, and 16). Those with a previous psychiatric history or other premorbid risk factors are particularly vulnerable to the pressure of organizational change. Too often, since extreme distress is felt to be justified by the unpleasant circumstances, no attempt is made to secure effective treatment. This problem is sometimes aggravated further by real or perceived financial limitations. Similarly, organizations will often fail to attend to the emotional needs of both laid-off and retained employees. The emotions and guilt attached to the events make it more difficult to see that rational therapeutic approaches to the distress can at least reduce the emotional damage.

Healing the Pain of Change

Attending to the needs of employees is an important part of realizing organizational goals. Leaders, officers, and managers must attend to members' emotional needs, especially during difficult times. They must hold the social fabric of the group together, preserve the essence of culture, and catalyze needed cultural change in an agreeable way. The following "treatments" are basic to surviving major organizational change.

Case Study 7

Daniel Steward was president of a long-established manufacturing firm, with no history of layoffs. After years of economic difficulty, Daniel and the board reluctantly decided to lay off a sizable part of the work force, including several popular managers. Daniel took active steps to prevent and control damage. He assembled his four most affected executives and met with them weekly. Those meetings focused on elicitation of their concerns, and reiteration of his support for their painful restructuring plans. Finally, he collected all their ideas for managing the change in a day-long brainstorming session. Next, Daniel and his four lieutenants held a three-day retreat for their twenty-eight junior managers. They met with the entire group, answering questions, and then met further in smaller working groups composed of managers from each division. As a result, morale dipped only transiently and recovered soon thereafter.

Most important in the change process was the president's demeanor. Daniel was an engineer by training and was emotionally removed by nature. Nonetheless, he put himself on the line and took charge of preserving his company's culture and morale. He listened quietly to a litany of complaints covering a host of issues. He even listened carefully about problems that antedated the downsizing. He withstood anger and responded to fear and sadness. Standing in front of several flip charts, Daniel wrote out a list of specific effects that the layoffs might have on people and on business. On one night of the retreat, he talked with his four lieutenants until four in the morning, and then met with everyone at eight A.M. Breakfast, lunch, and dinner were shared with a different group of managers each day. He personally spent many hours fielding questions from the twenty-eight low-ranking managers. And all the while, he talked of everything from his history with the company, to the spirit and vision that still animated him, to his conviction that the company would improve by the change. Those three days were often recalled over the following year. The company downsized, restructured, survived, and prospered.

Undertake Organizational Diagnosis

Accurate organizational diagnosis is an essential first step to solving organizational problems. Effective intervention requires knowledge about what the change means or does to affected employees. While this frequently involves the use of consultants, it can also be done within the organization. It requires: (1) earmarking time for data collection; (2) talking with a wide and representative employee sample; and (3) reviewing and considering the collected data (especially about emotional responses to the events; per Harry Levinson 1972). Supplementary data can also be collected by written surveys. Care must be taken. In the interest of straightforward furtherance of organizational goals, there is always the danger of discounting emotional reactions to change. Although it is possible to allow too much time for emotional recovery, more often there is too little time invested.

Encourage Communication

Employees and managers must be encouraged to talk more than their usual routine allows. The restorative expression of feelings can be helped by creation of ad hoc structures. For example, as large numbers of layoffs occurred, a large oil company arranged for consultants to lead weekly groups of ten managers, to address their reactions to the change. A good organization will always allow for expression of some grief through appropriate channels. Dysfunctional enterprises will often encourage denial, attempt to suppress the normal mourning process, and thus inadvertently intensify emotional distress and counteradaptation.

Offer Leadership Support and Guidance

During times of stressful change, leadership and management guidance are critical. Because the changes may also affect those in charge, guidance is even more difficult than usual. Public modeling of mature coping behavior is the premier and most powerful form of guidance. It entails a measure of self-discipline and the ability to differentiate destructive griping from the constructive expression of feeling and uncertainty. Excessive rage and futile complaining must be dealt with one on one and must be discouraged. Group settings are not ideal for such exaggerated emotions. Authority figures must expect more dependent and emotional employees, who seem to long for parents with all of the right answers, and who seem a bit less rational than usual. Management must make every effort to clarify events and their consequences for all concerned.

Carefully Assess Effects of Change

The stresses and consequences of change must be explicitly considered. Sources of data can include financial reports, productivity indicators, employee feedback, verbal and written surveys, medical department visits, and many more. Specific issues to consider include detailed consideration of emotional costs and consequences, presence of conspicuous fatigue, anxiety, or depression, and degree of communication between employees and with management. Permission must be given to bring up concerns and then attempts must be made to address them.

Maintain Organizational and Individual Mental Health

In times of major change, managers must manage themselves, as well as managing others. All that contributes to mental health is potentially at risk during even moderate change. Real attention must be paid to physical, emotional, and spiritual well-being. Often, a major life change brings long-neglected deeper values to the surface. Thus, religious faith and family values may be rediscovered, or returned to center stage. One senior manager, fired during a layoff, initially increased his already heavy drinking. For the first time ever, he sought the psychiatric help his wife and doctor had long urged. At a lower income one year later, he nonetheless felt happier than he had in two decades. He had repaired his long-damaged family relationships and was less prone to sacrifice everything for his career. His initial employer had helped by generous continuation of health benefits, and by extensive outplacement assistance.

When the earth moves under anyone's career path, relationships matter more than ever (see Chapter 8). Family members, old friends, and new friends can all offer support. Since close family members may also be overwhelmed, it is often helpful to renew dormant relationships and to expand the interpersonal network. A frequent danger is social avoidance because of guilt, shame, or sagging self-esteem. In other cases, withdrawal comes from guilt over successful survival of the change process. For example, one manager had to lay off 150 co-workers. He was guilt stricken, depressed, and withdrew from a social and religious life that involved many of his ex-co-workers. With therapy, he was able to regain his social life. He kept his regrets over time but overcame his depression.

Managers and employees will have a natural tendency to blame the organization for the painful changes at hand. Destructive acting out, passive-aggressive resistance, and even just pouting only make matters worse. As one executive put it somewhat coarsely, "Lead, follow, or get out of the way." Individuals who remain in a changed organization must direct all of their energies toward the organizational center. They must revivify the group culture and strengthen alliances among members. Here, leaders and followers have the same task: to adapt to and reshape the organization's new reality.

Too often, there are fears of unpleasant overtones in addressing the real causes of individual and organizational emotional distress. The word *stress* is a common and euphemistic shorthand that conveys the notion of causes external to the individual and organization. That makes the superficial emotions a lot easier to talk about, and a lot easier for the real causes to remain unaddressed. Thus, general considerations of pressure over an assignment, worry about moving the family, or adjusting to a reduced work force do not really say much about specific and idiosyncratic responses to stress by individuals. However, the most distressing reactions to change are always rooted in specific characteristics of individuals or of the organization. The appearance of organizational dysfunction or psychiatric symptoms always indicates a need to consider professional assistance. Many executives (and others) have trouble with this, experiencing a further drop in self-esteem as a consequence of "needing professional help." Success in securing optimal help for employees and organizations often depends on the sensitivity and skill of the referring manager. One human resources officer sent a troubled executive for a week-long seminar on groups, knowing that each participant had a 2-hour interview with the psychiatrist who led the groups. In that setting, the executive felt comfortable discussing his current difficulties and eagerly accepted a referral for treatment (see Chapter 1).

As with many other things, the best treatment is prevention. Many innovative organizations have reward systems in place for employees who exercise, meet weight targets, and do not smoke. In such places, health is a cultural value that is already in place if disruptive change occurs. A similar awareness of mental health tells employees that the organization cares enough about their emotional well-being. This fact in itself may provide a buffer for the effects of change. Having such resources as a norm is always preferable to creating them only in the face of change and stress.

SUMMARY

How people structure and change organizations devolves from human nature and from the experience of family socialization. No matter how technical the design or purpose of the organization, the "human equation" is always present. Employees' feelings and beliefs strongly influence their motivation and performance. Effective organizations replicate the best features of good families. They are supportive, authoritative but not authoritarian, and can create an organizational ideal that benefits from employees' highest aspirations.

Even when predicated on noble goals or future benefit, change is always difficult. Unaddressed, it can be more painful and destructive than necessary. Recognizing the potentially serious adverse effects on organizational mental health is an essential insight for surviving and successfully implementing change. Open, frank communication about the changes and their psychological impact is helpful at all levels of a changing organization. Unnecessarily constricted communication tends to foster excessive suspicion and regression among group members, and thus only worsens the adversity of change.

Bibliography
Buono, Anthony F., and James L. Bowditch. 1989. *The Human Side of Mergers and Acquisitions*. San Francisco: Jossey-Bass.
Hirschhorn, Larry. 1988. *The Workplace Within*. Cambridge, Mass.: MIT Press.
Jaques, Elliot. 1989. *Requisite Organization*. Arlington, Va.: Cason Hall and Co.
Kets de Vries, Manfred F. R., and Danny Miller. 1985. *The Neurotic Organization*. San Francisco: Jossey-Bass.
Levinson, Harry. 1972. *Organizational Diagnosis*. Cambridge, Mass.: Harvard University Press.
Levinson, Harry (ed.). 1989. *Designing and Managing Your Career*. Cambridge, Mass.: Harvard Business School Press.
Levinson, Harry, and Stuart Rosenthal. 1984. *CEO*. New York: Basic Books.
Peters, Thomas J., and Robert H. Waterman, Jr. 1982. *In Search of Excellence*. New York: Harper and Row.
Schein, Edgar H. 1989. *Organizational Culture and Leadership*. San Francisco: Jossey-Bass.
Shapiro, Edward R., and A. Wesley Carr. 1991. *Lost in Familiar Places*. New Haven, Conn.: Yale University Press.
Zaleznik, Abraham. 1990. *Executive's Guide to Motivating People*. Chicago: Bonus Books, Inc.
Zaleznik, Abraham, and Manfred F. R. Kets de Vries. 1975. *Power and the Corporate Mind*. Boston: Houghton Mifflin.

8

Job Loss and Employment Uncertainty

Nick Kates, M.B.B.S., FRCP(C), Barrie S. Greiff, M.D., and Duane Q. Hagen, M.D.

Portions of this chapter are adapted, with permission, from N. Kates, B. S. Greiff, and D. Q. Hagen. *The Psychosocial Impact of Job Loss.* Washington, D.C.: American Psychiatric Press, 1990.

ABSTRACT

As unemployment rates remain high, increasing numbers of workers face the possibility of losing their jobs. Job loss has many consequences for workers and their families. This chapter outlines ways in which losing a job can affect an individual. It then looks at interventions that can take place with individuals who are in danger of losing their jobs and outlines preventive programs that can be utilized in workplaces where layoffs or closures are pending.

INTRODUCTION

Layoffs, plant closures, and company mergers will continue to be a fact of economic life. Two out of three Americans will lose their job at some time during their working life. For some the effects will be minimal, particularly if they possess marketable skills or live in areas where there are plentiful work opportunities. For others, such as those with a strong emotional investment in their work or limited financial resources, employment may have a major impact on activities, relationships, and physical and emotional well-being.

To lose a job or to be excluded from the work force can erode self-confidence and create practical difficulties that can be overwhelming. Some people who lose their job find alternate work quickly with little disruption of their daily routine. For others, continuing joblessness can lead to a sense of isolation and alienation, and eventually to helplessness and despair. Whatever the duration of the period of unemployment, individuals who lose their job may develop physical and psychological symptoms of varying degrees of severity.

The effects of losing a job are complex and can affect every aspect of a person's life. While there is strong evidence of an association between job loss and emotional problems, the nature of this link is complicated. Losing a job is stressful in itself but can also set in motion a train of biological, psychosocial, and family changes that can lead to further difficulties. It can also expose or accentuate emotional, psychiatric, or family problems that predated the loss of the job.

Helping individuals who are about to lose their job presents many challenges for employers and clinicians. Clinicians need to appreciate the meaning a job can have and how the possibility of unemployment can affect the relationship between work, family, and social activities. They must be able to take a systemic or ecological view of the impact of losing a job, respecting the uniqueness of each individual's problem, while being aware of common issues that may affect all jobless people. They must be familiar with appropriate community resources and possess additional skills in history taking and in working collaboratively with social agencies. They must also recognize local, social, and political realities that can hinder both the development of needed programs and social reintegration for the more chronically unemployed individuals.

This chapter provides guidelines for those working with people in danger of losing their jobs, or those who have been recently terminated. It describes the impact of impending job loss and the ways in which these effects are transmitted. It outlines an approach to the assessment of an individual in this situation and preventive interventions both with individuals and within the workplace.

When considering the impact of job loss the clinician needs to bear in mind four recurring themes: (1) what a job can mean to an individual; (2) the interdependence of an individual's work, family, and social life; (3) multiple, interconnected, and often preexisting factors that can affect the outcome of a period of unemployment; and (4) the uniqueness of the experience for each individual who loses a job.

Case Example

Thomas O'Leary was a 49-year-old steel worker, referred to a psychiatric service for assessment of anxiety and depression. For as long as he could remember, he had always thrown himself into his work. This had always kept his chronic unhappiness under control. This time, though, he described a 4-month history of anxiety, depression, insomnia, and anorexia. At first he could not identify any cause for his distress, but further questioning revealed that his plant was threatened with large layoffs.

He was sure he wouldn't lose his job, but his work behavior had changed since news of the impending layoff leaked out. Trying to show that he was indispensable to the company, he had started to work overtime. But unlike his colleagues, he had made no attempt to find alternate work, or to prepare for possible unemployment. He had not discussed these issues with his wife or children, not wanting to bother them over a minor concern. But he had noticed his work performance starting to deteriorate. His concentration worsened, it took longer to complete routine tasks, he was irritable with co-workers, and they started to ignore him.

Tom's rigid interpersonal style, his intense job commitment, and his difficulty in coping with emotions had led him into a depression. He had denied the reality of his situation, avoided planning for unpleasant contingencies, and alienated himself from potential sources of support. An interview with Tom's wife pointed out their increasing marital stress, as well as his wife's unawareness of the threat to his job.

In treatment, Tom's depression responded promptly to psychotherapy and imipramine (an antidepressant medication). In therapy, Tom came to terms with the threat to his job and he started to make appropriate preparations. He became more aware of emotional and occupational support that was available from family and co-workers. He also talked about his fear of what might happen to his job, family, and himself, and his anger about potentially losing a job in which he had invested so much of himself. When he eventually did lose his job, he adjusted quickly and found new employment within 8 weeks. The feared financial impoverishment did not occur. But to again fend off his long-term fears of rejection and emotional impoverishment, Tom quickly became intensely dedicated to his new job.

THE IMPACT OF IMPENDING JOB LOSS

Most unemployed individuals will eventually adjust to job loss, make necessary changes, and find new work. For some, however, despair and feelings of helplessness will continue for months or years, with little optimism for the future. Emotional responses of the long-term unemployed change over time, as do the issues and problems that they confront (Harrison 1976; Borgen and Amundsen 1984; Kirsh 1983). Of greatest concern to employers is the anticipatory stage of employment uncertainty before a job is lost.

This stage is important because it is when emotional changes begin, and especially because it is when appropriate preparation and intervention can effectively change job loss outcomes. In some situations, employees might receive a warning a few months before their plant will close or they will lose their jobs. This allows them to make preparations for what may follow and to start a job search. In most instances, though, there is little advance warning or notice, particularly when it is only a small group of workers who are to be affected.

The anticipation stage can be a time of great anxiety and confusion, creating a sense of powerlessness or increased dependency that may result in extra demands on family and friends who may be unaware of what is taking place. Workers are often angry at what has happened to them but may have few outlets to ventilate this anger. The employer may be a remote or impersonal multinational corporation, immediate superiors may also be in danger of losing their jobs, and "acting out" may jeopardize opportunities for severance pay. For many workers this period is also a time for self-recrimination and blame.

Some workers deal better with stress and uncertainty; they accept the inevitable and prepare themselves for what they believe is to come. Some start to work harder, in the hope that they will make themselves indispensable to their employer, even volunteering for additional duties. And some, like Tom, choose to deny the reality of their situation, by refusing to believe that their job is at risk, or by believing that they will have no trouble finding new work. A reluctance to begin short-term adjustment or practical preparation during this period can have serious consequences after the job is lost.

Even before a closure or layoff is announced, there may be other sources of stress. Rumors abound in many workplaces, generating fear and uncertainty among all who might eventually be affected. This can increase rivalry and reduce solidarity and support among the work force, especially if some workers are privy to confidential information. It can also lead to a discrepancy within the workplace if upper management personnel are aware of an impending closure and start to plan for their own future, while the rest of the work force remains unaware of impending events.

HOW THE EFFECT IS TRANSMITTED

Disparate but complementary hypotheses have been proposed about how job loss affects an individual. The common mechanisms are summarized below.

Losses

When the many benefits that work offers are taken into consideration, it becomes apparent that job loss can lead to significant and substantive deprivations that will vary greatly from one situation to another. To fully appreciate this, it is necessary to understand what a job may have meant.

Economic Meaning
Remuneration from work pays for such essentials of day-to-day survival as food and shelter, as well as luxury items that can make life more comfortable. It also enables a worker to purchase material possessions that symbolize social standing or status, or that allow participation in leisure and social activities. Often, work also provides long-term financial security through pensions, supplementary income after retirement, and savings programs.

Some authors have suggested the greatest job loss hardships are loss of steady income, long-term career earnings, and long-term financial security (Aiken, Ferman, and Sheppard 1969; Gordus, Jarley, and Ferman 1981; Jacobsen 1987; Howland 1988). Unemployed workers with access to additional material resources seem to cope better with job loss and feel better about themselves (Jacobsen 1987). For those without other resources, the loss of an income may then lead to further deprivations when social activities must be curtailed or possessions must be sold.

Social Meaning

Work relationships offer opportunities for friendship, support, and social contact, and they can offer escape from a dissatisfying family or personal life. Work can also provide a sense of belonging and acceptance, as well as a clearly defined identity that extends beyond the workplace. In social settings, many people choose to define themselves by their job or work role. Talking about work can also establish fixed points or common ground in new relationships, especially at times when people feel unsure or vulnerable.

Work serves another function: It breaks up the hours in the day. If leisure is defined as the time spent not working, then without work there can be no leisure. And to a large extent, work and work behavior form the basis of societal organization.

Thus, the loss of a job can eliminate social contacts, friendships, and support from the workplace, as well as the daily structure that working brings. These losses cause feelings of sadness, anger, or guilt that in turn create a sense of isolation or alienation. If a worker and his or her family are forced to relocate to find new work, they may have to leave behind friends, a local neighborhood, and a familiar environment where they may have spent many contented years.

Psychological Meaning

Psychologically, work serves many functions. It may offer opportunities to express creative abilities, develop competence and mastery, and achieve responsibility, recognition, and respect. These functions are all landmarks of healthy emotional development.

Especially when work roles have perceived purpose and value, work helps to form and preserve internal identity, self-worth, and a sense of personal continuity. Behaviors and interactions that are part of the work role are internalized and they become an integral part of a self-image. Thus, a consistent aftereffect of job loss can be reduced self-esteem.

Other psychological factors are also relevant. The work ethic is instilled from birth and productive labor is held up as a social ideal. Work roles are modeled to children by parents, and they are consistently reinforced by educational and cultural experience.

Despite the advantages that work can bestow, not every job can meet psychological needs. Work can be stultifying, stressful, demeaning, and exploitative. In these cases, losing a job may be a relief or an escape. For some, being laid off provides an opportunity to pursue alternate career plans. It may challenge them to find a job that is better suited to their talents or to previously untapped abilities. In general, though, loss of a job entails multiple material, social, and emotional losses. The greater the emotional investment in a job, the greater the losses. Someone who loses a job may therefore be faced with many deprivations. The overall impact is cumulative, but the full impact may not be fully apparent until many weeks after job loss.

Role Changes

Changes in roles and role behaviors can be a useful way of conceptualizing job loss effects. The work role can serve many different social and interpersonal functions. At one level, the employer designates clearly defined job description obligations. These may be accompanied by spoken or unspoken expectations about associated behavior.

At another level, interpersonal contacts are a workplace opportunity to meet psychological needs. Self-esteem is enhanced by roles that allow personal growth, creativity, recognition, or respect. Those that are demeaning or stifling can have the opposite effect.

Change in Self-Esteem

However resilient or self-assured someone is, job loss or persistent unemployment can seriously undermine self-esteem and personal continuity. This process can start with feelings of rejection and can then be reinforced by further rebuffs from unsympathetic employers and insensitive acquaintances. Negative comments from family members and other sources of support can increase feelings of inadequacy. Over time, such changes in self-esteem can lead to a perception of diminished personal value, the status of a second-class citizen.

There is often a tendency for those who lose jobs to blame themselves, usually unnecessarily, for what has taken place. They portray their role in an uncontrollable unfolding of events in an ever worsening light. This self-blame further reduces self-esteem, already diminished by rejection and loss of a psychologically central work role and identity.

Increased Stress

Many sources of stress face someone who has lost a job. Stress can emanate from external demands, which may exceed material resources or coping abilities, or from internal pressures such as beliefs, values, and self-image. One of the most immediate pressures is the need to find a new job. Each of the steps involved in finding work, appraising one's personal skills and strengths, searching out opportunities, applying for jobs, and attending interviews, is potentially stressful. Pressures may mount as time passes, as personal hardships increase, and as the need to find work becomes more desperate. Many workers eventually reach a point where it seems futile to continue applying for jobs, risking inevitable disappointment, and so they give up the search.

Finding a new job may also involve additional expense or relocation to a new community. This is disruptive to family relationships, especially when other family members must stay behind for an interim period.

Unemployment is stressful in other ways. It is often difficult to apply for unemployment benefits. The shame of dealing with a welfare agency may also prevent some from utilizing available resources. If applying for social assistance becomes unavoidable, treatment with a lack of sensitivity or respect will reinforce feelings of inadequacy and failure.

Financial hardship is invariably a source of further stress and budgetary adjustments may not be sufficient to make ends meet. Jobless workers are faced with the prospect of having to sell possessions or make major financial sacrifices, in order to honor their daily commitments. This further reinforces feelings of failure and diminished self-worth, consequently impairing coping abilities.

Change in Social Support

Social relationships and community support are frequently disrupted when a job is lost. In part this results from the loss of support and social contacts that were previously available within the workplace. Other contributing factors include financially induced reduction in social activity, embarrassed avoidance of friends and former colleagues, and cessation of activities connected to the old job. The availability of community support and resources may also decrease at times of economic hardship or community disintegration. However, the perception of available support may be more significant in determining utilization than the amount of support that is actually available.

Change in Family Relationships

The loss of a job will affect every member of a worker's family. Changes in behavior of the unemployed worker will usually affect family relationships. Someone who is depressed may be short-tempered or withdrawn from other family members, while anxiety or stress may cause increased tension or reduced involvement in family activity.

Other changes, such as role adjustments, may be more subtle. Notably, families may need to adjust to increased amounts of time together. Every family member will be affected by financial cutbacks. A spouse may be forced to return to work or take on an extra job. Children may be aware that they can no longer afford to buy clothes or toys, or to continue certain longstanding social activities with their friends.

All family members may also be confronted with the stigma of unemployment. There may be shame or embarrassment that a family member is out of work, especially if the local community is ambivalent or critical. Children may also become aware of "differences" between their parents and other working parents, or they may be subjected to ridicule by their peers.

Unemployment should not, though, be seen as a solely negative experience. It can bring members closer together to face the common threat and challenges. The additional time together can lead to greater intimacy and strengthened emotional bonds. And there can be a shared sense of accomplishment when the family overcomes adversity and resolves its difficulties.

UNCOVERING PREEXISTING EMOTIONAL AND PSYCHIATRIC PROBLEMS

Preexisting physical, systemic, interpersonal, emotional, or psychiatric problems can be uncovered or heightened by job loss. Physical problems may deteriorate and may make it harder to return to work, especially for older workers. Workers who had adapted to physical disabilities may again be reminded of their impairments when looking for a new position. Impairments will also restrict the kinds of work that can be considered.

Preexisting psychological problems can include diminished confidence and self-esteem, poor coping skills, and more serious emotional, interpersonal, and psychiatric disturbances. These problems may not have been apparent in a previously secure job and predictable environment, but they may become heightened in new or less tolerant work environments.

Many people have chronic mild symptoms of depression, anxiety, and interpersonal dissatisfaction, to which they adapt through the emotional benefits of work and the work environment. Loss of this counterbalance will accentuate the underlying symptoms and may frequently lead to more pronounced psychiatric syndromes. The challenges of adjusting to job loss may also expose interpersonal weaknesses, exaggerate maladaptive personality traits, and aggravate preexisting marital and family problems. Concurrent personal stress can dramatically exaggerate the effects of job loss. It is essential to recognize emotional and psychiatric problems promptly and accurately.

AN INTEGRATED MODEL

The mechanisms described above are not exclusive. Indeed, they can be integrated into a simple model (Kates, Greiff, and Hagen 1990) that highlights their interrelationships and demonstrates how problems or weaknesses in one area can lead to further problems in other areas (Figure 8-1).

Protective factors reduce the impact of unemployment, or support and strengthen the individual. Provoking factors increase the impact of unem-

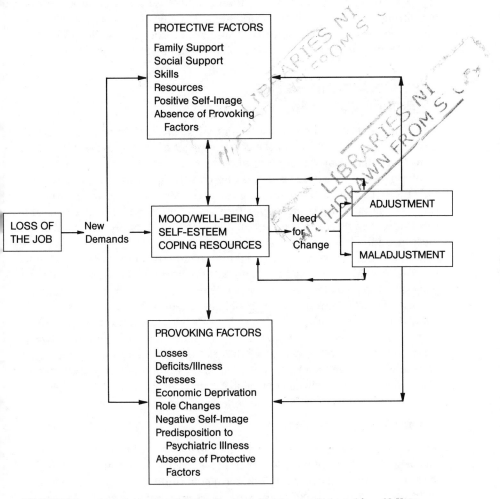

FIGURE 8-1.   An integrated model of the impact of job loss.   (Adapted from N. Kates, B. Greiff, and D. Hagen. 1990. *The Psychosocial Impact of Job Loss.* Washington, D.C.: American Psychiatric Press.)

ployment by making an individual more vulnerable. These factors are closely interconnected and are in a continuing state of flux. There are many ways of conceptualizing how these factors affect an individual, but changes in self-esteem are usually pivotal.

The stress and deprivation of unemployment threaten the ability to maintain a sense of personal continuity. Adjustments must be made to cope with stress, increase social support, manage change, and continue with day-to-day activities. If these adjustments are successful, they will reinforce the positive (protective) factors, thereby increasing self-confidence and permitting adaptation until new work is found. If adjustments are unsuccessful, there can be diminished self-worth and restriction in role flexibility and range, leading to an increased internal distress and further problems.

ASSESSING THE IMPACT OF IMPENDING JOB LOSS

The main goals of a clinical assessment are identification of risk for future problems and preparation for the consequences of unemployment. It is safe to assume that nearly everyone who loses a job will have at least some resulting problems. These problems often resolve spontaneously and require little more than support and information about available resources. Bringing the predicament into open recognition and confirming its reality can be a substantial benefit, even if little tangible help can be offered. Several areas must be addressed in a clinical assessment.

The clinician must recognize and understand the emotional response to job loss. Anger, anxiety, sadness, and fear are normal reactions that accompany the process of adapting to new realities. The clinician should be especially alert for more serious problems when the emotional response is out of proportion to the provoking event, or when the emotional distress fails to improve as pressures decrease. It is also essential to differentiate between actual and perceived impacts of job loss. Specific questions should elicit pertinent information on perceptual accuracy: recrimination, self-blame, and guilt about essentially uncontrollable events; and perceived loss of control.

Job and Work-Related Factors

The first step is to assess the importance and meaning of the individual's job. Important questions include length of the working day, amount of overtime, reasons for working, degree of long-term goal fulfillment, stressors encountered on the job, and extent of work interference with family and social activities. It is also worth asking about overall job satisfaction, attitudes toward the unemployed, impact of work role losses, and contingency plans already underway.

Personal Deficits and Preexisting Problems

An accurate assessment of preexisting problems or deficits is imperative for predicting emergent problems and high-risk individuals. Problems that might hinder progress include limited coping skills; limited material resources; limited work skills; physical impairment; and prior depression, anxiety, personality, and other psychiatric disorders.

Coping Skills

The ability to cope with the stress and problems of unemployment may be severely impaired by underlying psychological deficits. These deficits can include limited interpersonal skills, low self-confidence, reduced rejection tolerance, cognitive or intellectual impairment, and limited problem-solving skills. While any of these can increase vulnerability, low self-confidence can be a particular handicap, because so many events associated with job loss can reinforce feelings of inadequacy.

Limited Material Resources

The relative contribution of economic deprivation to the emotional and occupational outcome of job loss is debated. It is clear, though, that workers with fewer initial financial resources, and those who must effect major economic cutbacks, have more trouble coping with unemployment. It is worth asking about financial difficulties that predated and followed job loss. Mortgages and other major financial commitments have symbolic importance and may become increasingly hard to fulfill.

Limited Work Skills

Assessing work skills requires more than simply asking the individual what work he or she can do, or would prefer. Specific skills and strengths need to be assessed and their value for local employers must be understood. The assessment should also cover job search skills and preparedness for possible retraining or relocation. Limitations in any of these areas can hinder the search for new work.

Physical Impairment

Physical impairment invariably impedes efforts at reemployment, especially for older workers. A physical ailment that had been untroublesome might now become a problem for the first time. For example, a knee injury would not have interfered with a sedentary job, but becomes a handicap when considering manual labor. Sometimes, a preexisting health problem can be downplayed or can become less consequential when the need for work becomes paramount. A realistic health appraisal or a new treatment approach may help guide an unemployed worker toward a more appropriate or manageable job.

Prior Anxiety, Depression, Personality, and Other Psychiatric Disorders

When workers have a predisposition to emotional problems, the stress of job loss can often trigger an exacerbation of symptoms. Common chronic predisposing syndromes include atypical depression, drug and alcohol abuse, panic disorder, and other anxiety disorders (see other chapters for details). Similarly, personality disorders and styles will make reemployment and readaptation more stressful and more problematic (see Chapter 14). There might also be a history of acute psychiatric illnesses such as depression or psychosis. Importantly, most prior emotional and psychiatric diagnoses will have been previously undiagnosed. Many will not have been specifically apparent to the worker before diagnosis. Rather, workers might only have been aware of a vaguely distressful period or area of their life. Accurate psychiatric diagnosis requires substantial specific training and experience. It should not be attempted in the absence of proper qualifications or by self-report questionnaire.

Individual Strengths

Clinical assessment should include careful examination of personal strengths, resources, and supports. It can be extremely beneficial to ask the worker to list strengths and skills, pointing out how few have been affected by the job loss. This kind of approach enhances the sense of personal continuity, while pointing to potential solutions for particular problems. The value of other useful resources, such as owning a car, personal contacts, and knowledge of community supports, should also be identified.

Family Factors

Assessment should also include the effects of job loss and consequent problems on family life and interaction. Areas to cover include family members' awareness of each other's problems, family unit functioning, family life cycle stage attained, family activities, family financial situation, and the presence of other wage earners.

Social Supports

The assessment should also examine social support systems, including social activities, attitudes of social contacts, and knowledge of community resources. It is worth looking at whether changes are anticipated in social and community activities. Support network information can be gathered with a few key questions about principal social and professional relationships, their interpersonal roles, and their helpfulness. It is also important to find out what personal or organizational supports were previously available through the workplace.

An individual's perception of the availability and accessibility of support may differ from reality, but it is the perception that may more substantially determine whether supports are used. Large amounts of utilized support may not compensate for a lack of quality. Friends and former colleagues who are perceived as critical or as patronizingly sympathetic may be avoided, or may even have destructive effects. Supportive relationships, like effective psychotherapy, require empathic concern, emotional attentiveness, and practical awareness.

Most communities have established such services as vocational counseling and recreational centers that can meet some needs of the unemployed. It is worth checking whether the worker is aware of these programs and knows how to use these services, especially if unemployed for the first time. Avoidance of these services might be influenced by embarrassment or the need to maintain a sense of independence. Different kinds of vocational services are appropriate for workers from different types and levels of previous employment. Assembly-line workers and accountants need different kinds of advice or retraining.

Attitude Toward Work

It is important to assess effects of impending job loss on work attitudes, especially when residual anger interferes with ability to find support or new work. Some organizational cultures or specific circumstances will increase the chance of newly unemployed workers feeling unexpected guilt, remorse, or self-blame. The clinician should ask about causes and effects of previous unemployment episodes. Someone who has been fired more than once may develop what Triandis (1975) has called "ecosystem distrust." A gradual reduction in trust of authority figures and institutions will make it even harder to reintegrate this person into the work force. It is also important to understand local views of unemployment and of the unemployed, and perceptions of local community attitudes by the unemployed. An appreciation of these attitudes can help the unemployed accept the reality of their predicament and take advantage of available support.

The clinical assessment presented here is wide ranging, but it does not include all of the topical areas or depth of a detailed clinical psychiatric evaluation. Some parts will be appropriate only for some individuals. Each included topical area or question has been highlighted because it can unearth information that shows how the individual copes and can provide guidance for developing a management plan. In any difficult, problematic, or otherwise important case, a more detailed and comprehensive consultation should be arranged.

Impact on Those Who Remain at Work

It should be noted that layoffs can also be exceedingly stressful for those who retain their jobs as well as those who lose them. They are often expected to do more work or pick up the tasks of those whose jobs have disappeared. Often, this effort goes unrecognized by supervisors who may point to the good fortune of continuing employment.

Still employed workers may also have experienced a sense of lost control or helplessness before learning they would retain their jobs. This can be accompanied by a sense of loss or guilt for those who were laid off. There may also be bitterness or distrust of management, or fears of further employment problems. Ultimately, these individuals may emerge strengthened by the experience and may be more realistic about their long-term prospects.

INTERVENTION

There are three useful goals for clinicians who provide support or treatment to workers experiencing job loss or employment uncertainty:

- To provide support and advice about impending job loss.
- To identify appropriate resources outside the workplace.
- To identify emotional risk or distress requiring psychiatric referral.

Helping an Individual Cope

When helping someone cope with job loss, the following areas may be addressed.

Dealing with Deprivation

The ability to recognize, work through, and adapt to deprivations that follow job loss is very important. Although each individual loss may have a limited impact, cumulative effects can be magnified, and the losses may continue for a long time. The clinician can help recognize what has been lost, provide empathic support for emotional reactions, and help to focus on the specific adjustments needed. It is extremely helpful to put these reactions into a longitudinal time frame and to emphasize that the impact of distressing events will diminish over time. This perspective can also help maintain a sense of continuity and stability, despite ongoing social and financial disruptions.

Maintaining and Increasing Self-Esteem

Perhaps the single most important therapeutic task is to ensure that blows to self-esteem are overcome and confidence is restored. A clinician must be nonjudgmental and must allow ventilation of anger and anxiety. These feelings can often be partially eased simply by willingness to listen and to accept them at face value.

The emphasis should be on the preservation of a sense of personal continuity, encouraging the worker to recognize those things in life that will not change. Once again, putting present events into a longer-term time frame may be helpful. Personal strengths and skills should be identified and reinforced. Successes, however small, in any aspect of life should be pointed out and situations should be avoided where failure may be inevitable. Plans should be built on small, attainable targets rather than larger tasks that are less likely to be accomplished, however important they may seem.

Life situations, including the events that led up to the loss of the job, should be reviewed and reappraised. This exercise can show how there may have been uncontrollable events, thereby helping to dissipate inappropriate guilt. To offset feelings of helplessness, there should also be a focus on life areas where control and function are fully intact. When engaged in appropriate psychotherapy, attention should also be given to understanding contributory personal deficits, thereby increasing future control of circumstances.

Managing the Stress

To cope with the stress of unemployment, the worker should focus on practical issues and handling immediate problems, particularly during the initial crisis. Although it is important to address longer-term issues, many can be left until after the more pressing issues have been resolved. Problems that may arise can be predicted and management strategies can be developed.

A realistic approach to finances and budgeting is essential. Workers should be encouraged to make early adjustments before savings and other reserves are depleted. They should be dissuaded from maintaining a previous life-style simply to keep up appearances or to pretend that nothing has happened. Stress management and relaxation skills can offer some inexpensive temporary relief, often in support groups with others going through a similar experience. When needed and feasible, psychiatric consultation and psychotherapy can offer additional help.

Using Time Productively

Promptly establishing a new routine gives the day a focus, helps structure job hunting activities, limits demoralization, and establishes continuity. Efforts also need to be made to maintain the continuity of relationships, social and religious activities, and memberships.

Mobilizing Available Resources

It is essential to ensure that embarrassment or guilt feelings do not prevent use of available supports. The earlier an individual facing job loss can discuss concerns openly with family, the more helpful or understanding the family is likely to be. It can also give other family members a chance to talk about their own anxieties or needs. Individuals should take advantage of social supports or other networking contacts. Pride should not prevent asking for help or advice.

Exploring New Possibilities

Every encouragement should be provided to help find a new job. Job skills and options and long-term career plans should be reappraised before embarking on a job search. It is very helpful for workplace staff to have established active links with specialized community agencies that offer work programs.

The search for a new job should be taken as seriously as working itself, with sufficient time and energy devoted to the task. The clinician can offer simple tips such as how to put together a presentable resumé, how to prepare a personal information sheet that can be referred to when filling in job application forms, and how to build and take advantage of support networks and contacts. Many jobs are found by personal tips or word of mouth. Workers may also find it helpful to read about the experiences of others who have coped with a period of unemployment, recounted in books such as *What Color Is Your Parachute?* (Bolles 1978).

It may also be a time to look at different career options. For some workers a review of skills and abilities may help them recognize that many of their skills are transferable to a new career. Other displaced workers may see unemployment as presenting a window of opportunity, although they may need support and encouragement to take a chance at something different, In these cases, the loss of a job may ultimately prove liberating.

Linking with Community Agencies or Supports

Many community agencies provide services for the unemployed and their families. There are advantages if they can work closely with workplace personnel. Most communities have established information centers or clearinghouses that offer practical advice, counseling, support, and information for the unemployed. Many communities have also established emergency hot lines or crisis centers, often staffed by individuals who themselves have been unemployed, and who are trained and backed up by mental health workers. These services, though, should not be confused with psychiatric or other professional mental health care.

Self-help or mutual support groups for unemployed workers can serve many functions, providing support, solidarity, a sense of purpose, and information for their members. However, they need not only serve a support function. Job clubs, for example, enable unemployed workers to gather regularly to share information and leads on jobs that may be available. Such initiatives need to be actively supported by social agencies and organized labor. And a few individuals may benefit from a psychiatric referral to help them adjust to the effects of losing their job.

Agency contacts can also stimulate the development of collaborative programs in which several agencies contribute resources and expertise. One example might be a crisis line, run by volunteers who may be trained or backed up by staff of mental health services. Interagency contacts and cooperation can help staff of different services provide each other with much needed support and encouragement, as well as offering a forum for an exchange of ideas about solutions to common problems.

Identifying Those at Risk

Most of those who face job loss will find sufficient support from workplace, family, and community. Some people will experience more severe problems and may benefit from psychiatric referral. One or more of three kinds of situations may present themselves.

The first are situations where the workers are having an exaggerated response to the impending job loss. They may be excessively anxious, depressed, or angry. In coping with excessive internal distress, they experience a loss of perspective on the recent events.

The second are occasions when workers have preexisting vulnerabilities that may have required previous psychiatric attention. These might include a prior history of depression, anxiety, or other psychiatric disorders, difficulties in dealing with stress or change, problems in interpersonal relationships, or difficulties adjusting to previous job loss.

Third, it may be possible to recognize people who appear at risk because of social isolation, family dysfunction, limited coping skills, physical health problems, an excessive investment in their job, or other situations that suggest they will have trouble coping with further change.

It is useful for workplace staff to maintain working relationships with local psychiatric and mental health services. Their staff can often provide telephone advice or information if a clinician is in doubt as to whether psychiatric input is needed, which can then lead to a referral or suggestions for management.

PREVENTIVE INTERVENTION

Preventive interventions are feasible in situations where there is advance warning or a clear indication of the possibility of an imminent layoff or closure. The nature and speed of any response will depend on many specific local factors. These include the size of the community, the impact of the plant on a community's social and economic functioning, the attitude of the employer and the work force, financial resources, local leadership, and political will.

A variety of preventive interventions are discussed in this chapter. Not all will be applicable for each particular situation. From this array of options each community needs to choose those programs that best suit or can best be adapted to the local context. The greater the degree of local input in designing flexible programs that reflect the characteristics and needs of a particular community or workplace, the greater the chance of success. Cook (1987) reviewed early intervention programs in nine different plants across the United States. In each case, the more the program planners could take local geography, demography, traditions, and culture into consideration, the more successful the reemployment outcomes were for participants.

The goals of preventive workplace interventions are to help workers understand their predicament, regain a sense of control, learn about material and support resources that are available, and make adequate preparations for future eventualities (Stone and Kieffer 1984). Underlying this are the goals of strengthening the role of the workplace as a focus for these efforts and of building on strengths and resources that already exist. These interventions are much more likely to succeed if labor and management can collaborate to solve common problems.

While interventions within the workplace before job loss can prevent some immediate sequelae of unemployment, many workers fail to take advantage of those programs (Cook 1987; Gordus, Jarley, and Ferman 1981). Those workers who do so may be those who would already be more likely to make preparations or take the impending job loss more seriously. Workplace interventions apply mainly to situations where a major layoff or plant closure is planned, rather than where individual workers lose their jobs.

Interventions within the workplace mean that all affected workers can be reached. Problems can then be dealt with before they become disruptive. These interventions also provide a chance to identify workers who may require additional training or assistance, who may be failing to make appropriate preparations, or who are at risk of developing more serious problems.

The first and perhaps the most crucial intervention is to provide the work force with as much forewarning of layoffs and redundancies as possible. The provision of practical information is essential. This can be achieved through the dissemination of written materials and resource guides, one-to-one interviews with affected workers, and educational workshops or seminars.

Written materials should be easy to read and should contain relevant practical information on worker entitlements, how to apply for benefits, free recreation activities for workers and their families, training and retraining opportunities, and possible problems that may be faced. These materials can also provide information on community resources that might include financial and budgeting services, legal services, accommodations, counseling programs, health services, leisure and recreation services, and activities for all family members.

Educational workshops, with contributions from staff of different agencies and services, can also be an effective means of communicating this information. The content can focus on coping and dealing with the emotional and interpersonal aspects of losing a job or on the practical aspects of finding new work. In the former, the problems likely to be encountered can be reviewed and the preparations that workers can make to prevent these problems from happening can be discussed. Specific coping skills such as problem solving or stress management can also be taught. If relevant to participants, a workshop might choose to concentrate on a more specific issue such as coping with early retirement.

Helping workers cope with the emotional responses generated by job loss is often best handled in a group setting, although this may be seen by many workers as having little personal relevance. A group run by someone who is not connected to the workplace may provide workers with more of an opportunity to vent their feelings and prepare themselves for what may come.

Workshops on finding alternative work should cover ways of looking for a new job and the utilization of vocational services. Job search information can include the local availability of work alternatives, retraining programs or relocation schemes, ways of looking for new jobs, techniques for appraising skills, and the intake criteria of community agencies that help with specific work-related problems.

The workplace should also support efforts by workers to find new jobs by providing sufficiently flexible workdays to permit them to look for other jobs or attend interviews. One option is the establishment of an employer- or employer/union-sponsored job counseling or outplacement program, by which outside agencies help displaced workers find alternative employment. More private companies are now contracting to offer this service. Evidence from such programs across the United States stresses the need for flexibility in these initiatives. There is no one specific model or approach to be followed in every setting. Each community or workplace should develop programs that fit their own needs. Each should also assess efficacy as well as the implications of different forms of sponsorship (government, management, labor, private agencies, or through a collaborative effort). And if workers at risk are identified through this process, they can then be referred to more specialized services.

Clinicians and workplace staff must also remember that the psychological effects of job loss develop within a wider personal, social, and political context. Many interventions are unlikely to have any lasting impact unless the wider vulnerabilities are also addressed and the social conditions that can exaggerate job loss stress are improved.

SUMMARY

Workers who are faced with employment uncertainty or job loss will pass through several stages during adjustment. Clinical interventions require awareness of those stages and of the many meanings of a job and its loss. Job loss can increase stress, decrease emotional support, change family roles, decrease self-esteem, and uncover preexisting individual or family problems. A thorough assessment covers workplace, family, and environmental factors, as well as the skills and previous experiences of the worker faced with redundancy.

Preparatory intervention strategies can help people cope with the effects of job loss, link them with appropriate community resources, and identify those whose high risk of emotional problems may require psychiatric referral. Preventive programs should be considered when job losses can be predicted months in advance. Collaborative efforts by government, management, labor, and community agencies can help prepare workers emotionally, assist them in looking for new work, and provide information and support in dealing with other practical problems.

Bibliography

Aiken, M., L. Ferman, and H. Sheppard. 1969. *Economic Failure, Alienation and Extremism.* Ann Arbor: University of Michigan Press.

Bolles, R. 1978. *What Color Is Your Parachute?* Berkeley, Calif.: Ten Speed Press.

Borgen, W., and N. Amundsen. 1984. *The Experiences of Unemployment.* Scarborough, Ontario: Nelson Canada.

Cook, R. 1987. *Worker Dislocations: Case Studies of Causes and Cures.* Kalamazoo, Mich.: W. E. Upjohn Institute for Employment Research.

Gordus, J., P. Jarley, and L. Ferman. 1981. *Plant Closing and Dislocation.* Kalamazoo, Mich.: W. E. Upjohn Institute for Unemployment Research.

Harrison, R. 1976. The demoralizing experience of prolonged unemployment. *Canadian Department of Employment Gazette* (Aug.), pp. 339-348.

Howland, M. 1988. *Plant Closings and Worker Displacement.* Kalamazoo, Mich.: W. E. Upjohn Institute for Unemployment Research.

Jacobsen, D. 1987. Models of stress and meanings of unemployment: Reactions to job loss among technical professionals. *Social Science in Medicine* 24:13-21.

Kates, N., B. Greiff, and D. Hagen. 1990. *The Psychosocial Impact of Job Loss.* Washington, D.C.: American Psychiatric Press.

Kirsh, S. 1983. *Unemployment: Its Impact on Body and Soul.* Toronto: Canadian Mental Health Association.

Stone, J., and C. Kieffer. 1984. *Pre-Layoff Intervention: A Response to Unemployment.* Ann Arbor: Institute of Science and Technology, University of Michigan.

Triandis, H. 1975. Ecosystem distrust and the hard to employ. *Journal of Applied Psychology* 60:44-56.

9

Executive Development: People and Organizational Skills

Peter L. Brill, M.D.

ABSTRACT

Most executive development activity is designed for highly functional individuals without substantial psychopathology. The absence of overt symptoms makes it difficult to diagnose the type of maladaptive behavior or its severity for developmental purposes. Executive success often requires highly complex skills and high-risk individual initiative. Diagnosis for the purpose of executive development must always consider the organization's milieu. Organizational cultures are unique and can be misleading, unreasonable, and unpredictable.

One effective approach to diagnosis considers whether behaviors are counterproductive or inflexible. A psychiatrist should avoid drawing conclusions without comparing them to the greater business environment. Business environments present different perceptual realities, and as in any social system, accurate diagnosis is a complex process in which long-term behavioral consequences are not easily assessed.

Executive development can follow one or more of several paths. Many successful interventions have resulted from cognitive learning and a rational change process. In cases where these methods have failed to effect the desired changes in executive behavior, it may be helpful to address the interpersonal and intrapsychic conflicts that inhibit change. The clinical knowledge and insights of an occupational psychiatrist can be invaluable for resolving problems that are resistant to other forms of change.

INTRODUCTION

Personality disorders and other psychiatric problems often result in obvious symptoms and severe dysfunction. This chapter, however, focuses on a more subtle and common problem of well-functioning executives: the maladaptive effects of personality structure, adult identifications, and management skill limitations. The chapter addresses executive assessment and development needs within an organization.

Most executive development activities are designed to enhance professional growth and behavior, far from the overt symptoms addressed by ordinary psychotherapy. At the healthy and more functional end of the health/dysfunction continuum, accurate personality diagnosis becomes more difficult. Occupational psychiatrists must understand the source and accuracy of the information provided to them. Finally, an executive development consultation requires a theoretical structure for understanding each stage of the change process.

A *personality disorder,* for the purposes of this chapter, is psychological and behavioral dysfunction resulting from mental processes. Overt pathological symptoms are not required for a personality disorder to exist, just maladaptation within a given social environment. Clearly, a personality disorder does not represent a single continuum of cause, symptomatology, functional effects, treatment, and prognosis. For this discussion, though, it will sometimes be presented in that way. All social adaptation could be conceptualized as falling on or near a line, from severe dysfunction, to normal, to supernormal.

Range of Social Dysfunction and Adaptation

severe_____ moderate_____ slight_____ normal_____ supernormal

---

This model works quite well at the extremes of this continuum. Individuals with severe social maladaptation are frequently symptomatic, whereas individuals in the supernormal range of adaptation demonstrate a normal or better personality structure, are largely asymptomatic, and function well above average. One problem with this model is that substantial personality disorders may not be accompanied by symptomatology or apparent social maladaptation. As a result, the dysfunction may be difficult to document in the usual clinical setting, especially for individuals with supernormal adaptation.

APPLICATION OF PSYCHIATRY TO NORMAL BEHAVIOR

Psychiatry has traditionally focused on emotional distress, maladaptive behaviors, and diagnoses that warrant treatment. However, as the field expanded to accommodate the needs of adults in the mainstream, it became clear that most adults go through crises as a normal part of development. It also became apparent that reasoning solely along the axis of distress to diagnosis was questionable.

It is no longer clear that personalities are immutably fixed early in life. A recent study of several thousand managers has shown that personality is relatively fluid and that a rigid personality style is a sign of disorder rather than a natural consequence of childhood (cited in Smelser and Erikson 1980). Toward the supernormal side of the spectrum (see the model), personality disorders and social maladaptation are far more subtle. Highly technical and specialized methodologies must be employed to document problems and to make these problems amenable to change and improvement.

On its surface the standard clinical interview is essentially a self-report, in which patients describe their problems from their own point of view. This assumes that a self-report is a reliable source of information, a questionable assumption where family problems are involved. A similar potential for error exists in organizations, where multiple layers of influence and causation go beyond the individual's knowledge. In addition, an unwary clinician may assume that the environment (except in traumatic situations) is reasonable and predictable, and that a failure to function is caused by individual limitations. However, many organizational environments cannot be labeled as either reasonable or predictable. The discordance between the self-report and a comprehensive picture of reality can be even more problematic as maladaptation decreases. As a result, strict reliance on self-reported data can sometimes fail to document problems that are important and can even suggest a misdiagnosis.

DIAGNOSING AND DOCUMENTING A PERSONALITY DISORDER

Although a formally diagnosed personality disorder has a clearly defined constellation of behaviors, many of the personality problems that affect executives do not fall neatly into such categories. Further, even when a disorder is easily recognized, such as a compulsive personality disorder, the manner of presentation is often complex and the best mode of intervention may be difficult to determine.

Diverse personality styles can all be adaptive for high performance in specific situations. For example, the style of marketing executives can vary from hip-shooting, global, intuitive, and highly active to data-oriented, careful, and strategic. Successful presidents of companies also vary widely, from those who seek to control every aspect of the company to those who are quite humanistic and apt to delegate with ease. How can psychiatry know what is an adaptive personality given this wide range of successful styles?

Where maladaptive personality styles are present, the occupational psychiatrist is confronted with several questions. First, is it necessary to strive for a broad-scale personality change or can the focus be limited to the major maladaptive characteristics? Second, can compensatory structural changes be made and can increased skill or learning compensate for personality issues? Third, what methodologies will adequately describe the person, the objective situation, and the problem, so that appropriate action can be taken? And fourth, what form of information gathering is most likely to engage the executive in his or her own development process?

Personality disorders are usually asymptomatic to the individual involved. The individual may be unaware that his or her behavior is either counterproductive or harmful to others. Often the clinical interview and self-report will neither document the problem nor motivate change. A common observation of psychotherapists is that patients with personality disorders, but no self-obvious distress, lack the motivation needed for change. The problem is compounded when power or wealth is involved. Since those individuals have substantial resources to mold their environment to their own conscious and unconscious needs, the underlying distress can become nearly invisible.

For example, a company president with a narcissistic personality disorder may be so sensitive to criticism that her subordinates are afraid to advise her about potential adverse consequences of her decisions or to convey bad news. When failure comes, the blame attaches to the affected subordinate manager rather than to the president. Since the president is so powerful, no one confronts her regarding her part in the decision. She remains unaware of her behavior and how it adversely affects key decisions.

The *Diagnostic and Statistical Manual of Mental Disorders, Revised* (DSM-III-R) was largely developed for ordinary clinical practice. There is still a lack of an adequate formal nomenclature to categorize the more subtle forms of personality disorder. Even the term *personality disorder* implies a certain level of severity. Where executive development is involved, some of the most important personality issues are not properly classified as disorders. There may be specific emotionally determined components of behavior that are not viewed as a disorder, even when they severely hamper career performance and development.

CONFLICT NEGOTIATION STYLES

Case Study 1

Tom Retton, a senior division head, was having trouble fitting into the executive committee of a large high-tech firm. He had frequent conflicts with two other members of the committee and the president found him difficult to direct. When Tom took over the division it was losing money and making little progress toward a technology change vital to the future of the division and the firm. Two years later the change was completed and the division began to generate profits.

The head of another division, Jack Rice, was a long-term friend of the president. Jack was worried that Tom would surpass him and that he would end up working for Tom. Therefore, Jack competed with Tom in every way possible and with far greater subtlety. Tom was openly confrontational and competitive, whereas Jack would withhold cooperation in passive and indirect ways. The competition and lack of cooperation would get Tom angry. He would confront the problems in the executive committee, since working on them in private with Jack had proven fruitless. The president of the company disliked open conflict and blamed Tom for the problem.

Tom was the oldest of five children in a midwestern farm family. In high school he was an outstanding athlete and an excellent student. His career had been quite successful, and he enjoyed a happy and satisfying family life, a rich social life, and good friends. The success of his family life was confirmed by a direct interview with his spouse and by observation of the family. He knew about his successes and did not believe he had any maladaptation that needed help. However, he did have a problem with his approach to conflict resolution.

When Tom got into a conflict with a peer-level employee his first style was "Win or Lose," or 9/1 (the ratio of goal attainment concern to relationship preservation concern; see Figures 9-2 and 9-3 for explanation). As the oldest sibling, he was accustomed to a dominant position in conflicts. At school he encountered peers who would either attack or make fun of him, and he would fight back. In competitive athletic situations, it was important for him to compete vigorously in order maintain his position on the team.

Powerful individuals often compete over relatively unimportant matters. Tom was likely to fall into the same cycle of competitive behavior with anyone who competed against him (see Figure 9-1). The current situation was aggravated because Tom and Jack were expecting future competition. They thought that the CEO/president would one day separate his roles and appoint a president. They were competing for that job. For Tom the current situation was analogous to previous athletic competitions, where two people were competing for the same position on the football team.

To what extent this residual pattern was adaptive and to what extent it was counterproductive depends on the perspective. Competition between employees can be destructive when cooperation is necessary for each to adequately perform their function. Knowing that employees are motivated by competition for promotion, organizations will encourage some competition to maintain high motivational levels. From the point of view of employees, such competition is adaptive if their career objectives can be achieved without undue misery.

Does Tom have some sort of character pathology? His pattern of behavior and conflict resolution is rooted in childhood: unwitting and unconscious. But much of behavior is unconscious. The mere fact that it is unconscious, or rooted in earlier experience, is not sufficient to call it pathological. Clearly, Tom's social adaptation is in the supernormal range, for he is expected to make subtle distinctions and to solve complex technical and interpersonal problems related to his employment. Such distinctions and problems are outside the normal range for the average person.

In most interpersonal disagreements, an individual has two main con-

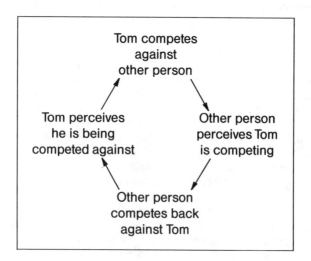

FIGURE 9-1.   When Tom perceives competition he is caught in a cycle.

cerns: concern for satisfactory attainment of some goal in the immediate disagreement and concern for preserving interpersonal relationships (see Figure 9-2).

In the illustration, a "nine" represents the highest concern for either goal attainment or preservation of the relationship. A "five" represents moderate concern and "one" represents the least concern. There are five important positions on this grid and each represents an approach to interpersonal conflict (see Figure 9-3).

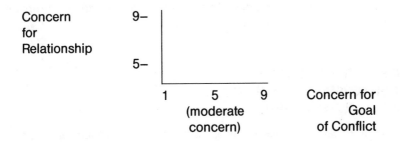

FIGURE 9-2. Conflict negotiation chart. (Based on 1969 conflict management survey for Teleometrics, International, Texas, conducted by Jay Hall.)

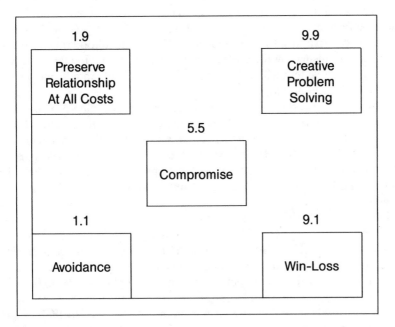

FIGURE 9-3. Conflict negotiation chart showing typical outcomes. (Based on 1969 conflict management survey for Teleometrics, International, Texas, conducted by Jay Hall.)

Creative problem solving (9/9; strong, equal goal/relationship concern levels) is the ideal solution. It attempts to resolve the disagreement in a way that satisfies both parties. Compromise (5/5) can help to resolve disagreements, but it is not as desirable as creative problem solving. Relationship preservation (1/9) requires giving in for the good of the relationship, but the disagreement will still exist. Win or Lose (9/1) is a power strategy that may defeat an opponent, but it contributes to ongoing interpersonal conflicts. Avoidance (1/1), involving withdrawal by both parties, is the least desirable of the solutions. It undermines what could be a worthwhile relationship because communication stops, feelings remain unprocessed, and the problem is locked into a static relationship.

INTERVENTION CRITERIA: COUNTERPRODUCTIVE AND INFLEXIBLE BEHAVIOR

Referring back to the case study, is Tom Retton's approach to competition counterproductive? In the short run his behavior is alienating the president of the company. The president blames Tom, the more active and visible person, rather than his old friend Jack Rice. Since the president's assessment affects Tom's ability to do his job, his behavior seems to be counterproductive. The long-term consequences are less promising. If Tom perseveres, he may either win or drive Jack from the company. But the likelihood that he will win is greatly diminished by the alienation of the president. He may be so valuable that the president will not fire him, but it is unlikely that he will achieve his goal and remain unscathed.

One way to ascertain if difficulties are personality related is to ask if a person's approach is both counterproductive and inflexible. Tom's difficulties fall within these criteria. As discussed above, his behavior is likely to be counterproductive. It is also inflexible, since it routinely reoccurs in his peer relationships. But before examining what steps could be taken to help Tom change and develop, it is necessary to understand the role of the organizational environment.

To ascertain which behaviors or styles warrant intervention requires more than simplistic assessment. Counterproductivity is determined partly by the individual's history, but also by the predicted outcome of particular business decisions. Admittedly, future consequences are difficult to predict. Predictions are harder still when an outside consultant applies an ideological view of an ideal world, rather than an empirical model of the particular real world. Moreover, problem behaviors that are counterproductive to the company may not immediately affect the individual. Inflexibility is a major criterion of personality-related problems within organizations. Inflexible individuals cannot change their style in response to changing circumstances, so that an otherwise productive style can become counterproductive. Both criteria must be met to indicate a personality problem.

Valid generalizations about personality-related phenomena are based on repeated, similar situations. For example, an individual may have a stimulus pattern that limits any generalization to encounters with strong male peers. But if no pattern of inflexibility is observed, then in what sense is the pattern related to personality? To what extent is apparently counterproductive behavior the result of an individual's temporary response or misperception, or a mistake by the consulting psychiatrist? It is only when both criteria are met that the problem can be related to personality.

DETERMINING REALITY OF SOCIAL ENVIRONMENTS

As seen in the case study, Tom Retton, Jack Rice, and the president differ in their sense of reality in this situation. While Tom's reality is that he is being dealt with in a competitive and manipulative manner, the president's reality is that Tom is difficult, unpleasant, and combative.

Personality and social environments are equally difficult to reduce to clear definitions, since to a great extent, reality is in the eye of the beholder. Organizations represent complex social environments, with perceptions of reality that vary according to one's level and function within the organization. Psychiatrists who have dealt with couples and families are used to dealing with this phenomenon.

To conclude simply that multiple realities exist and that one is no more accurate than another leaves the psychiatrist, the organization, and the executive with a lack of clarity. Clearly, procedural methods are needed to help determine an objective working reality. The fields of organizational development and management have developed methods precisely for that purpose.

Direct Observation

Direct observation will show the ways in which Tom Retton and Jack Rice are combative or cooperative. An observer can also chronicle the president's reaction to their confrontations, judge whether the president's response is helpful, and in turn, how other team members respond. The observer may find that Tom is not so competitive at all; he just thinks he is. If that is the case, his history of competitive relationships has probably oversensitized him to competitive cues.

Direct observation of behavior has distinct advantages. It is analogous to home visits in a family therapy situation, in which factors not obvious to the family members will be obvious to the observer.

Along with the advantages of direct observation there are potential pitfalls. First, if care is not taken, the training, experience, and biases of the observer can completely alter what is observed. For example, an observer who finds interpersonal aggression difficult may believe that the entire executive team is engaged in conflict. Business frequently tolerates far higher levels of direct aggression than health-related institutions. Conversely, a business veteran might be surprised by the high level of indirect aggression in hospitals.

Second, the participants may grossly alter their behavior when the observer is present. Most high-level participants in an organization have learned to adapt their style, to a greater or lesser extent, to fit any given circumstance. If the circumstance is one of observation, many are able for limited periods to alter what the observer sees. Third, since direct observations are not easily standardized or quantifiable, they cannot readily be compared across circumstances or organizations. Last, the cost of direct observation is often high, relative to the information obtained. When used as the sole strategy, it may require lengthy periods of observation by a highly trained specialist.

Quantitative Methods

A questionnaire measuring Tom Retton's leadership style was administered to his subordinates, peers, and superiors. Subordinates gave above average ratings to Tom's leadership style, compared to normative samples. In general, his peers perceived Tom as cooperative and effective in his way of dealing with them. However, two of Tom's peers saw him quite differently from the sample; their perceptions matched those of the president. Coincidentally, the executive committee included the president and those two members of the "old guard." While the questionnaires were anonymous, there may have been a self-reinforcing information flow, influenced by old guard members who saw Tom in a very different light.

Quantitative methods used in the field of organizational psychiatry include questionnaires that are completed either by a subgroup or by all members of an organization. Questionnaires vary in number, what they measure, and the specific properties of these measurements. Currently, many of these instruments are not validated as well as they should be.

Questionnaires fall into two types: those intended to measure something about an individual, such as leadership style, and those intended to measure something about the organization or unit, as in a climate survey. The advantages of the quantitative method are that it is relatively inexpensive and the information gathered allows for at least an approximate comparison between individuals or organizations. Further, it allows for the discovery of subgroups that are distinctly different from the sample at large. As long as anonymity is preserved, that information is relatively accurate.

Quantitative data have certain disadvantages. First, survey participants will respond within whatever categories exist. Therefore, if the survey instrument omits relevant questions, it may fall short of its objectives. Second, the results may depict a current situation, but may say nothing about its history or causal relationships. More sophisticated analyses may require longitudinal data from a potentially large survey population. Third, unless adequate data bases are available for comparison, the data may be interpreted according to a theoretical ideal, instead of what is possible in a specific environment.

Qualitative Methods

Qualitative information can be gathered from open-ended questions posed in a questionnaire or interview. If a questionnaire is prepared skillfully, the information gathered can be highly specific. Still, information of superior quality can be obtained through in-depth interviews conducted by organizationally knowledgeable, skilled interviewers. To preserve confidentiality and anonymity, the information is reported back to the individual or organization in group form.

The advantages of an interview are that it allows for cause and effect to be investigated, leading to a deeper understanding of current and past situations, the discovery of hidden alternatives, and the formation of a working relationship between the professional and interview participants.

Interviews have a cost disadvantage, since highly trained specialists may be needed for a lengthy period of time. In addition, it is not easy to compare interview findings from one organization or situation to another. Ultimately, the worth of an interview is entirely dependent on the skill of the interviewers.

Standardized Measurement of the Individual

Tom Retton's situation readily shows the utility of standardized measurement. Once his Win or Lose style was visualized on the conflict scale, it clarified what happened in his encounters. The theory behind the questionnaire helped both Tom and the psychiatrist understand the reality of his conflict resolution style and what could be done about it. Tom was able to use the consultation to his advantage, for when future differences arose, he reminded himself of his Win or Lose style and was often able to effect compromise. But whenever he accomplished this, he felt rather uneasy. In a follow-up consultation, the psychiatrist suggested that Tom consider insight-oriented psychotherapy if the uneasiness persisted, to understand and reduce it, and to further improve his managerial style.

There are many standardized tests designed to measure individual characteristics such as personality, leadership and management style, power preference, and intelligence. These methods are no substitute for the clinical interview, but they are often preferred because they are easier to administer and less time consuming. Each of these instruments has either a theoretical perspective or a method of empirical development.

The advantages of standardized tests depend on the test specifics. In general, they are inexpensive, give a deeper understanding of the person, provide a theoretical framework that is helpful both to the clinician and the executive, and provide useful feedback to the executive engaged in the change process. Further, if the executive wants the psychiatric consultation to remain confidential, these tests do not require the involvement of other people in the organization.

The largest single disadvantage of these instruments is that they are entirely based on a self-report that can be subject to enormous distortion. On managerial and leadership questionnaires, individuals rate themselves across various dimensions. The results are no better than the self-awareness of each individual. A comparison of peer and subordinate ratings against self-reported data quickly demonstrates that many executives are grossly unaware of their style. Further, while there are significant personality factors that affect leadership style, reasoning that proceeds directly from personality tests to leadership or management style is inaccurate. It can be shown that personality affects leadership style in complex ways, but not always in the way that intuition suggests.

WARNINGS

Reasoning from Personality to Organizational Decisions

Case Study 2

Sam Wise was the president of a large utility company in 1970. His case reflects the problem with reasoning from personality to organizational decisions. His company was in the process of deciding about a very large project and Sam seemed to be frightened and overwhelmed. He would hold repeated staff meetings with his top executives to discuss the project, always reaching the same conclusions. The economics of the decision overwhelmingly supported the project; in fact, if the organization did not go ahead with the project, it might not be able to compete in the years ahead. Sam had always been slow in making decisions, which was not generally a problem in the utilities industry. After a second meeting without progress, the board requested consultation with an occupational psychiatrist.

In brief, Sam had a history and clinical presentation of an obsessive character structure. Throughout his life Sam had been very detail oriented, slow in making decisions, and unable to handle emotion without difficulty. His major stated concern was uncertainty about environmental safety, despite the assurances provided by a succession of experts. In this respect he met the criteria for inflexibility. Further, it appeared that his personality structure had become counterproductive, for it utterly vitiated his ability to make a critical decision in a timely fashion. The consultation seemed unsuccessful and eventually Sam decided not to engage in the project.

In retrospect, Sam's obsessional personality style offered him a clearer long-term view of this particular decision. The decision was whether to build a nuclear power plant, and Sam's concern was the human and economic impact of a potential meltdown. The legitimacy of his concerns are now clear, but in 1970 his experts and top executives viewed them as unrealistic and alarmist.

Business exists in a complex milieu that has economic, social, legal, governmental, and technical realities. These factors take many years to understand and master for the particular business involved. Men or women of great vision often see things in the future that the average person fails to comprehend. Vision is a key characteristic of leadership and some leaders possess it to a degree that compensates for their other weaknesses.

The consulting psychiatrist must view the individual, the organization, and the process, but without forming opinions about organizational decisions. He or she is not qualified to take that perspective and doing so can be harmful. Therefore, when the issue is executive development, the occupational psychiatrist must be extremely vigilant about his or her own view of reality and of the organization's environment. Failing to do so can cause normal behavior or appropriate decisions to be labeled as pathological.

Confusing Lack of Knowledge or Skills with Personality Disorders

Lack of skill or knowledge can mimic personality problems. Purposeful behaviors are learned by watching others, by education or training, and by trial and error. Effective managers have learned from academic training, from managerial experience, and from being managed themselves. Inflexible personality styles can diminish the ability to develop an effective management and leadership style.

Skillful managing of people at work is every bit as complex as the diagnosis of psychiatric conditions. A psychiatrist would never expect a new medical student to diagnose psychiatric problems without appropriate education and direct supervision. However, many organizations place individuals in management positions with little or no training. Left to learn management on their own, they usually try to adopt a style that is comfortable and consistent with such existing role models as their parents, teachers, and previous managers.

An interesting line of inquiry when dealing with managers is to ask how and from whom they learned their management technique. Often they will say it is from a boss who they admired. Similarly, no student of psychiatry becomes a truly competent therapist by simply going to a course. It requires many years of practice and the integration of formal learning with actual experience. Even the earlier completion of a development course or program by no means guarantees that the appropriate conditions for learning ever existed. The real diagnostic dilemmas occur when there is both a lack of knowledge and some personality component.

MODEL OF EXECUTIVE DEVELOPMENT

The model in Figure 9-4 shows three paths of executive development activity (Paths 1, 2, and 3) that must often advance simultaneously in order to effect true change and growth.

Path 1: Cognitive Learning

Path 1 is the cognitive learning that results from intellectual input or from a change in one's understanding of a situation. All individuals use cognitive models to understand complex situations. For example, people who drive have a cognitive model of the highways that approach the nearest city. This model may or may not be accurate, but they have a model. Intellectual learning can sometimes suffice when a knowledge deficit exists. Individuals who get lost on the road can learn from a map without having to address personality factors. Clarification of the situation and use of an explanatory model often enable the individuals to understand their interaction with the organizational environment. There is a need for more knowledge in most developmental activities that involve character issues. A skilled occupational psychiatrist understands the organizational, management, and leadership road map, as well as individual psychodynamics and therapy. Where a cognitive approach is thought to be best, many executives do well with reading lists, coupled with discussions of how this knowledge applies to their situation. It is surprising to see how much behavioral change this approach can sometimes stimulate.

Path 2: The Rational Change Process

The rational change process involves a systematic investigation of the situation, the person, and the alternatives. This leads to a plan for change that is developed mutually by the executive and the psychiatrist.

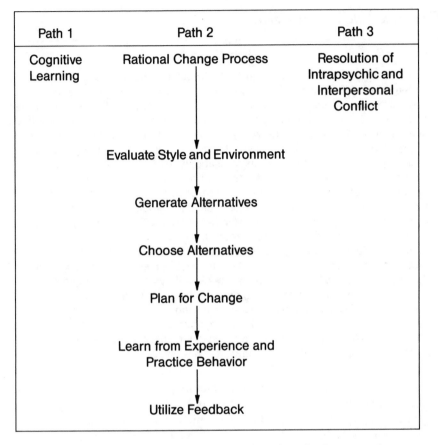

FIGURE 9-4.   Model of executive development: three simultaneous paths.

Case Study 3

A company president complained that he did not get good ideas from his subordinates. When asked what percentage of time he spent talking in staff meetings, he estimated 10–15 percent. Direct observation of his meetings determined that he was actually talking 65–75 percent of the time. He was unaware of his own behavior, its effect on staff meetings, and its effect on the perception of his operating style within the organization.

Path 2 describes the classical rational change process. Information must be gathered first, in order to understand the nature of a situation, to clarify what form of executive development is needed, and to identify the operating constraints that affect the executive and the organization.

Evaluate Style and Environment

Case Study 4

The Ozone Computer Corporation had a problem. The computer industry has undergone a striking change over the past 4 to 5 years. As new machines appeared, offering power and simplicity at reduced cost, the profits of the large computer companies decreased dramatically. The squeeze of competition has been fierce and will only intensify over time. Many companies have had to lay off employees.

The Ozone managers who remained had to find new ways to motivate employees, while coping with their own feelings of insecurity, inadequacy, anger, and blame. A program for their development focused on the clarification of changes in their environment and the implications of those changes to them as managers and leaders. A series of structured exercises asked the group to list the changes in the environment and to agree on the most important ones. Then the group determined the impact of these forces on their organization. Next they clarified the impact on them as leaders and managers: What should their style be and what new skills did they need to learn in response? A measurement of their style was obtained from their subordinates to help them decide how close they were to the needed approach. Finally, they were given a chance to discuss their own lives and feelings. What in their lives and feelings stood in the way of making the needed changes? They now had useful information about the Ozone organization, their management style, and themselves. Many new insights and behaviors resulted from their access to this information and their ability to integrate it in new situations.

The importance of information, strategies for gathering it, and the strengths and weaknesses of those strategies have been presented above. In general, it is necessary to gather information at a minimum of three levels: the individual's psychosocial history, the individual's management or leadership style, and the wider organizational environment.

Most psychiatrists and other therapists have had considerable experience in gathering psychosocial histories. The work history is especially important: It chronicles previous jobs; problems that occurred on those jobs; reasons for leaving or changing jobs; previous relationships with bosses, peers, and subordinates; and motivations for work. Determination of management or leadership style is best done by questionnaire or interview.

It is important to focus on the strengths and weaknesses of management or leadership style. Focusing solely on weaknesses of style can lower self-esteem and increase resistance to change. Management and leadership have some overlapping functions, but there are important distinctions. The typical functions of management are to plan, organize, direct, and control. In essence, the measurement of style reflects how these are done and the interpersonal sensitivity used in doing so. Leadership concerns vision, the articulation of goals for an organization or function, and the ability to build the strategy and network of motivated people necessary to achieve stated objectives.

Leadership does not always involve direct authority. As change accelerates and American organizations run on a more austere and decentralized basis, the need for leadership will increase. (For further information regarding the difference between management and leadership style, see the Bibliography.)

Finally, information regarding the environment of both the unit and the parent organization is necessary. A business organization competes in a complex, rapidly changing economic, technical, and social world. Large factors or forces in that world have an enormous impact on the day-to-day life of employees. In addition, the future needs of the job, its priorities, and specific work practices can all change radically because of evolving environmental circumstances.

Generate Alternatives

The next step in the development process is the generation of alternatives. Several factors can prevent the consideration of sufficiently broad alternatives. The first is a lack of knowledge. In management and leadership, there are often specialized skills and approaches that are necessary to handle particular situations. Frequently, these alternatives only become apparent when a problem or situation can be viewed from a different perspective, or when several alternatives can be contrasted. Consider the example of an employee who is constantly late for work, a more concrete problem than most. That employee may be suffering from a personality problem, such as a passive-aggressive or obsessive-compulsive personality. In addition, there may be personal problems at home, a lack of public transportation, a lack of motivation, a substance abuse problem, or a lack of competency for the job. Once such a problem has been determined to exist, an effort should be made to identify the cause.

When dealing with an organizational or developmental problem, the most important single factor in finding correct or desirable alternatives is the ability to choose appropriate perspectives for viewing the problem. Often this is difficult for an individual who is personally embroiled in the situation. Psychiatrists are trained to uncover and explain the complex and hidden interactions of individuals with their surroundings. However, there are two differences between ordinary psychotherapy and executive development. First, the search for alternatives is more active in executive coaching and development and has a shorter-term focus. Second, a knowledge of organizational and management theory is necessary to find certain alternatives, since many problems involve a mix of the individual and the organization.

Choose Alternatives

Conflict resolution often requires choice, the common denominator for change and for progress in executive development. Choice operates on at least two levels: in the real world and in the intrapsychic world of conscious and unconscious internal thoughts and feelings.

Often the real-world choices involved in executive development can be very complex. For example, which of two jobs should a vice-president choose? He is successful in his current job, but he is frustrated by a lack of autonomy and future potential. Another job would allow him the opportunity to be the president, but in a far more uncertain situation. The positive and negative consequences of both choices must be examined. These consequences could be labeled "real-world" issues.

Additional issues are raised by internal feelings and conflicts. They exist in an intrapsychic world that is familiar to the occupational psychiatrist. What present and past issues of emotional security are raised? How does the individual feel about the potential loss of relationships, and how has loss been handled in the past? The choice process is never entirely rational and emotional factors are intensified when choices are large. Their exploration is often vital and helpful to the development of the individual. Further, intrapsychic conflicts can reflect two inconsistent parts of the self, at least one of which is unconscious. Raising those issues to a conscious level allows for choice to take place, leading to resolution of the conflict.

Plan for Change

Case Study 5

An autocratic manager realized that his style was inhibiting the growth of his department. Current data and an analysis of future business needs made a clear case for decentralization, a concept that was inconsistent with his style. His style was partly the result of identification with a domineering father. In psychotherapy, he began to work through the internal issues that affected his ability to change. An unanticipated problem was that two of his direct subordinates had attained status, power, and security because they had successfully learned to cope with his style. If his style became more open, and if he was successful in decentralizing the department, their special relationship and power would be diminished. Therefore, they resisted the changes evolving in him and in the department. Thus, it is often necessary to plan the change process and its possible outcomes on multiple levels.

Managers faced with the need to alter their style are often faced with a complex problem. Besides overcoming the inertia of their own internal and character issues, the environment may initially resist or fail to support change.

Careful initial planning and periodic assessment of progress can be extremely important in keeping the development process on course.

Learn from Experience and Practice Behavior
There is a whole industry that provides materials and curricula for structured experiences that allow leaders and managers to practice new behaviors within a training environment. These vary from 1-hour sessions to 3-month and longer programs. A major consideration is the transferability of these experiences from the learning environment to the real world. Such materials provide an important opportunity to experience a problem in mock form and to practice new methods or behaviors in a safe classroom environment. This step is often necessary to initiate the development process, but it may not be sufficient to accomplish the necessary change.

As most psychiatrists are well aware, personality change is difficult to effect. Emotional and intrapsychic issues are often involved, so that simple experience and practice, removed from the real world, will fail to effect major behavioral change. Nonetheless the adult personality is often fluid and some form of learning does always takes place.

Developmental training experiences are of two basic types. The first is called a simulation, probably the most powerful kind of experience, if done correctly. This is a structured experience that elicits strong feelings and behaviors similar to the real-world situation in which new learning is needed. Since real-world consequences are absent, and since time can be taken to examine feelings and behaviors, a simulation is a powerful agent for change.

The second type of developmental training experience is a variation on practice or role playing. Practice of behaviors is very helpful, for awkward feelings that result from trying new behaviors are often easier to handle in a safe environment. Greater benefits accrue when there is video feedback to allow the individual to see himself as he is seen by others.

Utilize Feedback
Feedback is essential to the learning process, and the more complex the behavioral change, the more essential feedback becomes. Also, character change is unlikely without some type of ongoing feedback. Feedback can be by videotape, direct observation, repeat interviews, or questionnaires. The individual can also solicit feedback within his or her social network if the relationships allow candor.

It is vital for the occupational psychiatrist to discuss the ongoing change process with the individual involved and to develop a strategy for continuing feedback and reinforcement. Without this feature in the change process, the individual may have some early success, but may become frustrated by the lack of long-term change.

Path 3: Resolution of Intrapsychic and Interpersonal Conflict

The executive development model indicates that intrapsychic and interpersonal change are essential factors to recognize and address throughout the development process. Organizational frustration with the slow progress of executive development activity is commonplace but not surprising. Even extensive training programs usually will fail to address the central role of intrapsychic change (see Chapters 1 and 6). If patients have difficulty with emotional intimacy, they may interact more easily on an army reserve weekend than in an unhappy marriage. Their interpersonal skills are the same in each instance, but intrapsychic factors are heightened in the emotional setting of marriage. It should not be surprising, then, that a single training course dealing with new behaviors is unlikely to effect substantive change.

It is extremely important to view psychiatric knowledge and clinical insights in the context of organizations, management, and leadership. It is equally vital not to discount the importance of intrapsychic and interpersonal issues throughout the process of executive development.

SUMMARY

Diagnosis for the purpose of executive development is difficult. In most cases, the individuals have an overall level of social adaptation that is in the normal to supernormal range. However, they may show subtle maladaptive behaviors within complex organizational systems. Organizational dynamics can closely resemble those of families, so that psychological intervention often follows a family therapy model.

Viewing the individual outside of the social milieu can be highly misleading. Nor is it easy to learn enough about a work environment to be helpful. Organizations have idiosyncratic normative systems, with varying paths to the attainment of success and distribution of power. Many require highly complex skills and innovative individual initiatives.

An effective approach to executive development usually involves viewing behavior within the organizational context for its effect on the individual and company. Particular attention must be given to counterproductive or inflexible behaviors. Given the tension between short-term and long-term goal orientations, assessment of these concerns becomes even more complex.

Direct observation, as well as qualitative, quantitative, and standardized measurements, can be effective diagnostic tools for executive development. However, each has benefits and drawbacks. Executive development can take several paths. Many successful interventions have resulted from a cognitive approach to learning and a rational change process. When these techniques are not successful enough, psychiatric clinical knowledge and insight can provide invaluable support for intrapsychic and interpersonal conflict resolution.

Bibliography

Brill, P. L., and J. P. Hayes. 1981. *Taming Your Turmoil: Managing the Transitions of Adult Life.* Englewood Cliffs, N. J.: Prentice-Hall.

Greiff, B. S., et al. (in preparation). *Psychiatry in the World of Work.* Group for the Advancement of Psychiatry, Committee on Psychiatry in Industry.

Jacques, E. 1952. *The Changing Culture of a Factory.* New York: Dryden Press.

Kanter, R. M. 1980. *The Change Masters: Innovation for Productivity in American Corporations.* New York: Simon & Schuster.

Kotter, J. P. 1988. *The Leadership Factor.* New York: The Free Press.

Levinson, D. J. 1979. *The Seasons of a Man's Life.* New York: Ballantine Books.

Levinson, H. 1970. *Executive Stress.* New York: Harper, Row and Company.

McLean, A. A. 1979. *Work Stress.* Reading, Mass.: Addison-Wesley.

McLean, A. A. 1986. *High Tech Survival Kit: Managing Your Stress.* New York: Wiley & Sons.

Matteson, M. T., and J. M. Ivancevich. 1987. *Controlling Work Stress: Effective Human Resource and Management Strategies.* San Francisco: Jossey-Bass.

Mitchell, J. V. (ed.). 1983. *Tests in Print III.* Lincoln: Buros Institute of Mental Measurements, University of Nebraska.

Smelser, N. J., and E. H. Erikson (eds.). 1980. *Themes of Work and Love in Adulthood.* Cambridge, Mass.: Harvard University Press.

Vaillant, G. E. 1977. *Adaptation to Life.* Boston: Little, Brown & Company.

10

Emotional Crises in the Workplace

Stephen H. Heidel, M.D.

ABSTRACT

Emotional crises in the workplace involve disasters and emotionally traumatic events, aggression, substance abuse, depression and suicidal behavior, psychotic illness, and AIDS (acquired immunodeficiency syndrome). Crises may be caused by employees' outside emotional problems, or by problems in the work setting. These crises have a dramatic impact on individual employees and work groups. Organizations should develop policies and should inventory internal and external resources before an emergency occurs.

INTRODUCTION

Emotional crises in the workplace are increasingly common. These crises can include (1) emotionally traumatic disasters, such as earthquakes, fires, massacres, and serious accidents; (2) aggression, ranging from threats to physical acts; (3) substance abuse, causing an unsafe and disruptive workplace for millions of workers; (4) depression and suicidal behavior; (5) psychotic illnesses, causing peculiar or dangerous behavior; and (6) AIDS (acquired immunodeficiency syndrome), causing fear and anxiety among co-workers.

Despite the increasing frequency of emotional crises, companies often do not know how to recognize and respond when problems occur. Managers are often uncomfortable with emotional issues. Not knowing what to do, and afraid of making the situation worse, managers often avoid emotional problems and hope they will eventually correct themselves. Employees may be equally uncomfortable with emotional crises. Feeling awkward, they may find them hard to discuss or understand. They often react with silence. Employees in crisis may be afraid of looking weak if they seek help. As a result, emotional crises are too often denied, minimized, and even ignored. The most constructive approach requires acknowledgment, discussion, and proper action.

A healthy organization will accept the fact that emotional crises will affect them periodically. Companies can then develop policies, procedures, and resources to help deal with problems as they occur. First, each organization must predict which emotional crises they may face. Second, each should determine what procedures must be adopted to address those potential crises. Third, they should identify internal resources and supports to deal with these situations. Finally, they should identify what external resources are necessary to supplement their internal supports.

Emotional crises in the workplace can be divided into several categories. For each category in this chapter (emotional trauma, aggression, substance abuse, depression and suicide, psychotic behavior, and AIDS) there are case studies, discussion of the causes, effects on the workplace, and intervention approaches.

DISASTER AND EMOTIONAL TRAUMA

An earthquake jolted San Francisco. An airplane crashed in a cornfield in Sioux City. A fire ravaged Chicago. A nuclear power plant destructed on Three Mile Island. These are traumatic events, some natural and others accidental, that either cause or nearly cause a loss of life for many people. Individuals who live through these events are victims just as much as those who are killed. These survivors have experienced a severe stress, beyond the range of normal human experience, and they may well exhibit symptoms long after the incident has occurred.

A typical response to an emotionally traumatic event can involve six phases:

1. *Emotional shock*—being overwhelmed and stunned
2. *Denial*—not accepting that an event has happened
3. *Anger*—becoming frustrated, overwhelmed, and irate
4. *Remorse*—feeling sorrow and guilt for the incident
5. *Grief*—beginning the healing process
6. *Reconciliation*—integrating the event, getting on with life

Most people will follow some version of this process and then continue their lives. Some, though, will find themselves stuck somewhere in the middle of the process, unable to reconcile the event, and left with unresolved symptoms.

Case Study 1: Factory Fire

A machine caught fire at Geotech Chemical. Ten employees were evacuated when their area filled with smoke. After they left the building, they realized that the machine operator was still inside. Two employees reentered the building and helped the operator out. His clothes were on fire until he was wrapped in a blanket in the parking lot. He was admitted to a burn unit in critical condition and he died two days later.

Four days later the company was still in disarray. Management did not know what to do. Many employees had still not come back to work and production in the area had stopped. A psychiatrist was called in to meet with top management. He did the following: (1) listened to management describe in detail the events of the fire, including their own reactions and those of the employees; (2) described to the managers how people are affected by traumatic events; and (3) outlined a strategy to meet with employees in a series of group meetings.

Two large group meetings were held for all interested employees. Employees were encouraged to discuss their reactions. The first meeting concluded with a discussion of feelings that would be expected after a disaster, symptoms to be on the lookout for, and healthy coping mechanisms. A second meeting was attended by a smaller number of employees as a follow-up to the first meeting. Employees talked more about their reactions to the event, going back to work, and how to cope. The two employees who were still overwhelmed were then identified and referred for individual treatment.

There were nine people in the immediate work group. Three 2-hour confidential meetings were held with this group over a 2-week period. Participants were not to share this information with outside co-workers, management, or friends. One employee had severe anxiety and was not able to enter the fire area. Another was drinking a quart of vodka every night to fall asleep. A third had recurring visual images of the fire and could not concentrate. Another had recently lost both his mother and a friend and had become very depressed. Finally, one employee thought that the company was only trying to cover its own mistakes and he did not want to say anything at all. As a result of these meetings, symptoms subsided in all but one employee, who was then referred for individual treatment.

A final meeting was held with top management. By then, Geotech had become fully operational and the meeting served as a final report on the employees' progress. In case further efforts would be needed, management was given guidelines for detecting recurrent symptoms and workplace dysfunction. In a 6-month follow-up, all of the immediate work group members were performing well. None had quit their job and management reported that the organization had been running smoothly for 2 months.

Case Study 2: Plane Crash

A private plane took off in a dense fog. The pilot and two passengers were all principals of Eagleview Development. At a height of 200 feet, both engines caught on fire and there was not enough power to turn back to the airport. The plane began to descend, passed over a cliff, and came out of the cloud bank with the ocean visible below. The pilot crash landed the plane in the ocean. The three occupants escaped the plane before it sunk and were rescued by Navy helicopter. The three had very different reactions.

The chief operating officer, one of the passengers, felt it was a near-death experience. He was choked up and unable to express his feelings. Previously he had felt in control of his life, family, business, and he had been physically active. Now, though, he was unable to drive, jog, or go to work. He was embarrassed by his strong emotional reaction and was very nervous. He isolated himself at home, had nightmares, and became inexplicably angry at colleagues. At his wife's insistence, he saw a psychiatrist and was treated for panic disorder with desipramine (an antipanic drug) and psychotherapy. Much of the therapy focused on relationships with his estranged children. It took 6 weeks before he began to feel normal.

The pilot had a loss of concentration for one week. His herpes flared up and remained present continuously for weeks. Following the accident he had a greater appreciation for work, life, and beauty. He was able to return to flying and was nervous only for the start of his first subsequent flight. He felt more in control of himself than he had before.

The other passenger of the plane denied any significant reactions other than some mild insomnia. Others found him more withdrawn, confused, negative, and hard to work with. His depression did not clear until several months later.

Case Study 3: Bank Robbery

A man entered a Cielo Bank branch, pulled a gun from a bag, and pointed it at a teller. He demanded all the money she had, which was approximately $4,000. As a result of this incident, the individuals working in the bank were in a state of shock and fear. They felt a loss of control and felt they had been violated by the bank robber. The teller who was robbed had a variety of emotional reactions including feeling incompetent because she should not have had so much money available, guilt for somehow not stopping the robber from getting the money, anxiety and fearfulness about what might have happened to her, anger at the individual for having done what he did, and relief that no one had been injured. A number of employees experienced poor sleep, nightmares, and increased anxiety as a result of the bank robbery.

Response Determinants for an Emotionally Traumatic Event

People who experience a traumatic event will have widely differing reactions to it. Individual reactions differ for the following reasons:

1. *Severity of the event.*   The more severe the event, the greater the reaction. For example, if an employee is involved in an accident in which a co-worker is injured, that would precipitate a less severe reaction than if the same person was involved in an accident where many people were killed and injured.

2. *Previous trauma.*   If an individual has experienced traumatic events in the past, his or her reaction may be more severe than if no previous trauma had been experienced. A bank teller, for instance, who has experienced previous robberies would be more vulnerable than one who has not. The current trauma would be likely to cause a flooding of emotions from the previous events as well as the current traumatic incident. On the other hand, many people will be immunized by a trauma and thus less distressed by subsequent events.

3. *Psychiatric disorder or predisposition.*   Someone who suffers from or has a predisposition to a psychiatric disorder (i.e., anxiety, depression, substance abuse) will have more difficulty coping with a traumatic event than someone who does not. For example: A woman worked as a cashier for a convenience store. She had a longstanding depression, but she managed to function at a marginal level. Her store was robbed. She was held at gunpoint and was afraid she would die. Following that incident she had a worsening of her depression. With a few weeks of psychotherapy and antidepressant medication, she returned to work (and at a more functional level than before). Someone without her history of depression might have been able to return to work more quickly and easily.

4. *Social supports.*   A person with a strong nuclear family, close friends, and other community supports (e.g., church) will be better able to deal with trauma than someone without those supports. If a deliveryperson had an automobile accident causing serious physical problems, he or she would be much more apt to recover with the support of a spouse, a close-knit family, and several close friends than without close companions.

5. *Major life changes.*   A person who has sustained one or more major life changes (e.g., death of a spouse or friend, loss of a job, move from one location to another, major illness) in the past year will have more difficulty dealing with a traumatic event. In Case Study 1, the man whose mother and friend had died in the past month had more trouble dealing with the industrial fire as a result.

6. *Self-esteem.*   People who have high regard for themselves will be less devastated by a traumatic event than will those who do not have a good self-image. They are more able to recognize the difference between themselves and their circumstances.

7. *Protective role of a supportive and stable work environment.*   Some work environments are more supportive and nurturing than others. When a traumatic event occurs at a company that is perceived as caring for its staff, employees may recover more easily because they feel the support from their employer. When support services are offered to employees in need, they and their less-affected co-workers will be more able to resolve their problems, instead of reacting with anger, or inappropriately blaming the organization.

Effects

Every traumatic event in the workplace will be disruptive to the work force. At a minimum it will cause downtime for a few involved employees, but it may destroy the effectiveness of an entire organization. In the factory fire case it took 4 months for the company to regain its previous level of production. In the plane crash case, the entire organization was adrift for 6 weeks, until the chief operating officer regained his emotional stability. If management does not offer the chance to work through these emotional reactions, employees will be more likely to retain symptoms and will be more vulnerable to future events. They may harbor tension or resentment toward an employer seen as unsupportive.

Prevention and Intervention

Organizations that are at a low risk for traumatic incidents may only need to know where to find outside assistance in the unlikely event that it is needed. High-risk organizations include banks, retail stores, police and fire departments, airlines, and hospitals. They should have a strategy to deal with traumatic events. They should develop policies, procedures, and training programs for selected employees. Staff with responsibilities in the event of a trauma might be from personnel, safety, security, and the medical department. They need to know when to respond to traumatic events, how to control their own reactions, how to interact with victims, how to recognize symptoms, and when to call for professional help. Management plays an essential practical and symbolic role in organizing response to circumstances and in maintaining morale.

To the extent that external resources might be necessary, they should be identified in advance. There should be logical reasons for calling different resources. Resources might include police, ambulances, and professionals trained in trauma intervention and psychiatric emergencies.

AGGRESSIVE AND ASSAULTIVE BEHAVIOR

Aggressive and assaultive behavior among employees is not common, but it is a serious and increasing problem. A wide spectrum of behaviors is covered in this category, including challenging statements, verbal threats, physical altercations, and even deadly assault.

Case Study 4: Death Threat—Drugs

Art Carsten, a 32-year-old single male stock clerk at a manufacturing company, had a change in his behavior. He had started a basketball team and a photographic club at work. But he had alienated himself from co-workers by insisting that they share his enthusiasm. He became increasingly irritable. He made a threatening call to the personnel director at 5:30 A.M., threatened to steal the president's Porsche, and threatened to hurt co-workers. Art also threatened to kill his father. The next day he called work and said he was planning to resign and commit suicide. His mother called the personnel director and confirmed his threats. His girlfriend called to say that he had taken her car and disappeared with a gun. Over the ensuing days he called work several times, said that he was in hiding, and that if people tried to find him he would shoot first and ask questions later.

The company posted private-duty police inside and outside the company. After several days he was apprehended by the police. Co-workers remained frightened nonetheless. Art's urine test was positive for both marijuana and amphetamines. Though he had no history of psychiatric treatment, there was a family history of alcoholism and his mother had attempted suicide twice. Both the employee and his mother had been beaten by his father.

Case Study 5: Death Threats—Psychosis

Helen Davis, a 29-year-old woman, was referred for poor job performance. In the process of evaluation, she admitted to thoughts of killing her work supervisor. She spoke of this several times and in a disturbing way. As a result, the evaluator reported the threats to both the supervisor and the police. Helen was then referred for psychiatric treatment. She had two treatment sessions and she was given antipsychotic medication to control her paranoid ideas and uncontrolled anger. She was then released for return to work. Back at work, the company nurse was still worried about her stability and requested a repeat evaluation. During that interview the employee became angry, denied that she had ever made any threats toward her supervisor, and admitted that she was not taking the prescribed medication. Based on that information the psychiatrist no longer felt Helen was ready to return to work.

Case Study 6: Death Threats—Psychosis

Mike Sanjani, a 27-year-old single man working for an aerospace company, had a decline in his job performance over 3 months. One day he was noted to be incoherent and was referred to the medical department. He was paranoid and said he was planning to leave the plant early, stand outside the gate, and kill people indiscriminately with a machine gun as they came out. He then laughed inappropriately. He was immediately referred to a psychiatrist and hospitalized. Mike was diagnosed with paranoid schizophrenia, treated with appropriate medications, and his thought process returned to normal. He was able to return to work without violent thoughts and without anger directed toward co-workers.

Causes

When trying to understand the causes of assaultive behavior, one must consider both an individual's personal risk factors and also his or her environment. Individual risk factors include:

1. Male
2. Age 15-30
3. Childhood hyperactivity, enuresis, or temper tantrums

4. Past history of violence
   a. fighting or aggressiveness (age 8-12)
   b. history of aggressive crimes
   c. past or current aggressive acts
5. Verbal hostility
   a. threats of violence
   b. preoccupation with auditory hallucinations
   c. preoccupation with weapons
6. Antisocial personality disorder
7. History of drug or alcohol abuse
8. Social isolation

Environmental risk factors include:

1. Family: level of emotional support and acceptability of violent behavior
2. Peer: level of emotional support and acceptability of violent behavior
3. Job: level of employment stability and level of conflict with supervisors and co-workers
4. Stresses: external demands that may overwhelm internal coping resources

Prevention and Intervention

When confronted with a potentially assaultive employee at work, one must first assess his or her overall level of control. If the person is already assaultive and is out of control at that moment, a supervisor or manager must react accordingly, which might include calling security and/or police, and calling the medical department. When appropriate, an ambulance with extra attendants can help restrain and remove the individual without injury to either himself or others. It is important not to act heroically. Do not take unnecessary chances that might endanger yourself or others.

In assessing the severity of the threat, the following questions might be considered (never assume that any assessment of a violent threat is completely accurate):

1. What was the nature of the threat or assault?
2. How serious was the threatened conduct?
3. What is the behavior and emotion of the employee as he or she talks to you? Is the employee accepting personal responsibility for the threat or act and is this person able to describe a peaceful outcome?

4. What do you know about risk factors? Is the employee a male, age 15–30, who has been threatening or violent in the past, or who has a history of drug or alcohol abuse?

A decision must be made whether an employee can return to work, or if a psychiatric fitness-for-duty evaluation is needed. If the employee is cooperative and not out of control, talking can sometimes reduce the crisis. It helps to remind people that they really do not want to lose control of themselves and that help is available. At the same time, it is often wise to have security or another employee present as a precaution, and to reassure the employee that loss of control will not be permitted. When psychiatric evaluation is required, the employee should be escorted from work.

The evaluation might lead to hospitalization, treatment with psychiatric medications, or psychotherapy to help resolve the crisis and to ensure acceptable behavior on the job. When the treating psychiatrist feels an employee has gained control over his behavior, he will be released for return to work. The company should receive a fitness-for-duty report from either the treating psychiatrist or from the company's consultant. Follow-up communications between the company and the psychiatrist will help ensure continued participation in needed treatment (see Chapter 3), will help reassure the company about the employee's stability, and will allow the company to integrate the employee back into the workplace without undue safety risks.

SUBSTANCE ABUSE EMERGENCIES

Drug and alcohol abuse are devastating problems (see Chapters 15 and 16). On-the-job intoxication or drug withdrawal is often an emergency situation.

Case Study 7: Alcohol Withdrawal

Chuck Derossi, a 53-year-old married male and bank senior vice-president, had gone through an alcohol treatment program 3½ years ago. He said that he was then able to stop drinking alcohol. Now, though, he was not handling stress well and he had trouble concentrating at work. He rambled, had temper tantrums, and lacked attention to detail. He appeared to have blackouts, since he could not recall recent conversations. Confronted by the president of the bank, Chuck admitted to drinking and said he would stop. He did stop, but without any medical or psychiatric assistance. Two days later while at work he developed nausea, vomiting, profuse sweating, and severe abdominal pain. Paramedics rushed him to the emergency room where he was found to be in alcoholic withdrawal. He was admitted to the hospital under psychiatric care and three days later he was transferred to an evening alcohol treatment program. Six months later Chuck said that he would be dead if it were not for the bank president's intervention and for subsequent alcoholism treatment.

Case Study 8: Belligerent Intoxication

Doug Drover, a 44-year-old married male manufacturing company supervisor, was known to spend extended lunch hours at a local bar. After lunch he usually smelled of breath mints. It was well known within the production area that he would then be more belligerent. One day he became verbally and physically abusive while reviewing problems with a finished product. In addition to swearing at several employees, he began throwing equipment. The personnel manager met with a consultant for advice about how to handle Doug and then referred him for help. A meeting with Doug and his wife revealed a long history of alcohol abuse, including the consequent loss of a job 10 years before, an automobile accident while drunk, and a citation for driving under the influence. Doug agreed he had an alcohol problem and he entered an outpatient treatment program. Afterward, though, he refused to attend AA meetings and he only agreed to not drink during working hours. A 1-year follow-up showed that Doug had an improved job performance, was no longer belligerent, but was presumably still drinking alcohol.

Causes

Alcohol and drug abusers often have limited control over the timing of their habits. As a result, they may be acutely intoxicated at work or they may find themselves in withdrawal. Alcoholism then becomes a workplace crisis.

Effects

The effects of substance abuse in the workplace range from chronic to acute. Many substance-abusing employees seem to have a series of isolated incidents that are not emergencies and are not recognized as a real problem by co-workers. As an addiction progresses, employees and supervisors will often deny the seriousness of the problem. Workers may be afraid to speak up, unsure if management will support them and fearing reprisals from addicted employees. This can be especially problematic when drug-abusing employees are involved in drug sales, or are otherwise enmeshed in the drug culture. Employees must be assured that any comments given by them will be treated confidentially and with discretion.

Co-workers will make excuses or cover for an impaired employee. Supervisors will accept poor or erratic performance, delegate work assignments to co-workers, take on tasks themselves, and ultimately become frustrated and angry. After supervisors express their anger, the addict's job performance may improve temporarily, but only to then deteriorate further. Later, the addicted employee may suddenly show serious misjudgment, outrageous behavior, acute illness, or may incur serious accidents. Co-workers will become alarmed or fearful, especially in safety-sensitive areas. Ultimately morale deteriorates and the company is viewed as unwilling or unable to deal with the problem until an emergency arises. These events are clinical emergencies that can have major disruptive effects on the organization.

Prevention Intervention

Many companies anticipate drug and alcohol problems and make plans to deal with these problems as they occur. The preventive elements of a drug-free workplace include policy development, drug testing, education for employees, training for supervisors for workplace interventions, and treatment (see Chapters 15 and 16 for more detail).

When an employee is obviously intoxicated, action must be taken immediately. If the employee is belligerent, security or the local police may be needed to keep control of the situation (see earlier discussion of aggressive behavior). Intoxication will severely impair the capacity for rational discussion.

If an employee is mentally or physically impaired, it may be necessary to escort the employee away from the workplace. Decisions must be made about whether the employee should be escorted home, sent to the medical department, referred to an outside physician, required to take a drug test, scheduled to see an employee assistance counselor, or scheduled for a psychiatric fitness-for-duty exam. An employee who is having difficulty breathing or who is unresponsive may have overdosed on drugs or alcohol. Paramedics should be called and the employee should be brought to a hospital as quickly as possible.

SUICIDE EMERGENCIES

Depression, anxiety disorders, and substance abuse are suicide risk factors that are common in the workplace. The National Institute of Mental Health estimates that in any 6-month time period at least 6 percent of the U.S. adult population suffers from a diagnosable depression. Suicidal threats, gestures, and actions are commonplace in our society.

Case Study 9: Suicide—Co-Worker Effects

An employee jumped from the roof of his office building. Denise Harimoto, a co-worker with a longstanding depression, was the first person on the scene. Denise was flooded with emotions, felt angry and victimized by the event, and began talking about suicide. She was immediately taken to the medical department, assessed by a nurse, and referred to a psychiatrist. After one crisis intervention session, she no longer felt victimized and she no longer felt suicidal. Denise's longstanding depression fully resolved after a 4-month period of treatment with supportive psychotherapy and fluoxetine 20 mg (an antidepressant) taken daily.

Case Study 10: Suicide—Co-Worker Intervention Strategies

Laura Mendoza, a female machinist who was an excellent employee, committed suicide. Prior to the suicide, she had shot herself in the foot, reportedly while cleaning a gun at home. Laura also had three industrial accidents in a 1-month period, two of them on the same day. Several times, she told co-workers that it was very difficult for her to "go on." No one had ever directed her to the medical department or to a qualified professional.

Following the suicide, two support groups were held for co-workers. Some of these employees were not surprised when they learned of her suicide, but felt guilty and responsible for its occurrence. Some were angry at her for abandoning her husband and children. Others spoke of how Laura's death triggered thoughts of vulnerability and traumatic events in their own lives. Employees talked about previous social events and conversations with the deceased. One supervisor said how he remembered her fondly for her diligent work on an important project. Laura left a close friend a note saying, "I am sorry, but I can't go on anymore." Employees in her work group reported that they were not functioning well on the job since the suicide. After the support meetings, there was a large employee turnout for the funeral and many offers to help the bereaved family. The company nurse made a visit to the family afterward and encouraged the husband to seek family therapy.

Case Study 11: Provocative Suicidal Gestures

Stella Groban, a 29-year-old computer technician, had been an average worker for 4 years. She was moody, had poor interpersonal skills, and often talked about suicide. Sometimes she would show co-workers the razor in her pocketbook and then complain that nobody understands her. Twice she was on medical leave, returning once with scars on her wrists and the other time with vague comments about "taking too many pills." Her co-workers had always found Stella difficult to deal with and many had transferred to other work areas. Those who remained found themselves feeling constantly on guard, angry, and frightened whenever she was around. Morale and productivity were low.

This time, Stella had been loudly unhappy for 2 months, with uncontrollable crying, anger toward co-workers, and poor-quality work. Her co-workers stayed away from her, which made her feel less happy still. One day, she left her razor on her desktop, put her head down, cried openly, and threatened to kill herself when co-workers did try to help. At the supervisor's insistence, she was referred for immediate psychiatric evaluation. The consultant noted symptoms of acute major depression, chronic atypical depression, and borderline personality disorder. After 3 weeks of fluoxetine 20 mg (an antidepressant medication) taken daily and supportive psychotherapy, she returned to work. Though her severe depressive symptoms had subsided, her chaotic and angry interpersonal style was at first unchanged. Weekly psychoanalytic psychotherapy, with continuing medication, brought about gradual change. Stella was later able to apologize to co-workers for her anger and she gradually felt more accepted at work.

Causes

Risk factors for suicide include:

Direct verbal suicide threats
Suicide plans
Previous suicide attempts
Comments and behavior suggesting hopelessness or suicidal thoughts
Family history of suicide
Demographics—male, unmarried, unemployed, living alone
Loss of a relationship—widowed, separated, divorced, bereaved
Acute intoxication
Psychiatric illness—panic disorder, depression, psychosis, substance abuse,
    severe personality disorders
Physical illness

Suicidal behavior usually results from the interplay of life stresses and predisposing psychiatric problems. Events at work can be among those stresses but are not likely to provoke suicide attempts by themselves. Major organizational changes, such as rapid growth, mergers, and reductions in force, cause a loss of control, uncertainty, and emotional distress for involved employees (see Chapters 7 and 8). These may all contribute to depression, anxiety, and thus suicide risk. Critical, unresponsive, or distressed managers will further increase employees' distress.

Effects

The suicide of an employee leaves an emotional aftermath that should not be underestimated. Co-workers may feel grief, anger, and fear. They may feel guilty about the suicide and fearful for their own well-being. The effects on morale can be devastating. These effects are worsened still when the organizational culture does not allow recognition of the emotions, and their disruptive potential.

Prevention and Intervention

Before a manager or co-worker can recognize and help an employee at risk for suicide, he or she must first understand something about the nature of depression and anxiety symptoms, and their workplace manifestations. Employees must know where to turn; supervisors must know how to talk to a distressed or dysfunctional employee.

Every company should identify sources of support for crisis or time of need. The human resource, medical, security, and training departments may all be sources of support, as well as psychiatric consultants and employee assistance plans.

Key staff should be taught the symptoms of depression and how depression may manifest on the job. They must also be taught how to talk with employees exhibiting job performance problems and how to steer them to an appropriate resource where a thorough psychiatric assessment can be completed. It is not adequate to simply tell employees to seek help or to refer them to their family doctor (see Chapters 1 and 12). The chance that an employee would follow through on that kind of a referral is slight. Employees with an emotional problem should be seen by a psychiatric consultant for accurate diagnosis and effective treatment.

Finally, when an employee commits suicide, group meetings should be led by mental health professionals who understand suicide, diagnosis, and group process. This will allow employees to talk about the suicide, express their grief, support each other, and discuss how to appropriately help the surviving family. This supportive group process will help employees put the event behind them more quickly and reassuringly.

PSYCHOTIC BEHAVIOR

Occasionally an employee will make little sense or will appear to have lost contact with reality (see Chapter 17). This is clearly a psychiatric emergency. Possible causes include psychosis (of various kinds), medical illness, and substance abuse. Common symptoms of psychotic employees include incoherent speech or thought, grossly inappropriate emotions, paranoia (markedly unreasonable and unbending distrust), delusions (false beliefs maintained in the face of reason), and hallucinations (usually false voices).

Case Study 12: Schizophrenia

Louis Spakos, a 28-year-old single male aircraft assembler, had worked at his company for 7 years. He had been an average employee until he began showing strange behavior. For several months, he was verbally aggressive and stared into space. He was paranoid, feeling that people at work and home were following him.

Louis began talking about being Jesus Christ and commented to a co-worker that he might kill his supervisor. He was taken to the medical department and referred for emergency psychiatric hospitalization. He responded well to a short inpatient stay and thiothixene (an antipsychotic medication). Back at work, Louis was somewhat withdrawn but otherwise back to his old self.

Case Study 13: Bipolar Illness

Molly Brooks, a 35-year-old married airline stewardess, developed a higher level of energy at work and tremendous enthusiasm for her company. She went to one of the company's directors to give him some ideas for promoting the airline. Consequently, she was offered a job in the marketing department. On her last flight before her transfer she was inappropriately cheerful and sexually seductive, making passes at male passengers. While serving dessert, she shot whipped cream throughout the airplane. After the flight, Molly was grounded and referred for a psychiatric evaluation. She was euphoric, grandiose, and easily agitated. She said she had been talking to God and also that she had been drinking more alcohol than usual. She was diagnosed as having bipolar (manic depressive) illness, hospitalized, and treated with lithium 1200 mg (an antimanic medication) taken daily to normalize her mood and thought process. Molly successfully returned to work in the marketing department.

Case Study 14: Drug Dependencies

Pat Scranton, a 41-year-old married woman, complained of hearing music through the air-conditioning vents. Although her manager could not hear the music, he had the vent boarded up to block the sound. She continued to complain of music and was ultimately referred to a psychiatrist. Pat admitted to the psychiatrist that she was smoking crack cocaine every day. The cocaine was causing an auditory hallucination that went away when she stopped smoking. This psychiatric emergency was not initially recognized, but it was fortunately addressed before the psychosis worsened.

Case Study 15: Alcoholic Decompensation

Morse McCarron, a 55-year-old separated senior executive for a defense contractor, was sent to a management training program for 1 week. During the group sessions Morse was frequently unintelligible. He had a grandiose mood and felt that he was Jesus Christ. He was drinking six to ten martinis each evening during the conference. When he returned to work he was seen in consultation and was immediately hospitalized. He was gradually withdrawn from alcohol, at which point his mood stabilized and his delusions went away. Morse returned to work, stayed sober, and decided to try to reconcile with his wife.

Causes

There are many causes of psychotic behavior. The most common include schizophrenia, mania, depression, alcohol, cocaine, amphetamines, hallucinogens, prescription drug side effects, and medical illness. Although workplace stress might indirectly worsen a psychotic illness, psychosis is not generally work related. Too often, though, psychotic behavior is overlooked until there is a crisis.

Effects

When employees become psychotic they disrupt the workplace and may pose a threat of injury. Reactions of co-workers vary a great deal. They may be verbal in their concern or may simply withdraw from the affected employee. Most will be frightened or distressed. Some will not want to work or associate with psychotic employees. Other co-workers will take pity and try to help. Many will simply deny the significance of the situation and hope the problem will correct itself in time.

Prevention and Intervention

It is essential for employers to react quickly when emergencies of this nature occur. The internal and external resources must be mobilized immediately. When there is a risk of violence, security should be called. The employee with a psychotic disorder should be escorted from the workplace to an appropriate medical facility for an immediate psychiatric evaluation. There is a high likelihood that this employee will need hospitalization and treatment with psychiatric medications.

When the employee is stabilized and ready to return to work, a fitness-for-duty exam should be performed. This will give valuable information to the company about the nature of the problem and the employee's current level of functioning. When the employee is released to work, a return-to-work meeting should specify job expectations and what the employee's responsibilities are for continued psychiatric treatment (see Chapter 3). These might include medications, psychotherapy, and support groups. Side effects of prescribed medication should be specified. A release of information should be signed for the psychiatrist to contact the employer if the employee is noncompliant with treatment or if there is a change in the employee's clinical condition. All of this information should be summarized in a return-to-work agreement. Employees who have suffered a psychotic episode will be reassured that they will be helped to stay in control. Managers and supervisors must be given help to create a working environment that maximizes perceptions of support and stability.

AIDS

It is estimated that over 1.5 million Americans have an HIV (human immunodeficiency virus) infection and are at high risk for developing AIDS. Most of them are between the ages of 20 and 39 and are productive members of society. It is imperative that businesses prepare to deal with AIDS-afflicted employees and co-worker response. Co-workers may be afraid to work in close proximity, use the same toilet, eat in the same cafeteria, or drink from the same water fountain.

Case Study 16: AIDS-Related Harassment

Rodrigo Johnson, a 30-year-old married hemophiliac man, was a civil service agency safety director when he was diagnosed with transfusion-related AIDS. He developed some symptoms, including weight loss and lack of energy, and he was missing work regularly. At this point he began to receive harassment on the job. Rodrigo was asked to change from safety director to night supervisor. Then he was criticized for his work performance and was told that even as a supervisor he would have to start doing strenuous physical labor. Harassment continued until Rodrigo became too ill to work.

Case Study 17: AIDS-Related Company Closure

Gabe Hansen, a 38-year-old gay construction company owner, knew that he was HIV positive. He became tired, suffered a loss of memory, had blackouts, and had a significant weight loss. Trying to address the situation, Gabe told one senior employee that he was HIV positive and was having mild AIDS symptoms. He asked the employee to start assuming some additional managerial duties. Word spread, morale fell, anxiety rose, and several employees left the company. Since the situation had become emotionally uncomfortable and financially tenuous, Gabe closed the company.

Causes and Effects

AIDS is caused by the human immunodeficiency virus (HIV). HIV may be transmitted from one person to another via specific body fluids, including blood, semen, and vaginal fluids. HIV may be transmitted during intercourse, by either HIV-contaminated syringes or sharp objects that puncture the skin, and when HIV-infected blood is transferred to another person. There are several reasons why AIDS can evoke strong emotional reactions. It is a lingering yet fatal illness. Even though workplace contact poses very little risk, AIDS is recognized as a communicable disease. And AIDS is associated with issues of sexuality.

Due to medical advances, patients with AIDS are living longer and most want to keep their job. AIDS patients in the workplace have raised new concerns for employers, including strong reactions by co-workers and the need to accommodate ill or partially disabled employees. The high cost of AIDS treatment and consequent insurance coverage issues affect high-risk industries, such as those that hire a large percentage of gay men, and affected small companies. The real medical and financial concerns are amplified by the emotions attached to AIDS and its risk factors. When employees begin to exhibit symptoms of AIDS, employers may try to ignore or conceal the problem or may even encourage the employee to quit. AIDS concerns can explode into an emotional crisis regardless of the actual circumstances in a particular case.

Prevention and Intervention

Organizations should try to prevent the overreaction of employees when a co-worker is suspected of having AIDS. This can best be done by education. Managers should be given training programs that address their fears about AIDS before they are confronted with an HIV-infected employee. Employee education programs should address prevention of AIDS and the fact that there is no risk of contracting HIV in the workplace by casual contact.

It is wise for companies to develop a life-threatening illness policy that will cover all life-threatening illnesses, such as cancer, heart disease, and AIDS. This policy would state how companies make reasonable accommodations for those employees with physical disabilities. With AIDS this has come to mean a flexible work schedule, increased time off for medical appointments, and maintaining confidentiality of the diagnosis.

Training programs should be offered to supervisors and managers before employees contact AIDS. Then management will be able to deal effectively with cases as they arise in the future, both supporting the infected worker and calming the co-workers who may overreact.

SUMMARY

Emotional crises are becoming more commonplace in the workplace and organizations need to be prepared to deal with these situations when they occur. Organizations should first think about how they might inadvertently cause or contribute to emotional crises. Policies and procedures should be developed to guide organizations, utilize internal and external resources, and maintain awareness of policies and procedures. Planning will ensure that employees are promptly directed to needed professional help and that disruption in the workplace is minimized.

Bibliography
Aisner, James. June 1990. Trouble at the top: Senior executives in crisis. *Harvard Business School Bulletin* **66**(3):28-34.
Beckett, Joyce O. 1988. Plant closings: How older workers are affected. *Social Work* **33** (Jan.-Feb.):29-33.
Blanchard, Robert J., and D. Caroline Blanchard (eds.). 1986. *Advances in the Study of Aggression*. San Diego: Harcourt Brace Jovanovich.
Engel, Frema. 1987. Violence, crime, and trauma at work. *EAP Digest* **7**(5):29-33.
Figley, Charles R. (ed.). 1985. *Trauma and Its Wake*. New York: Brunner/Mazel.
Hinton, John W. (ed.). 1983. *Dangerousness: Problems of Assessment and Prediction*. London: George Allen & Unwin.
Hirschfeld, Robert, and Lucy Davidson. 1988. Clinical risk factors for suicide. *Psychiatric Annals* **18**(11):628-635.
Leana, Carrie R., and Daniel C. Feldman. 1988. Layoffs: How employees and companies cope. *Personnel Journal* **67**(Sept.):31-34.
Maltsberger, John T. 1986. *Suicide Risk: The Formulation of Clinical Judgment*. New York: New York University Press.
Monahan, John. 1981. *Predicting Violent Behavior*. Beverly Hills: Sage Publications.
National Institute of Mental Health. 1991. *What to Do When an Employee Is Depressed: A Guide for Supervisors*. Washington, D.C.: U.S. Department of Health and Human Services.
Utterback, Jim, and Jay Caldwell. 1989. Proactive and reactive approaches to PTSD in the aftermath of campus violence: Forming a traumatic stress react team. *Journal of Traumatic Stress* **2**(2):171-183.
Yandrick, Rudy M. 1988. Management of violent behavior. Collected articles from *Hospital and Community Psychiatry* **39**:1-62.
Yandrick, Rudy M. 1990. Critical incidents. *EAPA Exchange* **20**(1):18-23.
Yandrick, Rudy M. 1990. *Managing AIDS in the Workplace: An Executive Briefing*. Sponsored by California Council on Partnerships & California AIDS Leadership Committee, pp. 1-46.

11

Organizational Consequences of Family Problems

David E. Morrison, M.D., and David A. Deacon, M.B.A.

Introduction
Literature Review
Cases and Discussion
    Loss of Family Support
    Family Needs Interfering at Work
    The Workplace as a Substitute for Unmet Family Needs
    Motivation to Work Is Family Driven
Interventions
Summary

ABSTRACT

An unfortunate aspect of these exciting times is the increase in personal emotional problems. They beset everyone and the frequency of maladaptive responses to family problems keeps increasing. The adverse effects of work problems on family life are commonly discussed. But the equally common effects of family problems on the workplace are not always so carefully considered. Divorce, serious family illness, and the complexities of dual-career marriages are but a few examples. These and other common problems can have subtle and insidious workplace effects. More often than not, the relationship between family problems and workplace effects is altogether hidden to employers, employees, and families. As family problems increase and workplace change becomes a constant, effective attention to the workplace effects of family problems becomes ever more important. Sensitivity to these issues offers benefits for productivity, profitability, and employee mental health. Systematic review of common family problems (see Table 11-1) offers a framework for understanding organizational consequences.

INTRODUCTION

This chapter is about the impact in the workplace of problems that originate in the family. Business and mental health professionals hear and talk a lot about bringing work problems home from the office. For example, think about exhausted employees with no energy left over for the kids or, worse yet, employees who spend so much time at work or on the road that they hardly see their children at all. But this chapter looks at problems moving in the opposite direction, from the family to the workplace. Family problems can have adverse effects on productivity and morale, or trigger behavior that puts the organization at risk. Table 11-1 outlines four general categories of family problems and their many corresponding consequences.

Why is so much more heard about work's impact on the family than the family's impact on work? Part of the answer resides in a view that the work ethic of the industrial world has changed some functions of the family. Under this view, people are valued in terms of what they can add to the GNP (gross national product) as part of the work force, rather than for their functioning as mothers or fathers. A family (like a school) is thus evaluated for its ability to contribute to the nation's economy. Thus the family is where one gets ready to go to work.

One of the implicit functions of the family becomes rejuvenation of the individuals, so that they can give their all back at the office or shop. Family is then merely a setting where members can play out (both consciously and unconsciously) all of their problems—personal, family, or workplace—and all without getting in trouble with the boss. This is an expanded version of the "kicking the dog" syndrome, where the family becomes the frustration safety valve so that things do not explode at work.

Yet, if that was all there was to it, one would think there would be more research and clinical data about families' impact on work. In fact, there are other reasons why data have been limited. Companies do not measure people costs as much in depth as they measure other expenses. Costs of personal malfunction, if measured, are less likely to be broken down into malfunctions caused by family problems. Even such obvious problems as running dual-career families and geographical transfers are examined only superficially in the literature. Among social scientists, psychiatrists, and other therapists who consider family problems, it is generally more acceptable to discuss work effects on families than family effects on work. So both companies and clinicians tend to look at only part of the problem. But except for the most obvious cases, the problems stay hidden until they are looked for carefully.

Work is the arena of discipline, performance, and accountability. People need those experiences. And they get paid for what they do at work. Hence they are obliged to put out effort to keep personal problems from getting in

TABLE 11-1   **Family Problems: The More Subtle Organizational Consequences**

Loss of Family Support
    Depleted emotional energy
    Emotional unavailability for important interpersonal relationships
    Less capacity for ambiguity/more need for structure
    Narrower focus of attention
    Impaired judgment
    Acting out of anger
    Cognitive preoccupation
    Susceptibility to accidents
    Active or passive resistance to change
    De-skilling: loss of competence

Family Needs Interfering at Work
    Confusion among colleagues about changed attitudes to work
    Changes in what the workplace can expect from the impacted employee
    Employee resists changes that could impact the family
    Employee does not fulfill potential or sabotages own advancement
    Employee's work is undermined by family member's behavior
    Inappropriately risky or risk-averse behavior
    Exclusive focus on career advancement versus developing competence
    Vulnerability to burnout
    Ambivalence over employer values
    Deflated commitment
    Lack of self-confidence
    Grandiosity

Workplace as a Substitute for Unmet Family Needs
    Demands of work subverted by personal needs
    Feelings of guilt or shame over behavior
    Damaged self-esteem spills over to workplace
    Eventual loss of employee

Motivation to Work Is Family Driven
    Discord with colleagues
    Flimsy commitment
    Potential unfulfilled

the way of productivity. If not, they affect people beyond just their family. Others are counting on them to live up to their employment obligations. The others include not only fellow workers but also customers who buy the employer's goods and services, and the stakeholders (shareholders, creditors, taxpayers, etc.) who invest. "We should leave family problems at home" may be unrealistic when enforced in the extreme, but it is not the same as callous indifference to people.

Most of the time, families do a rather good job of supporting individuals so that they can competently meet their workplace obligations. Still, families can sometimes be distracting, distressing, or even pathogenic, and thus problems are created for work. Try as they might, people cannot always leave their family problems behind when they punch in every morning. Employees depressed about a poor marriage cannot come into work and say, "For now, I won't be depressed" (even though the diversion of work might brighten their spirit). Employees boiling over in anger after discovering a spouse's affair will certainly have moments of distraction, and diminished clarity of thought and expression. Most of the ways that family problems invade the workplace are more subtle than the above examples suggest. In fact, they are often altogether unconscious to employer, employee, and family alike. Everyone may know something is wrong, but the why's remain elusive.

Furthermore, it may be very difficult for people at work to discover the underlying problem. For example, consider an executive whose superiors are concerned that he has become aloof, risk averse, overcontrolling, and too concerned with form at the expense of substance. Nothing in the workplace or his career path offers any explanation. Nor has there been any apparent change in his personal life. Only in clinical consultation is it discovered that a daughter's 4-year history of juvenile diabetes has taxed his psyche and finances. He fears that if people at work knew about his sadness, they would see him as weak and would diminish his responsibilities. Moreover, the daughter's illness has also resurrected unconscious fears linked to his own mother's lengthy disability during his childhood. Referred by his company, he does open up in a confidential psychiatric consultation that looks at personal problems affecting his work. Because of his determination to keep co-workers in the dark, people at work have no way of knowing his distress. In fact, even he was unaware of the emotional links to his own childhood.

LITERATURE REVIEW

Interesting material on the organizational consequences of family problems can be found in both the popular and academic literature. The *Canadian Business Review* notes the now longstanding trend for women to want or need work, and also the growing trend among men to take a larger role in the family (MacBride-King and Paris 1989). The general point is that worker expectations vis-à-vis total life-style are changing, with potential effects on both family and workplace.

Preliminary data from a survey of Canadian employees by the Conference Board of Canada (cited in MacBride-King and Paris 1989) indicate that 66 percent of the survey sample experienced at least some difficulty in balancing the demands of work and home, with 20 percent reporting that balancing these demands was "very difficult" or "difficult." Also, nearly 80 percent of the respondents reported some level of stress or anxiety over the balance issue, with more than 25 percent indicating "a lot" or a "moderate degree." And specifically for work consequences, over 50 percent reported experiencing problems caused by absenteeism from colleagues' family responsibilities. Ten percent said they had left a position because of work/family conflicts, and 14 percent said they were considering leaving for such reasons. Just over 30 percent said that child or other dependent care responsibilities had limited their opportunities for advancement, which is a loss to the company as well as the individual.

In an article on the "Daddy Track," a more "family-sensitive" career track for fathers, *Industry Week* reported on a Robert Half International survey (McKenna 1990). Seventy-eight percent of the male and female respondents indicated that, given a choice, they would choose a slower career track with more flexible hours and more family time. *Industry Week* also cited a study done at AT&T. Seventy-three percent of men and 77 percent of women with children under 18 reported they had dealt with family issues while at work, with 25 percent of men and 48 percent of women reporting unproductive time at work because of child care issues in particular. In a companion piece in the same issue, *Industry Week's* editor argued: "We need all the good people we can find, so we'd better find out what the best and brightest can do, let 'em do it when they can do it, and get out of the way. About all that this 'track' foolishness will do is distract quality employees, and send them down another track—to some other organization that's smart enough to understand how the world of work is changing."

Much of the academic research literature focuses on the family consequences of work problems, rather than the organizational consequences of family problems. However, the attention given to the latter seems to be increasing. Kelly and Voydanoff (1985) consider the special problems of the female single-parent earner and her high level of job tension. They point out that these women sometimes have the burden of being the sole earner for their family, and they tend to be concentrated in the low-paying sectors of the market. And, they often join or rejoin the labor force under such unfavorable circumstances as separation, desertion, or death of a spouse. The higher job tension they experience can lead to decreased well-being of both parent and children. On the other hand, Burden (1986) found that single parents showed high levels of job satisfaction and no differences in absenteeism or other negative performance factors relative to other groups, despite being at risk for high job/family role strain.

Black and Stephens (1989) looked at American expatriates assigned to Pacific Rim locations, and the influence of the spouses on their adjustment and intent to stick with their assignments. They found that a spouse's favorable opinion about an overseas assignment is positively related to the spouse's adjustment, and the novelty of the foreign culture is negatively related to the spouse's adjustment. Furthermore, the adjustment of the spouse is positively related to that of the employee, and the adjustment of the spouse and of the employee are positively related to the intent of the employee to stay in the assignment. Though these results are not surprising, Black and Stephens point out that most employers consider the spouse to be an irrelevant factor in considering assignments. The authors recommend soliciting the opinion of the spouse, and providing training on living in the new culture to both spouse and employee. It would seem that the kind of thinking that Black and Stephens recommend for expatriate assignments could also be applied to domestic transfers and even other job changes such as promotions, where there can be a significant family impact working to the ultimate disadvantage of the company.

Morrison (1976) described the problems of emotional spillover between work and family, and of excessive separation between work, family, and self for city managers. Evans and Bartolome (1986) considered five different relationships between work and nonwork spheres. Though different from the framework used by this chapter (illustrated in Table 11-1), these relationships help illustrate a broad perspective on the important issues. Their five relationships are:

Spillover: Family satisfaction or dissatisfaction can impact work satisfaction or dissatisfaction, and vice versa.
Independence: The spheres of family and work are basically independent.
Conflict: Work and family are in conflict. For example, a happy home life requires sacrifices with respect to career advancement.
Instrumentality: One sphere is primarily a means by which to obtain something in the other sphere.
Compensation: One sphere compensates for the other. For example, work accomplishment can be a substitute for dissatisfaction at home.

Although Evans and Bartolome caution that there is no definitive way to describe the relationships between work and family life, their five relationships help provide a structure for understanding the various ways in which family issues have positive and negative effects on work. Burke (1986) agrees with the need to refine paradigms, and notes that empirical studies that get at the importance of nonwork factors as they affect work are limited. His comprehensive frame of reference for future research (Table 11-2) includes both objective and subjective measures of family considerations and workplace effects.

The cases in this chapter reflect some of the principles raised in the literature. They also go beyond the more superficial analyses underlying issues found particularly in the popular literature. The reader can use Burke's

TABLE 11-2　Family Impacts on Work

	Critical Factors in Family (Independent Variables)	Outcome Measures at Work (Dependent Variables)
OBJECTIVE	Financial need Wife's career position Social background and class Number of children/dependents Recency of critical events 　(e.g., death in family, 　divorce, separation) Quality of neighborhood Existence of child care facilities Ethnic background and traditions Family connections—social Type of marriage/family Stage in family life cycle	Absenteeism Number of rejections of 　promotion, transfer Level in hierarchy Performance and potential 　ratings
SUBJECTIVE	Degree of marital 　harmony/satisfaction Wife's career aspirations Degree of complementarity or 　conflict in couple's 　expectations, values, and 　commitment to the job Wife's personal beliefs and 　attitudes regarding work Family demands for time and 　energy Degree of social support Amount of emotional bonding 　and family adaptability 　(Olsen and McCubbin 1981) Family satisfaction with job Wife's adjustment to job 　location, transfers, 　promotion, etc.	Job satisfaction Job involvement Level of stress Work orientation Motivation Level of energy Performance Turnover intentions Willingness to travel, transfer Demands for/expectations of 　raises, promotions

Source: Burke (1986).

list to generate more examples. Cases below are organized into four main categories: loss of family support, family's needs interfering at work, the workplace as a substitute for unmet family needs, and motivation to work being family driven.

CASES AND DISCUSSION

The purpose of the following vignettes is to highlight some of the more common ways that work is impacted by family problems. Family and individual dynamics will not be discussed here, but rather the movement of family problems to work. The cases apply equally to men and women.

Loss of Family Support

Case Study 1: Loss of Family Support Due to Divorce

Jim Williams went through a very painful divorce. His ex-wife demanded more and more as the proceedings went on, and she succeeded in cutting Jim off from his children. He felt financially strapped, lonely, and betrayed. Meanwhile, Jim took a new job with a different employer. Alone, he moved to a new and unfamiliar town. He needed the new job to go well in order to get financially back on his feet and to renew his self-confidence. He started to get aggressive and impulsive. Eighteen months into the new job, Jim's boss confronted him with complaints from his peers that he was too pushy, self-interested, and defensive. His style was interfering with the teamwork that was necessary for his company to compete in a demanding new market.

Jim's divorce proceedings had left him emotionally and financially drained. Moving to a new job and a new town meant he left most of his support behind. The family is one of the most important support structures people take with them in a move. Jim's personal upheaval left him unprepared to tackle a critical challenge of any new job: building interpersonal relationships with colleagues at work. But perhaps the most important problem was that lack of support coupled with emotional depletion narrowed his focus. He was usually keenly attuned to relationship issues. One of his strengths in the past had been understanding the impact of his personality on other people. Now he was so preoccupied with his own need to get his life in order that the only relationships he could competently address at work were those with his own subordinates.

Everyone knows that divorce has effects on people that can show up in the workplace. Almost everyone can point to examples from their own experiences. But people face differing circumstances and react differently even to similar circumstances. Jim's divorce left him devoid of emotional resources to make adequate investments in his peers. He had to give of himself to get things off on the right foot, but he had little left to give.

Case Study 2: Loss of Support Due to Divorce

Steve Johnson, a first-line supervisor in a manufacturing company, had problems getting along with several supervisors 2 years ago. He profitably used professional consultation services provided by the company and he completely repaired the relationships. Six months ago, his manager said that he had made a "turnaround." His improvement was so great that he was asked to serve on a management/union committee that included some senior managers.

Last month, Steve's wife divorced him against his wishes. He became depressed and then he appeared inebriated at an important meeting of the management/union committee. In the middle of a discussion, and with a company attorney present, he made a lewd remark to a woman on the union team. In retrospect, people realized they had seen some evidence of probable excessive drinking in the previous several months.

Steve's circumstances and problems are different than Jim's. Steve is more stressed than depleted from his divorce, and the added stress from mixing with his seniors was enough to critically impair his judgment. His anger at his wife was acted out at work. The act was so obviously self-destructive that it also served as an expression of his guilt. He humiliated himself and was fired.

The unfortunate thing about Steve's case is that he was a good investment, a good bet, for his company. He had shown the willingness and ability to work on his problems and to change. One wonders if the earlier personal changes he had made to repair relationships with his supervisors did not also change the equilibrium in his marriage. There had not been a problem in his marriage before then. Steve's work affected his marriage, which then affected his work. Had the company been quicker in picking up the new signs of work and family problems, it might have saved a developing manager.

Case Study 3: Loss of Family Support Due to Illness of Family Member

Dick and Molly Black have always been mutually supportive. Recently, however, Molly became seriously ill, and the emotional support has been moving primarily in one direction. Dick, a semiskilled worker, has been preoccupied at work, and has suffered two minor injuries in 2 weeks.

Dick is worried about Molly and is not concentrating well on the job, even when he tries. His many concerns include financial resources; not showing his concern to Molly, the kids, or other family members; and what will happen to Molly. In addition to his worries, he has lost his most important source of emotional sustenance while having to put out more himself. Accidents have been well documented as an unconscious way to get out of an untenable situation (Group for the Advancement of Psychiatry 1977).

Case Study 4: Family Anger Directed at Work

Laurie Janison used to be able to use Pete as a sounding board for problems at work and he would help her put things in perspective. Pete liked her company and the people in it. He was one of those loyal spouses that companies want. However, recently Pete has become angry at his wife's company as it laid off people for the first time ever. Because of the tight economy, the company became leaner and demanded more time of its managers. Laurie has spent more and more time at work and company politics have become more intense.

Now when Laurie goes to Pete to complain, he jumps in to criticize the company with a vengeance. Laurie ends up defending her organization, which is the last thing she really wants to do. Instead of venting her anger with Pete like she used to, Laurie now plays it out in the workplace in the form of passive resistance to organizational change.

This situation is a more subtle form of loss of support. Pete is not aware of the impact his anger is having on his wife. He has cut her off from the one safe place she has to vent her frustrations. Laurie is not hostile toward her company—she just needs help with all of her feelings about the tough changes at work. She expresses less of her feelings at work because she feels vulnerable in the new, more risky environment. Laurie does not realize she is becoming passively resistant at work. Her colleagues know it all too well, but they have no idea it has anything to do with Pete.

Families are part of the organizational culture. They will support or undermine important cultural changes, because those changes modify the identities of the employees and family members who care about the organization. If they cannot understand why the organization made the changes, they feel betrayed. If the families are not supported at times of significant change, they will be less supportive of the employees doing the work of the organization.

Case Study 5: Loss of Direct Work-Related Family Support

Betty Stillman is a skilled technician in a professional organization who has never been much of a people person. She has always been able to rely on her husband Bill for counsel on people issues, which has kept her out of hot water. Bill's mother died recently and his own job is not going that well. He complains that he doesn't have the energy anymore to invest in Betty's work problems.

Lately, Betty has become "more like herself" at work, insensitive to other people's needs, ignoring organizational procedures to get what she wants, and turning her requests into demands. She has a short fuse and impulsively confronts anyone who stands in her way, even senior management. Betty has started going around her boss, who is becoming fed up with Betty's impact on morale.

Sometimes the support an individual receives from the family is more than emotional. In Betty's case, Bill actually filled in a specific work vulnerability. When she lost Bill's counsel, her poor understanding and management of people issues rose to the surface. Betty needed more than the usual amount of emotional support anyway, and now she had no place to ventilate, put things in perspective, or learn alternative approaches to workplace problems. Thus the problems evoked still further needs for support and started a destructive spiral.

Family Needs Interfering at Work

Case Study 6: Children and Dual Careers

Joanne and Carl Jones are a dual-career couple. Joanne's not assuming the traditional housewife's role has caused some minor problems. For example, there were squabbles over who should do the dishes or take out the garbage. But they've been able to negotiate the division of labor at home to their mutual satisfaction, and there haven't been any issues that would affect work one way or another. However, their recent first child has complicated the issue considerably. Joanne is anxious for Carl to assume an equal level of responsibility for dropping the baby off at day care and picking her up at the end of the day. On the other hand, Carl would like to see Joanne be more of a traditional mother and hence make more of a sacrifice in her work. Until they are able to renegotiate these issues, they've decided to both pull back to 8-hour days and curtail travel as much as they can. Besides, they want to enjoy their new daughter for a while and they'll worry about the mess later. Their respective employers are surprised at their sudden reduction in overtime hours and their unwillingness to travel.

All those involved in this situation have not had time to adjust: peers, subordinates, and superiors alike. Joanne and Carl's previous behaviors have created a set of unspoken expectations among their colleagues about how they will behave in the future. These expectations are a structure for their colleagues and these co-workers depend on the psychological contracts that the expectations constitute. What Joanne and Carl have done is unilaterally broken these contracts as they renegotiate their own. Befuddlement and exasperation ensue on an emotional level even though everyone "understands" intellectually why Joanne and Carl have changed. People at work will have to adjust to the new reality in their colleagues' lives.

Joanne and Carl also need to appreciate their responsibilities to the other people at work. They must organize their time to accommodate the new baby and work. They need to let people at work know if and when they can be expected to carry a regular load again. People at work have their own families with needs. They have all the problems presented above and more. People do not just take away from work or the organization when they reduce their performance. Organizations are made up of people. When one person gives less to work, co-workers must spend less time and energy on their own family interests.

Case Study 7: Spouse's Resistance to Changes at Work

Change is rampant in Lisa Greenwell's company, and she is expected to evolve out of her technical functions into a broader, business development role. This will involve more socializing and traveling, as well as a deepening of her knowledge about more ambiguous topics like politics and economics. This opportunity is a promising one for Lisa.

The problem is with her husband, John, a technical expert in the same industry. He likes Lisa the way she is. He is concerned that Lisa will be exposed to more "successful" men. "Will she still be my partner?" he wonders. He also worries about changes in their historical patterns of taking care of the kids, preparing meals, and doing housework. He tends to highlight the downside of Lisa's opportunity, and it's safe to say she would have accepted more promotions and progressed more quickly had it not been for his negativity.

This case could be seen as just another anecdote describing a man threatened by a competent woman. But this problem occurs with both sexes. It is the problem of one member of a relationship growing beyond the other because of the opportunities offered at work. Certainly the psychological contracts between the couple are changing in terms of taking care of the kids and the house. The problem, however, is John's emotional needs, not just the administrative needs of house and child management. The more important issue is his feeling of loss of his relative competence and the attendant shame. He fears that Lisa's support for him will change. Furthermore, he loves her the way she is; what will she be like if she changes?

John does not talk about any of those reasons or his worry that he will not be good enough for her after all her changes. It is hard for anybody to discuss such things. He may not even be aware of these feelings. Instead he gets defensive about men and competent women while his fear and envy undermine Lisa's chances to be as successful as possible at work.

Case Study 8: Spouse as a Specific Work Problem

Gene White is a salesperson who transferred from Boston to Cincinnati 3 years ago to develop new markets. When they were given news of the transfer, he and his wife, Phyllis, had just closed on the purchase of their dream house in Boston. Phyllis was a Boston native who thought of the city as the sophisticated cultural center of the country. Although upset and angry, she reluctantly agreed to the move.

Phyllis has openly criticized Cincinnati and Gene's company in front of other employees and even customers. In the community where Gene is trying to develop relationships, she makes disparaging comments as she compares Cincinnati to Boston. Gene's boss has told him that Phyllis's behavior is a liability with customers and he should "figure out how to manage her." Gene is afraid to confront her. The one time he broached the subject there was a fight that took a week to get over. The matter was never resolved.

In this case, the problem is not just lack of emotional support but inappropriate behavior caused by a spouse's emotions. Some family members have unrealistic views about what work can do for them. When a couple does accept a promotion and transfer, their house may represent all that they are leaving behind. It becomes all the more valuable in their eyes when they leave behind important emotional ties.

A spouse who feels self-righteously angry about a broken organizational "contract" can be an intimidating partner. Emotions become even more complicated when the transferred employee feels ambivalent about the move and guilty about the family ordeal. Both employee and family often need help in understanding the realities of work and the sacrifices required to move up or even remain in an organization. Saying that family members should be realistic about what they expect from an organization could be misunderstood as suggesting that companies be callously indifferent to family needs. The company must be concerned about the demands it makes on the people doing the work, if only for its own survival. The family members need to understand the realities of an organization surviving in a competitive global environment. Uninformed decisions can be hard to live with. When a family cannot live with their decisions, help in understanding and working through the feelings can reduce the risk of losing an otherwise effective worker.

Case Study 9: Spouse's Lifestyle Needs

Over the years, Carol Browder has earned more and more money in her job as a bond trader. In some years, her performance has been nothing less than spectacular. The problem is that her husband has adopted a more and more lavish life-style. She has gone into more and more debt to support it. Carol now finds herself in a position where she has to make at least as much as she did last year (one of her best years), and even that may not be enough.

Recently her behavior has been confusing to her boss and colleagues. She has alternated between aggressive and timid, animated and lethargic, outspoken and quiet. She is less articulate and confident in strategy meetings. She has missed obvious opportunities and pursued dubious ones. She seems to be having more trouble conceiving and sticking to her daily trading plans.

The family pressures here are obvious. Two somewhat subtle issues deserve comment. First, families that have a significant jump in income and no prior experience with such an income level may need support in personal financial planning. Even if the employee is a financial expert, he or she may have no experience with this level of personal finances. Also, there may be such intense work involvement that family concerns fall by the wayside. Work commitments and high incomes can be a way to avoid family conflicts, only to see the problems escalate. The company can help by offering personal financial planning and referral for therapy.

The second problem is the employee who puts the organization at risk. Often the best performers cause the most disastrous problems, because management does not watch them or does not want to (see Chapter 6). Management is primarily concerned with keeping them happy, thus missing the early signs of evolving problems in top performers.

Case Study 10: Spouse's Self-Esteem and Expectations

Tom Grant's wife, Anne, comes from a wealthy family with a long history of male family members holding top government and corporate executive positions. Anne puts a lot of pressure on Tom to succeed, and he is motivated as much by her expectations as he is by anything else. In a real sense, Tom works for his wife, not for his company! At work, he has built a reputation for pushiness and taking excessive risk. The recognition he demands is considered well above what his achievements would suggest. Most of Tom's colleagues regard him as a pain in the neck.

Human needs can be broken down into the spheres of work, family, and self. In Tom's case, Anne's personal needs supersede whatever Tom or his organization need. Tom is constrained by Anne from following and developing his own abilities, aspirations, and career at a more realistic pace. She contributes to his own commitment to a false self. As he focuses only on upward advancement, and ignores developing his true competence, he doesn't even consider whether the work itself is personally gratifying.

Such people can cause severe problems for organizations, particularly if they are successful in their ambitions and advance to senior management. They will be more vulnerable to burnout, because work has no gratification for them other than status and marital stability. They will provoke cynicism and distrust when they push others to be concerned about quality or commitment to the organization. Their own true values will be communicated by their behavior and mixed messages. As they focus on short-term gains on their way up the corporate ladder, others will have to clean up the longer-term consequences of their actions. They are interested in what is best for their career (appearance of success) and not what is best for the organization.

Case Study 11: Fear of Surpassing the Spouse

Lynn Fox's career is on the brink of skyrocketing, but she is fearful of having a more successful career than her husband. He has told her that he is particularly sensitive to outperformance by a woman. It now seems that every time Lynn is about to get promoted, she heads it off with an uncharacteristically stupid mistake.

In this case, once again, the spouse's personal needs get in the way of setting appropriate goals in the workplace and maximal career fulfillment.

Of course, the mistakes Lynn makes are not mistakes at all but unconscious attempts at self-sabotage in the interest of protecting her marriage and her spouse's self-esteem.

Case Study 12: Values Conflict

Mike Castle is a highly successful investment banker who earns a lot of money and advises at the upper echelons of corporate decision making. Mike's wife, Heidi, is a psychologist who has always leaned to the left politically. She sees money as increasingly important to Mike, and she doesn't like what she perceives as the capitalist mindset of his clients. She has any number of complaints about them: "exploitation of the people doing the work," "interest in profits to the detriment of everything else important," and "environmental irresponsibility." She has never been interested in business and doesn't understand Mike's work, let alone what it does for society and people. Furthermore, she isn't interested in learning anything about his work or business.

As a result, Mike starts to doubt the validity of his work and he acts defensively. That provokes Heidi to take an even more aggressive position and Mike makes extreme arguments in return. As he has begun to second guess his motives, he has become much more timid and is tentative in his decision making.

The issue here is a fundamental conflict in values between Heidi and Mike. These kinds of conflicts can be especially incendiary, in that they cut to the issue of basic identity. By taking a moralistic position, Heidi succeeds in shaming Mike. He adopts a moralistic defense of his work, but begins to doubt his genuine moral values and the value of his dedication. His new uncertainties are reflected in declining performance at work.

This case also points out that work is implicitly and explicitly charged with values that employees do not necessarily accept. And when family members focus on seeming value conflicts for their own emotional reasons, there can be serious consequences for organizational function. The organization can help through genuine concern for the broader contexts of society and the environment, and for the inherent value of its own goals. Leaders need to articulate the organizational contributions to larger societal concerns. When this understanding is communicated to families, the strain of apparent value conflicts may diminish, while underlying emotional tension is focused elsewhere.

Case Study 13: Work Fulfillment Displaced

Ralph Merton is a skilled laborer with little opportunity to move up. His wife has seen work only as a place where Ralph gets a paycheck. For her, the church is where people should give all their true effort. Her own church has a particularly charismatic pastor. She has recently encouraged Ralph to become heavily involved in church administration activities, which has provided him with a heightened sense of mission and accomplishment. At work, Ralph is in a greater rush to leave at night and has begun to cut some corners in his production.

But Ralph's company competes in an industry troubled by foreign competition and customer dissatisfaction with quality and cost. The organizations that survive will have to make dramatic changes. And there won't be just a few changes. Industry analysts believe the companies that will be successful will be those that are able to constantly change as the realities of technology and markets change. Ralph, though, doesn't want to attend after-hour courses and team meetings. He and his wife just don't see how manufacturing techniques and quality control have any real meaning for them, and they don't want any limitations on their church work.

There is a more important problem for organizations in this case than just dealing with people who are not interested in their employer's work. Ralph has been pulled away from seeing his work as personally meaningful at a time when he will be asked to intensify his efforts, change his approach, and develop new skills. Potentially, his work will become more meaningful for him, but it will first feel like an intrusion into the things he really wants to do. So he will be one of those people who resists needed changes unless he gets some help.

Obviously, nonwork activities (civic, church, or whatever) are enriching experiences. And, they often enhance workplace performance by energizing the employee or developing transferable skills. The problem for the organization occurs when nonwork activities compensate for what is missing at work (remember Evans and Bartolome's descriptions of different relationships between work and nonwork), because these activities can detract from employees' emotional investment and commitment. There are particular stresses during times of change. However, Ralph's nonwork activities might develop attitudes and skills that would facilitate his ability to change and grow. The difference depends on whether his company can find a way to make his work meaningful to him again. Then, too, it would be helpful if his wife could see his work as more than just a paycheck.

Case Study 14: Family Encourages Maladaptive Behavior

Lou Wilson's wife, Mary, idealizes him and encourages his grandiose and omnipotent fantasies. She has raised the kids to do the same. Lou has carried a "king-of-the-hill" attitude into the workplace, to the annoyance of his peers and to the concern of his bosses. They have observed him skipping details where he shouldn't, being insufficiently sensitive to customer needs, and acting in other ways that suggest his perceived superiority.

People are happiest in their families when they receive support from them and when the family helps them be who they are. But overestimation of competence can be damaging to work just as underestimation can. Overestimation is more likely to cause problems for the organization. Such individuals can put the company in serious risk as they do not plan, cross-check, adequately prepare, or submit to policies and procedures. In this case, Lou's family is reinforcing his unrealistic evaluation of himself and his worth, which may be the main reason he married his wife in the first place. Family members can be expected to act to neutralize any required confrontations he receives at work. Any efforts at getting Lou to make changes in his personal behavior will also have to consider the role of his family.

The Workplace as a Substitute for Unmet Family Needs

Case Study 15: Declining Intimacy at Home Resulting in an Affair at Work

Sue Hanson's marriage has been weak for some time now and keeps getting worse. Emotional intimacy is absent altogether, and the couple's sexual relations are hollow and perfunctory. Even though her husband doesn't particularly care for her, he doesn't believe in divorce. As a result of her frustrated personal needs, Sue started working more. Soon the only people she really knew well were at work.

After several years, when more and more of her life became centered at work, she started an affair with a manager in another department. He cares for her and understands her work (something her husband never bothered to do). They spend most of their time together talking about personal things. Sue has come to realize she never did much of that before, and it has given her something she only vaguely knew was missing. But it is not without its cost. Sue is starting to feel guilty, but more about breaking company policy than her commitment to a dead marriage. She is thinking about quitting her job.

This is another example of compensation. Sue is not getting her emotional and sexual needs met with her husband, and she has found a man at work who provides them. As more and more of waking hours become worktime, particularly for white-collar workers, needs for intimacy surface prominently in the workplace. Sexual intimacy is often part of the equation. It does no good to merely set policies against these workplace relationships. The issues are too complex for that simplistic an approach. Individuals need to work through their own needs, frustrations, and interpersonal realities in a setting that contributes to sound decisions.

Many people will need the confidential assistance of a professional who can help them look at underlying psychological dynamics. When the employee feels caught in an unresolvable dilemma over emotional needs, the organization also suffers.

Case Study 16: Family Assaults on Fragile Self-Esteem

Joe Taylor is from a blue-collar background, but he has succeeded in making it to middle management in his company. He is often self-conscious about his roots. At the present time, relationships with his children seem to be falling apart on all fronts. He feels like a failure as a father and his wife supplements the children's rebellions with plenty of her own criticism. She even taunts him about his newfound uptown ways.

As his self-esteem has dropped, Joe's usual fear of being "found out" at work has increased. He fears his colleagues will realize he is less competent than they are. As a result, he has been extra careful about the quality of his work, but his productivity has suffered.

Joe's self-esteem gets undermined by events at home that exacerbate the insecurity that has always been tugging at him at work. This in turn undermines his performance. It is not uncommon for upwardly mobile people to feel insecure when working with those from higher socioeconomic backgrounds. Even employees with top-notch educations can be so concerned about their status that they focus exclusively on work. Thus, they do not develop themselves as spouses or parents, and they do not confront their anxieties about family intimacy. The developing incompetence in the family adds to their insecurity, and once again there is a downward spiral.

A spouse from a similar background may not only feel abandoned in the task of making the family work but may also feel intimidated about the new social circles. The spouse then expresses worries by nagging and eventually by angry attacks, and also has difficulty understanding the demands of the work. One professional in a rather sophisticated service organization complained, "If I was a cab driver my wife would know what I do. As it is, she thinks I don't have any real responsibilities, and she can't see why I won't take off in the middle of the day to pick up the laundry or do some errand for her."

Motivation to Work Is Family Driven

Case Study 17: Elder Care

Jane Gale's parents are living at her home with her and her husband. They require more and more time and energy. As a result, Jane sees work not only as a source of funds for supporting her parents but also as a haven where she can relax a bit. In a sense, she goes to work to get some rest.

Jane's motivation in working is not to maintain her sense of mastery and self-esteem by playing out her aggressive and creative drives. Rather it is to finance something outside of work and to get away from it all. This is not necessarily a problem for the organization, but its members will need to be sensitive to the impact of any significant changes in her work demands. For example, Jane may be talented enough to be considered for promotion or a transfer. In many organizations, if managers turn down such an opportunity, it is held against them, which would be a mistake in Jane's case. While the organization should give her a chance to say if she wants the promotion or transfer at this time, it should also understand her reasons if she declines the offer. If there is another opportunity when her family life has changed, she can be asked again. The same points would hold true for a parent with very small children.

Case Study 18: Financial Pressures at Home

Peggy Delaney is a nurse. Her colleagues call her the "leisure nurse" because she works primarily to finance expensive vacations with her husband, Norm. She would just as soon stay at home as a housewife, but both she and her husband Norm enjoy a little extravagance around vacation time, and Norm doesn't make quite enough money. He has pressed her to go back to work so they can keep taking the vacations, and she has reluctantly decided to take a job in her old profession. The other nurses at the clinic where Peggy works don't begrudge her working just for money, but they recognize Peggy's resentment and are bothered that she's not the caring professional that they are.

As in the case of Jane, Peggy is motivated almost exclusively by family and personal considerations. However, the clash that this causes with her peers is more dramatic than in the case of Jane, where the consequences of her elder care responsibilities may not even be noticed in the workplace. In Peggy's case, the chances are greater that her disinterest will collide with the key value of the organization, which is the professional health care of others.

Management needs to attend to the behavior of Peggy and her work group but not to Peggy's motives. It is certainly legitimate for someone to work just to finance vacations. The organizational concern is for personal behavior and effects on morale. Unnecessary comments or behavior that provoke co-worker envy should be confronted. However, if Peggy is an adequate performer her peers need to understand her contribution. She may not be worthy of promotion, but her feelings should not generate resentment.

INTERVENTIONS

To the same extent that businesses are sensitive to the impact in the workplace of medical problems, they need to become attuned to the usually more elusive impact of family problems and the other sorts of psychiatric problems covered in this book. It is in their best economic interests to do so.

Emotional problems are always more complex than they appear. Hence they are a significant challenge for businesses. One temptation may be to merely try being more sensitive, relying solely on good instinct, and becoming, in essence, an amateur psychologist. Being more sensitive is certainly a necessity, but when potential effects are substantial, professionals need to be involved early on. Comprehensive diagnosis and appropriate treatment require not only special skills but also detachment from the workplace environment. Employers should focus on the quality of work, raising red flags early, and seeking outside consultation when the issue is more than just a routine workplace conflict (see Chapter 1). Of course, employees often do not know when they have a family problem affecting their work.

Beyond increasing workplace sensitivity, the most important thing employers can do is make it safe for employees to come to them with emotional problems. Common wisdom dictates to employees that they keep their personal problems out of the workplace. In fact, it is precisely this attitude that often makes the consequences of the problem worse. The means by which business can begin to chip away at this attitude and turn it around is simple communication of its commitment to provide a helping hand. An effective method is face-to-face sessions conducted by informed bosses, whereby people can sense the dedication of the organization. The more people see that dedication, the safer they will feel in seeking help for their problems.

Communications should include more than just a stated commitment, however. They should also include the mechanics and procedures for people to follow when they have a problem, and the kinds of services the company will be making available. With such details, employees have a structure to follow that will make them feel less tentative about coming forward. Everyone does better when options are laid out.

SUMMARY

Sooner or later, family problems affect everyone at their work. Most of the time, these problems are not that significant, and only a few close co-workers know about them. Yet there are times when the organizational consequences of family problems are very significant, but no one sees or looks for underlying causes. At these times, the family's impact on work becomes more than an expected cost of doing business. It becomes an excessive cost that needs to be addressed. Family problems of this dimension are a legitimate concern for employers.

When family-driven problems at work occur, they are, on average, more significant than the literature suggests. This downplay occurs because the nature of emotional problems is usually subtle, as the preceding cases illustrate. Some of the more subtle organizational consequences of family problems are summarized in Table 11-1. Because in the real world each case has its own unique twist, the table does not purport to be complete, but is only reflective of the cases presented in this chapter. Employers need to be sensitive to the many motivations underlying employees' work, and the many implications for their commitment and sense of responsibility. Families affect motivations in both positive and negative ways.

Bibliography

Black, J. Stewart, and K. Gregory Stephens. 1989. The influence of the spouse on American expatriate adjustment and intent to stay in Pacific rim overseas assignments. *Journal of Management* **15**(4):529-544.

Burden, Dianne S. 1986. Single parents and the work setting: The impact of multiple job and home life responsibilities. *Family Relations* **35**:37-43.

Burke, Ronald J. 1986. Occupational and life stress and the family: Conceptual frameworks and research findings. *International Review of Applied Psychology* **35**:347-368.

Evans, Paul, and Fernando Bartolome. 1986. The dynamics of work-family relationships in managerial lives. *International Review of Applied Psychology* **35**:371-395.

Group for the Advancement of Psychiatry, Committee on Psychiatry in Industry. 1977. *What Price Compensation?* Vol. 9, Publication No. 99.

Kelly, Robert F, and Patricia Voydanoff. 1985. Work/family role strain among employed parents. *Family Relations* **34**:367-374.

MacBride-King, Judith, and Helene Paris. 1989. Balancing work and family responsibilities. *Canadian Business Review* **16**(3):17-21.

McKenna, Joseph F. 1990. The daddy track. *Industry Week* **239**(5):11-21.

Morrison, David E. 1976. Focus on the family. *Public Management* **58**(3):2-8.

Olson, D. H., and H. I. McCubbin. 1981. Circumplex model of marital and family systems, VI: Application to family stress and crisis intervention. In *Family Stress Coping and Social Support Theory, Research and Practice for Family Health Professionals*, H. I. McCubbin (ed.). New York: Praeger.

Potter, Joyce M. 1989. Family-related programs: Strategic issues. *Canadian Business Review* **16**(3):37-30.

III

Common Employee Problems

12

Anxiety and Stress

Dan J. Stein, M.B., and Eric Hollander, M.D.

Effects
Workplace Management
Psychiatric Management
Summary

ABSTRACT

Psychiatric knowledge of the anxiety disorders has increased rapidly in the past few years. This chapter reviews these conditions and how they manifest themselves in the workplace. The differences between ordinary anxiety and the anxiety disorders are outlined, and the most common anxiety disorders are discussed. Adjustment disorder with anxiety, generalized anxiety disorder (tension), panic disorder (phobias and intense anxiety), social phobia (stage fright and shyness), obsessive-compulsive disorder, and posttraumatic stress disorder are each considered in turn. These disorders are seen commonly in the workplace and may be profoundly disabling. However, appropriate psychiatric evaluation and treatment will usually provide prompt and effective treatment, with benefits for both the worker and the workplace.

INTRODUCTION

Few workers will disagree that the workplace is a source of stress and anxiety. Work is performed in accordance with particular goals; there are deadlines to be met and productivity standards to be maintained. Work also involves relationships that have particular requirements; interactions with employers, employees, co-workers, and clients can all cause stress.

A good argument can be made that some degree of stress and anxiety in the workplace is not only inevitable but is also beneficial insofar as it is motivating. The goal of stress management, then, is not the elimination of stress but rather the fostering of positive and constructive responses to stress.

This common-sense notion of stress, anxiety, and their management has been found useful and is widely held. Nevertheless, in workers who think they are merely suffering from stress, anxiety may lead to unbearable subjective distress or to substantial impairment of work. The common-sense model may be unsuitable for such workers and ordinary stress management programs may be ineffective.

Instead, such workers may benefit from a more thorough perspective. When anxiety at work leads to unbearable subjective distress or to substantial impairment of work, then workers may not merely be suffering from stress, but may instead have an anxiety disorder. The anxiety disorders are extremely common and include the panic and anxiety disorders (panic disorder, generalized anxiety disorder, and adjustment disorder with anxious mood), the phobic disorders (agoraphobia, social phobia, and simple phobia), obsessive-compulsive disorder, and posttraumatic stress disorder.

Each anxiety disorder has specific characteristics that allow it to be diagnosed, and each has particular causes that are addressed with specific treatments. In fact, many of the most important advances in clinical knowledge in recent decades have occurred in the area of anxiety disorders, and a range of new treatment options have become available. In the following sections, current knowledge about each of the anxiety disorders will be discussed within the context of the workplace.

ADJUSTMENT DISORDER WITH ANXIETY, GENERALIZED ANXIETY DISORDER, AND OTHER TENSION STATES

Although stress and anxiety may be considered universal phenomena, there are times when the distress of anxiety, or its effect on social and occupational functioning, leads the sufferer to seek help. The presentation of anxiety may, in general, be either acute or chronic.

Adjustment disorder with anxious mood (ADAM) may be considered an acute form of anxiety. This syndrome is defined in DSM-III-R as an acute response to a stressor that is characterized by nervousness, worry, and jitteriness in excess of a "normal and expectable reaction" and involving impaired social or occupational functioning. In cases where anxiety follows a stressor, but where symptoms are not in excess of a normal and expectable reaction or where functioning is not impaired, the clinician may use the DSM-III-R categories of "other interpersonal problem" or "phase-of-life problem or other life circumstance problem."

Generalized anxiety disorder (GAD) may be considered a chronic and severe form of anxiety. Those who suffer from this disorder may complain either of various worries or of physical symptoms. The most common spheres of preoccupation are the family, work, money, and illness. Physical symptoms include motor tension, autonomic hyperactivity, and hyperarousal. Motor tension is manifested in tremulousness, muscle aches, easy fatigability, or restlessness. Autonomic hyperactivity symptoms include shortness of breath, palpitations, sweating, dry mouth, dizziness, gastrointestinal complaints, flushes or chills, frequent urination, and trouble swallowing. Evidence of hyperarousal is feeling keyed up or on edge, an exaggerated startle response, difficulty concentrating, trouble falling asleep or staying asleep, and irritability.

Case Study 1

Bob Woodrow is a 42-year-old teacher who has had an outstanding record for many years. His students have consistently performed well on standardized examinations, and his fellow staff have thought of him as someone who is able to instill a love for learning. In the most recent examinations, however, Bob's students did fairly poorly. Soon after learning this, Bob began feeling increasingly anxious about his teaching. He worried continuously about whether he had prepared adequately for class, about whether he had any ability as a teacher, and about how his students would do on the next examination.

Bob's perpetual jitteriness began to be noticed by other teachers. At times his worries kept Bob awake, and on the following days he was too exhausted to teach class. This came to the attention of the principal, who hinted that perhaps Bob needed a leave of absence. Bob took this suggestion and went on a trip, but his absence from the school only made him feel more anxious. When he returned from his vacation, he elected to seek professional help.

Bob was diagnosed as having adjustment disorder with anxious mood. He was given a brief course of cognitive therapy to help change his overly negative thoughts. At the beginning of the therapy, when Bob was having difficulty falling asleep, he elected to take medication for a few nights.

Case Study 2

Fred Fassi is a 32-year-old printer, who as long as he can remember has considered himself a worrier. If he isn't worried about the standard of his work (which is good), then he worries about his children (who are all doing fine), or about his finances (which are in good shape). He feels keyed up and tense from the time he wakes up, and at night he has difficulty falling asleep. Furthermore, he often has muscle aches, gets tired easily, and invariably has one bodily symptom or the other—dizziness, nausea, or palpitations. While feeling sad at times, he can be cheered up if something good happens.

Although Fred gets his work done, at times he is so worried that he is unable to focus on his projects. In addition, he is reluctant to accept challenging assignments, as in the past these have only increased his worry load and given him even more trouble falling asleep.

During an evaluation session with his supervisor, the two agreed that Fred's ability far exceeded his performance. Fred's supervisor suggested that a psychiatrist might be able to help him.

Fred was diagnosed as having generalized anxiety disorder. His psychiatrist suggested a combined treatment comprising an insight-oriented psychotherapy and a course of antianxiety medication.

Diagnosis

The DSM-III-R diagnosis of adjustment disorder with anxious mood is made when a reaction to an identifiable psychosocial stressor or stressors occurs within 3 months of onset of the stressor(s); when the response of nervousness, worry, and jitteriness is in excess of a normal and expectable reaction to the stressor; and when there is social or occupational dysfunction as a result. When the symptoms are thought to be normal, or when symptoms do not interfere with functioning, the diagnostician may use a DSM-III-R V code such as "other interpersonal problem" or "phase-of-life problem or other life circumstance problem."

The DSM-III-R diagnosis of generalized anxiety disorder is made when at least two unrealistic or excessive worries are present for at least 6 months, and when at least six somatic symptoms accompany the anxiety. The diagnosis should not be made when the worries are secondary to another DSM-III-R axis I disorder or to a specific organic factor. GAD needs to be differentiated from a variety of psychiatric disorders with anxiety symptoms, including depressive disorders (especially anxious depressions with morbid ruminations), somatization disorders (such as hypochondriasis), eating disorders, and other anxiety disorders (such as obsessive-compulsive disorder). Both physical disorders such as hyperthyroidism and organic mental disorders such as caffeinism can mimic GAD.

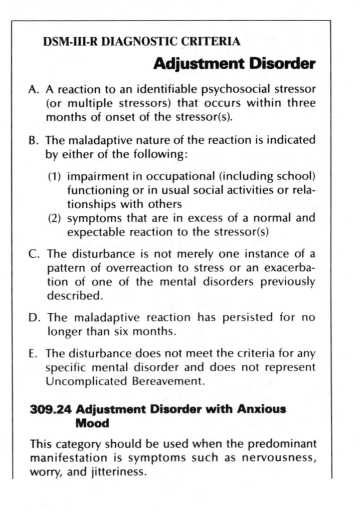

DSM-III-R DIAGNOSTIC CRITERIA

Adjustment Disorder

A. A reaction to an identifiable psychosocial stressor (or multiple stressors) that occurs within three months of onset of the stressor(s).

B. The maladaptive nature of the reaction is indicated by either of the following:

    (1) impairment in occupational (including school) functioning or in usual social activities or relationships with others

    (2) symptoms that are in excess of a normal and expectable reaction to the stressor(s)

C. The disturbance is not merely one instance of a pattern of overreaction to stress or an exacerbation of one of the mental disorders previously described.

D. The maladaptive reaction has persisted for no longer than six months.

E. The disturbance does not meet the criteria for any specific mental disorder and does not represent Uncomplicated Bereavement.

309.24 Adjustment Disorder with Anxious Mood

This category should be used when the predominant manifestation is symptoms such as nervousness, worry, and jitteriness.

300.02 Generalized Anxiety Disorder

A. Unrealistic or excessive anxiety and worry (apprehensive expectation) about two or more life circumstances, e.g., worry about possible misfortune to one's child (who is in no danger) and worry about finances (for no good reason), for a period of six months or longer, during which the person has been bothered more days than not by these concerns. In children and adolescents, this may take the form of anxiety and worry about academic, athletic, and social performance.

B. If another Axis I disorder is present, the focus of the anxiety and worry in A is unrelated to it, e.g., the anxiety or worry is not about having a panic attack (as in Panic Disorder), being embarrassed in public (as in Social Phobia), being contaminated (as in Obsessive Compulsive Disorder), or gaining weight (as in Anorexia Nervosa).

C. The disturbance does not occur only during the course of a Mood Disorder or a psychotic disorder.

D. At least 6 of the following 18 symptoms are often present when anxious (do not include symptoms present only during panic attacks):

Motor tension

   (1) trembling, twitching, or feeling shaky
   (2) muscle tension, aches, or soreness
   (3) restlessness
   (4) easy fatigability

Autonomic hyperactivity

   (5) shortness of breath or smothering sensations
   (6) palpitations or accelerated heart rate (tachycardia)
   (7) sweating, or cold clammy hands
   (8) dry mouth
   (9) dizziness or lightheadedness
  (10) nausea, diarrhea, or other abdominal distress
  (11) flushes (hot flashes) or chills
  (12) frequent urination
  (13) trouble swallowing or "lump in throat"

Vigilance and scanning

(14) feeling keyed up or on edge
(15) exaggerated startle response
(16) difficulty concentrating or "mind going blank" because of anxiety
(17) trouble falling or staying asleep
(18) irritability

E. It cannot be established that an organic factor initiated and maintained the disturbance, e.g., hyperthyroidism, Caffeine Intoxication.

Reprinted with permission from the *Diagnostic and Statistical Manual of Mental Disorders*, 3d ed. rev.; copyright 1987 by the American Psychiatric Association.

Causes

A number of different factors may be involved in the etiology of acute and chronic anxiety. Social, psychological, and biological factors will be considered in turn.

A variety of social stressors can initiate and exacerbate anxiety, and among these are the stressors of the workplace. One classification divides crises into the situational and the transitional. The former originate in material or environmental problems, personal or physical problems, and interpersonal or social problems. The latter originate in life-cycle or developmental transitions, and in shifts in social status.

In addition, psychological factors contribute to the initiation and maintenance of anxiety. Freud's psychoanalytic theory gave a central role to anxiety, which he conceived in terms of the forces of the mind. In this model, unconscious mental conflicts can result in hidden fears and thus anxiety. A subsequent behavioral model also centralized anxiety, which was conceived of as conditioned by fear of environmental stimuli. In this model, particular learning experiences also lead to hidden fears and anxiety. Although there are some differences in the way psychodynamically oriented and behaviorally oriented practitioners think about anxiety, there is an increasing convergence of these models. Notably, most clinicians would agree that people learn to think and feel about themselves and others in particular ways during their childhoods. These patterns of mental processing continue to be important in adulthood, but they may take place outside of awareness. Exploration of these kinds of mental processes may lead to an understanding of the person's anxiety (see Chapter 1).

Finally, a number of biological systems have been proposed as contributing to the etiology of anxiety. The locus coeruleus, an area in the brain, can be stimulated by many anxiety-causing drugs and inhibited by many antianxiety drugs. The effectiveness of benzodiazepines in the treatment of ADAM and GAD, and the discovery of a brain benzodiazepine receptor, suggest the existence of brain chemicals that block the receptor and cause anxiety. Finally, there is evidence that both the serotonergic and noradrenergic neurotransmitter systems are involved in the production of anxiety. Common to these various biological models is the possibility that a resetting of response levels of the nervous system, or sensitization, is responsible for the production of symptoms of anxiety.

Effects

The worker who suffers from ADAM or from GAD may not only suffer from subjective distress but may also be unable to perform at an optimal level. Especially in GAD, the motor tension, autonomic overactivity, hyperarousal, and often chronic insomnia of the disorder lead to easy fatigability, a variety of bodily symptoms, and poor concentration. The worker may attempt to relieve these by using a variety of medications. Substance abuse may begin in an attempt to self-medicate the symptoms, but will in all likelihood only make them worse (see Chapters 15 and 16). Finally, symptoms of depression may set in and further exacerbate the situation.

At the workplace, the sufferer from ADAM or GAD may be thought of as a worrier who requires a great deal of reassurance. At times, all that is noticed is a certain preoccupation or "spaciness." In some instances, bodily symptoms or impaired performance will be the first indication of the disorder. If stressors are identified by co-workers, then these people may extend support.

Workplace Management

As always, the best treatment lies in prevention. The workplace can help in the early identification of stressors, and in the provision of programs to help with anxiety management. These may include the teaching of relaxation techniques and skills training and coping. Ongoing identification of stressors at work may lead to valuable changes in the workplace.

Once ADAM and GAD develop, they will be detected at work if the worker is open about his or her worries, if bodily symptoms are obvious, or if there is interference with performance. The workplace may offer reassurance and a system of social supports, and may offer referral to a mental health professional.

Psychiatric Management

Psychiatric management of ADAM and GAD may entail the use of relaxation techniques, such as relaxation tapes, hypnosis, biofeedback, and meditation. Psychotherapy may be helpful in exploring mental processes that contribute to the anxiety, whether this is done using a psychodynamic or a cognitive-behavioral approach. Brief psychotherapy, with a more directed focus on specific symptoms and on the here and now, may be sufficient for some.

Finally, the use of antianxiety medications such as the following benzodiazepines can prove invaluable in the management of these disorders:

Generic Name	Trade Name
Alprazolam	Xanax
Chlordiazepoxide	Librium
Chlorazepate	Tranxene
Clonazepam	Klonopin
Diazepam	Valium
Lorazepam	Ativan
Oxazepam	Serax

The successful use of other techniques often requires that the most debilitating symptoms be first eradicated pharmacologically. The long-term use of benzodiazepines remains a subject of some dispute. Recent studies (e.g., Roth, Noyes, and Burrows 1988) indicate that abuse of the benzodiazepines has been overestimated, that the medications are safe, and that tolerance probably does not develop. Nevertheless, workers should be informed of the side effect of sedation, and withdrawal should be undertaken very slowly and with medical supervision. Further study of long-term treatment is necessary. Buspirone (BuSpar), a new nonbenzodiazepine nonaddicting antianxiety medication, appears to have less sedative property than the benzodiazepines and less potential for abuse. Preliminary studies (e.g., Hollander, Liebowitz, and Gorman 1989) indicate that tricyclic antidepressants may also be effective in chronically anxious patients even in the absence of depressive symptoms or overt panic disorder.

PANIC DISORDER: PHOBIAS
AND INTENSE ANXIETY

Thanks to the efforts of psychiatric researchers, panic disorder has in recent decades become recognized as a specific psychiatric disorder, with a particular biological substrate that responds to medication. The disorder is now also recognized as fairly common, with a 6-month prevalence of at least 0.6 to 1.0 percent (Myers et al. 1984). Panic disorder typically begins in the patient's late twenties. The person may be performing any one of his or her daily activities when suddenly, out of the blue, he or she is overcome with a sense of intense anxiety and impending doom. At the same time, a number of bodily symptoms are present, including shortness of breath, dizziness or faintness, palpitations or fast heartbeat, trembling or shaking, sweating, choking, nausea, and chest pain. Attacks usually last from a few seconds to 20 minutes.

Although the first attack often occurs during a routine activity, attacks are also associated with a number of events. These include life-threatening illnesses, accidents, separation from home (i.e., going to college, getting married, moving away to a new job), and the real or symbolic loss of an important relationship. Attacks may also begin with the use of mind-altering drugs, especially marijuana, LSD, sedatives, cocaine, and amphetamines. These stressors may act as triggers to provoke the onset of panic disorder in predisposed patients.

DSM-III-R DIAGNOSTIC CRITERIA

Panic Disorder (with and without Agoraphobia)

A. At some time during the disturbance, one or more panic attacks (discrete periods of intense fear or discomfort) have occurred that were (1) unexpected, i.e., did not occur immediately before or on exposure to a situation that almost always caused anxiety, and (2) not triggered by situations in which the person was the focus of others' attention.

B. Either four attacks, as defined in criterion A, have occurred within a four-week period, or one or more attacks have been followed by a period of at least a month of persistent fear of having another attack.

C. At least four of the following symptoms developed
   during at least one of the attacks:

   (1) shortness of breath (dyspnea) or smothering
       sensations
   (2) dizziness, unsteady feelings, or faintness
   (3) palpitations or accelerated heart rate (ta-
       chycardia)
   (4) trembling or shaking
   (5) sweating
   (6) choking
   (7) nausea or abdominal distress
   (8) depersonalization or derealization
   (9) numbness or tingling sensations (paresthe-
       sias)
   (10) flushes (hot flashes) or chills
   (11) chest pain or discomfort
   (12) fear of dying
   (13) fear of going crazy or of doing something
        uncontrolled

   Note: Attacks involving four or more symptoms
   are panic attacks; attacks involving fewer than four
   symptoms are limited symptom attacks

D. During at least some of the attacks, at least four of
   the C symptoms developed suddenly and increased in intensity within ten minutes of the beginning of the first C symptom noticed in the attack.

E. It cannot be established that an organic factor initiated and maintained the disturbance, e.g.,
   Amphetamine or Caffeine Intoxication, hyperthyroidism.

   Note: Mitral valve prolapse may be an associated
   condition, but does not preclude a diagnosis of
   Panic Disorder.

Subtypes of Panic Disorder

300.21 with agoraphobia

A. Meets the criteria for Panic Disorder.

B. Agoraphobia: Fear of being in places or situations
   from which escape might be difficult (or embar-

rassing) or in which help might not be available in the event of a panic attack. (Include cases in which persistent avoidance behavior originated during an active phase of Panic Disorder, even if the person does not attribute the avoidance behavior to fear of having a panic attack.) As a result of this fear, the person either restricts travel or needs a companion when away from home, or else endures agoraphobic situations despite intense anxiety. Common agoraphobic situations include being outside the home alone, being in a crowd or standing in a line, being on a bridge, and traveling in a bus, train, or car.

Specify current severity of agoraphobic avoidance:

Mild: Some avoidance (or endurance with distress), but relatively normal life-style, e.g., travels unaccompanied when necessary, such as to work or to shop; otherwise avoids traveling alone.

Moderate: Avoidance results in constricted life-style, e.g., the person is able to leave the house alone, but not to go more than a few miles unaccompanied.

Severe: Avoidance results in being nearly or completely housebound or unable to leave the house unaccompanied.

In Partial Remission: No current agoraphobic avoidance, but some agoraphobic avoidance during the past six months.

In Full Remission: No current agoraphobic avoidance and none during the past six months.

Specify current severity of panic attacks:

Mild: During the past month, either all attacks have been limited symptom attacks (i.e., fewer than four symptoms), or there has been no more than one panic attack.

Moderate: During the past month attacks have been intermediate between "mild" and "severe."

Severe: During the past month, there have been at least eight panic attacks.

In Partial Remission: The condition has been intermediate between "In Full Remission" and "Mild."

In Full Remission: During the past six months, there have been no panic or limited symptom attacks.

300.01 without agoraphobia

A. Meets the criteria for Panic Disorder.

B. Absence of Agoraphobia, as defined above.

Specify current severity of panic attacks, as defined above.

Reprinted with permission from the *Diagnostic and Statistical Manual of Mental Disorders,* 3d ed. rev.; copyright 1987 by the American Psychiatric Association.

Patients experiencing their first panic attack often interpret it as a heart attack or stroke. Upon arrival in the emergency room, nothing is found other than perhaps a fast heartbeat. Patients may receive extensive medical work-ups or may be summarily dismissed with the advice that it is all in the mind.

If the panic attacks continue, patients may begin to dread the experience of having attacks, and may begin to develop anticipatory anxiety. This may lead to phobic avoidance or agoraphobic fears of leaving home, of being alone, or of being in a situation where one is trapped or cannot escape, or where help is not easily available. Typical fears are of using public transportation or being in crowded places. The severity of these fears may range from mild distress over solo travel, to severe incapacitation with an inability to leave home.

Case Study 3

Gail Dresden is a successful insurance salesperson, who recently turned 36. She has always considered herself in excellent physical and mental health. Last fall, Gail was given a new and potentially lucrative sales district. On the day she drove to the location, while speeding along the interstate, she suddenly felt like her heart was pounding. She pulled over, but her heart continued to race. In addition, she felt short of breath and had chest pain and palpitations. She thought she was about to die or go crazy. After about 10 minutes, the symptoms had diminished enough to allow her to drive to a nearby hospital. The doctor assured her that she had not suffered a heart attack, and she felt relieved and reassured.

Nevertheless, in subsequent weeks, Gail had a similar attack every other day. She began to feel nervous about going on long trips where there was no access to medical help, and she requested that she be reassigned to an office sales job. She became fearful of leaving her apartment and preferred to travel with other people rather than by herself.

Of course, it was not always possible to arrange for someone to accompany her, and at such times Gail stayed at home and made excuses. This resulted in a marked drop in her sales, and she appeared in imminent danger of losing her job. Fortunately, one afternoon Gail was watching television when she came across a program on panic disorder, and she diagnosed herself as having this condition.

Gail's psychiatrist confirmed this diagnosis. When she questioned Gail in more detail about her life, Gail recalled that she had great difficulty in separating from her mother when first going to nursery school. Gail knew from the television program that antidepressants were often helpful for panic disorder, and she elected to begin medication and psychotherapy.

Diagnosis

The diagnosis of panic disorder by DSM-III-R criteria is made when panic attacks or the fear of them persist, and when at least four somatic symptoms are present during a panic attack. The diagnosis should not be made when the panic attacks are secondary to a physical disorder such as pheochromo-cytoma or to a substance such as cocaine or amphetamines. Certain disorders such as agitated depression, depersonalization disorders, and substance withdrawal can mimic panic disorder. Similarly, fear of leaving home and avoidance of being alone may be seen in paranoid and psychotic states, depressive disorders, and posttraumatic stress disorder.

Causes

The finding that people with panic disorder can have attacks provoked in a laboratory setting has allowed researchers to better understand the neurobiology of panic. Lactate infusions and carbon dioxide inhalations provoke panic attacks in people with panic disorder, but not in people without panic disorder. These procedures are thought to stimulate the locus coeruleus, an area that contains more than half the noradrenergic neurons of the brain, so resulting in the autonomic discharge that characterizes a panic attack. The nucleus has connections with other parts of the brain such as the limbic lobe and the prefrontal cortex that may be responsible for anticipatory anxiety and phobic avoidance. Panic attacks may be blocked by medication that inhibits the nucleus, and anxiety may be lessened by medication that acts at limbic sites.

Psychoanalysts have emphasized the connection between separation issues and subsequent panic. Researchers have indeed found that a large percentage of patients with panic disorder recall having separation anxiety as children. Furthermore, the initial panic attack is sometimes preceded by real or threatened loss of a significant relationship. These phenomena may also fit with biological findings; thus the biological substrate for normal separation anxiety may be aberrant in panic disorder with agoraphobia.

Freud also noted the connection between agoraphobia and anxiety attacks. While conditioning does not appear to account for the initiation of panic disorders, learning theory is useful in explaining the anticipatory anxiety that develops in panic disorder.

Certain events at the workplace may involve separation issues and trigger panic attacks. These include job transfers, promotion or demotion, the employment of new workers, or the laying off of old workers. Later on, certain situations at work may come to be particularly feared by the worker. These include airline travel, commuting to work, and meetings in which the worker feels physically or emotionally trapped.

Effects

While panic attacks themselves may be extremely uncomfortable, the development of anticipatory anxiety inevitably leads to poor work function and personal distress. In many panic patients, agoraphobia develops. Travel, for example, may become overwhelming. Severe disability often results. Such symptoms frequently lead to demoralization, and workers may begin to use substances in an attempt to obtain relief. Unfortunately, people with this disorder may be sufficiently distressed to be driven to suicide.

Although workers with panic attacks often feel that their symptoms are conspicuous, co-workers are usually not aware of the occurrence of such attacks. Occasionally, a period of muscular stiffening followed by relaxation is observed. As anticipatory anxiety increases, work may suffer. With the development of agoraphobic concerns, the worker may turn down assignments that involve traveling or feeling trapped.

Workplace Management

Panic disorder is usually detected only when anticipatory anxiety distracts the worker, or when agoraphobic concerns become incapacitating. Management in the workplace comprises education about the disorder and reassurance that the prognosis is excellent with appropriate treatment. While treatment is initiated, the workplace can help diminish avoidance behaviors, for example, by assisting the worker with travel arrangements.

Psychiatric Management

Workers with panic disorder can benefit from a combination of pharmacological and psychotherapeutic interventions. The following medications block panic attacks:

Generic Name	Trade Name
Antidepressants	
Amitriptyline	Elavil
Desipramine	Norpramin
Imipramine	Tofranil
Nortriptyline	Pamelor
Clorimipramine	Anafranil
Phenelzine	Nardil
Tranylcypromine	Parnate
Fluoxetine	Prozac
Benzodiazepines	
Clonazepam	Klonopin
Alprazolam	Xanax

It is important to remember that such other benzodiazepines as diazepam (Valium) are not usually helpful. The presence of depressed mood is not a requirement for antidepressants to be effective. Treatment of panic disorder with antidepressants should be initiated at low doses, since these patients may initially experience paradoxical anxiety or jitteriness, and they are sensitive to side effects of medication. It is helpful to inform the patient of potential side effects to avoid interpretation of somatic symptoms as imminent panic attacks. Blocking panic attacks will not necessarily lead to any diminution in the intervening anticipatory anxiety or phobic avoidance. A daily diary of anxiety and panic symptoms may help the patient learn this differentiation.

Anticipatory anxiety may be helped by a benzodiazepine. Phobic avoidance may respond to firm encouragement to face the feared situations. It is helpful to point out that the medications will block panic and lessen anxiety, but they will not diminish phobic avoidance. Many patients may need additional psychotherapy or behavioral therapy. Behavioral techniques include breathing retraining to eliminate hyperventilation, relaxation, and cognitive restructuring to give physical symptoms a more benign interpretation. Psychodynamic treatment may focus on possible relationships between the exacerbation of panic disorder and real, threatened, or symbolic separations.

Medication is usually given for about 6 months before a taper is begun. High-potency benzodiazepines work quickly, but there is a risk of withdrawal symptoms if they are discontinued too quickly. Several studies (e.g., Hollander, Leibowitz, and Gorman 1989) suggest that up to two thirds of patients will not relapse immediately after cessation of antidepressant medication.

SOCIAL PHOBIA: STAGE FRIGHT AND SHYNESS

A phobia is the persistent, irrational fear of a specific object, activity, or situation that results in a compelling desire to avoid the dreaded object, activity, or situation (the phobic stimulus). Most commonly the person does actually avoid the object, activity, or situation, though he or she recognizes that the fear is out of proportion to the danger.

DSM-III-R DIAGNOSTIC CRITERIA

300.23 Social Phobia

A. A persistent fear of one or more situations (the social phobic situations) in which the person is exposed to possible scrutiny by others and fears that he or she may do something or act in a way that will be humiliating or embarrassing. Examples include: being unable to continue talking while speaking in public, choking on food when eating in front of others, being unable to urinate in a public lavatory, hand-trembling when writing in the presence of others, and saying foolish things or not being able to answer questions in social situations.

B. If an Axis III or another Axis I disorder is present, the fear in A is unrelated to it, e.g., the fear is not of having a panic attack (Panic Disorder), stuttering (Stuttering), trembling (Parkinson's disease), or exhibiting abnormal eating behavior (Anorexia Nervosa or Bulimia Nervosa).

C. During some phase of the disturbance, exposure to the specific phobic stimulus (or stimuli) almost invariably provokes an immediate anxiety response.

D. The phobic situation(s) is avoided, or is endured with intense anxiety.

E. The avoidant behavior interferes with occupational functioning or with usual social activities or relationships with others, or there is marked distress about having the fear.

F. The person recognizes that his or her fear is excessive or unreasonable.

G. If the person is under 18, the disturbance does not
meet the criteria for Avoidant Disorder of Childhood or Adolescence.

Specify generalized type if the phobic situation includes most social situations, and also consider the
additional diagnosis of Avoidant Personality Disorder.

Reprinted with permission from the *Diagnostic and Statistical
Manual of Mental Disorders,* 3d ed. rev.; copyright 1987 by the
American Psychiatric Association.

In social phobia the person's central fear is of acting in front of others in a
way that will be humiliating or embarrassing. Typical situations that social
phobics fear or avoid include speaking, eating, or writing in public, using
public lavatories, and attending parties or interviews. An individual may have
one or more social phobias.

When forced or surprised into the phobic situation, the person feels
intense anxiety, accompanied by a variety of somatic symptoms. Although
these may often be similar to the symptoms of a spontaneous panic attack,
they differ in that blushing is common in social phobia but not in panic, while
the reverse holds for chest pain. Furthermore, paroxysmal onset is characteristic of panic disorder but not of social phobia.

Phobias are also fairly common disorders, with a 6-month prevalence of
1.2 to 2.2 percent for social phobia and of 4.5 to 4.7 percent for simple phobia
(Myers et al. 1984).

Case Study 4

James Storch is a 42-year-old accountant who is occasionally required to make
presentations to his department. Since high school, this kind of public speaking
has made James anxious, but he has forced himself to do his job. Recently, however,
James was asked to give a series of talks to representatives from another company.

During the week before the first presentation he was so worried by the thought of
embarrassing himself while giving the talk that he was unable to sleep. On the day of
the presentation, even though he succeeded in answering most of the questions, he
found himself feeling extremely anxious, sweating, and trembling. His mouth was so
dry that he frequently had to take sips of water. Just before the second presentation,

James called work to say that he had laryngitis and he arranged for a colleague to present for him. Although this excuse provided him with great relief, James knew that this was a short-term answer to a longstanding problem. He asked the medical department for the name of a psychiatrist. The psychiatrist found that James had social phobia, advised a course of phenelzine (an antidepressant medication effective for social phobia), and suggested a series of behavioral strategies to decrease his anxiety.

Diagnosis

There appear to be two types of social phobia: discrete (performance) social phobia and generalized social phobia. Discrete social phobia only involves anxiety and avoidance in performance situations, whereas generalized social phobia may involve anxiety and avoidance in all social situations. Social phobia may be differentiated from simple phobias (circumscribed fears of specific objects, situations, or activities) in which humiliation and embarrassment are not involved. Avoidance of certain social situations is seen as a part of avoidant and paranoid personalities, agoraphobia and obsessive-compulsive disorder, depressive disorders, schizophrenia, and paranoid disorders. The well-trained diagnostician can usually distinguish such disorders from social phobia.

Causes

Psychoanalysts have hypothesized that phobic symptoms occur when intense hidden emotions are controlled by displacing them onto avoided external objects or situations. Behaviorists have shown that it is possible to create and treat a phobia through conditioning and deconditioning techniques. Ethologically minded theorists have suggested that phobias are an example of evolutionarily prepared learning. While these different models may be applicable to some patients with social phobia, their clinical utility may vary.

The efficacy of medication for social phobia has given support to hypotheses that this disorder has an important biological component. It has been hypothesized that certain brain neurochemicals may be involved in human response to social approval and disapproval. It is possible that medication acts on these substances, and thereby decreases sensitivity to criticism and rejection.

Again, the workplace is unlikely to cause social phobia, but certain tasks at work, such as giving presentations or interacting with a group, may be feared and avoided by the social phobic. Organizational environments that are either overtly critical or superficially friendly can exacerbate social phobia.

Effects

Some people with social phobias may be asymptomatic unless faced with their phobic situation, at which time they will experience intense anticipatory anxiety. Others develop a fear that people will sense their anxiety in a social situation and will ridicule them. A vicious cycle may be set up, with fear leading to anxiety that impairs performance. Such developments may lead to social isolation, severe impairment, and abuse of alcohol or sedatives to self-medicate these symptoms.

In the workplace, social phobia may lead to few difficulties if the phobic situation is avoidable. The worker with social phobia may simply be considered shy by co-workers. Avoidance may, however, limit career advancement. If the worker has multiple fears, anxiety and avoidance may make impossible any work requiring social interaction. It should also be remembered that some workers will initially respond counterphobically to their fears. An example is the driven salesperson who has learned to control and thus utilize his or her fear of embarrassment.

Workplace Management

Social phobia may be seen initially during job interviews. Social phobia will be detected if an important work-related social situation is avoided, if anticipatory anxiety is sufficiently high to interfere with performance, or it can be suggested by marked shyness. Programs that prepare and practice the worker for performance and speaking situations can be very helpful. A diminution in overt criticism of workers may be helpful. Education about the disorder and reassurance that the prognosis is good with treatment are appropriate.

Psychiatric Management

Combined psychotherapy and pharmacotherapy can be extremely helpful for social phobia. Monoamine oxidase inhibitors (such as phenelzine and tranylcypromine) are a group of antidepressants that are a well-documented treatment for social phobic symptoms. Fluoxetine (Prozac) has not been as well studied, but may be similarly helpful. Beta-blockers (such as propranolol and atenolol) can be used for prompt management of discrete performance anxiety. Systematic desensitization, cognitive restructuring, and social skills training are also helpful. Psychodynamic psychotherapy of social phobia will often focus on reducing interpersonal fears, and will be most effective after medication benefits have started.

OBSESSIVE-COMPULSIVE DISORDER

Obsessions are defined as recurrent, persistent ideas, thoughts, impulses, or images that are experienced, at least initially, as intrusive and senseless. The person who suffers from obsessions attempts to ignore or suppress them, or to neutralize them with some other thought or action. Compulsions are repetitive, purposeful, and intentional behaviors that are performed in response to an obsession, or according to certain rules, or in a stereotyped fashion. The behavior is designed to neutralize or to prevent discomfort or some dreaded event or situation, but either the activity is not connected in a realistic way with that which it is designed to prevent, or it is excessive, and, at least at first, this is recognized by the person.

DSM-III-R DIAGNOSTIC CRITERIA

300.30 Obsessive Compulsive Disorder (or Obsessive Compulsive Neurosis)

A. Either obsessions or compulsions:

Obsessions: (1), (2), (3), and (4):

(1) recurrent and persistent ideas, thoughts, impulses, or images that are experienced, at least initially, as intrusive and senseless, e.g., a parent's having repeated impulses to kill loved child, a religious person's having recurrent blasphemous thoughts

(2) the person attempts to ignore or suppress such thoughts or impulses or to neutralize them with some other thought or action

(3) the person recognizes that the obsessions are the product of his or her own mind, not imposed from without (as in thought insertion)

(4) if another Axis I disorder is present, the content of the obsession is unrelated to it, e.g., the ideas, thoughts, impulses, or images are not about food in the presence of an Eating Disorder, about drugs in the presence of a Psychoactive Substance Use Disorder, or guilty thoughts in the presence of a Major Depression

Compulsions: (1), (2), and (3):

(1) repetitive, purposeful, and intentional behaviors that are performed in response to an ob-

---

session, or according to certain rules or in a stereotyped fashion

(2) the behavior is designed to neutralize or to prevent discomfort or some dreaded event or situation; however, either the activity is not connected in a realistic way with what it is designed to neutralize or prevent, or it is clearly excessive

(3) the person recognizes that his or her behavior is excessive or unreasonable (this may not be true for young children; it may no longer be true for people whose obsessions have evolved into overvalued ideas)

B. The obsessions or compulsions cause marked distress, are time-consuming (take more than an hour a day), or significantly interfere with the person's normal routine, occupational functioning, or usual social activities or relationships with others.

A patient with obsessive-compulsive disorder may suffer from either obsessions or compulsions. There are several commonly found subtypes of OCD, each with distinctive symptoms. One subtype includes patients with obsessions about dirt and contamination, with compulsions of ritual washing or avoidance of contaminated objects. A second subtype includes patients with pathological counting and compulsive checking. A third group includes patients with pure obsessions and no compulsions. There is a subtype of OCD with primary obsessional slowness, where patients spend many hours performing the tasks of daily life. Other patients with OCD, known as hoarders, are unable to throw out anything for fear they might someday need something they discarded. Usually these groups of symptoms overlap or develop sequentially.

The phrase *obsessive-compulsive* may conjure up an image of a worker who is a perfectionist: overly neat and overly rigid. Such a person is, however, unlikely to have OCD, and is more likely to have an obsessional personality disorder (see Chapter 14).

OCD itself has only recently been recognized as a quite common psychiatric disorder. It is now thought to have a 6-month prevalence of 1 to 2 percent (Myers et al. 1984).

Case Study 5

Milly Schmidt is a 28-year-old secretary for a partner in a law firm. Since adolescence, Milly has felt compelled to do certain things in a repetitive fashion. At one point she went through a stage of door checking: spending much of her day wondering whether she had locked her apartment door, fearing that someone had robbed her apartment, and having to return home, often more than once a day, in order to check that the door was locked.

Over the last year or so, Milly noticed that her repetitive behaviors were appearing at work. Before beginning work, she felt compelled to arrange the stationery on her desk in a particular orderly and symmetrical fashion. Initially this kept her desk tidy, but now this ritual was occupying far more time than it was worth. In addition, she felt an absolute urge to check the letters that she wrote at least six or seven times. On the one hand, this meant that she never made mistakes, but on the other hand, she knew that it was senseless to spend so much time doing this, and her efficiency had gradually but steadily deteriorated.

The partner became increasingly concerned. He had become quite aware of her inefficiency, and besides, Milly seemed a little off to him. An important legal contract was not submitted on time and three more just barely made it. The partner considered the options with the firm's administrator. Rather than just dismissing Milly, he instead gave Milly the name of a psychiatrist he knew. With a diagnosis of obsessive-compulsive disorder, Milly began treatment with clomipramine (an antiobsessional medication) and cognitive behavioral therapy. Some weeks later, the worst symptoms had improved, and Milly also began to discuss her recent engagement and European honeymoon plans, as well as her hopes of escaping from her chronically angry parents.

Diagnosis

The diagnosis of OCD is made when obsessions and compulsions cause significant distress, are time-consuming, or significantly interfere with social or occupational functioning. Although activities such as eating, sexual behavior, gambling, or drinking may be performed excessively, or compulsively, these are experienced as pleasurable by the person and are more akin to addictions than to true compulsions. The morbid ruminations or preoccupations frequently found in depression are unpleasant, but they are regarded as meaningful by the person, whereas the obsessions of OCD are viewed as senseless. OCD should be differentiated from obsessive-compulsive personality disorder, which is characterized by perfectionism, orderliness, and inflexibility. These traits are egosyntonic; they are regarded as realistic and not resisted or struggled against. It is also necessary to differentiate OCD from schizophrenia and phobia.

Causes

One psychoanalytic view might say that OCD is caused by a combination of hidden emotions and biological factors. The usual goal-oriented organization of motivation is replaced with hidden aggressive and hostile impulses, and by particular psychological defenses against the emergence of those impulses. Other psychoanalytic models would add the role of a harsh and unforgiving superego (conscience) in OCD, and also the central importance of issues of control in interpersonal relations. Psychoanalytic theory is useful insofar as it provides a detailed description of OCD symptoms and of some central mental processes in OCD, including the involvement of aggression and of control issues.

The behavioral model may also be useful in treating certain aspects of OCD. Thus behaviorists have offered detailed accounts of how rituals develop into learned habits via a reduction in anxiety. Behavioral treatment aims at breaking the learned habits.

Contemporary researchers have made progress in finding the biological factors hypothesized by earlier writers such as Freud. Two biological models of OCD have been proposed. The first is the neurotransmitter model. This model involves neurotransmitter dysregulation, especially of the serotonin system. People with OCD may have high spinal fluid levels of serotonin metabolites. When serotonergic medications (such as clomipramine or fluoxetine) are prescribed and symptoms decrease, there is a corresponding decrease in serotonin metabolite levels. Similarly, drugs that activate the brain serotonin system appear to exacerbate OCD symptoms. After successful pharmacological treatment, patients lose their sensitivity to such drugs. Serotonin does not, however, appear to be the only neurotransmitter involved in OCD, and perhaps alterations of serotonin function offset abnormalities in other neurotransmitter systems.

The second is the neuroanatomic model, which involves structural brain abnormalities in the basal ganglia or frontal lobe. OCD may be initiated by a variety of neurological disorders (trauma, infection, anoxia), and is associated with several diseases of the basal ganglia. Finally, patients with OCD may have abnormalities upon various neurological examinations and upon brain imaging.

These explanations are not necessarily incompatible, with structural damage and neurotransmitter dysregulation being causally related. Biological explanations are further bolstered by family studies that suggest a genetic component.

Obsessive-compulsive disorder is unlikely to be caused by the workplace. However, obsessive-compulsive symptoms fluctuate and may be exacerbated by both personal and workplace stresses. Further, particular management styles may be associated with an increase in anger-provoking struggles for control, and this may exacerbate obsessive-compulsive symptoms.

Effects

OCD may begin in childhood or early adolescence. The onset is insidious, often with a chronic or progressive course. The effect on the worker may be extremely debilitating. People with OCD may be socially isolated, marry at an older age, have a high celibacy rate, and have a low fertility rate. Nevertheless, new developments in behavioral and pharmacological treatment have led to vastly improved prognosis.

Compulsions may be recognized at the workplace in the form of ritualistic behavior, or in the form of impaired performance. Repetitive obsessive thoughts can also impair attention and concentration. Workers with OCD may have rigid ideas or approaches that persist inappropriately. Sometimes workers with OCD display excessive anger. While some obsessive-compulsive personality traits may be useful in some jobs, OCD is most likely to be dysfunctional.

Workplace Management

OCD will be detected if ritualistic behavior is observed, or if obsessions and compulsions lead to impaired functioning. The use of management styles and organizational structures that allow the negotiation of anger-provoking control issues may be helpful. Management in the workplace may also comprise education about the medical nature of the disorder, and reassurance that workers with OCD are not crazy and it is not all in their head. Finally, appropriate referral to a psychiatrist skilled in the treatment of OCD is essential.

Psychiatric Management

Until recent medication advances, OCD was often considered extremely difficult to treat. Clinical research now suggests that patients with OCD should receive medication. The serotonergic antidepressants (such as chlorimipramine, fluoxetine, fluvoxamine, or sertraline) are the medications of choice. Patients need to build up to high doses and to remain on the medication for as long as 12 weeks before a full effect is seen. If the patient is partially improved, these medications are often augmented with fenfluramine, buspirone, lithium, or a neuroleptic.

Optimal psychiatric management of OCD usually involves psychotherapy in addition to medication. Cognitive-behavioral treatment comprises exposure procedures that aim to expose patients to their feared objects (e.g., exposure to dirt) until they see that their discomfort does not last but eventually ceases, and response prevention techniques (e.g., prevention of washing) that aim to decrease the frequency of compulsive rituals. Psychodynamic interventions often focus on greater insight into underlying aggression or control issues, precipitating emotional stresses, and family dynamics.

POSTTRAUMATIC STRESS DISORDER

Posttraumatic stress disorder (PTSD) comprises a characteristic set of symptoms that occurs after a psychologically distressing event that is outside the usual range of human experience. The stressor is one that would be considered traumatic to almost anyone, and the event invariably involves fear and helplessness. The characteristic symptoms include reexperiencing the event, avoidance of stimuli associated with the event, psychic numbing, and increased arousal.

DSM-III-R DIAGNOSTIC CRITERIA

309.89 Post-traumatic Stress Disorder

A. The person has experienced an event that is outside the range of usual human experience and that would be markedly distressing to almost anyone, e.g., serious threat to one's life or physical integrity; serious threat or harm to one's children, spouse, or other close relatives and friends; sudden destruction of one's home or community; or seeing another person who has recently been, or is being, seriously injured or killed as the result of an accident or physical violence.

B. The traumatic event is persistently reexperienced in at least one of the following ways:

(1) recurrent and intrusive distressing recollections of the event (in young children, re-

---

petitive play in which themes or aspects of the
trauma are expressed)

(2) recurrent distressing dreams of the event
(3) sudden acting or feeling as if the traumatic
event were recurring (includes a sense of reliving the experience, illusions, hallucinations,
and dissociative [flashback] episodes, even
those that occur upon awakening or when intoxicated)
(4) intense psychological distress at exposure to
events that symbolize or resemble an aspect of
the traumatic event, including anniversaries of
the trauma

C. Persistent avoidance of stimuli associated with the
trauma or numbing of general responsiveness (not
present before the trauma), as indicated by at least
three of the following:

(1) efforts to avoid thoughts or feelings associated
with the trauma
(2) efforts to avoid activities or situations that
arouse recollections of the trauma
(3) inability to recall an important aspect of the
trauma (psychogenic amnesia)
(4) markedly diminished interest in significant activities (in young children, loss of recently acquired developmental skills such as toilet
training or language skills)
(5) feeling of detachment or estrangement from
others
(6) restricted range of affect, e.g., unable to have
loving feelings
(7) sense of a foreshortened future, e.g., does not
expect to have a career, marriage, or children,
or a long life

D. Persistent symptoms of increased arousal (not present before the trauma), as indicated by at least
two of the following:

(1) difficulty falling or staying asleep
(2) irritability or outbursts of anger
(3) difficulty concentrating
(4) hypervigilance
(5) exaggerated startle response

> (6) physiologic reactivity upon exposure to events that symbolize or resemble an aspect of the traumatic event (e.g., a woman who was raped in an elevator breaks out in a sweat when entering any elevator)
>
> E. Duration of the disturbance (symptoms in B, C, and D) of at least one month.
>
> **Specify delayed onset** if the onset of symptoms was at least six months after the trauma.
>
> Reprinted with permission from the *Diagnostic and Statistical Manual of Mental Disorders,* 3d ed. rev.; copyright 1987 by the American Psychiatric Association.

Stressors that are outside the usual range of human experience include participating in combat, environmental disasters or severe accidents, and other threats to limb and life. The trauma is reexperienced in the form of recurrent painful, intrusive recollections, daydreams, or nightmares. Occasionally there are dissociative states in which the event is relived. Psychic numbing or emotional anesthesia is manifest by diminished responsiveness to the external world, with feelings of being detached from others, loss of interest in usual activities and in the future, and inability to feel such emotions as tenderness or love. At times the victim of trauma suppresses all thoughts and feelings associated with the event and avoids activities or situations that may lead to remembering the event. Symptoms of excessive arousal include difficulty sleeping, irritability and explosive anger, difficulty concentrating, hypervigilance, and an exaggerated startle response. Other symptoms may include guilt at having survived, depression, anxiety, panic attacks, shame, and rage. The disorder may be complicated by substance abuse or suicidal actions. The onset of PTSD may be delayed until some months following the event; this is more likely in survivors of major catastrophes rather than ordinary accidents.

Case Study 6

Jane Segal is a 26-year-old insurance broker. Two months ago, Jane and her 4-year-old daughter Susan had a terrifying experience. On the way home from their local grocery, a man sprang out from behind a tree, held a gun to Susan's head, and demanded Jane's purse. When Jane gave him the purse, he opened it, was disappointed by how little money there was, and made several more threats before finally taking off.

Afterward, thoughts of the episode kept intruding into Jane's mind. At night she had difficulty sleeping and would have nightmares about being held up. During the day she was on edge, lost her usual cheerfulness, and would not walk along the route of the holdup. She became demoralized and started drinking heavily to help her sleep. Some of her accounts sensed that something was wrong, and Jane couldn't be as dedicated to her work as she wanted to be. A broker who was close to Jane advised her to seek help at a local health center. Jane was diagnosed as having posttraumatic stress disorder and her psychiatrist encouraged her to talk about the traumatic experience. The psychiatrist also prescribed alprazolam 0.5 mg (a mildly sedating antianxiety and antipanic medication), which Jane occasionally took when she was unable to sleep.

Diagnosis

Diagnosis is made when symptoms following a severely distressing event last for longer than a month. In adjustment disorder the stressor is within the range of common experience, and the characteristic symptoms of PTSD are absent. It may be noted, however, that certain authors (e.g., Horowitz 1986) hold that even stressors within the range of usual human experience, such as bereavement, may lead to a syndrome of reexperiencing the trauma. Various organic mental disorders resulting from brain injury or to substance abuse may mimic PTSD. PTSD may mimic phobia and panic disorder, and indeed has been considered a variant of the latter condition. Major depression and generalized anxiety disorder may develop secondary to PTSD. Especially where there are existing or potential legal issues or entitlements, factitious disorder and malingering (conscious deception and feigning of illness; see Chapter 18) should be ruled out.

Causes

Individuals show marked differences in how they react to stress. It has been argued that the more previous trauma experienced by a person, the more likely he or she is to develop symptoms following a stressful event. People with high premorbid anxiety levels may be more likely to respond with pathological anxiety. When stressors become extreme, however, even in the absence of preexisting conditions, the rate of morbidity increases significantly. A disruptive recovery environment may further increase the level of impairment.

PTSD may also be modeled using biological and ethological constructs. Thus animals prevented from escaping from acute stress develop a syndrome of learned helplessness that parallels the symptoms of PTSD. Autonomic stimulation occurs in situations of helplessness and involves activation of the noradrenergic system and depletion of central noradrenaline. Animals who have previously been exposed to inescapable shock are more sensitive to noradrenaline depletion. Such a model is supported by the finding that PTSD responds to clonidine, a noradrenergic agonist.

Effects

The clinical course of PTSD may involve three stages. Stage I is the response to trauma. Nonsusceptible people may experience adrenergic symptoms immediately after the trauma, but they do not dwell on the event. Predisposed people with high anxiety levels may have an exaggerated response and they continue to ruminate about the event. If symptoms persist past 4 to 6 weeks, stage II, or acute PTSD, is present. Feelings of helplessness and loss of control, symptoms of arousal, and reliving of the trauma occur. The person's life becomes centered around the trauma, leading to changes in personality, interpersonal relations, and occupational functioning. In stage III, chronic PTSD develops, with disability, demoralization, and despondency. The person is now preoccupied with the physical disability resulting from the trauma. Somatic symptoms, anxiety and depression, substance abuse, disturbed relations, and unemployment may occur.

The symptoms of posttraumatic stress disorder may affect many areas. Not only may there be intense subjective distress from recollections of the event but the combination of excessive arousal and psychic numbing may lead to difficulties in concentration and performance and to strained interpersonal relations.

Recently, PTSD has been an increasingly presented cause for disability claims and lawsuits (see Chapter 5). This has resulted in high costs for employers and insurance carriers, as well as expensive litigation and disruptive workplace effects. It is essential to ensure that preexisting conditions have been fully and accurately assessed, that diagnostic criteria are met, that malingering is not present, and that optimal treatment has been conducted with full patient compliance. Both sophisticated psychotherapy and medication are often needed.

Workplace Management

Early intervention after intensely stressful events may be effective in both reducing immediate distress and in preventing chronic responses. Workers may be referred for crisis therapy, which should strike a balance between early supportive intervention to minimize the traumatic state and later working through of the trauma. Establishment of a safe and communicative relationship, reappraisal of the traumatic event, revision of the patient's inner model of himself or herself and the world, and planning for termination with a reexperiencing of loss are important issues in this model of the management of PTSD. Once symptoms of PTSD have appeared, however, referral for symptomatic control should be made.

Psychiatric Management

Symptomatic management may involve psychotherapy and psychopharmacological intervention. Psychotherapeutic approaches include review of the traumatic event, understanding the emotional response, and understanding both the emotional antecedents and consequences. Various cognitive-behavioral techniques have been shown to be helpful in PTSD. Furthermore, in small open clinical research trials, a variety of medications have been used. These include antidepressants, clonidine, beta-blockers, and benzodiazepines. While there are few controlled trials of any form of therapy in people with PTSD, antidepressant medication may prove helpful if insomnia or depression are present. Similarly, PTSD-associated panic attacks can be treated with suitable antipanic medications.

SUMMARY

This chapter reviews the anxiety disorders from the perspective of modern psychiatry. The symptoms of these disorders manifest in specific ways at the workplace. Such symptoms may be exacerbated by work-related stress, and they may also lead to substantial interference with work performance. Early recognition of these specific disorders at the workplace, with appropriate workplace and psychiatric management, may be of great benefit in reducing their occupational impact, and may lead to a greatly improved prognosis.

Bibliography
Barlow, David. 1988. *Anxiety and Its Disorders: The Nature and Treatment of Anxiety and Panic.* New York: Guilford.
Hollander, Eric, Michael Liebowitz, and Jack Gorman. 1989. Anxiety disorders. In *Textbook of Psychiatry,* John Talbott, Robert Hales, and Stuart Yudofsky (eds.). Washington, D.C.: American Psychiatric Press.
Horowitz, Mardi. 1986. *Stress Response Syndromes,* 2d ed. Northvale, N.J.: Jason Aronson.
Klein, Donald, and Judith Rabkin (eds.). 1981. *Anxiety: New Research and Changing Concepts.* New York: Raven Press.
Marks, Isaac. 1987. *Fears, Phobias, and Rituals: Panic, Anxiety, and Their Disorders.* New York: Oxford University Press.
Myers, J. K., M. M. Weissman, G. L. Tischler, C. E. Holzer, P. J. Leaf, H. Orvaschel, J. C. Anthony, J. H. Boyd, J. D. Burke, M. Kramer, and R. Stoltzman. 1984.

Six-month prevalence of psychiatric disorders in three communities. *Archives of General Psychiatry* **41**:959-967.

Roth, Martin, Russell Noyes, and Graham Burrows (eds.). 1988. *Handbook of Anxiety.* New York: Elsevier.

Taylor, Charles, and Bruce Arnow. 1988. *The Nature and Treatment of Anxiety Disorders.* New York: The Free Press.

Weissman, M. M., G. L. Klerman, J. S. Markowitz, and R. Ouellette. 1989. Suicidal ideation and suicide attempts in panic disorder and attacks. *New England Journal of Medicine* **321**(18):1209-1214.

13

Depression and Burnout

David A. Van Liew, M.D.

ABSTRACT

In this chapter, the term *depression* is used to signify not a transitory mood but a mood disorder that requires professional treatment. At least 20 percent of the U.S. population will experience significant depression in their lifetime, a disease process involving the entire body and mind. Depression is a very treatable disease and is highly recognizable in the workplace. It often presents itself as fatigue, absenteeism, decreased productivity, accidents, and unexplained illness, as well as alcohol and substance abuse. However, 70 percent of depressed people do not receive treatment. Greater awareness of depressive disorders (causes, symptoms, and typical progression) will ensure prompt and appropriate treatment, and in turn will minimize effects on the worker and workplace. Optimal treatment requires psychiatric evaluation, diagnosis, and treatment. Prompt treatment with psychotherapy, often combined with antidepressant medication, will usually relieve many symptoms within 3 weeks. Full resolution follows in 4 to 12 months. Regardless of severity, nearly all properly diagnosed depressions will show significant response to appropriate treatment.

INTRODUCTION

Definitions of Depression and Burnout

The word *depression* means different things to different people. When used loosely, it often refers to passing phases of sadness or a reaction to difficult life experiences. When psychiatrists diagnose depressions, they mean particular disorders, with specific signs and symptoms, that are sufficiently prolonged to impair daily functioning. A distinction must be made between clinical depressions and the ordinary lows of everyday life. It is possible to feel very unhappy as one moves along a normal continuum of moods. In this chapter, the term *depression* will signify a mood disorder that requires professional treatment.

The term *burnout* is used so frequently that it has lost much of its original meaning. As originally used, burnout meant a mild degree of stress-induced unhappiness. Ultimately, it was used to describe many distressing situations: everything from fatigue to an episode of major depression. The word *burnout* seems to have become an alternative word for *depression,* but with a less serious significance. When it is used in this chapter, it is equated with adjustment disorder with depressed mood.

Incidence and Effects of Depression

Depression, excluding temporary blue moods and periods of grief and bereavement, is one of the most common mental health problems in the workplace. Recent research (e.g., Dubovsky 1988) suggests that in industrialized countries the incidence of depression has increased with each decade since 1910, and the age at which someone is likely to become depressed has dropped with every generation born after 1940. Depressive illnesses are common and serious, taking a tremendous toll on both workers and workplace. Two out of ten workers can expect a depression during their lifetime, and women are one and a half times more likely than men to become depressed. One out of ten workers will develop a clinical depression serious enough to require time off from work.

Understanding depression as an illness is necessary for promoting organizational mental health. Despite considerable popular press about depression, and common popular usage of the term, 80 percent of people fail to recognize their own serious depression. Moreover, fewer than 25 percent of depressions receive treatment, and most of that treatment is from nonpsychiatric personnel (American Psychiatric Association, *Facts About: Depression*). In the midst of these facts, there are reasons for optimism: First, the signs of depression can be very clear; and second, the vast majority of depressions will respond to appropriate psychiatric care.

Symptoms and Diagnosis of Depression

The symptoms of depression frequently surface first at work. They are often noticed by co-workers, manifesting as changes in the depressed person's work patterns, moods, thinking processes, physical functioning, and behavior. The depressed employee's mood becomes markedly negative, with sadness, irritability, defensiveness, and fits of anger coming to the fore. Sometimes the first sign of depression is the throwing of a wrench, the ripping up of a memo, or eruptive cursing. Other distinct signs of possible depression include crying, touchiness (being easily hurt or angered), fatigue, decreased ability to concentrate, decreased physical coordination, increased incidence of accidents, absenteeism, and physical illness.

Depression nearly always has a compromising effect on social behavior. In addition to having reduced interpersonal awareness, the depressed employee engages in fewer conversations and is less inclined to cooperate with others. These behavioral changes have considerable impact on the person's relationships with family, friends, and colleagues. Resulting disruptions range from mild (misunderstandings) to extreme (job termination, separation, and divorce).

Internally, depressed employees usually think negative thoughts about themselves, their job, and the future. They experience a diminished ability to concentrate, make decisions, or remember things. They frequently have exaggerated guilt, fear, and a sense of impending doom. As depression deepens, people feel worthless, helpless, and hopeless. They often think of suicide. In the most severe cases, they may develop psychotic beliefs with catastrophic fantasies of terminal illness, financial ruin, or serious moral impropriety (see Chapter 17).

A true depression is not merely a passing blue mood. It is not a sign of personal weakness or a condition that can be willed away by sheer determination. People with depressive illness cannot simply cheer up and get better. Without treatment, the condition can last for months or even years. Although depressed employees visit medical clinics two to three times as frequently as other workers, the depression itself may remain masked and undiagnosed.

The emotional state of depression is almost always sad, anxious, or depressed. If a person does not appear depressed, the depression may have already progressed to a more serious state, where indifference becomes the chief attitude toward any activity or social overture. People who are experiencing a passing case of the blues or normal grief usually experience some symptoms of depression, although they continue to function almost normally. However, they too can develop a full-blown depressive disorder that requires treatment.

A depressive disorder is a whole body disorder, pervading one's physical self as well as one's mind and emotions. The body no longer functions smoothly; sleeping and eating patterns change, sometimes dramatically. Energy and productivity levels drop. The immune system becomes suppressed, thus increasing vulnerability to illness. While interest in athletic or sexual activity typically wanes, paradoxical obsession with such activities sometimes develops as an unwitting avoidance of the depressed feelings. Facial expressions and body language reflect the depressed person's inner process: Shoulders droop, body movements slow down, and smiles are rare.

Accounts of depression appear in personal diaries throughout history, confirming the human universality of this experience. Abraham Lincoln depicted his depression with vivid immediacy:

> I am now the most miserable man living. If what I feel were equally distributed to the whole human family, there would not be one cheerful face on earth. Whether shall I ever be better, I cannot tell; I awfully forbode I shall not. To remain as I am is impossible. I must die or be better, it appears to me. (Greist and Jefferson 1984, p. 6)

Common Types of Depressive Disorders

Depressive illnesses come in a wide variety of forms. The four major categories discussed in this chapter are:

1. *Adjustment disorder:* Adjustment disorders are the least severe class of depressive disorders. Essentially, an adjustment disorder is a maladaptive reaction to identifiable psychosocial stressors, occurring within 3 months after the onset of the stressor and lasting no longer than 6 months. The mood disturbance is temporary and remits soon after the stressor ceases, or when the person is able to develop a new level of adjustment. In its original meaning, occupational burnout is most appropriately considered a subset of this classification. Bereavement, grief, and demoralization are conditions with depressive symptoms. They are discussed in this section, even though there is neither social nor occupational impairment, nor symptoms beyond a normal and expected reaction. There is no absolute definition of a normal reaction, so clinical judgment is often required.

2. *Major depression:* The essential features of a major depressive episode are depressed mood or loss of interest or pleasure in almost all activities for most of the day, for a period of at least 2 weeks. Major depression comes on quickly, and symptoms are more severe than can be explained by life circumstances. There are major changes in mood, thinking, bodily functions, and behavior, as evidenced by drastic changes in appetite, sleep patterns, energy level, concentration, and decision making, along with persistent feelings of worthlessness and hopelessness.

Melancholia is a variation with significant weight loss, lack of positive responses, excessive worry, and early-morning waking. Seasonal affective disorder is a seasonal depression. Psychotic depressions are diagnosed when the symptoms no longer have their basis in fact or reality (see Chapter 17).

3. *Dysthymic disorder:* Dysthymia (atypical depression, depressive neurosis, depressive personality) is a chronic mood disturbance persisting for most of the day, more days than not, for a minimum of 2 years. This disorder usually begins early in life, and is sometimes referred to as *depressive personality.*

Although it has many of the same symptoms as major depression, overall impairment is usually milder and is due more to symptom chronicity than severity. Atypical depression is an important common variant that includes increased sleep and appetite, decreased energy, reactive mood, and increased sensitivity to interpersonal rejection.

4. *Bipolar (manic depressive) disorder:* Bipolar disorder, formerly known as manic depressive disorder, consists of recurrent, cyclic episodes of mania and depression, characterized by a sudden onset (within several days), and lasting from any number of weeks to months. Because of the severity of this illness and the possible medical and social consequences of the person's mood and behavior, prompt diagnosis and treatment are absolutely essential.

Causes of Depression

Depression is almost always caused by a complex combination of factors including genetic predisposition, familial patterns, developmental experiences (such as early loss of a parent), biological dysfunction, environmental stress (such as dealing with an emotionally or physically demanding job), and emotional stress (such as intense grief). Every individual has a unique pattern of biological, psychological, and environmental/circumstantial factors that together make a depression more or less likely to occur.

Biological
Medical research has contributed a great deal to our understanding of the biochemistry underlying depression. Depression is thought to reflect an imbalance of neurotransmitters, the natural biochemicals that allow brain cells to communicate with each other. An irregularity in these chemicals may cause a wide variety of psychological and physical changes; hence the popular coining of the term *chemical imbalance* to describe depression.

Genetic factors are important in many cases of mood disorder, and for bipolar disorder in particular. Mood disorders tend to run in families, follow Mendelian dominance, and run true to form. If one identical twin has depression, there is a 70 percent chance that the other twin will also develop depression. Children, parents, and siblings of a depressed person have a 15 percent chance of developing depression (Griest and Jefferson 1984, p. 7). If a parent has a particular type of depressive disorder, the children are likely to acquire the same disorder, and they may also respond similarly to specific medications.

Psychological
Psychological causes of depression are generated by a complex combination of early significant losses, family environment, developmental experience,

life-style, relationship choices, and adjustment skills. People who experience an early loss, or losses, of significant people may develop a predisposition to depression. Previous life experiences concerning the handling of loss, grief, and anger will have a great effect on current risk for depression, as well as on response to the illness. Personality and temperament are also highly predictive of reactions to loss and grief. People who are dogmatic and rigid in their life philosophy and thought processes (the "all or nothing" or "right or wrong" approach) tend to experience more frequent and more severe depressions (see Chapter 9). Similarly vulnerable are those with a history of interpersonal conflicts and those who have habitual negative expectations (sometimes called *learned helplessness*).

Learned adjustment and coping skills play a key role in adaptation to relationship and environmental stresses. When life experience is limited, stress is unremitting, and opportunities for developing new perspectives and coping skills are scarce, depression is more likely to occur and to persist. Not surprisingly, the employee most likely to suffer depression is the young, poor, single mother of small children. The incidence of depression also increases dramatically as employees grow older and as they move through difficult developmental periods. This is particularly true for older men nearing retirement. Any change in life circumstance, promotion, demotion, transfer, marriage, divorce, or death can potentially trigger a depression.

Environmental/Circumstantial
While depression can be caused by troubled relationships, job problems, or financial stress, depression can also be a major cause of those same problems. In the work environment, it is often difficult to separate the cause from the effect. However, it is important to keep in mind that, despite the profoundly disruptive effects of clinical depression, depressed people should not be blamed for a medical illness they cannot control. Equally important is the fact that treatment will help most depressed people, even when the causes are unclear. At the same time, the presence of recognizable risk factors does not make depression inevitable. The chances of depression are increased when the stressors are severe, unexpected, multiple, chronic, uncontrollable, associated with physical illness, or damaging to personal identity, integrity, or self-worth.

Alcohol, marijuana, narcotics, sedatives, and tranquilizers can cause or considerably worsen depression. Depression also typically follows withdrawal from cocaine, amphetamines, and even nicotine. Prescription medications (including antihypertensives, steroids such as cortisone, body-building steroids, and birth control pills), as well as many medical illnesses (such as hepatitis, infectious mononucleosis, cancer, or abnormal thyroid hormone levels), can also cause or complicate depression.

Workplace Recognition and
Referral of Depressive Disorders

While recognition of characteristic depressive disorder changes seems straightforward, even trained professionals will often find it initially difficult to gauge the type, extent, and causes of the disorder. That some form of depression exists can be readily detected through workplace observations. In general, psychiatric problems manifest as difficulties involving comprehension, personal interaction, and productivity. In particular, mood changes (signaling a depressive disorder) appear in the form of diminished good humor, dissatisfaction, and distinct unhappiness. There may be a tired, washed-out look. Physiologically, there may be signs of poor eating, sleep disturbance, and other health problems. Psychologically, there can be irritability, negativity, indecisiveness, and self-doubt. Depressed people cannot and do not work as effectively as they would under normal conditions. Productivity levels drop through inability to complete tasks, as well as inability to stay at the job.

There is much more to referral than simply handing over the name of a psychiatrist or the company doctor. Some people still think of mental illness as a weakness or a personal failing. This is particularly true of depressed patients, whose sense of self-worth is at a low ebb. Referrals are far more likely to be effective when the patient recognizes a legitimate problem that needs treatment. The following four guidelines can help assure effective referral for therapy (see also Chapter 1):

1. *Offer affirmative and supportive guidance.* Be concerned, friendly, candid, and direct. Strong and stable guideposts are essential during depression. Bolster emotional strength by providing practical means of finding the best resources.
2. *Locate the best resources.* In times of crisis it is difficult to see the possibilities. Even those depressed employees with seemingly considerable psychological and social resources will often need help in finding appropriate treatment. Take the time to find the name of a specific referral.
3. *Act concretely.* Give the employee something tangible to hang onto: a pamphlet, the practitioner's business card, or a handwritten note with instructions and telephone numbers on it. During depression, it is all too easy to think that no real help is at hand.
4. *Follow through with the referral.* Once you have given out the referral name and number, be sure to check with the employee a day or two later to assess progress. Many times, effective referral will require further efforts or professional intervention. A friendly attitude of firmness, composure, and expected compliance is helpful. Get help if there are

problems. In case of emergency situations that involve threats of violence or self-harm, do not hesitate to call company security or the police.

Treatment

Mood disorders are very treatable. With professional psychiatric care, almost all depressions will improve significantly. Most symptoms can be relieved in a few weeks, with more complete psychological recovery in 4 to 12 months. The most effective treatment for depression is a combination of psychotherapy and antidepressant medication. In general, people with the most severe depressions are the most responsive to medication.

Hospitalization may speed the recovery process. In a hospital setting, the levels of antidepressant medication can be raised more rapidly, and the psychotherapy (including group and individual therapy) is generally more intensive. The decision to hospitalize a depressed person is usually based on concerns about the person's safety, or the cause, depth, and intensity of the depression. The course of hospitalization usually runs 2 to 4 weeks, with weekly follow-ups afterward. The overall outcome of treatment for depression on either an inpatient or an outpatient basis is about the same.

Psychotherapy

The initial role of the psychiatrist is to give helpful guidance in understanding and dealing with depression. Psychotherapy then soon addresses prevention of recurrent depression by looking at coping skills, and thought and behavior patterns. Psychotherapeutic support is always beneficial during the suffering of depression, and especially when there is delayed response to needed medication. There are a variety of different psychotherapies, but in the treatment of depression, most fall under three categories (see also Chapter 1):

1. *Insight-oriented and interpersonal psychotherapy:* This treatment relates depressive symptoms to unresolved early childhood losses and conflicts. It aims for both resolution of deeper problems and practical solutions for the issues at hand. It may combine exploratory psychotherapy, establishment of coping skills, and antidepressant medication.
2. *Cognitive therapy:* The emphasis is on learning new ways of thinking and behaving, in order to replace habitual negativity. It is a highly structured and directive approach.
3. *Behavior therapy:* The focus is on specific goals to increase the depressed person's activity level, capacity for enjoyment, and ability to relax (via specific relaxation techniques).

Relevance of certain psychotherapeutic techniques to specific depressive disorders follows in each section.

Medication

While adjustment disorders usually do not require medication, antidepressant medications are a front-line treatment for other depressions. Antidepressants generally become fully effective in 3 to 6 weeks, are continued for a 4- to 12-month course of treatment, and are not habit forming. There are two major types of medication used to treat depression: the heterocyclics (including tricyclics and serotonin reuptake inhibitors) and the monoamine oxidase inhibitors (MAOIs).

Heterocyclics are the most frequently prescribed and are indicated for people whose depressions are characterized by insomnia, fatigue, exhaustion, hopelessness, and loss of appetite and weight. The tricyclics (such as imipramine and nortriptyline) have been used for decades and are thought to act on several different neurotransmitter sites. A more recent class of antidepressants acts only on serotonin neurotransmitter sites. Since these serotonin reuptake inhibitors (such as fluoxetine and sertraline) act at more specific sites, they may have fewer side effects. Fluoxetine is especially effective for atypical depression (see section on dysthymia).

MAOIs are used to treat depression in patients who are intolerant of or unresponsive to heterocyclics, but they have a potential for serious chemical interactions with certain foods and other medications. MAOIs should only be prescribed by a physician familiar with their use. Patients taking MAOIs are restricted from eating tyramine-containing foods as diverse as aged cheese, avocados, pickles, red wine, and beer (see Table 13-1). The MAOIs are also used for atypical depression, panic disorder, and posttraumatic stress disorder.

Infrequently, such stimulants as dextroamphetamine, methylphenidate, or pemoline are used for medically ill patients and others who cannot tolerate standard antidepressants. Patients who respond to stimulants do so in a few days. Because there is some risk of tolerance and dependence, dosage and duration are carefully monitored.

Long-term, continuous medication may be necessary to prevent or lessen recurring depressions. Lithium has long been the medication of choice for treatment and prevention of bipolar (manic depressive) disorders. Recent research (e.g., Kaplan and Sadock 1990, p. 94) suggests that carbamazepine and valproic acid may be similarly effective.

Perfect prediction of antidepressant response and side effects is not possible. Medication choice depends on type of depression, side effect profile, latency of medication onset, and concurrent medical illness (Table 13-1). In general, antidepressant side effects are more bothersome than

TABLE 13-1 Antidepressant Medication

Generic Name	Trade Name	Daily Dose (mg)		Side Effects			Other Precautions
		Start	Usual	Sedation	Anti-cholinergic	Hypotension	
Tricylics (Heterocyclics)							
Imipramine	Tofranil	75	150-300	+3	+3	+3	
Desipramine	Pertofrane						
	Norpramin	50	100-300	+1	+1	+2	
Amitriptyline	Elavil						
	Endep	75	150-300	+3	+4	+4	
Nortriptyline	Aventyl						
	Pamelor	50	50-125	+1	+1	+2	
Protriptyline	Vivactil	15	15-60	+1	+4	+3	
Doxepin	Sinequan						
	Adapin	75	75-300	+4	+2	+4	
Trimipramine	Surmontil	75	50-200	+4	+2	+3	
Clomipramine	Anafranil	25	150-250	+2	+1	+1	
Dibenzoxazepines							
Amoxapine	Asendin	150	150-400	+1	+1	+1	

(continued)

TABLE 13-1 Antidepressant Medication—Continued

Generic Name	Trade Name	Daily Dose (mg) Start	Daily Dose (mg) Usual	Side Effects Sedation	Side Effects Anti-cholinergic	Side Effects Hypotension	Other Precautions
Monoamine Oxidase Inhibitors							
Hydrazines							
Phenelzine	Nardil	45	45–90	+1	+2	+3	[a]
Isocarboxazid	Marplan	20	20–60	+2	+1	+3	[a]
Nonhydrazines							
Tranylcypromine	Parnate	20	20–80	+1	+1	+2	[a]
Tetracyclics							
Maprotiline	Ludiomil	75	125–225	+3	+1	+1	
Triazolopyridine							
Trazodone	Desyrel	150	150–400	+3	+0	+3	
Stimulants							
Dextroamphetamine	Dexedrine	2.5	10–20	0	+2	+1	[b]
Methylphenidate	Ritalin	5	20–30	0	+2	+1	[b]
Pemoline	Cylert	18.75	56.25–75	0	+2	+1	[b]
Serotonin Reuptake Inhibitors							
Fluoxetine	Prozac	20	20–40	+1	+/0	+/0	
Sertraline	Zoloft	50	50–200	+1	+/0	+/0	
Aminoketones							
Bupropion	Wellbutrin	200	150–400	0	0	0	
Lithium		600	600–1500	+2	+/0	0	[b,c]

Antidepressants typically require 3 to 6 weeks for therapeutic response.
[a] Strict dietary restriction.
[b] Given only under strict medical supervision.
[c] Primarily used as adjunctive treatment.

life-threatening. The most common side effects are drowsiness and such anticholinergenic problems as dry mouth, rapid or uneven heartbeat, difficulty urinating, constipation, and blurred vision. Orthostatic hypotension that causes fainting is a particular problem in the elderly. Insomnia sometimes responds quickly to a sedating antidepressant at bedtime. An antidepressant with a low sedative effect will maximize alertness.

Most depressions respond well to appropriate outpatient psychotherapy and antidepressant medication. Once the antidepressant is given, there can be some reduction of insomnia and anxiety in a few days. The major antidepressant response occurs after 3 or 4 weeks. Sleep, appetite, energy, and concentration will typically improve first. Improvements in attitude, optimism, and judgment follow soon after. Within 4 to 6 weeks, there is usually a distinct lift in spirits. Moments of positive thoughts and feelings will become increasingly frequent. Within several months, the psychological sequelae will usually resolve, although vulnerability to stressors may still be greater than before. Complete biochemical and psychological readjustment may take a year.

Psychiatric follow-up is extremely important, both for antidepressant medication management and for psychotherapy. There is a tendency for patients with major depression to stop treatment once the antidepressants start to take effect and mood begins to improve. This is not only untimely but unhelpful for the recovery process. Full recovery and the establishment of preventive coping skills require persistent effort and a certain amount of trial and error. Actively encouraging the patient to follow through on both medication and psychotherapy will ensure maximal recovery.

Workplace Management

Depressive disorders have major effects on worker and workplace. A passing blue mood does not necessarily require psychiatric evaluation or treatment. Unfortunately, many severe depressions are never appropriately treated. Prompt recognition of symptoms and timely referral for psychiatric evaluation ensure optimal improvement. Once depression has been diagnosed, management can help with recovery. It is important to recognize the physical symptoms and limitations of depression, the increased sensitivity to stress, and the need for compliance with treatment. Equally, it is important to bring the employee back up to speed at the earliest reasonable time. More generally, companies that provide job security, reasonable measures of independence and responsibility, physical comfort and safety, and readily available avenues for resolving problems or conflicts will thus create a psychologically supportive environment. To the extent that management style can help recovery or prevent depression, organizations can offer clear feedback, appropriate acknowledgment and praise, and a realistically optimistic corporate culture.

ADJUSTMENT DISORDER
WITH DEPRESSED MOOD

Diagnostic Overview

An adjustment disorder with depressed mood means that there is a depressive adjustment to specific, identifiable psychosocial stressors. Typically, the depressed mood is transient. The nature of the adjustment disorder assumes that the disturbance will remit after the stressor ceases, or when individual adaptations are made. The stressors may be single or multiple, periodic or continuous. They often occur in a family or workplace setting. Stressors may affect only a particular individual, or they may affect a group or community. Some stressors may accompany specific developmental events such as going to school, leaving the parental home, getting married, becoming a parent, making rank, failing to attain occupational goals, and retiring from the work force.

DSM-III-R DIAGNOSTIC CRITERIA

Adjustment Disorder

A. A reaction to an identifiable psychosocial stressor (or multiple stressors) that occurs within three months of onset of the stressor(s).

B. The maladaptive nature of the reaction is indicated by either of the following:

   (1) impairment in occupational (including school) functioning or in usual social activities or relationships with others
   (2) symptoms that are in excess of a normal and expectable reaction to the stressor(s)

C. The disturbance is not merely one instance of a pattern of overreaction to stress or an exacerbation of one of the mental disorders previously described.

D. The maladaptive reaction has persisted for no longer than six months.

E. The disturbance does not meet the criteria for any specific mental disorder and does not represent Uncomplicated Bereavement.

309.00 Adjustment Disorder with Depressed Mood

This category should be used when the predominant manifestation is symptoms such as depressed mood, tearfulness, and feelings of hopelessness.

Reprinted with permission from the *Diagnostic and Statistical Manual of Mental Disorders,* 3d ed. rev.; copyright 1987 by the American Psychiatric Association.

Bereavement and grief bring about such specific adjustments of body and mind that they have their own diagnostic category. Because the reaction to death of a loved one is so common and universal, the ensuing bereavement is considered a normal reaction (Table 13-2). Survivors may have thoughts that they would be better off dead, or that they should have died instead of the loved one. Bereavement may be delayed, but rarely occurs after 2 to 3 months. Duration varies considerably, with the acute phase resolving in 1 to 1½ months, and the overall bereavement lasting 6 to 24 months. A full-blown depressive syndrome can develop from the depressed mood of bereavement, but this would then involve more complicated symptoms, such as a persistently poor appetite, weight loss, insomnia, pervasive guilt and self-blame, and no sense of resolution.

Grief, which closely resembles bereavement, occurs following the loss of a job, romantic relationship, cherished pet, favorite memento, or something that has great value to the individual. Most characteristically, it emerges after the breakup of a personal, intimate relationship, or the ending of a significant task or job.

Demoralization is an increasingly common cause of depressed mood for intensely goal- and career-oriented individuals. This mood disorder frequently goes unrecognized and undiagnosed, although it can have the same depressive symptoms as bereavement and grief. Employees and companies are often unaware of the profoundly negative impact that adverse workplace changes can have on both workers and the organization.

TABLE 13-2   Comparison of Depression and Grief

Index	Depression	Grief
Timing	6–12 months	1–24 months following a loss
Symptoms	Worse in morning if diurnal mood variation is present	Worse in afternoon, as patient faces the day without the lost person
Depressive vegetative signs	Typical: insomnia, anorexia, lethargy	Less common
Thought	Guilt, self-deprecation	Thoughts, hallucinations of deceased relative are sometimes normal
Guilt	Pervasive guilt and self-blame	Limited to feelings about what patient should have done differently or about having survived when another person has not
Self-esteem	Lowered self-esteem and self-confidence	Intact self-esteem except for anxiety about living without the lost person or thing
Resolution by expressing feeling	Only 50% of cases resolve with nonspecific encouragement to express feelings	Sadness resolves when patient expresses feelings about the loss
Resolution	No sense of resolution	Feeling of aceptance
Abatement	Spontaneous improvement takes 6–12 months	Acute phase abates in 4–6 weeks
Recurrences	Become more severe and long-lasting with time	Primarily at important holidays and anniversaries

Case Anecdotes

Case Study 1: Adjustment Disorder with Depressed Mood

Coe MacIntyre is a 32-year-old associate in a law firm. Two months ago, her boyfriend Patrick walked out on her, ending a 4-year relationship. Coe was hurt and shocked. She thought it was ultimately for the best, since Patrick had been jealous of her devotion to work. Yet since then, she has had the flu twice, lost 12 pounds, and used up all of her sick leave and vacation days. Her fellow employees have begun avoiding her, because she can't stop crying and talking about how mean, hurtful, and irresponsible Patrick was. To compound matters, she has been sending terse, angry messages on the electronic mail, and her office manager is trying to decide what to do. Even so, Coe has been sleeping well, enjoying the food that she does eat, and laughing with close friends about old times and future boyfriends.

Adjustment disorders develop rapidly in response to change. This can pose a particularly sudden challenge for managers. Romantic relationship difficulties have great potential for destabilizing emotional equilibrium and they are a major source of adjustment disorders. Rationally, Coe thinks it is best to let go of her relationship with Patrick. Emotionally, she finds it difficult to break a 4-year bond. Her depressive symptoms, along with the resentment and anger expressed through tears, words, and memos, are characteristic of an adjustment disorder.

Case Study 2: Bereavement

Mark Boudreau is a 27-year-old computer programmer, whose mother died of ovarian cancer 2 months ago. Although he was never especially close to her, as her eldest son he had helped her financially and emotionally over the last 2 years. During the past week he has spent several evenings reviewing medical and hospital records to see if he and the doctors did everything they could to prevent her death. For weeks he has suffered from anxiety, worry, fatigue, insomnia, anorexia, apathy, and difficulty concentrating at work. Unwilling to worry any other members of his family, Mark finally asked his boss whether he should quit, change jobs, or take a leave of absence.

Mark is going through bereavement, a normal grieving process that follows the death of a loved one. However, the more this process is delayed by internally conflicted feelings about the deceased, or by such external circumstances as an unrecovered body, the more problematic bereavement can become. In Mark's case, emotional ambivalence about his mother has resulted in a painful suspension of bereavement. This process involves phases of admission, acceptance, mourning, and readjustment to a life without the loved one. With understanding and timely referral for treatment, Mark would be able to get the psychiatric support and guidance necessary to complete his grieving process. Otherwise, he might easily develop a major depression.

Case Study 3: Demoralization

Ben Steinberg is a 44-year-old electrical engineer who has been working for the same aerospace company for 20 years. For the past 2 years, his company has not made money, and so it was announced that all engineers' wages would be frozen. Ben said that he understood perfectly well why he did not get a raise, and noted that his wife would be able to earn the tuition for their handicapped daughter's special school. Nevertheless, in staff meetings he complained loudly about the bitterness of the coffee and the scarcity of office supplies, and he frequently focused on minutiae. He went to the personnel office, demanded to see everyone's salaries, and then played hurtful practical jokes on co-workers. When Ben failed to show up for work 2 days in a row, his colleagues became alarmed and called the personnel director.

Demoralization is a highly individualized emotional reaction to real or perceived issues. In Ben's case, the money is not the real issue. However, his desire to support his family without his wife working is important to his self-image, so the news of no raise hit him particularly hard. Deeply felt personal needs and desires can be hard to understand for the individual and can be difficult to communicate to others. An inner sense of demoralization can surface in the workplace as disruptive behavior, obnoxious comments, nitpicking complaints, or extreme sensitivity to criticism. For all of these reasons, a manager needs to approach demoralized employees with an extra measure of both understanding and firmness.

Causes

In most cases, employee vulnerability is a more significant contributor than the stressor itself. Vulnerability increases when stressful events involve difficult adult developmental phases. Recurrent, continuous, and multiple stressors have a cumulative effect. Personal concerns about security, self-esteem, desire for approval, and empowerment can swiftly overwhelm the individual, without anyone realizing just what has happened. Interpersonal relationships have a great deal to do with a sense of well-being. Any disruption of a relationship with a spouse, parent, lover, friend, or colleague typically has a ripple effect on other relationships and functioning. The most traumatic stressors affect personal safety concerns, such as accidents, burglaries, and auto vandalism. Similarly, natural or human disasters can be profoundly stressful, particularly when they are violent, unjust, or uncontrollable.

Although environmental and circumstantial stressors are sometimes easy to recognize, they are often not sufficient explanation for a marked reaction. Sometimes the smallest change within the workplace can trigger an adjustment disorder. New job assignments, supervisory changes, departmental transfers, demotions, and even promotions call for adaptation. Emotional trauma caused by mergers, acquisitions, and the downsizing of companies is common (see Chapter 7). Use of objective grades and point systems can sometimes be unintentionally traumatic. There can also be stressful seasonal business cycles, for example, in the retail and travel industries.

Treatment

The good news about adjustment disorders with depression is that they are eminently treatable. In fact, treatment usually proves successful in fewer than 12 psychotherapy sessions. The psychiatrist will help patients to identify both the role of the stressor and their particular vulnerability. The reduction or elimination of the stressor is a necessary first step in order to create a comfort zone in which the person feels safe enough to fully acknowledge and accept personal vulnerability. If the patient is interested, therapy can then go beyond the current situation, and additional coping and adaptational skills for future stressors can be developed.

Antidepressant or antianxiety medications are occasionally prescribed during the initial crisis. Psychological testing can help the person perceive the problem more quickly. A patient's written narrative of the problem and potential solutions can speed up the process. Psychotherapy sessions are concentrated during the initial several weeks of treatment, then gradually cut back to weekly and monthly appointments. Follow-up is extremely important in ensuring optimal resolution and attainment of appropriate coping and adjustment skills.

Workplace Recognition, Effects, Management, and Prognosis

Both positive and negative changes call for psychological adjustment. Twenty-five percent of people can easily adjust to highly stressful changes; another 50 percent adjust in a matter of weeks. Experience has shown that the remaining 25 percent have difficulty and may develop adjustment reactions. Since the underlying problem can be intimate or interpersonal, direct consideration of the problem can be uncomfortable for employee, co-workers, and supervisors alike. Accurate prediction of impairment magnitude, duration, or consequences is not always possible. Direct observation of employee emotions, moods, attitudes, conduct, and productivity, combined with support and direct feedback, is the most effective way to deal with adjustment disorders.

Employees with possible adjustment disorders should be referred for professional evaluation as soon as severe symptoms or stressors become evident. Strong encouragement may be needed. Often employees will think that they should be able to handle life's challenges without outside help. Psychiatrists and employee assistance programs are helpful in distinguishing between the personal, relational, and psychological causes. Mental health professionals also are adept at understanding the nuances and consequences of personal change, and they will take the necessary time to understand both the uniqueness and the universality of the problem at hand.

The greatest effects on worker and workplace occur when adjustment reactions take place without anyone's awareness. When the underlying disorder remains hidden, the problem becomes externalized. Tensions increase, sides are chosen, and both the employee and employers start pointing fingers. The behavioral symptoms of the transient depression usually become the focus of the problem. When the affected employee has difficulty setting agendas or problem solving, a supervisor can inadvertently worsen matters by focusing on the shortcomings. Ideally, when a worker has difficulty with focus, teamwork, and productive effort, a supervisor needs to realize that there are underlying causes for the outward changes in behavior. In practice, however, tensions often rise, and there is a tendency toward either inaction or overreaction on both sides.

Adjustment disorders have a good prognosis, since the symptoms go away after the stressor ceases or after a new level of adaptation is reached. Extensive loss of work time is not usual. When work is missed, it is usually for patching up relationships, dealing with parental concerns, or working on legal or financial matters. Regular Monday absences, extended breaks, and other time loss issues do need to be addressed. Emotional adaptation takes time. It is helpful to clarify employer expectations, to foster resolution of the stressors, and sometimes to allow time off to effect prompt solutions.

Since some limited dysfunction can occur for a short time, special care should be taken in work situations that involve major responsibilities or physical risk. Decisions may have to be postponed and safety protocols must be followed with particular care. Expectations and communications should be extremely clear. They should be conveyed verbally first, and followed up with written reminders.

MAJOR DEPRESSION

Diagnostic Overview

Major depressive disorder (MDD) is the best known form of depression. Variously called clinical, endogenous, or biochemical depression, there are also subtypes including melancholia, seasonal affective disorder (SAD), postpartum depression, and depressive psychoses. MDD is often popularly described as a nervous breakdown or chemical imbalance.

DSM-III-R DIAGNOSTIC CRITERIA

Major Depressive Episode

Note: A "Major Depressive Syndrome" is defined as criterion A below.

A. At least five of the following symptoms have been present during the same two-week period and represent a change from previous functioning; at least one of the symptoms is either (1) depressed mood, or (2) loss of interest or pleasure. (Do not include symptoms that are clearly due to a physical condi-

---

tion, mood-incongruent delusions or hallucinations, incoherence, or marked loosening of associations.)

(1) depressed mood (or can be irritable mood in children and adolescents) most of the day, nearly every day, as indicated either by subjective account or observation by others

(2) markedly diminished interest or pleasure in all, or almost all, activities most of the day, nearly every day (as indicated either by subjective account or observation by others of apathy most of the time)

(3) significant weight loss or weight gain when not dieting (e.g., more than 5% of body weight in a month), or decrease or increase in appetite nearly every day (in children, consider failure to make expected weight gains)

(4) insomnia or hypersomnia nearly every day

(5) psychomotor agitation or retardation nearly every day (observable by others, not merely subjective feelings of restlessness or being slowed down)

(6) fatigue or loss of energy nearly every day

(7) feelings of worthlessness or excessive or inappropriate guilt (which may be delusional) nearly every day (not merely self-reproach or guilt about being sick)

(8) diminished ability to think or concentrate, or indecisiveness, nearly every day (either by subjective account or as observed by others)

(9) recurrent thoughts of death (not just fear of dying), recurrent suicidal ideation without a specific plan, or a suicide attempt or a specific plan for committing suicide

B. (1) It cannot be established that an organic factor initiated and maintained the disturbance

(2) The disturbance is not a normal reaction to the death of a loved one (Uncomplicated Bereavement)

Note: Morbid preoccupation with worthlessness, suicidal ideation, marked functional impairment or psychomotor retardation, or prolonged duration suggest bereavement complicated by Major Depression.

C. At no time during the disturbance have there been delusions or hallucinations for as long as two weeks in the absence of prominent mood symptoms (i.e., before the mood symptoms developed or after they have remitted).

D. Not superimposed on Schizophrenia, Schizophreniform Disorder, Delusional Disorder, or Psychotic Disorder NOS.

Major depressive episode codes: fifth-digit code numbers and criteria for severity of current state of Bipolar Disorder, Depressed, or Major Depression:

1–Mild: Few, if any, symptoms in excess of those required to make the diagnosis, **and** symptoms result in only minor impairment in occupational functioning or in usual social activities or relationships with others.

2–Moderate: Symptoms or functional impairment between "mild" and "severe."

3–Severe, without Psychotic Features: Several symptoms in excess of those required to make the diagnosis, **and** symptoms markedly interfere with occupational functioning or with usual social activities or relationships with others.

4–With Psychotic Features: Delusions or hallucinations. If possible, **specify** whether the psychotic features are *mood-congruent* or *mood-incongruent*.

Mood-congruent psychotic features: Delusions or hallucinations whose content is entirely consistent with the typical depressive themes of personal inadequacy, guilt, disease, death, nihilism, or deserved punishment.

Mood-incongruent psychotic features: Delusions or hallucinations whose content does *not* involve typical depressive themes of personal inadequacy, guilt, disease, death, nihilism, or deserved punishment. Included here are such symptoms as persecutory delusions (not directly related to depressive themes), thought insertion, thought broadcasting, and delusions of control.

5–In Partial Remission: Intermediate between "In Full Remission" and "Mild," **and** no previous Dysthymia. (If Major Depressive Episode was superimposed on Dysthymia, the diagnosis of Dysthymia alone is given once the full criteria for a Major Depressive Episode are no longer met.)

6—In Full Remission: During the past six months no significant signs or symptoms of the disturbance.

0—Unspecified.

Specify chronic if current episode has lasted two consecutive years without a period of two months or longer during which there were no significant depressive symptoms.

Specify if current episode is **Melancholic Type.**

Diagnostic criteria for Melancholic Type

The presence of at least five of the following:

    (1) loss of interest or pleasure in all, or almost all, activities

    (2) lack of reactivity to usually pleasurable stimuli (does not feel much better, even temporarily, when something good happens)

    (3) depression regularly worse in the morning

    (4) early morning awakening (at least two hours before usual time of awakening)

    (5) psychomotor retardation or agitation (not merely subjective complaints)

    (6) significant anorexia or weight loss (e.g., more than 5% of body weight in a month)

    (7) no significant personality disturbance before first major depressive episode

    (8) one or more previous major depressive episodes followed by complete, or nearly complete, recovery

    (9) previous good response to specific and adequate somatic antidepressant therapy, e.g., tricyclics, ECT, MAOI, lithium

Major depression can develop in as short a time as 2 weeks, and in its early stages it can masquerade as anxiety or stress. There is usually some precipitating stressful event, such as the death of a loved one, divorce, or business failure. Even so, development of MDD is more often rooted in personal reactions to the emotional trauma. In the workplace, early stages of MDD may be evidenced by increased anxiety and inability to concentrate on the work at hand. Characteristically, there will also be withdrawal, isolation, decreased productivity, and fatigue. There can often be persistent physical pain, especially headache, backache, and muscle pain.

In diagnostic terms, the primary symptom of MDD is depressed mood or markedly diminished interest or pleasure in everyday activities for at least 2 weeks. There are also significant changes in appetite, weight, sleep, and daily tasks. Inwardly, feelings of worthlessness and guilt develop, along with recurring thoughts of death and a diminished ability to think and concentrate. As the depression deepens, there is increasing withdrawal from social situations and negativism. Avoiding or actively refusing professional help often emerges as part of the picture. One of the cruel things about MDD is that intense awareness of despair and suffering is combined with profound disheartenment about the value of treatment. Past happiness is forgotten and future happiness is considered unattainable. But effective help is available, and the sooner depression is recognized and treated, the better for all concerned.

Case Anecdotes

Case Study 4: Major Depressive Disorder Following Separation

Three weeks after Gwendolyn Turner reached 50, she started her own imported clothing boutique. On Christmas Eve, 5 weeks after that, her husband announced that he had been in love with another woman for the past 10 years. On New Year's Day he moved out while their youngest son went back to college. During the next month, Gwendolyn became increasingly despondent and slept fitfully 3 to 4 hours a night. She woke up early, with a feeling of dread about the future, and tried to figure out how she could have kept her husband from leaving her. Although she couldn't think clearly, and continued to toss and turn, she felt too tired to get out of bed. She became apathetic about her new business venture. She made mistakes on the computerized ledgers and missed several days of work. Carol, her business associate and close friend, became alarmed when Gwendolyn announced plans to review her life insurance policy and take 3 weeks off. Carol tried to call Gwendolyn's estranged husband, but he was unreachable on a sailboat in the Virgin Islands. Carol finally decided to call a psychiatrist to find out what could be done. Gwendolyn agreed to a consultation, talked about her suicide plans, and was hospitalized for 2 weeks. Treatment with nortriptyline, 50 mg twice a day, and intensive psychotherapy brought her through the worst of her depression within a month. Within 3 months, she had her business on track and had resumed a satisfying social life.

Relationships are the most satisfying of human experiences and they also have the greatest potential for causing distress. One of the most difficult stresses of all is the loss of a spouse through separation, divorce, or death. The effects are intensified when extramarital affairs or child custody issues are involved. Consequent depressions can often progress from adjustment disorders to a major depression. The intensity of Gwendolyn's despair was compounded by the new business, disclosure of the extramarital affair, abrupt departure of her husband, her son's simultaneous return to college, and the occurrence of a major holiday (when people, consciously or unconsciously, expect to be happier than usual).

Although Gwendolyn was career oriented and owner of the new store, the shock of her husband's desertion was so acute that she was not only unable to do her work but was also oblivious to the fact that she had developed a serious depression. The actual recognition of depression is often left to a spouse, friend, or business associate. Depression prevents people from thinking, concentrating, or making decisions as well as usual. Thus it is vital to communicate with them in very specific terms, both verbally and in a written letter of concern or a thoughtful evaluation. This should be done as early as possible, to ensure timely medical and psychiatric evaluation.

Case Study 5: Major Depressive Disorder with Melancholia

Karl Jensen was 62 when he learned that his wife had breast cancer, shortly before they left for a long anticipated Caribbean cruise. Two months after their return, Karl's wife died. In the next 7 months, Karl had increasing trouble keeping up with his work schedule, despite overtime work and 35 years of experience as a machinist. His physical movements were noticeably slower. Even though he double-checked his figures, he made several costly mistakes. He lost interest in his outside activities and felt especially bad in the mornings. Instead of joining his buddies for lunch, he spent lunch hour sleeping in his car. Noticing that Karl looked worried, thin, ill, and very tired, a co-worker asked about his health. Although Karl said he felt all right, he admitted that he was having stomach problems, waking up worried every morning at three A.M., and he had lost 18 pounds. He knew he wasn't working up to par, but thought he needed to put in extra hours to have money for a memorial. Several days later, the supervisor smelled beer on Karl's breath, reprimanded him, and started the paperwork for Karl's discharge. The co-worker then convinced Karl to go for help. Karl was able to stop drinking when he began outpatient treatment. He was started on trazodone, 50 mg three times a day, and psychotherapy twice a week. Since a routine pretreatment electrocardiogram revealed a mild first-degree heart block, a follow-up study was done to confirm medication safety.

Alcohol use is frequently associated with depression. Depression can lead to drinking, and drinking can also cause or worsen depression. Giving up drinking will not allay the depressive process; but if it does not stop, depression is almost impossible to treat (see Chapter 16). Although grief and bereavement would be expected after death of a spouse, the type, intensity, and prolongation of Karl's symptoms indicated a more severe illness. Karl's underlying problem was major depression with melancholia. He used alcohol both to ease the blow of his wife's death and to hide the severity of his depressive symptoms. His susceptibility to major depression was increased by his age and by the circumstances surrounding her death. Karl and his wife had fulfilled their lifetime dream of a Caribbean cruise, but only to find themselves with the nightmare of her sudden illness and death.

Causes

MDD has many contributing causes. Emergence, severity, and timing of MDD depend on biology, personality, and circumstance. The physical symptoms of MDD and frequent resistance to psychotherapeutic treatment alone have long suggested a major biological component. When antidepressant medication first became available in the 1950s, the nature of medication response provided further support for a biological mechanism. Unlike abused drugs, they do not induce a high, and neither do they correct unhappy circumstances. Antidepressants are thought to act on brain neurotransmitter symptoms to relieve MDD symptoms. Since the mid 1970s, much antidepressant research has focused on chemicals that prevent cells from reabsorbing the neurotransmitter serotonin (e.g., Fuller 1991). Serotonin thus remains longer at nerve endings and it has a greater effect. These increased levels of serotonin seem to alleviate MDD symptoms. There is some evidence that predisposition toward depression can be inherited, perhaps through variations in neurotransmitter systems. MDD occurs generation after generation in some families, but it can also appear where there is no prior family history.

There are many other biological causes and triggers of depression, including many physical illnesses, medications, abused drugs (and alcohol), hormonal pattern changes, and sleep pattern changes. A severe accident, shock, or other environmental stressors can also act as biological triggers for depression. As in all emotional illnesses, the psychological and biological dimensions of MDD are closely intertwined.

Personality and emotional makeup play an equally important role in vulnerability to major depression. Particularly vulnerable to MDD are people who have frequent or sustained interpersonal conflicts, unrealistic expectations, extreme idealism, ignorance of life limits, unresolved grief, or unexpressed anger. Similarly prone to depression are people with low self-esteem, habitual pessimism about themselves and the world, or easily overwhelmed life adjustment under stress. Traumatic relationships and such losses as divorce, illness, or death can trigger depression. Strained family relationships, marital discord, extramarital affairs, and children's problems are among the most severe stressors.

Any significant life pattern change can trigger a depressive episode. Even if there is a strong hereditary or personality disposition, MDD is usually triggered by some specific event. While the event is sometimes clearly recognizable and concrete, it is often subtle or highly symbolized. A neighbor's move to another state, the birth of a niece, or a colleague's promotion are all less apparent stressors than divorce or parental illness.

Increasingly, the workplace is a trigger for depressive episodes. As more families include two parents with full-time jobs, work takes a more central role in emotional well-being. Job security, satisfaction, social status, income, and even seemingly minor perks such as a reserved parking space can become potent symbols of self-worth. Accordingly, if these elements are threatened or lost, there is diminished reliance on internal and family supports, and depression can result. The problem intensifies when there is also a sudden awareness of missing social and family relationships. Other work-related factors such as long hours, physical overexertion, time pressure, conflict with co-workers, inconsistent supervision, and responsibility without commensurate authority can contribute to susceptibility for depression.

Treatment

Treatment for major depression has improved dramatically and is constantly improving. Continuing research has defined subtypes of depression, allowing for specifically effective treatment. The first antidepressant medications became available in the 1950s, and they are now complemented by many new medications with more specific effects and fewer side effects. Even psychotherapy has improved, with greater awareness of the importance of emotional intimacy and some specific approaches to depression. Although depression remains a serious illness, most people find effective relief. Public awareness of effective treatment also leads to earlier recognition and treatment. Psychotherapy and antidepressant medication are the most common treatments for MDD, and they are best used in combination. Medication provides relatively fast symptomatic relief, and it enables psychotherapy to provide longer-term assistance with self-knowledge and improved coping skills. Depressed patients often find psychotherapy alone unhelpful, and they find medication alone neither immediately reassuring nor useful in addressing their circumstances.

Since depression is a complex and multidetermined illness, complete medical and psychiatric evaluation is essential before treatment begins. The evaluation includes a medical and psychiatric history outlining physical and emotional background, and a mental status examination that uncovers changes in the individual's moods, thoughts, speech, and memory. Specific symptoms are used to look for depressive subtypes and concurrent psychiatric and medical diagnoses. The psychiatrist will typically perform or order a physical exam and blood tests to check for undiagnosed medical problems.

Psychological tests are also used to assess the symptoms, severity, and type of depression, as well as to point to accompanying psychiatric conditions and personality patterns.

Psychotherapy is a science and an art. A psychiatrist tries to absorb what the patient is feeling as well as saying, and then chooses the most promising psychotherapeutic approach. In the course of treatment, patient and psychotherapist talk about the present and past experiences, relationships, and goals; and about the thoughts, feelings, and behaviors that they produce. Hidden fear and anger can contribute to depression onset and continuance. Understanding the hidden beliefs and feelings that cause distress produces distinct emotional relief and enhanced ability to find practical solutions to problems at hand. For this reason, psychotherapy is often called "talk therapy."

Psychotherapy is usually most effective for less severe major depression, which forms the larger part of the MDD spectrum. Psychotherapy provides a relationship with a doctor who has worked with other depressed patients. Through this relationship, the therapist initially provides information about depression, therapy, and medication, and provides supportive guidance for individual and family. Explanation of the illness and treatment offers hope, and it allows collaborative pursuit of a definite and individualized treatment. Understanding the perceptual and behavioral patterns that may have led to depression reduces the risk of future recurrence. Although therapy is less effective in the depths of a more severe depression, it still provides support, and patients can become more engaged after antidepressant response.

Antidepressant medications play a vital role in the treatment of major depression. These medications are initially most effective in reducing insomnia, anorexia, depressed mood, and anxiety. They treat MDD symptoms, but without inducing any particular emotional state. They do not make people feel high, and they do not correct unpleasant circumstances. They do make it easier to see circumstances for what they really are: no better and no worse. Some MDD symptoms may show a mild response within a week, but it usually takes at least 3 weeks for an overall response to become evident. Patients are often tempted to stop taking antidepressants too soon, because antidepressant effects are not immediate and there may be side effects. Once medication response begins, the antidepressant is usually continued for another 4 to 12 months. An attempt should then be made to discontinue the medication slowly, while monitoring the individual for the return of depression.

Occasionally used are electroconvulsive therapy (ECT) and such experimental somatic approaches as bright light, sleep deprivation, sleep phase changes, and exercise. While contemporary ECT is considered safer and more effective than other treatments of severe MDD, it is also controversial. It is most often used for upper-income patients who need to return to work as quickly and safely as possible, or as a last resort for treatment-resistant or medically complicated depression. Bright light therapy is effective for seasonal affective disorder.

Workplace Recognition, Effects, Management, and Prognosis

Major depression has far greater effects on employees and organizations than are usually recognized. Depression is common, and commonly unrecognized. Along with unhappy expression, depression leads to general dissatisfaction and loss of interest and pleasure in the workplace. Isolation from co-workers and avoidance of office gatherings create an atmosphere of discomfort and distrust. Overall behavior is less productive, less purposeful, and less helpful. Tardiness, absenteeism, alcohol and drug abuse, and multiple illness and accidents affect the morale of the whole workplace. Perhaps most significantly, unrecognized depression can impair judgment, engender poor decisions, or produce ineffective management style.

Although MDD will often evoke feelings of sympathetic concern, that concern does not necessarily lead to effective referral and treatment. Well-meaning co-workers and managers may want to "protect" the employee from recognition of a serious illness, or from treatments perceived as intrusive. Instead of prompt referral for optimal treatment, MDD can thus escape recognition or can be addressed with minimal treatment approaches. Depression often comes on so slowly or surreptitiously that the employee remains unaware of the problem until crisis, confrontation, suicide, or accident supervenes. Major depression demands early detection and prompt referral.

During treatment, and after recovery, it is helpful to talk directly about symptoms, medications, medical leave, time for medical appointments, and any workplace restrictions. Care must be taken to avoid intrusiveness. Suggestions or instructions should be simple and direct. Clearly defined work tasks, objectives, and report-back systems are also helpful during this adjustment time. Frequently, a reduced initial work schedule will ease readjustment to the workplace and will demonstrate concern and support. For others, it is easier to return to a full work schedule and is demeaning to feel treated as an invalid.

Although antidepressant medications continue to improve, side effects can include drowsiness, dryness of the mouth, and the temporary lowering of blood pressure. Patients on antidepressants may need to get up or move around more slowly at work. Vehicles, machinery, and heavy equipment may require extra precautions. Intellectual and cognitive functioning may be mildly compromised before treatment response, causing some difficulty in concentration or decision making. Again, direct questions, explicit statements of support, and constructive suggestions can help overcome these temporary complications for workers not on medical leave. With appropriate care, depression responds fully to treatment, and odds of future episodes can be considerably reduced.

DYSTHYMIA AND ATYPICAL DEPRESSION

Diagnostic Overview

Dysthymia, roughly translated from the Greek as "ill humored," describes a chronic, intermittent, low-grade depressive mood disorder that frequently recurs, or never completely disappears. The symptoms are persistent though often mild. Social or occupational dysfunction is subtle, but it can substantially color personality and can increase under stress or over time. Dysthymia includes a complex set of symptoms: joylessness, low energy levels, low self-esteem, and impaired concentration and decision making. Moreover, dysthymia can lead to workplace negativism, irritability, and complaining. Friends and co-workers tend to see a seriously flawed personality rather than a treatable depressive disorder.

DSM-III-R DIAGNOSTIC CRITERIA

300.40 Dysthymia (or Depressive Neurosis)

A. Depressed mood (or can be irritable mood in children and adolescents) for most of the day, more days than not, as indicated either by subjective account or observation by others, for at least two years (one year for children and adolescents)

B. Presence, while depressed, of at least two of the following:
   (1) poor appetite or overeating
   (2) insomnia or hypersomnia
   (3) low energy or fatigue
   (4) low self-esteem
   (5) poor concentration or difficulty making decisions
   (6) feelings of hopelessness

C. During a two-year period (one-year for children and adolescents) of the disturbance, never without the symptoms in A for more than two months at a time.

D. No evidence of an unequivocal Major Depressive Episode during the first two years (one year for children and adolescents) of the disturbance.

Note: There may have been a previous Major Depressive Episode, provided there was a full remission (no significant signs or symptoms for six months) before development of the Dysthymia. In addition, after these two years (one year in children or adolescents) of Dysthymia, there may be superimposed episodes of Major Depression, in which case both diagnoses are given.

E. Has never had a Manic Episode or an unequivocal Hypomanic Episode

F. Not superimposed on a chronic psychotic disorder, such as Schizophrenia or Delusional Disorder.

G. It cannot be established that an organic factor initiated and maintained the disturbance, e.g., prolonged administration of an antihypertensive medication.

Reprinted with permission from the *Diagnostic and Statistical Manual of Mental Disorders,* 3d ed. rev.; copyright 1987 by the American Psychiatric Association.

Since dysthymia can look like a learned pattern or style, it was once known as depressive personality. While frequently associated with the anxiety disorders (see Chapter 12), and itself a risk factor for other syndromes, dysthymia is thought to be a biologically distinct syndrome. Some of the associated syndromes respond to the same treatments, whereas others require additional attention.

Dysthymia typically begins between ages 20 and 30. Symptoms intensify over time and they tend to be worse in the evening. Dysthymia is exacerbated by acute loss and by chronic stress. Four percent of the general population experiences dysthymia, with women more frequently and more chronically symptomatic (Jonas and Schaumburg 1991). Some affected men and women may hide away their depressive symptoms under intensified work effort or outward hostility. In crisis, though, they can become acutely aware of their sadness.

Dysthymia commonly contributes to such other disorders as substance abuse, alcoholism, personality disorder, and even major depression. Dysthymia is considered a primary syndrome, unless the depressive symptoms are due to such problems as anorexia nervosa, somatization disorder, rheumatoid arthritis, or substance abuse. As with other types of depression, a thorough medical evaluation is always important.

Case Anecdotes

Case Study 6: Dysthymia with Physical Illness

Joseph Carpino is a 28-year-old mechanical engineer who was promoted to management 2 years ago. He had always hoped that supervisory work would be more satisfying than the assembly line, but the increased demands of the new job have made him increasingly fatigued. As soon as he gets home, he falls asleep in front of the television, but then he can't fall asleep in bed.

In the past few months, Joseph has had more physical illnesses and medical problems than in his entire life. He has sensations of tightness and pressure in his throat, headaches and tightness, poor appetite, and upset stomach. His backache hasn't gone away for more than 2 months. During his most recent visit to the company medical department, the doctor recommended that he see a psychiatrist. But Joseph refused because he knew he "wasn't nuts." However, when his wife complained about his increasing withdrawal, Joseph confessed that he felt totally drained and defeated, and he didn't see how he could continue working. Even so, he decided to drown his distress in overtime work on a new project.

Joseph displays the characteristics typically found in dysthymia. He has fought against continuing unhappiness by hoping that job promotion would improve his general frame of mind, as well as advancing his career. But when the promotion brought new and stressful responsibilities, he began to develop the depressive symptoms of exhaustion, sleep problems, and frequent physical illness. In his distressed state, he couldn't see the connections between depression, stress, and physical illness, and so he saw no point in seeking help.

Case Study 7: Atypical Depression

Sharon Branigan has been depressed for almost all of her 37 years. Her first marriage was a painful experience, but she now has high hopes for her second partner. Unfortunately, Sharon and her husband haven't agreed on timing for children. She has wanted a first child quickly, but her husband pays child support to his former wife and counts on Sharon's income to support their standard of living. Besides, he argues, another child would keep them from getting ahead. Two years of marriage counseling have not helped much.

After 5 years of marriage, Sharon feels her biological clock may keep her from ever having a child. She feels rejected by her husband, and her usual depression, pessimism, and irritability are getting worse. She sleeps and naps most weekends and evenings, and has such low energy that television is her only activity. Although Sharon tries to diet, she has gained 15 pounds on her snack bar runs for doughnuts, bagels, and especially chocolate chip ice cream. She is overly sensitive to criticism at work, but deprecates herself, her colleagues, and her company. Whenever work assignments keep her from lunch with co-workers, she feels angry and abandoned by them, and then feels still more depressed. She has become the center of several personality conflicts in the office. Recently, the situation has intensified, with arguments, blistering memos, and an inability to take suggestions. The office administrator called in a psychiatric consultant, who soon referred Sharon for treatment. On fluoxetine, 20 mg daily, she was still unhappy, but felt more "normal" than ever before. Renewed couples therapy was now able to start resolving some of her marital problems. Co-workers gradually noticed a new and happier Sharon.

Feeling emotionally rejected at home, at work, and even by her childless state, Sharon developed an exacerbation of her chronic atypical depression. She gained weight despite her diet, and she pushed people away despite wanting closeness and understanding. Many people with atypical depression find themselves disciplined or on probation at work, rather than referred for treatment. It is very easy to confuse personality, interpersonal conflict, circumstances, and biochemical depression. For this reason, professional assessment is vital.

Causes

Dysthymia is caused by a complex combination of psychological stressors, biological vulnerability, and environmental factors. People who have had dysfunctional families, abuse, or childhood emotional deprivation are more prone to dysthymia. Similarly susceptible are those who have had severe disappointments in interpersonal relationships. By the time dysthymia is presented in the psychiatrist's office, the many contributors are so thoroughly enmeshed that it is difficult to separate them.

There is increasing evidence for a biological factor, both from genetic research and from the evidence of many patients who respond well to antidepressants. There also seems to be a link between dysthymia and many physical illnesses. Two thirds of dysthymic patients also have physical illness or chronic pain.

Although the primary causes for dysthymia are personal psychological vulnerability and physiological stressors, the workplace can also cause or exacerbate symptoms. For example, uncertain job security, conflicts with co-workers or authority figures, and excessive or unwelcome competition can bring on dysthymic symptoms. When there is a threatened or actual loss of income, or symbols of status or privilege, dysthymia can develop. Notably, real, perceived, and symbolic interpersonal rejections are most potent of all.

Treatment

Dysthymia is a chronic recurring illness that usually responds best to combined treatment with psychotherapy and medication. While short-term psychotherapies can be very helpful in crisis, they should not be confused with careful evaluation and specific treatment. Similarly, while antidepressants are helpful in two thirds of cases, they do not offer full benefit without psychotherapy. The treatment of dysthymia is a gradual recovery process that can effect full recovery but not necessarily a permanent cure.

Insight-oriented psychotherapy focuses on both eliminating dysthymic symptoms and developing preventive learning skills. Symptoms can improve with psychodynamic interpretations, and also in response to appropriate changes in work or living arrangements. Long-term remission from dysthymia is much more likely when the causes are understood and acknowledged; when stressors are controlled, avoided, or eliminated; and when healthful life patterns are solidly established. Often, as certain causes are discovered, isolated, and addressed, other related or deeper issues will appear. The more limited the treatment modality in terms of time and resources, the more attentive patient and therapist must be to learning, integrating, and following up on the recovery process.

Dysthymia is a relatively mild form of depression that responds best to the same doses and durations of antidepressant medication used for major depression. Symptoms start to improve in 3 weeks, with full benefit in 2 months. Medication is continued with psychotherapy for 6 months before tapering is attempted. The psychotherapy continues until the depression is in remission or the symptoms are under control, and until the individual has learned adequate coping skills. MAOIs, serotonin reuptake inhibitors such as fluoxetine, and buproprion have particular value, although other antidepressants and lithium are sometimes effective. MAOIs are the best studied, but they have more side effects. Optimal treatment often requires several medication trials, or use of adjunctive medication. Some associated anxiety symptoms may also be treated with clonazepam or alprazolam. Hospitalization is rarely required.

Medication for atypical depression is usually specific, despite symptoms that can be more intense and causes that are less well defined. MAOIs and fluoxetine are the treatments of choice. MAOIs require careful management because of possible drug toxicity and the need for a restrictive diet. Some psychiatrists have special expertise in depressive and anxiety disorders, including available medications, current scientific information, and specialized psychotherapeutic methods.

Workplace Recognition, Effects, Management, and Prognosis

Recognition of dysthymia is more difficult than it might seem. Dysthymic symptoms and patterns become a functionally normal, if chronically depressed, way of life. Co-workers and family members may have long been accustomed to the decreased productivity and general dysfunction. Most often, the diagnosis is made after some crisis, often related to workplace issues. Other times, a major depression or substance abuse problem may point to a prior history of dysthymia. As with all mood disorders, referrals for dysthymia should include a thorough medical examination and psychiatric evaluation, along with practical suggestions about current problems and specific guidelines for preventing recurrent symptoms.

Because dysthymia does not have a clear initial onset phase, other complicating factors are likely to have developed by the time diagnosis is made. Potential concomitants cover a wide spectrum, including alcoholism, substance abuse, physical illness, family problems, conflicts with co-workers, productivity problems, and major depressive disorder.

The inward psychological effects of dysthymia on affected workers are similar to other depressions. However, because of dysthymia's chronicity and pervasive effects on relationships, the most observable workplace dysfunctions will be in the area of ineffective or problematic personal interactions. There may be inner sadness, worry, and fatigue, which surfaces on the job as impatience, restlessness, complaining, and uncooperativeness. At the extreme, externalized rejection sensitivity and sadness can appear in the workplace as repeated confrontations; continuous dissatisfaction with assignments or company policies; or exaggerated concerns about bona fide problems of discrimination. Overall, dysthymia can be a subtle but powerful influence, out of the worker's conscious control, but affecting many co-workers.

The most common medical effects are increased physical illness and sick days. Frequent aches and pains (especially in the lower back and neck), injuries, and accidents are always evidence of stress, and they frequently reflect dysthymia. Monday morning absenteeism is cause to consider dysthymia, as well as family problems and alcohol or substance abuse.

Treatment for dysthymia does not usually require a medical leave. Occasionally, 1 or 2 weeks off will reduce the level of personal stress and accommodate severe anergy while antidepressant medication takes effect. Since follow-up treatment is essential for resolving symptoms of dysthymia, managing medication, and learning preventive coping skills, time off from work for weekly sessions may be necessary for several months. While it is best for supervisors to stay out of the treatment process, it is appropriate and advisable to know if medications are likely to cause cognitive or physical problems on the job. Some extra attention should be paid to work behavior and productivity, along with support and specific recommendations. Because dysthymia is a chronic illness and habit patterns take time to break, recurrences are common. Acknowledge treatment efforts and progress, and encourage readaptation to the workplace.

BIPOLAR (MANIC-DEPRESSIVE) DISORDER

Diagnostic Overview

Bipolar disorder (BPD) is a disorder in which mood swings between extreme highs and lows. Commonly called manic depressive disorder, it is the most distinctive and dramatic of the depressive illnesses. While major depression can occur at any age, BPD onset generally occurs by the age of 35. Left untreated, it is a lifetime illness with recurrent episodes that become more frequent in later years.

DSM-III-R DIAGNOSTIC CRITERIA

Manic Episode

Note: A "Manic Syndrome" is defined as including criteria A, B, and C below. A "Hypomanic Syndrome" is defined as including criteria A and B, but not C, i.e., no marked impairment.

A. A distinct period of abnormally and persistently elevated, expansive, or irritable mood.

B. During the period of mood disturbance, at least three of the following symptoms have persisted (four if the mood is only irritable) and have been present to a significant degree:

   (1) inflated self-esteem or grandiosity
   (2) decreased need for sleep, e.g., feels rested after only three hours of sleep
   (3) more talkative than usual or pressure to keep talking
   (4) flight of ideas or subjective experience that thoughts are racing
   (5) distractibility, i.e., attention too easily drawn to unimportant or irrelevant external stimuli
   (6) increase in goal-directed activity (either socially, at work or school, or sexually) or psychomotor agitation
   (7) excessive involvement in pleasurable activities which have a high potential for painful consequences, e.g., the person engages in unrestrained buying sprees, sexual indiscretions, or foolish business investments

C. Mood disturbance sufficiently severe to cause marked impairment in occupational functioning or in usual social activities or relationships with others, or to necessitate hospitalization to prevent harm to self or others.

D. At no time during the disturbance have there been delusions or hallucinations for as long as two weeks in the absence of prominent mood symptoms (i.e., before the mood symptoms developed or after they have remitted).

E. Not superimposed on Schizophrenia, Schizophreniform Disorder, Delusional Disorder, or Psychotic Disorder NOS.

F. It cannot be established that an organic factor initiated and maintained the disturbance. **Note:** Somatic antidepressant treatment (e.g., drugs, ECT) that apparently precipitates a mood disturbance should not be considered an etiologic organic factor.

Manic Episode codes: fifth-digit code numbers and criteria for severity of current state of Bipolar Disorder, Manic or Mixed:

1–Mild: Meets minimum symptom criteria for a Manic Episode (or almost meets symptom criteria if there has been a previous Manic Episode).

2–Moderate: Extreme increase in activity or impairment in judgment.

3–Severe, without Psychotic Features: Almost continual supervision required in order to prevent physical harm to self or others.

4–With Psychotic Features: Delusions, hallucinations, or catatonic symptoms. If possible, **specify** whether the psychotic features are *mood-congruent* or *mood-incongruent*.

Mood-congruent psychotic features: Delusions or hallucinations whose content is entirely consistent with the typical manic themes of inflated worth, power, knowledge, identity, or special relationship to a deity or famous person.

Mood-incongruent psychotic features: Either (a) or (b):

(a) Delusions or hallucinations whose content does *not* involve the typical manic themes of inflated worth, power, knowledge, identity, or special relationship to a deity or famous person. Included are such symptoms as persecutory delusions (not directly related to grandiose ideas or themes), thought insertion, and delusions of being controlled.

(b) Catatonic symptoms, e.g., stupor, mutism, negativism, posturing.

5–In Partial Remission: Full criteria were previously, but are not currently, met; some signs or symptoms of the disturbance have persisted.

6–In Full Remission: Full criteria were previously met, but there have been no significant signs or symptoms of the disturbance for at least six months.

0–Unspecified.

Reprinted with permission from the *Diagnostic and Statistical Manual of Mental Disorders*, 3d ed. rev.; copyright 1987 by the American Psychiatric Association.

The acute manic state of bipolar disorder creates a chaos like no other mental illness. A person with mania has a highly infectious, although often macabre, sense of vitality and joie de vivre. The expansive, manic symptoms make other people in the vicinity feel exhilarated until they realize that the manic person is careening uncontrollably through hyperactivity, grandiosity, hostility, and bizarre diversions. While the characteristic elation of mania is the most noticeable phase of BPD, there are usually episodes of profound depression as well. Moods swing on a cycle between depressive and manic poles, generally with periods of normal mood in between. The dramatic mood swings of BPD can dominate a social or work environment. The symptoms of the depressive phase of a bipolar cycle closely resemble other depressive disorders. Melancholic major depressions do commonly occur, but recent research also suggests shared characteristics of bipolar and atypical depressions.

Manic patients will state, "I've never felt better in my entire life," and "I feel like I'm on top of the world!" As the manic episode escalates, thoughts race, sleep becomes minimal, physical activity increases, and reckless financial and sexual behavior emerges. Ordinary communication seems too slow. Rapid speech, grandiose ideas, multiple conversations, and back-to-back meetings are used to accelerate the pace, while quick decisions and fast action are demanded from others. Unfortunately, thoughts become incoherent, projects remain incomplete, relationships quickly deteriorate, and there is a pronounced lack of judgment. Even though true mania is highly destructive to any constructive task, nothing can change the euphoric mood. There may also be sudden anger, rage, irritability, suicide, and paranoia. Mania is a psychiatric emergency requiring prompt referral, evaluation, and treatment.

Cyclothymia is a diagnosis used to describe milder cycles that do not cause marked impairment in social or occupational functioning. Hypomania is a milder form of mania, characterized by high energy, spontaneity, creativity, and optimism. It is not certain that these two diagnoses are always true variants of bipolar disorder.

Case Anecdotes

Case Study 8: Bipolar Disorder, Manic, with Psychotic Features

Jim Braithwaite was the 32-year-old co-owner of a highly successful insurance agency. Jim was the most effective salesperson, as well as the resident business genius. One day, he startled his partners by announcing that he had found the key to their future success. Without their knowledge, he had bought out a failing business. He assured them that he could turn it around quickly, and with extraordinary 20-hour workdays, the new acquisition was profitable in 4 weeks.

Buoyed by this success, Jim decided he could save his city from slow deterioration. He abruptly donated half of his $300,000 savings to charity and announced plans to run for mayor. He put intense pressure on his best clients to "give until it hurts," and many of them left the agency. He became furious when his partners questioned his activities, and they quickly forced him out of the company.

Feeling angry, discouraged, and victimized, Jim left his wife behind and moved to Washington, D.C. He spent most of the next month sleeping in a seedy motel room. Very soon, though, he felt a familiar surge of energy and began looking up lobbyists and senators, and visiting the hot singles bars. Hearing the voice of God, he decided to run for Congress to save the world. He called everyone he knew for political support. Many of the calls were late at night and incoherent. He was always turned down, and each time he would hurl insults before hanging up in midsentence.

One evening at a singles bar, Jim started dancing on a table. When he started stripping off his clothes, the police took him to a hospital. Over the course of a 6-week stay, his delusions disappeared with haloperidol, 5 mg three times a day, and his mania responded within 10 days to lithium, 300 mg four times a day. While there, he learned for the first time of his grandfather's many nervous breakdowns. Although Jim felt embarrassed by his own behavior, at first he could not see any real need for treatment compliance. Back home, he did agree to stay on lithium and to remain in therapy, and he started to make amends with his wife and partners.

Jim Braithwaite has a bipolar illness with mania and mood-congruent psychosis. His delusions and hallucinations reflect typically manic thoughts of inflated self-worth and a special relationship to a deity. He cycles from high to low every few months. Although his expansive and reckless behavior was at first productive, it soon caused serious damage to his agency, partners, finances, family, and personal reputation. As long as he remains compliant with treatment, the odds of another manic episode are greatly reduced. Unfortunately, he is not yet fully convinced that he really has a problem.

Case Study 9: Bipolar Disorder, Mixed

Martha Levine is a 29-year-old with a brilliant mind and a photographic memory. Though moody, averse to material belongings, and romantically inexperienced, she had always been the life of the party. She finished college with the highest honors, and then took a year off before an equally stellar law school performance. After a whirlwind relationship in her senior year, she married a materialistic and successful investment executive.

A few months after the wedding, Martha failed the bar exam. Shocked and angry about this first major career failure, she began to experience wildly fluctuating moods every few days. Some days she would be so down in the dumps that she wouldn't make it out of bed. Other days she would stay up most of the night and go on wild spending sprees. One time she bought several thousand dollars of underwear on a whim. After 6 months of fluctuations, she decided to take a clerk's job with the sexual abuse unit of the public defender's office. Everyone was delighted to have someone so positive and active in the office, and overlooked her frequent absences and occasional confusion. Her supervisor rewarded her enthusiasm with unusual and challenging cases.

Although Martha soon used up her sick time, she often worked 12-hour days, frequently taking her clients out to long lunches and the office staff to cocktails. She also began to press for major changes in the office. Then, at the office holiday party, Martha gathered an audience and explicitly described a weekend sexual adventure with a co-worker while her husband was away. Realizing that something was very wrong here, Martha's supervisor called a city attorney for advice the following day. Martha was placed on medical leave pending evaluation. The psychiatrist first recommended lithium, then added clonazepam, and initially saw Martha three times a week in therapy. The therapy addressed Martha's practiced avoidance of emotional intimacy and material belongings, and her driven preoccupation with academic goals. Her usual style had come unglued by the emotional reality of marriage and the prospect of a well-paying adult job.

Martha was at a stressful, susceptible time in her life, with simultaneous changes in her career, income, and marital status. Shifting every few days from mania to depression, she showed a rapid cycling pattern of bipolar disorder. Depression was largely hidden by days off from work, while manic behavior became increasingly visible in the workplace. Unwitting colleagues initially encouraged what looked like productive energy. Only Martha's most outrageous behavior finally caused her supervisor to recognize the severity of the problem and call for legal help. Mania is commonly first viewed as a social, moral, or legal problem, rather than as a psychiatric disorder.

Causes

Recent studies show convincing evidence of a genetic factor in bipolar disorder. While the actual physiology is not yet understood, medication response provides additional evidence for biochemical mechanisms. Even among identical twins of BPD patients, not all are affected. Psychological factors also play important causal roles, particularly for individuals who come from close but dysfunctional family units. Emotional triggers also determine the timing of manic and depressive episodes, though the actual stressors are not always obvious during the initial interview.

Workplace stresses can trigger episodes of bipolar disorder in predisposed employees. Some authors believe that susceptible individuals are especially energetic and hardworking. They originate new ideas and are aggressive risk takers. Organizations appreciate and often encourage these traits. However, in manic degree, these tendencies are destructive for both employee and organization. Contributory workplace factors include extended work hours, work involving intensive efforts and high stakes, physically dangerous occupations, professions focusing on public image and the media, and social service professions. Some medications and drugs can trigger bipolar episodes, including antidepressants, steroids, stimulants, alcohol, and cocaine.

Treatment

Although it can be difficult to establish a therapeutic alliance with the bipolar patient, the vast majority of patients respond well to the combined support of medication and psychotherapy. Extensive medical, psychotherapeutic, and psychopharmacological background is essential. Effective treatment requires the close medical supervision of lithium effects and side effects, well integrated with ongoing psychotherapy. Lithium carbonate successfully reduces the number and intensity of manic episodes for 75 percent of those who take the medication properly. Extremely effective for treating the acute manic phase, lithium also appears to prevent repeated episodes of depression. Full treatment compliance will sometimes offer complete long-term remission of symptoms. Those who respond best to lithium are patients who have periods of relatively normal mood between their manic and

TABLE 13-3   Antimanic Medication

Generic Name	Trade Name	Usual Daily Starting Dose (mg)	Usual Daily Effective Dose (mg)
Lithium carbonate	Eskalith Lithane	300-600	600-1500
Lithium citrate	Cibalith S	300-600	600-1500
Carbamezepine	Tegretol	900	400-2200
Valproic Acid	Depakane	250	1200-1500
Clonazepam	Klonopin		

Notes: Antimanic medications typically require at least 5 to 10 days before therapeutic response. Sedating antipsychotic medications are sometimes used in the interim.
Strict medical supervision may require: (a) careful dose adjustment; (b) monthly serum drug levels; (c) blood counts; (d) kidney function tests.

depressive phases. Several other medications have also proved successful as second-line treatments for mania (Table 13-3), and multiple medications may be necessary to control symptoms.

Lithium is usually prescribed in 300-mg tablets, with a typical daily maintenance dose of 600 to 1500 mg. Dose is adjusted to maintain therapeutic blood levels. Lithium must be carefully monitored for its many side effects. Among frequent side effects are weight gain, excessive thirst and urination, stomach and intestinal irritation, muscular weakness, and hand tremors. If the blood level of lithium becomes too high (due to overdose, concurrent illness, or dehydration), resulting serious complications can include confusion, delirium, seizures, coma, and death. When properly monitored, lithium will safely provide the opportunity for a normal life, which would otherwise not be possible.

The manic belief in extraordinary talents and entitlement to special treatment extends well into psychotherapy. Typically, the patient wants to be in charge of the treatment process itself. Psychotherapy provides pivotal assistance at times of crisis, as well as helping to maintain daily emotional equilibrium. Through psychotherapy the patient works out the problems created by the disorder in practical steps, reestablishing relationships and a healthy self-image. Interpersonal boundaries and roles are carefully established, and the need for medication compliance is continually discussed.

Bipolar illness can cause profound disruptions in family relationships. Mental health treatment facilities often have special programs and support groups established for family members, to help them understand, adjust to, and support the bipolar patient. Family members can learn coping skills, as well as becoming an active part of the treatment team.

Workplace Recognition, Effects, Management, and Prognosis

Nothing stirs up the workplace like a case of full-blown mania. At best, it is disturbing; at worst, it is extremely disruptive. If the person with mania is a rapid cycler, with moods changing every few hours or days, his or her accompanying behavior will leave fellow employees bewildered and scared. Mania must not be viewed as a social or legal problem. Psychiatric treatment is absolutely essential at the first manic sign. Even if mania abates and a period of normalcy follows, a depressive phase will soon begin. Without treatment, mania can last as long as 3 months, during which time the manic individual can do irreparable physical, mental, social, and financial damage to himself (or herself) and to others. By the time mania is detected, there may be extreme grandiosity and rejection of mundane normal rules of behavior. It may be impossible to create recognition of the seriousness of the situation and of the need for treatment.

The fact remains, however, that mania is a psychiatric emergency. It is necessary to get the manic worker into a protective environment. If there is resistance to referral, or irritability, anger, or paranoia, do not attempt to handle the situation alone. Call for help. Often the mere presence of an official in uniform is enough reassurance and external control to moderate mania and to induce cooperation. Be prompt and firm in taking action, but physical force may only provoke resistance and physical reaction.

Organizations can appear to benefit from the first stage of mania. The affected individual is still coherent enough to be effective, and the characteristic optimism and high energy can even increase the enthusiasm of other employees. However, things soon begin to fall apart. Mistakes and misjudgments appear; the manic individual becomes increasingly irritable, stubborn, and aggressive; and what had seemed to be shared productive activity becomes a loud, frantic, paper-pushing nightmare. Sometimes the manic worker is the first one to try to put on the brakes, sensing that the situation has gotten out of control. Nevertheless, there may be sudden resentment, rage, or paranoia, often from thoughts of being denied sufficient credit for the productivity boom, or else from feeling just plain misunderstood.

The depressive phase that typically follows a manic episode can also have a significant effect on co-workers. The worker's depressed mood can be as infectious as the emphatically upbeat mood that preceded it, and a generally lower morale and diminished level of productivity may ensue. The effects of bipolar disorder in the workplace are confusing and potentially pervasive and disturbing. They must be dealt with promptly and frankly.

Bipolar disorder usually requires a medical leave, but return to work is often possible within a few weeks. Restoring the worker's immediate work environment and co-worker relationships to a smoothly functioning state can take longer. Following a manic episode, self-esteem and quality of interpersonal relationships are often at an unprecedented low. Moreover, there may have been behavior that resulted in disastrous consequences for relationships, finances, and work. Even so, bipolar patients are characteristically highly motivated, productive employees who enjoy their work. They will generally readjust to the workplace quickly and appropriately.

In general, guidelines for managing workers recovering from mania are similar to those for depression. Management should minimize stress and stimulation, streamline responsibilities wherever possible, and check to make sure that psychiatric medication and therapy are continuing. Responsibilities should be increased as soon as reasonably possible and medically appropriate.

SUMMARY

Transitory feelings of sadness are commonplace and unremarkable. In situations of profound personal loss, such as bereavement, feelings of extreme sadness and even despair are normal. However, when people cannot emerge from these feelings, or do not find these feelings improving, they may be suffering from one of several depressive disorders. One out of four women and one out of ten men can expect to develop a depressive disorder during their lifetime. Depressive episodes may occur suddenly, for no reason. More commonly, however, they are triggered by a known or unrecognized specific event.

In the workplace, depression is both the most common as well as the most treatable serious emotional illness. Unfortunately, many individuals do not recognize their illness or do not get treatment to alleviate their suffering. Instead, they may attribute physical symptoms to a case of the flu, sleeping and eating problems to general stress, and emotional problems to lack of sleep. In fact, depression is a whole body illness, affecting not only feelings but thought, behavior, physical health, and fundamental safety.

Symptoms of depression surface in the form of frequent illness and excessive fatigue, decreased productivity, interpersonal conflicts and negativism, safety problems and accidents, alcohol and substance abuse, and absenteeism. Because the symptoms can be so varied and puzzling, thorough psychiatric evaluation is necessary to obtain an accurate diagnosis and to tailor an optimal treatment program.

The most effective treatment is usually a combination of psychotherapy and antidepressant medication. Antidepressants usually start helping within 3 to 4 weeks. Continued psychotherapy during the recovery process is valuable for guidance through the illness, and for new coping skills and increased self-understanding to help prevent recurrence. Eighty percent of clinically diagnosed severe depressions will improve significantly within weeks. In most cases, early diagnosis and treatment will allow outpatient treatment, thereby avoiding the lost work time and high costs of prolonged treatment and hospitalization.

Bibliography

Bartlett, K. 1990. Depression at work: Costly but treatable. *Journal of Psychosocial Nursing and Mental Health Services* **28**(11):5.

Cameron, P. M. 1989. Psychodynamic psychotherapy for the depressive syndrome. *Psychiatric Journal of the University of Ottawa* **14**(2):397-402, 409-412.

Clayton, P. J. 1990. Bereavement and depression. *Journal of Clinical Psychiatry* **51**(July, suppl.):34-38, 39-40.

Dubovsky, Steven L. 1988. *Clinical Psychiatry.* Washington, D.C.: American Psychiatric Press.

Finlayson, R. 1989. Recognition and management of dysthymic disorder. *American Family Physician* **40**(4):229-238.

Fuller, Ray W. 1991. Role of serotonin in therapy of depression and related disorders. *Journal of Clinical Psychiatry* **52**(May, suppl.):53.

Gelenberg, Alan J. 1991. The clinician's challenge: Strategies for treatment of depression in the 1990s. *Journal of Clinical Psychiatry* **52**(June, suppl.)

Greist, John H., and James W. Jefferson. *Depression and Its Treatment.* New York: Warner Books.

Jonas, Jeffrey M., and Ron Schaumberg. *Everything You Need to Know About Prozac.* New York: Bantam Books.

Kaplan, Harold I., and Benjamin J. Sadock. 1990. *Pocket Handbook of Clinical Psychiatry.* Baltimore: Williams & Wilkins.

Keller, M. B., and L. A. Baker. 1991. Bipolar disorder: Epidemiology, course, diagnosis, and treatment. *Bulletin of the Menninger Clinic* **55**(2):172-181.

Larson, K. B. 1990. Activity patterns and life changes in people with depression. *American Journal of Occupational Therapy* **44**(10):902-906.

Phelan, J., J. E. Schwartz, E. J. Bromet, M. D. Dew, D. K. Parkinson, H. C. Schulbert, L. O. Dunn, H. Blane, and E. C. Curtis. 1991. Work stress, family stress, and depression in professional and managerial employees. *Psychological Medicine* **21**(4):999-1012.

Physicians Postgraduate Press. 1991. The changing horizon in the treatment of depression and related disorders. *Journal of Clinical Psychiatry* **52**(May, suppl.).

Physicians Postgraduate Press. 1991. *Evolving Standards of Antidepressant Therapy.* Journal of Clinical Psychiatry Monograph Series, vol. 9, no. 1.

Potter, W. Z., M. V. Rudorfer, and H. Manji. 1991. The pharmacologic treatment of depression. *New England Journal of Medicine* **325**(9):633-642.

Prien, R. F. 1990. Efficacy of continuation drug therapy of depression and anxiety: Issues and methodologies. *Journal of Clinical Psychopharmacology* **10**(3, suppl.): 865-905.

Tollefson, G. D. 1990. Recognition and treatment of major depression. *American Family Physician* **42**(5, suppl.):59S-66S, 69S.

14

Personalities, Personal Style, and Trouble Getting Along

Mark P. Unterberg, M.D.

ABSTRACT

Everyone has a personality type. Personality disorders, personal style, and trouble getting along can all be considered in an organized and clinically useful way. Of all the psychiatric problems that face organizations today, one of the most insidious can be the otherwise high-functioning individual with a severe personality disorder. These individuals create multilevel problems that defy easy detection and definition, due to the intermingling of their health and pathology. They are usually much harder to recognize than the obvious depressive or alcoholic. Their personality causes repeated but subtle disruption in the work force and in decision-making processes. This chapter discusses the major categories of personality disorders and styles, gives illustrative case examples, and suggests appropriate approaches by psychiatrist and employer. It also reviews the organizational problems in trying to address problem individuals at any organizational level.

INTRODUCTION

All business is personal. Whether on the assembly line or in the corporate board room, the workplace is made up of people with complex combinations of personality traits. Success in the workplace requires technical abilities as well as professional presence, but it is most profoundly determined by personality. Other than computers talking with each other, there is no workplace situation that does not involve personal and subjective aspects of the individual. The common expression, "It's nothing personal, just business," is interesting just because it attempts to deny the significant contribution of personality to the workplace.

Decisions are constantly made out of a personal frame of reference that determines workplace perceptions. No matter how hard the effort, even the most determinedly "objective" decisions are ultimately affected by personality style. Productive organizations and employee mental health thus both require careful attention to individual personality traits and difficulties.

This chapter focuses primarily on maladaptive personality traits of otherwise ordinary individuals, and the consequent effects both on themselves and on their workplace environment. There is always a subtle interplay of the environment with both adaptive and maladaptive traits. As circumstances and individuals change, personality assets and strengths of a relatively healthy employee can become destructive to the team effort. Employees who suffer from more recognizable depression, psychosis, and even substance abuse may create more obvious problems for the organization. But, personality traits that become problematic under stress can create insidious and slowly progressive havoc. Even senior mental health professionals will sometimes leave maladaptive personality traits unrecognized. It is essential to maintain business and mental health professionals' awareness of the subtle and sometimes destructive effects of personality in the organizational setting.

There is no way to avoid bringing personality traits to the workplace. The psychological structures that define unique and separate individuals can be neither eliminated nor avoided. Personality is a reflection of emotional defenses (ways of operating) that individuals evolve in reaction to interpersonal circumstances over the years. These defenses can be what are called compromise formations, derived from the unwitting need to create a balance between internal emotional needs and the demands of external reality. There are always needs and instinctual desires to be gratified. Under ideal circumstances, personality helps ensure balance and calmness that allows maximal productivity, creativity, and enjoyment.

Established patterns of emotional defenses form personality traits that seek the most harmonious possible adaptation to external realities and that present a unique individual to the world. Initially formed in childhood, defenses can be modified by later experience. The most adaptive personalities are flexible in response to changing internal and external circumstances. Loss, growth, distress, pleasure, and change are ever present. Although much has been written about interpersonal relationships in the social arena, there has been less attention to personality adaptation at work.

Personality disorders represent defects in emotional defenses and resultant compromise formations (see Chapter 1). The psychological structure that was set in place to help the individual achieve maximum potential in a given environment can be poorly adapted to newer circumstances. Perceptions and decisions become nonproductive and even repetitively self-destructive. Unwittingly, maladaptive personality traits now prevent attainment of desired goals. It is important to remember the difference between personality traits and disorders. Pronounced personality traits can exist without a personality disorder. Personality disorders exist when there is a distinct pattern of excessive, inflexible, and consistently self-destructive personality traits (see Chapter 9).

Adaptive individuals can modify their personality traits through experience. Actions lead to consequences, and assessment of those consequences is used to modify responses to similar problems in the future. In varying degrees, this process goes on throughout life and allows a high degree of balance and well-being. Life in both social and work arenas goes pretty well. But when there is a personality disorder, actions are unresponsive to their consequences. Faced with adverse feedback from the environment, the same behaviors are still repeated over and over. There is a defect in the feedback loop. Adverse consequences are either ignored or not perceived, or else there is an inability to modify behavior. Most people with personality disorders tend to think that the problem resides with others or in the environment, and not within themselves. This helps put workplace problems in perspective. Even so, employees with personality disorders always have positive personality traits and characteristics. Otherwise, they would not have been hired in the first place. However, the maladaptive and inflexible patterns can emerge under stress.

Figuring out what to do requires good clinical data and judgment, to accurately assess personality issues in the workplace, and to best help the employee make necessary changes to become a productive worker. More sophisticated understanding of underlying mechanisms allows the clinical information to be organized into useful and understandable findings and recommendations.

The case studies are intended to highlight the individual diagnostic categories. The cases thus have a slightly exaggerated quality. And in reality, personality is usually more subtle and complex than these descriptions permit. Most readers will find at least one case that sounds a little bit like them. Although this might be frightening at first, it is important to remember that personality styles are on a continuum of severity. The individual with a personality disorder makes decisions that are typically nonproductive but designed to provide immediate emotional relief. At times there seems to be little reflection about the real problems, while there is a repetitive quality to the counterproductive behaviors. Those behaviors are based more on internal emotional needs (from past experiences) than on present external realities. Decisions are thus both inappropriate and painful. These two points are the most obvious guidelines that can be used in distinguishing personality style and disorder. Sometimes what happens, though, is that the inappropriate decision affects others, and it causes problems for co-workers and the workplace.

OBSESSIVE-COMPULSIVE: OVERINVOLVED/UNDERACHIEVING EMPLOYEES

Case Study 1

Herbert Kroft is a 34-year-old single man who was hired to head up the accounting section of a medium-size firm. He replaced a recently retired, popular department head, and was assigned the task of revamping the accounting department's collection methods. He dressed impeccably and spoke in a very articulate, clear, and precise manner. After 6 months, though, four out of nine employees tendered their resignations. They complained that Herbert was impossible to work with, and that no matter what they did it was never good enough. Management and Herbert's supervisor found that their own interactions usually went well, and that a major overhaul of the department was proceeding quickly and precisely.

In the next 6 months, three more people left. Two of them complained that the office atmosphere was oppressive. Although Herbert surprised management by his marathon work hours, his leadership reputation continued to suffer. His accusers called him moralistic, judgmental, and almost tyrannically perfectionistic. They felt that his only concern was for the production of his section, with little concern for employee morale. He would cancel vacations on short notice and would be clearly irritated by leave requests for personal problems. Despite Herbert's work hours, the next year saw more and more overdue reports and projects. Herbert also started a pattern of frequent visits to his supervisor's office to discuss minute details of accounting system flaws, sometimes in heated terms. Herbert was starting to miss the big picture.

Events came to a head on the day his entire department threatened to resign en masse if the supervisor didn't do something about Herbert's effect on department morale. Biting the bullet, the supervisor called Herbert in. And as usual, Herbert didn't budge. He figured that his subordinates were only trying to shirk their responsibilities. He couldn't see their point of view, or even acknowledge that they might have some legitimate grievances. After talking with the CEO, the supervisor recommended that Herbert see a consulting psychiatrist, or accept suspension until the situation was reviewed.

In treatment, Herbert began to understand that he had a problem. With much work, he was able to start changing his usual approaches to people at work. Gradually, he became more appropriate and less of a problem for his supervisor. He was still more concerned with fine details than others, but therapy helped him to use this skill for productive work. Herbert also learned to recognize that even his less obsessional subordinates could do a first-rate job, if only he let them. Although his workers gradually noticed the change, his reputation lasted far longer. Herbert stayed in individual therapy for a year and a half. He was happy enough with his experience that he went on to recommend treatment to others.

Obsessive-compulsive personality style is usually a career asset, because of the intense dedication to work that it may entail, often to the exclusion of family and other outside life. When the traits become excessive, however, there can be a detrimental increase in inflexibility and perfectionism, and an emotional need to make the world conform to a personal perception. Since obsessional traits make it hard to see what went wrong, further difficulties can result from confrontation, isolation, or termination.

DSM-III-R DIAGNOSTIC CRITERIA

301.40 Obsessive Compulsive Personality Disorder

A pervasive pattern of perfectionism and inflexibility, beginning by early adulthood and present in a variety of contexts, as indicated by at least *five* of the following:

(1) perfectionism that interferes with task completion, e.g., inability to complete a project because own overly strict standards are not met

(2) preoccupation with details, rules, lists, order, organization, or schedules to the extent that the major point of the activity is lost

(3) unreasonable insistence that others submit to exactly his or her way of doing things, **or** unreasonable reluctance to allow others to do things because of the conviction that they will not do them correctly

(4) excessive devotion to work and productivity to the exclusion of leisure activities and friendships (not accounted for by obvious economic necessity)

(5) indecisiveness: decision making is either avoided, postponed, or protracted, e.g., the person cannot get assignments done on time because of ruminating about priorities (do not include if indecisiveness is due to excessive need for advice or reassurance from others)

(6) overconscientiousness, scrupulousness, and inflexibility about matters of morality, ethics, or values (not accounted for by cultural or religious identification)

(7) restricted expression of affection

(8) lack of generosity in giving time, money, or gifts when no personal gain is likely to result

(9) inability to discard worn-out or worthless objects even when they have no sentimental value

Obsessive-compulsive personality is not the same as obsessive-compulsive disorder (OCD; see Chapter 12). OCD can be an incapacitating syndrome, where overwhelming obsessions or compulsions preclude normal functioning. OCD symptoms can become sufficiently overt, extreme, or bizarre that behavior appears abnormal and idiosyncratic to peers. Obsessive-compulsive personality traits, on the other hand, do not grossly interfere with functioning, although they can certainly impede productivity and interpersonal relationships. OCD and obsessive-compulsive personality also differ in the degree of outward anxiety and response to medication. OCD is accompanied by intense anxiety about obsessions and compulsions that responds to such specific anti-OCD medication as clomipramine and fluoxetine. Obsessive-compulsive personality is not accompanied by such anxiety. In fact, the personality style is felt as quite appropriate, while others are blamed for any problems.

The etiology of obsessive-compulsive personality disorder is uncertain, but it is thought to derive primarily from early emotional environment. In the workplace, traits can be exacerbated by increasing intensity, complexity, or importance of work, or by a perceived decrease in support from superiors. There is always a push for perfection, and with more variables it gets harder to "tie up all the loose ends." Perhaps more importantly, a perceived loss of support intensifies inner emotions and need for perfection. Too often, the forest cannot be seen for the trees. Increasing brittleness and tension begin to have a strong effect on co-workers, who then see a humorless, difficult, moralistic, or aggressive colleague.

Goals of Psychotherapy

The initial consultation reviews the current problem and past history, and looks for associated life events and mood disorders that may have made things worse. Once a need for psychotherapy has been established, the initial phase of therapy is used to establish a nonthreatening atmosphere. Obsessive-compulsive traits have typically been used for emotional self-protection since childhood. The early phase of treatment also allows initial recognition of counterproductive behaviors and of their associated emotions. The counterproductive traits are often intensely driven psychological defenses against threatening hidden emotions and fears. A central goal of psychotherapy is to uncover fears of what would happen if behavior was modified, and if a more balanced life were then attempted. In particular, therapy focuses on interactions with other people.

General Management Approach

Obsessive-compulsive employees are difficult to recognize in the workplace. They usually work hard, see themselves as productive and appropriate, and blame others who they see as less than perfect. Problems are most commonly pointed out by co-workers and subordinates, and are less often immediately recognizable by superiors. And it is not always easy to discuss the problems with someone who sees the causes lying elsewhere. When usual performance evaluation and management approaches are not sufficient, referral for psychiatric evaluation may be helpful. The prognosis for introspective employees is good. The ability to recognize their contribution to the problems is essential to modification and understanding of counterproductive behavior. In fact, modification of personality defenses will often permit a higher level of productivity and personableness than before. Recognition of change requires careful supervisory awareness, as well as attention to possible future problems.

HISTRIONIC: OVEREMOTIONAL/ OVERREACTIVE EMPLOYEES

Case Study 2

Sandra Green is a 27-year-old single woman who was hired for a middle management position in the marketing department. She came with excellent references and had impressed the head of marketing with her intelligence, quick wit, and extremely attractive appearance. Sandra quickly became part of the group. Within days she had personally sought out each of her colleagues, introducing herself and winning them over with her humor, personality, style, and helpfulness to the department. She dressed better than anyone else at the office and was especially well liked by her male co-workers. Despite her recent arrival, she quickly established herself at meetings by presenting novel ideas that needed lengthy discussion. Even so, Sandra didn't actually seem to get much done.

Over the next few months, it became increasingly clear to some co-workers that she needed inordinate amounts of attention. Sandra kept finding ways to put herself on "center stage." She started to date three male co-workers simultaneously, while her female colleagues found her increasingly competitive, uncooperative, and unsympathetic. A crisis developed when Sandra complained hysterically to her male supervisor that the other women in the office had not invited her to a Friday evening happy hour. She angrily decried how badly she was treated by the other women in the department, despite her own unusually considerate efforts. In dramatic terms, Sandra described how she was a helpless victim of jealous and competitive female colleagues. She was very convincing.

The supervisor called an office meeting. Sandra subtly castigated some other employees for not appreciating her work. Several people asked her not to monopolize discussion time at business meetings. Some also complained that she spent more time at coffee breaks with men than on group projects. After the meeting was over, Sandra stormed into the supervisor's office. She demanded that a couple of people be threatened with termination if they tried to interfere with her performances or social life. She also suggested that a closer relationship with the supervisor could help them both, and suggested continuing the discussion over lunch or dinner. Flattered at first, the supervisor suddenly became aware of Sandra's seductiveness and her effects on morale. He realized, too, that her work lacked the quality and depth that her references and initial plans had seemed to predict. The next week, he asked her to seek a consultation.

In consultation, the psychiatrist recognized the full spectrum of histrionic personality traits, as well as symptoms of a chronic mild atypical depression (see

Chapter 13). Importantly, he also discovered that she had left her previous job after failure of a long-term romance with a colleague there. Although that relationship had always been rocky, she felt devastated by the breakup and increasingly despondent about her future social prospects. Sandra was referred for individual and group psychotherapy, and was started on phenelzine (a monoamine oxidase inhibitor antidepressant). When her mood started to improve within 3 weeks, there was a marked reduction in office tensions.

Even so, Sandra had great difficulty recognizing and accepting that she played a significant role in her problems. When she was able to see this as a product of early childhood fears and wishes, though, she gradually began to make corrections. Her dress became more appropriate, and she no longer needed quite so much attention. She became increasingly aware of her oversensitivity to others and was able to respond appropriately. In less than a year, co-workers were well aware of the new Sandra. Her work improved, and her romantic life was outside of the office. Although she still took up a lot of meeting time, she could catch the hint to finish, and would often end a speech with humor.

Employees with histrionic traits may initially come across as particularly attractive or seductive. Dress, behavior, and demeanor all contribute to an emotional, or even sexual, allure. Without their own awareness, they will often use their attractiveness to achieve other goals or wishes. Co-workers often perceive an immature or infantile inability to recognize failings, or even to acknowledge the potential validity of other people's observations. Instead, there appears to be an insatiable appetite for attention and a dramatically embellished manner of speaking. More problems arise in the workplace when exaggerated emotions bother other employees, stir up competitive and jealous feelings, lead to excessive controversy, or contribute to overblown promises and incomplete assignments.

DSM-III-R DIAGNOSTIC CRITERIA

301.50 Histrionic Personality Disorder

A pervasive pattern of excessive emotionality and attention-seeking, beginning by early adulthood and present in a variety of contexts, as indicated by at least *four* of the following:

(1) constantly seeks or demands reassurance, approval, or praise
(2) is inappropriately sexually seductive in appearance or behavior
(3) is overly concerned with physical attractiveness

(4) expresses emotion with inappropriate exaggeration, e.g., embraces casual acquaintances
with excessive ardor, uncontrollable sobbing
on minor sentimental occasions, has temper
tantrums

(5) is uncomfortable in situations in which he or
she is not the center of attention

(6) displays rapidly shifting and shallow expression of emotions

(7) is self-centered, actions being directed toward
obtaining immediate satisfaction; has no tolerance for the frustration of delayed gratification

(8) has a style of speech that is excessively impressionistic and lacking in detail, e.g., when
asked to describe mother, can be no more
specific than, "She was a beautiful person."

Reprinted with permission from the *Diagnostic and Statistical
Manual of Mental Disorders,* 3d ed. rev.; copyright 1987 by the
American Psychiatric Association.

Histrionic personality traits are commonly demonstrated through overly
emotional reactions to normal, everyday situations. Tension and emotional
excitability are combined with inappropriate exaggeration of relatively normal happy, sad, or angry feelings. Histrionic traits are commonly exaggerated under the stress of personal or work problems, or if there is a concurrent
depression or anxiety disorder. In particular, atypical depression (formerly
called hysteroid dysphoria) can be associated with exacerbated histrionic
traits. It is important to remember, though, that these two syndromes are
thought to have differing causes and treatments.

Goals of Psychotherapy

When therapy begins, the patient will often feel very upset about undeserved
criticisms or losses. There may be substantial, if partially unwitting, attempts
to convince the therapist to offer sympathy for the perceived victimization.
Unprovoked, behaviors and perceptions from outside soon start to appear
within the therapy itself. Drawing a parallel to behaviors at work and at
home, the patient can now begin to recognize counterproductive behaviors
and painful underlying emotions. It is important for the therapist to remain
empathic with the patient's distress, yet not be unduly influenced by the

intensely expressed emotions. In fact, therapist awareness of some of the feelings generated will offer data about how others react to the patient outside of the therapeutic setting. Gradually, by using observations of present behaviors along with exploration of how these may be connected with the past, the therapist can eventually help address the self-destructive traits, while recognizing the positive and engaging elements.

General Management Approach

Histrionic personality traits give an appearance of immaturity. Employees may feel that their attractive qualities entitle them to special treatment, and they may feel angry if someone more emotionally stable is over them. That anger can lead to unwitting manipulations, designed to attract attention from those in authority. Initially, management should help to set boundaries by providing employees with clear rules, expectations, feedback, and modeling. Referral for consultation can be useful when problems persist. As with other personality disorders, histrionic employees may take the stance that the problems are caused by other people. It may be especially difficult in the workplace to address any problems of inappropriate relationships, personal dress, or seductive style. The prognosis is quite good when there are strengths that can enhance social and work activities, and when there is a capacity to develop introspection and change.

ANTISOCIAL: CRIMINAL/ AGGRESSIVE EMPLOYEES

Case Study 3

Phil Dixon is a 35-year-old recently divorced shipping department employee who had impressed the job interviewer with his intelligence and style. Phil worked hard at first and impressed his supervisor. However, within several months he started a pattern of calling in sick and taking family leave days. Sometimes when a personal crisis pulled him away in midday, his job assignments got fouled up or had to be completed by someone else. There were increasing reports to the supervisor about Phil's lack of consideration for co-workers. The complaints were mostly that Phil was avoiding work. And since his arrival, several expensive items had disappeared from the shipping department. Although Phil was a likable man who socialized with the others, he would sometimes get irritable and aggressive. Since this would happen when people disagreed with him or crossed him, he found it easy to get personal loans from co-workers, as well as advances on his salary.

Phil's difficulties culminated when housekeeping discovered some of the missing items in his locker during routine cleaning. Phil was confronted and claimed that someone must have planted the items there in order to sabotage his job status. His explanation was so tearful and convincing that the supervisor thought he was telling the truth. But co-workers had long suspected Phil and had not had much luck getting their money back from him. Some of their things were missing, too. When Phil met with the supervisor again, he became irate and threatened to walk off the job immediately. Feeling confused and threatened, and recognizing a significant personality problem, the supervisor asked Phil to see a psychiatric consultant. Phil said that he was going for therapy, but it was nearly a month before the supervisor realized that Phil never even went for the consultation.

Case Study 4

At 46, Tom Newman was a senior vice-president of the Zeilig Manufacturing Company. His adroit accomplishments had been recognized by the busy CEO and Tom had risen rapidly through the ranks. Although there had long been quiet rumors about possibly improper activities, the stories were passed off by a CEO preoccupied with other concerns. After all, the stories came mostly from disgruntled former subordinates. Eventually, though, a former female employee filed suit against Tom and the company, claiming he had intimidated her into a sexual relationship. The director of human resources was then surprised to hear similar stories from four other past and present employees.

Further investigation included review of Tom's extravagant travel expenses. Despite some records that disappeared, it looked like he had padded or "dummied" as much as $80,000 over 4 years. Careful review of Tom's initial job application revealed that he had been suspended twice from college for cheating and theft, that he hadn't actually gone to graduate school at all, and that he had failed to acknowledge a conviction for tax fraud in his twenties. When confronted with some of these allegations, Tom denied any impropriety. But when his explanations were questioned, he became irate and implored the CEO to fire the individuals who had confronted him. He attempted to fire a few of them himself, but was blocked by human resources. As the CEO's information file grew, he put Tom on leave and considered whether to bring legal action.

Basically, sociopaths in the organization want to beat the system. They will try to satisfy their own sense of entitlement, with little concern for the personal or professional effects on others. Notably, there is an apparent absence of guilt about these behaviors. Assessment of antisocial personality must consider past history, as well as recent events. The pattern begins in adolescence and typically encompasses all spheres of activity. Antisocial patterns are likely to be present from school, other employers, and at home. It is important not to confuse isolated dishonest behavior under emotional stress (see Chapter 6) with the more pervasive and intractable behaviors of antisocial personality.

DSM-III-R DIAGNOSTIC CRITERIA

301.70 Antisocial Personality Disorder

A. Current age at least 18.

B. Evidence of Conduct Disorder with onset before age 15, as indicated by a history of *three* or more of the following:

   (1) was often truant

   (2) ran away from home overnight at least twice while living in parental or parental surrogate home (or once without returning)

   (3) often initiated physical fights

   (4) used a weapon in more than one fight

   (5) forced someone into sexual activity with him or her

   (6) was physically cruel to animals

   (7) was physically cruel to other people

   (8) deliberately destroyed others' property (other than by fire-setting)

   (9) deliberately engaged in fire-setting

  (10) often lied (other than to avoid physical or sexual abuse)

  (11) has stolen without confrontation of a victim on more than one occasion (including forgery)

  (12) has stolen with confrontation of a victim (e.g., mugging, purse-snatching, extortion, armed robbery)

C. A pattern of irresponsible and antisocial behavior since the age of 15, as indicated by at least *four* of the following:

   (1) is unable to sustain consistent work behavior, as indicated by any of the following (including similar behavior in academic settings if the person is a student):

     (a) significant unemployment for six months or more within five years when expected to work and work was available

     (b) repeated absences from work unexplained by illness in self or family

     (c) abandonment of several jobs without realistic plans for others

(2) fails to conform to social norms with respect to lawful behavior, as indicated by repeatedly performing antisocial acts that are grounds for arrest (whether arrested or not), e.g., destroying property, harassing others, stealing, pursuing an illegal occupation

(3) is irritable and aggressive, as indicated by repeated physical fights or assaults (not required by one's job or to defend someone or oneself), including spouse- or child-beating

(4) repeatedly fails to honor financial obligations, as indicated by defaulting on debts or failing to provide child support or support for other dependents on a regular basis

(5) fails to plan ahead, or is impulsive, as indicated by one or both of the following:

  (a) traveling from place to place without a prearranged job or clear goal for the period of travel or clear idea about when the travel will terminate

  (b) lack of a fixed address for a month or more

(6) has no regard for the truth, as indicated by repeated lying, use of aliases, or "conning" others for personal profit or pleasure

(7) is reckless regarding his or her own or others' personal safety, as indicated by driving while intoxicated, or recurrent speeding

(8) if a parent or guardian, lacks ability to function as a responsible parent, as indicated by one or more of the following:

  (a) malnutrition of child

  (b) child's illness resulting from lack of minimal hygiene

  (c) failure to obtain medical care for a seriously ill child

  (d) child's dependence on neighbors or non-resident relatives for food or shelter

  (e) failure to arrange for a caretaker for young child when parent is away from home

  (f) repeated squandering, on personal items, of money required for household necessities

> (9) has never sustained a totally monogamous relationship for more than one year
> (10) lacks remorse (feels justified in having hurt, mistreated, or stolen from another)
>
> D. Occurrence of antisocial behavior not exclusively during the course of Schizophrenia or Manic Episodes.
>
> Reprinted with permission from the *Diagnostic and Statistical Manual of Mental Disorders*, 3d ed. rev.; copyright 1987 by the American Psychiatric Association.

Causes for antisocial personality disorder are uncertain. Antisocial patterns may partially reflect maladaptive adult role models from childhood or adverse socioeconomic factors. They may also be an extreme variant of narcissistic personality traits, with cold detachment from other people and feelings of angry entitlement. An inherited component has been suggested, possibly associated with somatization disorder (Briquet's syndrome; see Chapter 18).

Goals of Psychotherapy

True antisocial traits present a problem for psychotherapy. Employees may agree to therapy solely because it is less painful than losing a job or going to jail. Characteristically, they present with "pseudocompliance" as a conscious resistance to treatment. It is important, then, to have as much clinical data as possible from outside sources (which does not necessarily mean breaching patient confidentiality). Since antisocial individuals do not always share the same emotional and behavioral monitoring system as others, they can quite readily agree with any interpretations and comments about their behavior. This gives the appearance of participation in therapy, but without true introspection, insight, or change. Ultimately, change requires that the patient realize intellectually that existing behavior patterns will lead to dreadful pain and suffering. Antisocial patients are far more likely to be concerned about their own pain than the pain they cause others. At least a year of consistent therapy is usually needed for any chance of deep emotional change. Ideally, treatment also enables the patient to incorporate some of the psychiatrist's values through emotional attachment and emulation.

General Management Approach

Antisocial personality traits wreak havoc in the workplace. Not only are the antisocial behaviors themselves destructive but their occurrence can insidiously undermine morale. Manipulations, cons, and improper conduct are hidden at first, then earnestly denied. The apparent lack of guilt about harm to others can be especially destructive. Workplace recognition usually follows the overt association of a problem or pattern of problems with the responsible party. When the responsibility does become clear, management must be quite firm and must set clearly defined rules of conduct. If the employee stays with the organization, close supervision and carefully structured work responsibilities are necessities. In particular, the employee should not be allowed to make unsupervised decisions that could hurt other employees or the organization. Significant antisocial personality traits are an indication for prompt referral for nonjudgmental treatment.

Without both treatment and careful reinforcement of workplace rules, there is little hope for change in antisocial personality disorder. Even so, prognosis is always guarded, since there is limited ability to even recognize that a problem exists and there are few internal safeguards to prevent manipulation of the treatment itself. Return to work is possible only when the damage done is minor and future risk is small. Otherwise, morale can be seriously affected by the anger of co-workers and supervisors over past behaviors and ongoing concern about the betrayal of others. Prognosis is far better when there has been only an isolated episode of dishonesty, in the absence of true antisocial personality.

PARANOID: ISOLATED/LITIGIOUS EMPLOYEES

Case Study 5

Ethan Waterman is a 34-year-old married man who was recently elected union shop steward, after 7 years at his firm. Ethan had been known as a good worker, but he had always seemed quiet, humorless, and a bit discontented. Though cordial to his superiors, he tended to keep his distance. He was more comfortable talking to one or two people than a larger group. Even before his election, Ethan would get angry about management and would occasionally raise questions that imputed prejudiced motivations. Eventually, after he became enraged during a meeting with company managers, he was referred for a confidential consultation.

After several interviews, it was clear that Ethan harbored tremendous resentment of authorities at work, within his union, in politics, and in his family. And his questions of the psychiatrist were at first belligerent and accusatory. Ethan felt that there was no relationship between his intensified anger on the one hand, and the near simultaneous arrival of elective office and of a first child on the other. He said that his anger had increased because of a new realization about the depth of company efforts against him. Ethan saw no reason to continue in treatment.

Even without specific information, Ethan was convinced that the company exploited and harmed union employees. He often used the power of the union shop to deliver attacks without any substantial basis in reality. Much of his angry fire was directed at managers who had previously offered him advice, helpful supervision, or construc-tive criticism. He was also spending far more time rallying workers against the company than trying to constructively resolve the perceived problems. He spent even less time completing his work assignments. Finally, Ethan angrily threatened to sue the vice-president of human resources. In front of other people, he also made obscene comments and appeared physically intimidating.

Faced with the prospect of termination, and aware now that something was troubling him, Ethan agreed to enter treatment. Early discussion of Ethan's earlier combativeness with the psychiatrist led to some awareness of his adversarial view of authority figures. He realized that his view of management had been colored by emotions from his personal life and upbringing. Gradually, he became better able to separate his emotions from his perceptions of the company. Even though Ethan remained more suspicious of company motivations than others, he could now assess each situation individually.

Paranoid personality traits are more commonly heightened by accom-plishments than by criticisms. The newly elevated role feels more precarious and more subject to the malevolence of others. To a limited extent, this can be a realistic consideration. For example, managers and leaders draw more attention than employees with less authority. But a paranoid perception can make newfound attention feel like attack.

DSM-III-R DIAGNOSTIC CRITERIA

301.00 Paranoid Personality Disorder

A. A pervasive and unwarranted tendency, beginning by early adulthood and present in a variety of con-texts, to interpret the actions of people as deliber-ately demeaning or threatening, as indicated by at least *four* of the following:

(1) expects, without sufficient basis, to be ex-ploited or harmed by others
(2) questions, without justification, the loyalty or trustworthiness of friends or associates

(3) reads hidden demeaning or threatening meanings into benign remarks or events, e.g., sus-
pects that a neighbor put out trash early to
annoy him
(4) bears grudges or is unforgiving of insults or
slights
(5) is reluctant to confide in others because of
unwarranted fear that the information will be
used against him or her
(6) is easily slighted and quick to react with anger
or to counterattack
(7) questions, without justification, fidelity of
spouse or sexual partner

B. Occurrence not exclusively during the course of
Schizophrenia or a Delusional Disorder.

Reprinted with permission from the *Diagnostic and Statistical
Manual of Mental Disorders,* 3d ed. rev.; copyright 1987 by the
American Psychiatric Association.

Paranoid personality disorder is different from paranoid psychosis (see
Chapter 17). Psychotic disorders allow little capacity for reality testing, are
more likely to appear bizarre, pose a greater risk of danger, and usually need
medication or hospitalization. A psychotic employee, who talks to others
solely through his own fantasies, is often recognizable to everyone.

Paranoid personality traits lead to constant concern about potentially
harmful environments and people. Paranoid traits are thought to derive from
early failure of emotionally intimate relationships. Rather than feel abandoned by other people, paranoid traits allow substitution of an adversarial
attachment. But there is an ongoing mistrust of friends, colleagues, and
family. Feelings are strongly projected onto others, with the possibility of
"hair trigger" reactions to perceived anger or harm. Since the anger can be
palpable to others, it can lead unwittingly to adversarial relationships and
can thus become a self-fulfilling prophecy. Paranoid personality traits make
some appear like lone wolves. Kindness and a soft underside beneath the
angry exterior can invite friendship and helpfulness. Unfortunately, paranoid traits carry a deeply felt fear of hostile intentions and friendly efforts
will sometimes stir up an angry reaction.

Hypervigilance and self-protective data gathering can also be major
assets. High-functioning employees with paranoid traits are often able to

make accurate observations about other individuals. These are commonly critical observations, perceived from a hostile position, conveyed as objective truth, and designed for self-protection. Colleagues may find it difficult to determine the frame of reference, especially of someone in a position of power. And apprehensiveness about people in general can include particular mistrust of those who are more trusting.

Goals of Psychotherapy

As with any personality style, the initial task of treatment is formation of a treatment alliance, based on the therapist's ability to instill a sense of trust, stability, and reliability in the relationship. The task is complicated because the general mistrust of others applies to therapists too, though careful perseverance can allow even this obstacle to be minimized. It is helpful to acknowledge how real the mistrustful perceptions are, but without challenging their accuracy. After an alliance has been formed, work can begin on recognizing the general mistrust of others and the reality that not everyone is actually hostile or even paying attention. A focus is also placed on learning to differentiate between reality and fearful perceptions. Greater change is accomplished through further understanding of hidden emotions and their childhood origins. Not infrequently, concurrent depressive or anxiety disorders require use of medication as well.

General Management Approach

People with paranoid traits are often most comfortable in a relationship that is supportive, consistent, fair, and emotionally nonintimate. That kind of anchoring relationship offers a degree of emotional stability and reality testing. Although a treating psychiatrist can fill that role, treatment also involves ultimate discussion of deeper emotional concerns. In the workplace, a manager can set up periodic brief meetings to discuss ongoing projects and organizational concerns. Those meetings also serve as a safe place to confidentially express grievances without fear of reprisal. Unlike a therapy session, the focus is entirely on work projects, without consideration of emotional relationships at home or in the workplace. Objective data collection and feedback is often reassuring. This kind of process can be effective only if the paranoid employee has sufficient trust in the supervisor to tolerate a differing opinion. Care must be taken not to get caught up in paranoid beliefs. Even though optimal treatment and management may still leave some continuing fears of persecution, consistent reality testing can keep them in check and minimize effects on workplace relationships.

BORDERLINE: IMPULSIVE/DIVISIVE EMPLOYEES

Case Study 6

Jane Tryen is a 37-year-old, somewhat overweight former sales clerk, who joined Payplastic Stores at an entry-level management position. She had always been an underachiever, but got this new job through hard work and intelligence, and because of a company effort to have well-seasoned sales personnel in lower management. A few months later, her office seemed to be struggling with morale. Projects that required teamwork and collaboration were falling behind. When employees were interviewed individually about the problems, they kept mentioning Jane.

Jane would take provocative and angry positions against opposing views, while at the same time gathering passionate supporters for her side. In effect, she played people off against each other. Even in social interactions, co-workers would sometimes feel angry at each other, until they realized that Jane had somehow set up their disagreement. Jane liked to gossip about people, but was pretty much unaware of her effects on them, or the extent of their discussion about her. She did feel that there were co-workers who were causing problems for her. She would laugh and gossip with them, even while campaigning secretly for their dismissal.

Jane felt that any criticism of her was unfair, especially considering her current personal crises. After her recent third divorce, her ex-husband was not making alimony payments. They would sometimes argue late into the night and Jane would be tired and tense the next day at work. Actually, she had always had a complicated personal life. Her emotions would shift from one extreme to the other, it took little to provoke her anger, and there was always the desperate loneliness. Increasingly estranged from co-workers, and spending her limited funds on proper business attire, Jane now felt both emotionally and financially impoverished. Eventually, she became so enraged that she abruptly threw some of her files across the room. Later that week, she stormed out of a meeting with her supervisor and left for home.

The supervisor realized that Jane had become an increasing liability and a cause of other employees' dissatisfaction. Co-workers were spending enormous amounts of time and energy dealing with Jane and with the results of her actions. Even so, the company had invested considerable time and energy in her training and she had completed some very successful projects. When Jane was referred for consultation, she loudly ridiculed the idea to anyone in the office who would listen.

Borderline personality traits can have seriously disruptive effects in the workplace. Intense emotions, impulsive behavior, subtle divisiveness, and disaffection all contribute to discord and disunity. Causes of borderline personality are thought to include unstable or disruptive early childhood relationships, as well as comorbid anxiety and depressive disorders (see Chapters 12 and 13). Panic disorder is especially common. Clinical observations have noted that borderline personality disorder is associated with certain characteristic styles of emotional defenses. For instance, hidden anger at expectations of emotional rejection and despair is diffused through such mechanisms as splitting (divisiveness) and overidealization and devaluation (seeing people as either all good or all bad).

DSM-III-R DIAGNOSTIC CRITERIA

301.83 Borderline Personality Disorder

A pervasive pattern of instability of mood, interpersonal relationships, and self-image, beginning by early adulthood and present in a variety of contexts, as indicated by at least *five* of the following:

(1) a pattern of unstable and intense interpersonal relationships characterized by alternating between extremes of overidealization and devaluation

(2) impulsiveness in at least two areas that are potentially self-damaging, e.g., spending, sex, substance use, shoplifting, reckless driving, binge eating (Do not include suicidal or self-mutilating behavior covered in [5].)

(3) affective instability: marked shifts from baseline mood to depression, irritability, or anxiety, usually lasting a few hours and only rarely more than a few days

(4) inappropriate, intense anger or lack of control of anger, e.g., frequent displays of temper, constant anger, recurrent physical fights

(5) recurrent suicidal threats, gestures, or behavior, or self-mutilating behavior

(6) marked and persistent identity disturbance manifested by uncertainty about at least two of the following: self-image, sexual orientation, long-term goals or career choice, type of friends desired, preferred values

(7) chronic feelings of emptiness or boredom

(8) frantic efforts to avoid real or imagined abandonment (Do not include suicidal or self-mutilating behavior covered in [5].)

Goals of Psychotherapy

Treatment of borderline personality disorder is always a complex process. Since circumstances and other people tend to be seen in all good or all bad terms, there can be difficulty in recognizing that most people have both strengths and weaknesses. Impulsive and angry behaviors are also common complications. Intense emotions combine with inner despair and limited self-controls on behavior to make for behavioral problems in all relationships, and the therapeutic relationship will similarly follow a stormy course. The psychiatrist will be seen alternately in idealized and in highly critical ways. One early goal of therapy is to foster a therapeutic alliance and to point out that other people should be viewed in a more realistic way. Ultimately, the underlying mistrust of relationships and consequent anger at other people must be explored. It should be noted that depressive and anxiety disorders are extremely common in these patients, but are commonly unrecognized. Psychotherapy alone, without appropriate medication for those syndromes, will usually have only limited benefits.

General Management Approach

Employees with borderline personality traits are just as challenging for management. Although there can sometimes be overt evidence of impulsive or disruptive behavior, the problems are more often manifest in more subtle ways. Unwittingly, the employee can have a divisive influence on co-workers. For instance, there can be persuasive and emphatic expression about how other people have either been helpful or harmful to them. Appropriate limit setting is essential, with a focus on proper workplace conduct, completion of assigned tasks, and due consideration of co-worker feelings. Supervisors must also be ready for angry protests and must even be tolerant of the possibility that the employee will be angry at them. Problems and complaints should be discussed specifically and with specific suggestions for improvement. Supervisory meetings should not deteriorate into arguments.

NARCISSISTIC: GRANDIOSE/ DEMANDING EMPLOYEES

Case Study 7

Bill Chang is a 41-year-old vice-president of manufacturing operations. He had been promoted over several other managers after only 10 years with the company. More than a few colleagues had the feeling that Bill's prestigious position came more through office politics and ingratiation of the president than it did from significant personal accomplishment. Although a few people were resentful, most were impressed by his looks, bearing, charm, and achievement. Bill's wife is extremely attractive, well positioned in society, and the mother of their two beautiful children. Supposedly, his expensive cars, showy house, and exclusive country club were paid for more by his wife's family than by his own income or investments.

Gradually, there were increasing complaints from Bill's subordinates. Mostly, people thought that Bill was unconcerned about their well-being. They also thought that their assignments seemed mostly designed to advance Bill's position in the organization, and that he was sacrificing production quality and efficiency for his own short-term benefit. Bill sometimes used departmental meetings merely as a platform for his grandiose ideas, or even for outright discussions of his personal power, brilliance, and future success. And despite his dazzling success, he was hypersensitive to criticism. Almost everyone agreed that he was intolerant of even the most constructive advice. Still, Bill had quite a following. He sought out the "in crowd," and those in positions of power. Although he tolerated subordinates who might be useful to him, he had little apparent concern for anyone beneath him. Those who would feel appreciated for a while would eventually end up feeling used.

After several months of the growing complaints, the president realized that some of Bill's character traits had been exaggerated by the promotion. Besides the obvious impairment of departmental enthusiasm and morale, there were questions about management style and direction. He shared his concerns with Bill and referred him to a consulting psychiatrist. Although the president figured that Bill needed work on some superficial behaviors, his overall respect for him was un-diminished. Bill, though, felt rejected and a bit humiliated at first. Later on, he realized the importance of the president's referral. In the near term, he was able to start paying more deliberate attention to his subordinate's concerns and to long-term planning for his department. Only much later did Bill start to understand how his emotional sensitivity had made him seek admiration as a substitute for affection.

Narcissistic individuals can have strongly detrimental effects on the workplace. Through charm, intelligence, and very real contributions, they can advance a highly personal agenda that precludes actual concern for others or for organizational goals. Recognition of the problem can be difficult, especially if the narcissistic traits are in powerful individuals. Ultimately, destructive self-serving behavior creates significant adverse consequences. So, it is usually better to handle the problems sooner than later. At the same time, it is important to remember that there is an important difference between ambition and healthy self-advancement and destructive self-aggrandizement.

Narcissism is best thought of as a reflection of an underlying inability to find or tolerate emotional intimacy. Instead, narcissistic traits develop as protection against underlying loneliness, fear, and anger. They also offer a means of finding substitutes for the missing affection. The replacements can range from preoccupation with power, wealth, and material things, or with such personal assets as intelligence, beauty, and physical strength. These reassurances offer a fragile stability, but they are subject to disruption by their loss or by almost any manner of life changes. Major depression and self-destructive behavior are common consequences.

DSM-III-R DIAGNOSTIC CRITERIA

301.81 Narcissistic Personality Disorder

A pervasive pattern of grandiosity (in fantasy or behavior), lack of empathy, and hypersensitivity to the evaluation of others, beginning by early adulthood and present in a variety of contexts, as indicated by at least *five* of the following:

(1) reacts to criticism with feelings of rage, shame, or humiliation (even if not expressed)

(2) is interpersonally exploitative: takes advantage of others to achieve his or her own ends

(3) has a grandiose sense of self-importance, e.g., exaggerates achievements and talents, expects to be noticed as "special" without appropriate achievement

(4) believes that his or her problems are unique and can be understood only by other special people

(5) is preoccupied with fantasies of unlimited success, power, brilliance, beauty, or ideal love

(6) has a sense of entitlement: unreasonable expectation of especially favorable treatment, e.g., assumes that he or she does not have to wait in line when others must do so

(7) requires constant attention and admiration, e.g., keeps fishing for compliments

(8) lack of empathy: inability to recognize and experience how others feel, e.g., annoyance and surprise when a friend who is seriously ill cancels a date

(9) is preoccupied with feelings of envy

Reprinted with permission from the *Diagnostic and Statistical Manual of Mental Disorders,* 3d ed. rev.; copyright 1987 by the American Psychiatric Association.

Goals of Psychotherapy

Here, too, psychotherapy initially fosters a therapeutic alliance and focuses then on developing a fuller life-style. The narcissistic preoccupations are not challenged directly. Rather, they ultimately fade in importance as the quality of emotional relationships improves. At the same time, though, initial reality testing is often important. Helping patients see that their behaviors and emotional distancing do have effects on other people, and that those effects can hurt them in turn, is essential for their future success. Frequently, it can be helpful to point out conscious conflicts of narcissistically related behaviors with personal moral or religious beliefs.

General Management Approach

Narcissistic individuals often present organizations with a real dilemma. They can be very motivated and creative, and they have much to contribute to the organization. But ultimately, whatever they do, it is really for themselves. They may see themselves as indispensable and others as unimportant. They may feel such a need to appear perfect that they cannot let themselves seek help. Narcissistic employees need to be approached in a gentle, nonthreatening manner to prevent further blows to their ego and to avoid further reaction on their part. Correction should be put in a constructive light and must be balanced by positive input from the supervisor. It is always important to leave these individuals with something positive, particularly their self-respect.

PASSIVE-AGGRESSIVE: COMPLIANT/UNDERACHIEVING EMPLOYEES

Case Study 8

Richard Sanders is a 45-year-old, heavy-set man, who has been with the company for over 20 years. He has held the same secure clerical position for the past 10 years, and his career advancement has probably already peaked. His section, which had fallen behind in a changing business environment, needed to be turned around. After 15 years on the job, the old supervisor was terminated for poor departmental productivity and because of his inability to recruit fresh talent. Richard was not getting along well with the new supervisor. The new supervisor was trying to reorganize the department and complained to human resources that Richard was one of the main impediments to change. Though he couldn't put his finger on it, he felt frustrated by Richard's apparent avoidance of work, and was even more frustrated because he couldn't really document the details. Richard would be quite agreeable to efforts upon supervisory advice, but there was always a slackening of his output afterward.

On the surface, Richard got along fairly well with others in the department. He had even evolved into a kind of leadership position, although it was unclear exactly where he was leading everyone else. His inactivity seemed to inspire theirs. He had little investment in initiating and completing his assigned tasks. Richard seemed to take longer with his work and turned it in later than anyone else, although always with some sort of rational explanation. At times he would be difficult, coming in late to work, or leaving essential papers at home. And his computer had far more frequent destructive hard-disk crashes than anyone else in the office. But because of his positions at both the company and at the union, extra data would be needed to terminate him. So far, it had been difficult to obtain clear data that he was avoiding or resisting work. Mostly, he just left people feeling angry at him.

Recently, the supervisor proposed a new and potentially exciting direction for the department. Richard's silent opposition to these changes made it difficult to maintain enthusiasm and excitement from everyone else. Moreover, the supervisor noticed that Richard's activities were focusing more and more on gathering support for his resentment and oppositionalism. When Richard was eventually referred for counseling, he had to be pushed for weeks before he made an appointment.

Passive-aggressive traits are difficult to recognize, since most of the resistance is hidden. A key characteristic is the increasing frustration of co-workers and supervisors who try to encourage more productive activity. Meanwhile, passive-aggressive employees seem to move calmly on, apparently unaffected by the inefficiency and irritation around them. These employees will seem unaware of creating anger or expressing aggression by passivity, and will even be surprised by any confrontation about their behavior.

DSM-III-R DIAGNOSTIC CRITERIA

301.84 Passive Aggressive Personality Disorder

A pervasive pattern of passive resistance to demands for adequate social and occupational performance, beginning by early adulthood and present in a variety of contexts, as indicated by at least *five* of the following:

    (1) procrastinates, i.e., puts off things that need to be done so that deadlines are not met

    (2) becomes sulky, irritable, or argumentative when asked to do something he or she does not want to do

    (3) seems to work deliberately slowly or to do a bad job on tasks that he or she really does not want to do

    (4) protests, without justification, that others make unreasonable demands on him or her

    (5) avoids obligations by claiming to have "forgotten"

    (6) believes that he or she is doing a much better job than others think he or she is doing

(7) resents useful suggestions from others concerning how he or she could be more productive
(8) obstructs the efforts of others by failing to do his or her share of the work
(9) unreasonably criticizes or scorns people in positions of authority

Reprinted with permission from the *Diagnostic and Statistical Manual of Mental Disorders*, 3d ed. rev.; copyright 1987 by the American Psychiatric Association.

Goals of Psychotherapy

While all personality styles tend to be self-perpetuating, passive-aggressive traits may lead to particularly heightened passive resistance in response to advice or to initial psychotherapeutic efforts. Since passive-aggressive personality traits are usually positively self-perceived ("egosyntonic"), the impetus for change does not at first originate inside the patient. As a result, the best way to initiate therapy is to point out behaviors that will lead to difficulties and suffering. Appealing to concern for others is usually fruitless. As long as other people are seen as uncaring or hostile, it is hard to elicit sincere empathic behavior. Eventually, though, intelligence and self-preservation allow most to seek more flexible and adaptive personality traits.

Objective data about maladaptive behavior are especially important early in treatment. Otherwise, the patient will try to rationalize away the details, minimize the nature of the problem, and justify a lack of commitment to treatment and change. Genuine change is no small feat. Childlike emotional defenses need to be discussed in a clear and nonembarrassing manner, pointing out when current problems are a reenactment of early childhood relationships. In varying degree, the difficulties tend to occur in all relationships: at work, socially, and at home. Effective psychotherapy will be a gradual process, sometimes over an extended period. Changes in passive-aggressive behavior are significant for both the organization and the employee.

General Management Approach

Employees with passive-aggressive traits can be very difficult to manage. The harder you try to push them, the less they seem to get done. There may be very reasonable explanations for individual episodes, but in the long run, the supervisory process feels more and more frustrating. To make matters more complicated, the employee is usually unaware of the subtle aggression in his or her inactivity. Documentation of complaints, low productivity, effects on co-workers, and resistance to change is important. In particular, these data are useful in giving feedback to employees on their behavior and its effects. Documentation is also essential when further action is indicated, such as referral for treatment or probationary work periods. Sometimes, it is easier for an employee to understand the problem if there is similar feedback from co-workers. At other times, though, this can also lead to greater feelings of resentment and passivity.

SUMMARY

This chapter reviews the most significant categories of personality disorder and style that are seen in the workplace. Though there are many variations, the personality disorders each include at least three elements. First, the behavior patterns are both inappropriate and painful to the self or to others. Second, the maladaptive patterns are substantially unaffected by external inducements to change. And third, little by little the patterns create problems for the organization and for co-workers. The workplace effects of personality disorders and styles are initially more subtle than the effects of more overt problems such as depression or alcoholism.

This chapter reviews some emotional aspects of personality; recognition of personality patterns; contributing factors; effects on employees, workplace, and organizational productivity; and approaches effecting change. Not included in this chapter are such other DSM-III-R categories as impulsive, immature, dependent, and avoidant personality disorders.

Acknowledgment   With grateful acknowledgment to Welda Vance, whose exceptional editing skills contributed significantly to this effort.

Bibliography

Bellak, L., and P. Faithorn. 1981. *Crises and Special Problems in Psychoanalysis and Psychotherapy.* New York: Brunner/Mazel.

Colarusso, C. A., and R. A. Nemiroff. 1981. *Adult Development.* New York: Plenum Press.

Freud, S. 1954. *The Standard Edition of the Complete Psychological Works of Sigmund Freud.* London: Hogarth Press.

Kaplan, H. I., and B. J. Sadock. 1990. *Synopsis of Psychiatry,* 6th ed. Baltimore: Williams & Wilkins.

Kernberg, O. 1984. *Severe Personality Disorders: Psychotherapeutic Strategies.* New Haven, Conn.: Yale University Press.

Levinson, D. J. 1978. *The Seasons of a Man's Life.* New York: Ballantine Books.

Nicholi, A. M., Jr. 1978. *The Harvard Guide to Modern Psychiatry.* Cambridge, Mass.: The Belknap Press of Harvard University Press.

Vaillant, G. E. 1977. *Adaptation to Life.* Boston: Little, Brown and Company.

15

Drug Abuse and Dependence

Jeffrey S. Rosecan, M.D.

ABSTRACT

Drug abuse is a major problem in the American workplace. In this chapter the terms *drug abuse, drug dependence,* and *drug addiction* are defined, and guidelines for identifying and managing drug abuse in the workplace are reviewed. Individual drug abuse syndromes are described and illustrated with case studies. Guidelines for urine testing are provided, as is a sample corporate substance abuse policy.

INTRODUCTION

Drug abuse continues to be a major social problem in the United States in the 1990s. It is estimated that the direct costs to industry of alcohol and drug abuse are close to $80 billion per year, that 14 percent of Americans abuse or

346

are dependent on alcohol, and that 5 percent of Americans abuse or are dependent on other drugs. In addition, drug abuse has been linked to other major societal problems, including AIDS (acquired immunodeficiency syndrome), homelessness, and crime. This chapter focuses on the problems of drug abuse in the workplace. Aside from the staggering cost to business, drug abuse is directly responsible for problems including injury, accidents, disability, lateness, absenteeism, theft, embezzlement, and overall reduction in performance and morale. Co-workers who do not use drugs, employers, and the general public all pay the price for these consequences of drug abuse in the workplace.

Why is drug abuse so common in the workplace? Many drug-abusing employees in their thirties and forties have liberal attitudes toward the use of illicit drugs, especially marijuana. As cocaine increased in popularity in the 1970s and 1980s, it too became acceptable as a recreational drug, and many believed it was safe and nonaddicting. Many employees erroneously assume that alcohol, marijuana, or cocaine use outside of the workplace (i.e., at home or on weekends) will not affect their job performance. They believe that it is their choice or right to use drugs socially or recreationally in their private time. Many businesses have developed drug abuse and urine testing policies, which are reviewed in this chapter. This is a controversial area and reflects the difficulty of differentiating an individual's rights from his or her workplace responsibilities.

The response of business has increasingly been the development of employee assistance programs (EAPs), where the overall approach is to identify and treat the drug-abusing employee, rather than to fire him or her. EAPs provide job-based evaluation and referrals, and some also provide substance abuse treatment. EAPs are valuable for workers in that they provide a nonthreatening place to obtain alcohol and drug abuse information and counseling. They give employees the message that their companies would rather help them with their problems than fire them.

But by definition, EAPs are in a difficult position. They are the advocate of the employee, yet at the same time they must protect the interests of the employer. They often serve as the intermediary between the two during the period of substance abuse treatment. As with all types of mental health treatment, patient confidentiality must be preserved (see Chapter 3). Yet for the EAP to be effective, there must be some degree of communication with the employee's supervisor, union, or personnel office. It is important that the guidelines for communication of this type be clear at the very beginning of treatment. In most programs, the employer communicates with the EAP regarding job performance, and the EAP provides the employer with periodic progress reports without divulging confidential information.

Employers are generally in favor of the EAP system since they feel that in the long run it is more cost effective to treat employees than to fire them and retrain new ones. It is also helpful for company morale to see recovering alcoholics and drug abusers return to work, happier and more productive. Insurance companies are also generally in favor of EAPs since successful substance abuse treatment has been shown to reduce overall medical costs.

However, there are several important limitations to EAPs. Many executives, upper-level managers, and company presidents do not seek treatment for substance abuse through their EAPs. They often prefer off-site treatment programs or clinicians since (1) their substance abuse may involve an illicit drug rather than alcohol, (2) company morale would suffer if it became known, for example, that the CEO was a cocaine addict, and (3) it is difficult to be treated by someone you employ. The EAP focus on substance abuse often means less broadly trained clinicians and less careful attention to other emotional and psychiatric problems.

USE, ABUSE, AND ADDICTION

All drug use is not abuse and, as is discussed later, urine testing of employees does not help to distinguish the drug user from the abuser. What is drug abuse or addiction, and how can companies deal effectively with this problem? The terms *drug abuse, dependence,* and *addiction* are often used interchangeably, but there are important technical differences between them. The scientific community would prefer not to use the term addiction, but it is widely used to imply a severe drug dependence. In the 1980 DSM-III, substance abuse was classified as a pathological pattern of use resulting in some form of social or occupational impairment, lasting for at least a month. In order to meet criteria for DSM-III substance dependence, there also had to be a physiological dependence on the drug, manifested by either tolerance or a withdrawal syndrome.

In the revised 1987 version of DSM-III-R, the criteria for substance dependence no longer require physiological dependence. Instead, an individual is considered dependent on a psychoactive substance if three of nine listed symptoms are found by the examining doctor. The key feature of this classification is impaired control over substance use, not physiological dependence. These criteria are valid for all of the commonly seen drugs of abuse, including cocaine, amphetamines, marijuana, barbiturates and other tranquilizers, and opiates including codeine, morphine and its derivatives, and heroin. In DSM-III-R, psychoactive substance abuse is a less severe form of substance dependence. It is a residual category for individuals who have a maladaptive pattern of use, but who do not meet full criteria for psychoactive substance dependence. The DSM-III-R criteria for psychoactive substance dependence are shown in the boxed copy. It is important to note that not all nine symptoms must be present for the diagnosis of substance dependence. The diagnosis requires that the symptoms persist for at least one month, or that they have recurred repeatedly over a long period of time, as in binge cocaine use. Another important factor to note is that it is rare to find an abuser of just one drug. The majority of substance abusers are polysubstance abusers. Common drug combinations include stimulants (e.g., cocaine, amphetamines, diet pills) with depressants (e.g., alcohol, tranquilizers), although clinically one sees drug combinations of all types. Dependence on legal or medically prescribed drugs is still psychoactive substance dependence, and DSM-III-R wisely does not make this distinction in its diagnostic criteria.

DSM-III-R DIAGNOSTIC CRITERIA

Psychoactive Substance Dependence

A. At least three of the following:

(1) substance often taken in larger amounts or over a longer period than the person intended

(2) persistent desire or one or more unsuccessful efforts to cut down or control substance use

(3) a great deal of time spent in activities necessary to get the substance (e.g., theft), taking the substance (e.g., chain smoking), or recovering from its effects

(4) frequent intoxication or withdrawal symptoms when expected to fulfill major role obligations at work, school, or home (e.g., does not go to work because hung over, goes to school or work "high," intoxicated while taking care of his or her children), or when substance use is physically hazardous (e.g., drives when intoxicated)

(5) important social, occupational, or recreational activities given up or reduced because of substance use

(6) continued substance use despite knowledge of having a persistent or recurrent social, psychological, or physical problem that is caused or exacerbated by the use of the substance (e.g., keeps using heroin despite family arguments about it, cocaine-induced depression, or having an ulcer made worse by drinking)

(7) marked tolerance: need for markedly increased amounts of the substance (i.e., at least

a 50% increase) in order to achieve intoxication or desired effect, or markedly diminished effect with continued use of the same amount

Note: The following items may not apply to cannabis, hallucinogens, or phencyclidine (PCP):

(8) characteristic withdrawal symptoms (see specific withdrawal syndromes under Psychoactive Substance-induced Organic Mental Disorders)

(9) substance often taken to relieve or avoid withdrawal symptoms

B. Some symptoms of the disturbance have persisted for at least one month, or have occurred repeatedly over a longer period of time.

Criteria for severity of Psychoactive Substance Dependence:

Mild: Few, if any, symptoms in excess of those required to make the diagnosis, and the symptoms result in only mild impairment in occupational functioning or in usual social activities or relationships with others.

Moderate: Symptoms or functional impairment intermediate between "mild" and "severe."

Severe: Many symptoms in excess of those required to make the diagnosis, and the symptoms markedly interfere with occupational functioning or with usual social activities or relationships with others.[1]

In Partial Remission: During the past six months, some use of the substance and some symptoms of dependence.

In Full Remission: During the past six months, either no use of the substance, or use of the substance and no symptoms of dependence.

Psychoactive Substance Abuse

A. A maladaptive pattern of psychoactive substance use indicated by at least one of the following:

(1) continued use despite knowledge of having a persistent or recurrent social, occupational, psychological, or physical problem that is caused or exacerbated by use of the psychoactive substance

(2) recurrent use in situations in which use is physically hazardous (e.g., driving while intoxicated)

B. Some symptoms of the disturbance have persisted for at least one month, or have occurred repeatedly over a longer period of time.

C. Never met the criteria for Psychoactive Substance Dependence for this substance.

Reprinted with permission from the *Diagnostic and Statistical Manual of Mental Disorders,* 3d ed. rev.; copyright 1987 by the American Psychiatric Association.

A more practical definition that is widely used looks at four main criteria for drug addiction: compulsion, continued use despite adverse consequences, loss of control, and denial. Compulsion is a preoccupation with the drug. The addict spends most of his or her time thinking about the drug (where to obtain it, how to buy it, how to conceal it, where to use it), using the drug, and withdrawing from the drug. Clearly this leaves little time for work or anything else. Many addicts in the workplace are able to conceal their drug use for years, and to the outside observer they can appear to be functional. It is only when they are confronted with their drug abuse, and forced to enter treatment, that the full extent of their compulsion to use drugs is revealed.

Another feature of drug addiction is continued use despite adverse consequences. The addict is unwilling (usually earlier in the course of the addiction) or unable (in the later stages) to stop drug use. Despite threats to the marriage, financial losses directly attributable to drugs, or medical complications of drug abuse, the addict continues drug use. Spouses can threaten divorce, creditors can sue or take away credit cards, and doctors can warn their drug-abusing patients. Ironically, it is the employer who can say "Get help or you're fired" who often has the greatest leverage.

Loss of control is an important criterion for drug addiction, and it is one of the more confusing aspects for employers to comprehend. If the addict can show up and work reliably some of the time, why not all of the time? Why can some drug abusers appear to be conscientious employees Monday through Friday and then binge nonstop on drugs throughout the weekend? Why doesn't the addict just have the willpower to not use drugs? The problem is that once the addict starts using drugs, it becomes increasingly difficult to stop. Loss of control may not be apparent until a period of time has passed, because of the principle of progression of the addiction. Over time, untreated drug use progresses from social and recreational use, to more problematic heavy use, and finally to out-of-control addiction. In order to understand the loss of control the addict experiences, addiction must be looked at as a progressive, not static, illness.

It follows that denial of the problem is a related symptom of the addiction. If the addict was able to control his or her drug use in the past (i.e., early in the progression), why not in the present? If one has apparent control over the drug use for a period of time, it is difficult to accept the eventual loss of control. The addict at first minimizes the damage the drug abuse has caused in his marriage and relationships with family and friends. He will typically blame others or circumstances outside of his control (e.g., "My wife doesn't understand me"; "My boss passed me over unfairly for a promotion") as justification for his continued drug abuse. He becomes quite adept at rationalizing his behavior (e.g., "Cocaine isn't addictive anyway"; "These pills are prescribed by my doctor") and minimizing the problem. The first step toward successful treatment of alcohol or drug addiction in the workplace is the direct confrontation of the denial. The employer or partners often have more leverage and more emotional neutrality than a family member. Drug abusers are usually unwilling to seek help on their own and must be made to see the adverse consequences of not stopping drug use (e.g., loss of job, filing for divorce). The employee is given the choice of treatment or termination, and the usual result is a referral to an EAP or other treatment provider.

A helpful way to conceptualize addiction to any substance is to view it as an interaction between the individual, the environment, and the substance (Figure 15-1). All three factors are important, but in certain situations one

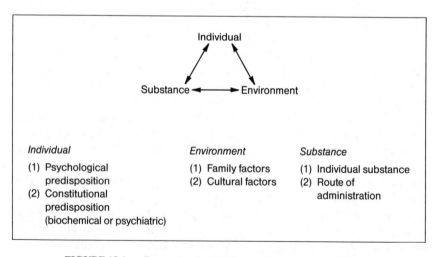

FIGURE 15-1.   Factors involved in the development of an addiction.

factor outweighs the others. This approach is related to the biopsychosocial approach to illness, where biological, psychological, and social factors are all important in the etiology and treatment of human illness.

The Individual

Certain individuals have psychological traits that leave them predisposed to addiction. Many employees use drugs as self-medication for such painful emotional states as the breakup of a marriage, a family crisis, or a financial loss. Alcohol, marijuana, cocaine, prescription analgesics, and tranquilizers are the drugs most commonly used to medicate life's stresses and anxieties. Over time, susceptible individuals can thus develop an addiction. It is important to note that many employees become psychologically dependent on legal or illegal drugs, before the physical dependence sets in.

Other individuals are at risk for the development of drug dependence because of their biochemical or psychiatric predisposition. Those employees with strong family histories of alcoholism or depression may be at higher risk, although the data are not definitive. Since alcoholism and drug abuse often coexist with anxiety or depressive disorders, a comprehensive psychiatric examination is necessary for accurate diagnosis and successful treatment.

The Environment

The workplace, whether it is the boardroom or the mailroom, is where the employee's drug attitudes meet the employer's. Each workplace has its own personality and its own view of drug use. Some are militantly antidrug, with mandatory urine testing policies, active EAP programs, and employee outreach services. Others are relatively laissez-faire, where "soft" drug use and drinking are openly tolerated.

The family is the mediator between the individual and his or her culture, and the family environment is where attitudes toward drugs are first learned. Family factors are important in the development and treatment of drug dependence. For example, an employee may honestly feel that marijuana is safe and nonaddicting if she was brought up in a family where it was grown and smoked openly. Drug dependence may be one of the indicators of family dysfunction; hence treatment will not be successful without active involvement of the family.

For adolescents and younger adults in the work force, the peer group supplants the family as the primary determinant of attitudes toward alcohol and drug use. It is understandably difficult for young adults to abstain from drugs if all of their friends are users. It is an important principle of drug abuse treatment for the abuser to avoid the people, places, and things associated with drugs. In order to do this successfully, most employees need to form new friendships and new support systems through treatment programs and 12-step programs like Alcoholics Anonymous (AA), Narcotics Anonymous (NA), and Cocaine Anonymous (CA) (see Chapter 16).

The Substance

The individual substance and its route of administration are important determinants of the progression of social drug use to drug dependence. Alcohol is a drug with a relatively low potential for dependence, yet alcoholism remains by far the major substance abuse problem in the United States, responsible for over 100,000 deaths per year (see Chapter 16). Only 10 percent to 15 percent of alcohol users will progress on to alcoholism, whereas an estimated 75 percent to 90 percent of freebase cocaine and crack users will become addicts (the number is significantly lower for nasal users) (Group for the Advancement of Psychiatry, Committee on Alcoholism and the Addictions). With freebase cocaine or crack, individual factors and the environment are less important than the substance itself in determining the development of the addiction. With alcohol, familial, cultural, and genetic factors appear to be more important than the drug.

INDIVIDUAL DRUG DEPENDENCE SYNDROMES

Stimulants (Cocaine, Amphetamines, Diet Pills)

Stimulant dependence, like most forms of drug dependence, is difficult to detect in the workplace. Unlike alcohol or marijuana, there is no odor or hangover. Cocaine abuse is the most common form of stimulant abuse, and there are several clinical features to watch for. Personality changes are commonly seen in cocaine abusers. They become depressed, irritable, and sometimes quite paranoid (see Chapter 17). Mood swings and temper outbursts can occur for no apparent reason. Stimulants are often used as appetite suppressants or "pep pills," and initially a loss in weight and an improvement in mood or energy level are seen. Many women who develop stimulant dependence first started using these substances for their appetite-suppressant effects. Users of cocaine initially can report euphoria and an increased sense of well-being, well described by Sigmund Freud in 1884:

> The psychic effect of cocaine . . . consists of exhilaration and lasting euphoria, which does not differ in any way from the normal euphoria of a healthy
> person. . . . One senses an increase of self-control and feels more vigorous and more capable of work. . . . One is simply normal, and soon finds it difficult to believe that one is under the influence of any drug at all. (Cited in Byck 1974)

Although the initial effects of stimulants are positive for some individuals, with chronic use there are invariable personality changes and adverse psychological effects as described above. Stimulant abusers can gain or lose weight, and can become trapped in a cycle of insomnia at night and oversleeping during the day. It is common for abusers of stimulants to use depressants such as alcohol, tranquilizers, or marijuana to counteract overstimulation. This often leads to cross-addiction, where there is dependence on both a stimulant and a depressant. People who were once industrious workers find that they have difficulty concentrating and staying alert. With cocaine abuse, nosebleeds, sore throats, chronic sinusitis, skin excoriations, shortness of breath, and chronic cough (especially in freebase or crack users) are common. All of the stimulants dilate the pupils, raise the pulse and blood pressure, and can cause palpitations and profuse sweating. Frequent unexplained absences, lateness, inability to sit still, and excessive trips to the restroom, along with the above physical and psychological symptoms, should lead the employer to suspect stimulant, especially cocaine, abuse.

Case Study 1

David Harrison is a 26-year-old attorney who was seen in consultation with a senior partner from his law firm and his mother. David had a relatively normal suburban upper-middle-class childhood and adolescence. He had many friends and outside interests. By the time he was in high school, he knew that he wanted to be a lawyer like his father, and he was soon working for his father's firm in the summer. David experimented with marijuana, but like his father, he preferred to "wind down" with several beers after tennis or at a party. In David's last year of law school, his father died suddenly of a heart attack. Although David applied for a prestigious clerkship at a federal agency, he withdrew his application, and after the funeral he asked his father's partners if he could join the firm.

David's first year at the firm was a disappointment. He worked constantly but never seemed to catch up. He became anxious and lonely, and lost touch with his college and law school friends. One day after work he snorted a few lines of cocaine offered to him by a colleague. He felt relaxed and euphoric, and he was able to work all night. He was surprised at how effortlessly he completed his project. David bought a gram of cocaine for himself and began to use it regularly. His mood was much better, he was talkative and outgoing, and he found his confidence and sense of humor returning.

After several months be began a romantic relationship with Susan Wing, a 25-year-old lawyer from another firm, and he began to socialize with her friends. Many of these new friends used cocaine socially, and Susan always seemed to have it around. David began using it several times a week, and after several months he found he needed it to wake up and get to work on time. He began having trouble sleeping. He would smoke pot or have a few beers every night to get to sleep. Susan noticed that he became irritated easily, and they began to argue. When she suspected that David was more interested in using cocaine than in having sex, she insisted that they both stop using cocaine "until things are better." While Susan was able to stop easily, David found the first week without cocaine terrible. He was depressed, lethargic, and he called in sick twice because he couldn't get out of bed. Finally, he bought more cocaine and used it every morning, deceiving Susan. One evening Susan found a vial of cocaine in his pocket and confronted him. David broke down in tears and promised to seek professional help if he ever used cocaine again.

Over the next few days, David craved cocaine continuously. He felt tense and exhausted. He suspected that Susan was watching him constantly, and he believed she was talking behind his back at his firm. When he angrily confronted her, she denied everything, told him he was paranoid, and said she wanted to end their relationship. David was crushed. He felt numb but was unable to cry. He bought a quarter ounce of cocaine and snorted it continuously alone; he called in sick 3 days in a row. He was despondent, he hadn't eaten or slept in days, and he had lost 15 pounds. He called a senior partner at work, one of his father's closest friends, and said he was quitting. He locked himself in his apartment, took the phone off the hook, and began to think that suicide would be better than facing his family or colleagues again. Several hours later, the partner and David's mother arrived.

David entered a private psychiatric outpatient abuse program and was started on imipramine (an antidepressant medication). He was seen in individual, group, and family therapy, and he began to improve after several weeks. David became involved in Cocaine Anonymous and began to attend meetings regularly. His performance at work also improved, and after several months David decided to leave the firm and reapply to the federal agency in which he was originally interested.

In David's case, one problem was that he joined the firm for the wrong reasons (i.e., guilt over his father's death). He was lucky that his relationship with his superiors was such that he was not fired when his cocaine dependence was discovered. His performance at work was certainly improved by cocaine initially, but 8 months later he was nonfunctional. David's firm has since decided to set up a program to deal with problems of alcohol and drug abuse among employees.

Marijuana (Cannabis)

Marijuana is the most commonly used illicit drug; because of its pungent odor, it is not usually smoked openly in the workplace, yet its use is widespread. The active metabolite of marijuana is delta-9-tetrahydrocannabinol (THC). The THC content of illicit marijuana has increased dramatically in recent years, reaching 10-15 percent, from 1-5 percent in the late 1960s. This is the presumed reason that there are now more DSM-III-R cannabis-dependent individuals than in the past, even though there are fewer users in national surveys. THC is lipid soluble, meaning that it accumulates in the fatty tissue of the body, including the brain. For this reason, THC can be measured in the urine up to several months after cessation of chronic use. In occasional users (less than once a week), urine can still test positive for THC for extended periods, even though these users may show no social or occupational impairment.

Case Study 2

Melvin Gold is a 42-year-old bus driver who has been working for the county for 19 years. He is married, has two children, is a model company employee, and is an active volunteer for local charities. Since his graduation from high school, Melvin has been a social drinker and marijuana user. Although his wife of 15 years initially objected to the marijuana, she now occasionally smokes it with him. Five years ago, Melvin's union agreed to a drug testing policy where county employees have their urine tested for drugs during the annual physical examination. Melvin's tests have all been negative, since he stops smoking marijuana several weeks before the urine test each year.

Recently, Melvin was involved in an accident where he seriously injured an 11-year-old girl who had chased a ball in front of his bus. Melvin was unable to stop in time. Because of a state law requiring testing for alcohol and drugs at the time of a bus accident, Melvin was tested and was found to have traces of marijuana in his blood and urine. He was arrested, and after a lengthy public trial, was fined, had his driver's license revoked, and was reassigned to a desk job at the bus company. The 11-year-old girl recovered after a lengthy hospital stay.

Melvin does not appear to fit DSM-III-R criteria for marijuana dependence, though it is unclear just how impaired he was at the time of the accident. Perhaps if he were drug-free his reflexes would have been milliseconds faster, allowing him to brake before hitting the girl.

The marijuana-dependent individual who smokes daily will have deficits in vocational, social, and psychological functioning. Common findings include inability to concentrate, difficulty with judgment and fine motor coordination, memory impairment, and social withdrawal. Lethargy, depression, and a loss of goal-directed behavior are common. In the workplace, the results can be dangerous to the individual user, co-workers, and the general public, depending on the occupation. A marijuana-dependent bus driver, security guard, factory worker, or air traffic controller can endanger the health and even lives of co-workers and the public.

How can an employer determine if a worker is marijuana-dependent? Physical signs include red eyes (conjunctival injection) with a glazed stare, dry mouth and throat with a chronic hoarse cough, a rapid pulse (tachycardia), and occasional weight gain (because of increased appetite for sweets). These signs in combination with the psychological changes above should lead the employer to suspect marijuana dependence. An analysis of the urine or blood is necessary to confirm the suspicion.

Opiate Narcotics

The opiate narcotics can be arbitrarily divided into two classes, the illicit and the medically prescribed. The pharmacologic effects and potential for abuse and dependence are independent of this arbitrary division, and both are major problems in the workplace. Heroin is the major illicit opiate narcotic in the United States. It is predominantly injected intravenously, although it can also be inhaled nasally or smoked. Heroin produces a rapid and powerful physiological dependence with tolerance (increasing amounts needed to achieve the desired euphoria) and a withdrawal syndrome (when supplies are interrupted). The withdrawal syndrome includes nausea, vomiting, diarrhea, muscle aches, abdominal cramps, and cravings for more heroin (which will alleviate the withdrawal). Once the heroin dependence is established, procurement of the drug becomes the focus of the addict's life.

There are many medical complications of intravenous heroin dependence, most notably respiratory arrest from overdose, infections from contaminated needles and nonsterile conditions, and HIV (human immunodeficiency virus) infection from shared needles. In the workplace, the heroin addict is frequently absent and late. He or she is prone to accidents because of heroin intoxication (lethargy, somnolence, difficulty concentrating, impaired motor coordination and judgment) or withdrawal. Injuries resulting in disability, and theft or embezzlement to support the dependence, are common.

The legal medically prescribed opiates, such as codeine, hydromorphine, meperidine, oxycodone, and morphine, are also abused in the workplace. They are more difficult to detect, because they are usually taken in pill form (the analgesics) or in syrups (the cough suppressants). Regular use of these substances leads to a high level of tolerance, and to a withdrawal syndrome identical to that of heroin. Dependence on illicit opiates is difficult to evaluate and treat when there is a medical disorder requiring analgesia or cough suppression.

The employee initially obtains the opioid by prescription from a physician, but gradually increases the dose on his or her own because of tolerance. Eventually the employee makes procurement of medication the focus of his or her life, and frequently obtains prescriptions from multiple doctors or illicit sources. Optimal psychiatric evaluation and treatment requires familiarity with drug dependence and pain control, and careful coordination with other treating physicians. One approach is to make the psychiatrist solely responsible for prescribing appropriate narcotic medication.

Case Study 3

Sylvia Wheat is a 35-year-old single nurse anesthetist at a local hospital. She was brought to employee health after fainting in the operating room while at work. Review of her personnel record showed a pattern of lateness and excessive absenteeism. A supervisor had filed incident reports indicating missing narcotics from Sylvia's nursing station during the past year. When confronted with these findings, Sylvia admitted addiction to intravenous meperidine (Demerol), which she had taken from the narcotics cabinet. The director of the anesthesia service at the hospital consulted with the personnel director and the employee health director. They suggested that Sylvia be hospitalized at another hospital for a 28-day detoxification and rehabilitation program. If she refused hospitalization she would be terminated. In addition, the legal department felt that it was the hospital's obligation to notify the state nursing board. Sylvia agreed to be hospitalized and did well in the inpatient chemical dependency program. She entered the outpatient program after discharge, began individual and group therapy, was urine drug tested twice a week, and went to frequent NA (Narcotics Anonymous) meetings. At a hearing where she appeared before the nursing board, Sylvia was ordered to remain in the outpatient program for 2 years, with twice weekly urine testing. She was told that if she failed any drug tests, her license to practice nursing would be suspended. Sylvia did well, and after her 2 years were completed, she entered a certified alcoholism counselor (CAC) degree program. She is now the director of nursing at the same hospital where she had been a patient.

Tranquilizers (Sedative, Hypnotic, and Antianxiety Drugs)

Minor tranquilizers are the most commonly prescribed psychoactive medications. Benzodiazepines are approved for the treatment of insomnia and anxiety, and in the case of alprazolam, panic disorder. As is the case with the prescription opioids, employees become adept at concealing their dependence on these medications. They are taken orally as pills and are usually legally prescribed by physicians. The intoxication syndrome consists of oversedation, lethargy, and impaired coordination. This can be quite dangerous if the employee is required to drive, operate equipment, or perform complex tasks in a pressured work environment. These medications are commonly combined with alcohol, another central nervous system depressant, potentiating the adverse effects. The withdrawal syndrome typically begins within hours to days upon abrupt discontinuation, and it consists of extreme anxiety, agitation, insomnia, nausea, tremors, and in extreme cases, seizures. The pulse and blood pressure are elevated, and the employee is clearly in distress. Urgent medical treatment is advised.

Sedative-hypnotic dependence is similar to medically prescribed opioid dependence, in that there is usually an initially valid medical or psychiatric indication for the medications. The employee gradually increases the dose on his or her own because of tolerance and the need to prevent withdrawal. When dependence finally develops, pill-seeking behavior becomes prominent. A psychiatrist experienced in treating anxiety and depression and familiar with substance dependence should coordinate treatment of the employee in these cases.

Case Study 4

Maureen Newton is a 32-year-old secretary for a suburban bank, who went to the employee health service complaining of insomnia. Upon questioning by the doctor, it was clear that she was agitated and upset over a recent breakup with her boyfriend. She had lost 10 pounds in the past month and was complaining of abdominal pain and bloating. The doctor ordered laboratory tests and x-rays, including an upper GI series. She was given prescriptions for several ulcer medications and for alprazolam at bedtime and as needed during the day for anxiety.

Within days, Maureen began to feel better physically. She was also sleeping better and feeling calmer during the day. Although she was still hesitant to date or attend singles events, she began to socialize with co-workers and twice a week she had several drinks after work. At this point she was taking alprazolam 0.5 mg three times a day, without adverse effects. After unexpectedly running into her ex-boyfriend at the bar one evening, she became agitated, went home, and took several extra alprazolam. Over the next week, she increased her dose to 1.0 mg three times a day. When she ran out of medication, her doctor telephoned in a prescription with five refills. Over the next few months, Maureen continued to do well at work. Her ulcer apparently healed. When she ran out of medication, she decided she was feeling much better and no longer needed it. Within 24 hours Maureen became extremely shaky and jittery. She was nauseous and light-headed, and felt her heart racing. When she woke up in the emergency room that evening she was told that she had a seizure due to alprazolam withdrawal.

Although Maureen does not fit criteria for DSM-III-R sedative dependence, she experienced a severe withdrawal syndrome because of physical dependence on alprazolam. Maureen was admitted to the hospital and gradually detoxified. Employee health then referred her for continuing psychiatric treatment. She was seen in weekly psychotherapy and her psychiatrist coordinated treatment with her internist.

URINE TESTING

Preemployment and periodic mandatory urine testing for illicit drugs has become a controversial topic in recent years. Some pros and cons of mandatory workplace urine testing are as follows:

Pros:	*Cons:*
Deterrent to drug use	Might be unconstitutional
Permits early identification of abusers	Can be inaccurate
Drug-free workplace safer and more productive	Does not differentiate drug use from abuse
Drug-free high-risk occupations (e.g., airline pilot) promote public safety	Job performance should govern employment, not drug use.

The main argument in favor of mandatory urine testing is deterrence of illicit drug use, at both work and home. Drug-using employees are required to stop, and employees unable to stop are identified and referred for evaluation and treatment. A safe and drug-free workplace is increasingly viewed as a right by both employees and organizations. Employees feel that substance-abusing co-workers jeopardize everyone's safety (e.g., on an assembly line or in a power plant) and invite criminal behavior in the workplace (see Chapter 10). Companies are aware of the enormous financial losses from drug-related absenteeism, pilferage, poor performance, and accidents. Many would like to see a drug-free workplace as the first step toward a drug-free society. Feasibility and even desirability are questions that society as a whole must answer.

Those who are opposed to mandatory urine testing say that it is a violation of constitutional rights to privacy. What people do in their private time, including illicit drug use, should not concern an employer. They feel that job performance is what matters, not the presence or absence of drugs in the urine. Even with safeguards, concerns are also raised about reporting errors and potential breaches of confidentiality.

An employee's right to privacy must be balanced with society's best interests. If public safety is involved, should certain professions or occupations be subject to mandatory drug testing? For example, should airline pilots, air traffic controllers, or anesthesiologists be required to have mandatory urine testing? Society, through its legal and judicial system, will answer these questions.

An additional concern is the accuracy of the urine tests themselves. There are always limitations on accuracy, and an employee's career, reputation, and livelihood can be mistakenly jeopardized. While it is possible to repeat all positive urine tests, and then confirm them with more accurate blood tests, there is no present guarantee that this will be done.

Urine tests do not distinguish drug use from drug abuse or dependence. This can only be done with a comprehensive medical and psychiatric history, and physical examination. At best, laboratory tests are adjunctive and provide diagnostic confirmation. It is accepted in the treatment community that urine testing is a useful adjunct in the treatment of the drug-dependent individual, but not all drug users are abusers.

SUMMARY

The American workplace has not been immune to the growing problem of substance abuse, which has profoundly adverse effects on the physical and mental health, productivity, and morale of employees. Effective approaches to the problems of illegal drug use require careful attention to recognition, management, and treatment, and to associated psychiatric diagnoses. Careful attention must also be given to the importance of social relationships in perpetuating or resolving drug problems. Drug abuse, drug dependence, and drug addiction are terms with distinct and specific meanings, and individual drug abuse syndromes have differing characteristics. Prevention can include a deliberate corporate substance abuse policy, and urine testing programs are sometimes appropriate.

APPENDIX: SAMPLE CORPORATE SUBSTANCE ABUSE POLICY*

The company is committed to providing a safe and productive work environment for all employees. Substance abuse by an employee can adversely affect the employee's productivity, jeopardize the safety of the employee and others, and damage the reputation of the company. The company developed this substance abuse policy to maintain a work force free from the use of illegal drugs and controlled substances, and to assure the elimination of drugs and drug-related activities in the workplace. The company will apply

*Prepared by the author.

the terms of this policy strictly to all covered employees and applicants. Employees and applicants are provided a copy of this policy and copies of the attached consent forms for urine (and/or blood) testing and for release of medical information.

Policy

The company strictly prohibits the unlawful manufacture, distribution, possession, or sale of controlled substances, or the use of controlled substances in a manner not medically authorized, on company premises, or while engaged in company business, or during work hours. The presence of an illegal drug or its metabolite in an employee's system while on company premises, while engaged in company business, or during work hours is also strictly prohibited.

Use of prescribed drugs in accordance with a physician is not prohibited under company policy; however, employees taking prescribed drugs are responsible for any effect the medication may have on their performance.

The company recognizes that drug dependency is an illness, and that early recognition and treatment is the key to successful rehabilitation. The company maintains an EAP to assist employees with substance abuse problems by making referrals to appropriate treatment programs, and employees who feel they need help with substance abuse problems should contact the director of human resources. Employees voluntarily seeking assistance for a substance abuse problem through the EAP or a qualified outside professional resource will not be disciplined for seeking such assistance, and the treatment will be handled in confidence. Employees who request leave of absence to participate in a treatment program will be given favorable consideration. However, if an employee has not volunteered for treatment and is found to have violated company policy, he or she may not avoid discipline by volunteering to participate in a treatment program. Moreover, participation in a voluntary treatment program will not excuse violation of the company's policy.

The company will provide education for supervisory personnel to assist in identifying and addressing substance abuse by employees. Supervisors will be provided with guidelines for maintaining confidentiality of all substance abuse-related information and for referring employees to our EAP or appropriate treatment.

Drug Testing

All applicants for employment are subject to testing for drug abuse. Any job offer made by the company is contingent upon the applicant consenting to taking and passing the test. Refusal of the applicant to comply with the testing procedure will disqualify the applicant from consideration for employment.

Current employees may be required to submit to drug testing if in the opinion of their supervisor there is a strong suspicion of drug abuse or other breach of this policy. If this is the case, the supervisor notifies the director of human resources who then notifies our EAP. Our EAP and its medical director will then decide if a drug test is warranted. Any employee who refuses to submit to testing may be subject to immediate discharge. If the drug test is positive, our EAP and its medical director, in consultation with the director of human resources, will decide on a recommended course of action. If the employee refuses to comply with this course of action (e.g., drug abuse treatment) this may be grounds for immediate dismissal.

Procedure

Specimen collection for a drug test will be accomplished in a dignified and private matter. Collection will take place at the company medical facility, and in the case of urine testing, will be observed by same-sex medical facility personnel. Appropriate chain-of-custody procedures will be employed, and the tests will be conducted by a laboratory satisfying forensic standards. The laboratory will preserve for 6 months an aliquot of specimen sufficient to permit independent confirmatory testing at the request of the applicant. The laboratory will endeavor to notify the company of positive test results within 2 days after receipt of the specimen. An applicant or employee may request a retest within 3 days from notice of positive test results.

I hereby acknowledge that I have received the company's drug abuse policy, have read and understood it, and consent to drug testing for substance abuse as outlined in the policy.

Date: Signature: Witness:

___/___/___   _____   _____

Bibliography

Byck, R. (ed.). 1974. S. Freud: Über Coca, in *Cocaine Papers,* pp. 49-73. New York: Stonehill Publishing.

Group for the Advancement of Psychiatry, Committee on Alcoholism and the Addictions. 1991. Substance abuse disorders: A psychiatric priority. *American Journal of Psychiatry* **148:**1291-1300.

Millman, R. 1986. Drug abuse and dependence. In *American Psychiatric Association Annual Review,* vol. 5, A. Frances and R. Hales (eds.). Washington, D.C.: American Psychiatric Press.

Schukit, M. 1989. *Drug and Alcohol Abuse: A Clinical Guide to Diagnosis and Treatment,* 3d ed. New York: Plenum.

Spitz, H., and J. Rosecan (eds.). 1987. *Cocaine Abuse: New Directions in Treatment and Research.* New York: Brunner-Mazel.

16

Alcohol Abuse and Dependence

Carlotta L. Schuster, M.D.

ABSTRACT

Alcohol abuse and dependence occur frequently in the workplace, at great cost to productivity, health, and morale. This chapter discusses alcoholism, and offers guidelines for workplace recognition, management, and referral; differentiation from other illnesses including comorbid psychiatric diagnoses; and both outpatient and inpatient treatment approaches. Alcohol abuse recognition must be combined with optimal treatment techniques.

INTRODUCTION

According to the *Seventh Special Report to Congress,* one out of three deaths in 1990 was directly or indirectly linked to alcoholism. Cirrhosis was the ninth leading cause of death in the United States. Alcoholism was associated with 25 percent of all general hospital admissions, costing the nation $130 billion. The cost to industry in decreased productivity of alcoholic workers can be reduced by early treatment intervention.

The etiology of alcoholism is complicated. While there are genetic, psychodynamic, and social influences that can contribute to the development of alcoholism, every at-risk individual will have a different pattern of contributors. For example, Cloninger (1987) showed that adopted-away sons of male alcoholics (who were not living with alcoholic families) have a fourfold to fivefold greater chance of alcoholism than controls. This effect is especially strong if the onset of alcoholism was early in life and was preceded by a history of antisocial behavior. Those sons of male alcoholics with late onset and no antisocial traits were more heavily influenced by such environmental factors as behavior of their adoptive parents, stress response, and peer pressure, rather than by genetic factors.

Adopted-away daughters of male alcoholics were no more likely to develop alcoholism than controls. Cloninger (1987) also showed that adopted-away daughters of female alcoholics had a threefold greater chance of developing alcoholism than controls. However, most studies of women suggest a greater influence of environmental than genetic influences on the development of alcoholism. Recently there have been attempts to locate a specific gene or group of genes involved in the transmission of alcoholism. This subject is currently a matter of hot debate in the scientific literature (Blum et al. 1990; Comings et al. 1991; Cloninger 1991; Gerlenter et al. 1991).

DSM-III-R DIAGNOSTIC CRITERIA

Psychoactive Substance Dependence

A. At least three of the following:

    (1) substance often taken in larger amounts or over a longer period than the person intended

    (2) persistent desire or one or more unsuccessful efforts to cut down or control substance use

    (3) a great deal of time spent in activities necessary to get the substance (e.g., theft), taking the substance (e.g., chain smoking), or recovering from its effects

(4) frequent intoxication or withdrawal symptoms when expected to fulfill major role obligations at work, school, or home (e.g., does not go to work because hung over, goes to school or work "high," intoxicated while taking care of his or her children), or when substance use is physically hazardous (e.g., drives when intoxicated)

(5) important social, occupational, or recreational activities given up or reduced because of substance use

(6) continued substance use despite knowledge of having a persistent or recurrent social, psychological, or physical problem that is caused or exacerbated by the use of the substance (e.g., keeps using heroin despite family arguments about it, cocaine-induced depression, or having an ulcer made worse by drinking)

(7) marked tolerance: need for markedly increased amounts of the substance (i.e., at least a 50% increase) in order to achieve intoxication or desired effect, or markedly diminished effect with continued use of the same amount

Note: The following items may not apply to cannabis, hallucinogens, or phencyclidine (PCP):

(8) characteristic withdrawal symptoms (see specific withdrawal syndromes under Psychoactive Substance-induced Organic Mental Disorders)

(9) substance often taken to relieve or avoid withdrawal symptoms

B. Some symptoms of the disturbance have persisted for at least one month, or have occurred repeatedly over a longer period of time.

Psychoactive Substance Abuse

A. A maladaptive pattern of psychoactive substance use indicated by at least one of the following:

(1) continued use despite knowledge of having a persistent or recurrent social, occupational, psychological, or physical problem that is caused or exacerbated by use of the psychoactive substance

(2) recurrent use in situations in which use is physically hazardous (e.g., driving while intoxicated)

B. Some symptoms of the disturbance have persisted for at least one month, or have occurred repeatedly over a longer period of time.

C. Never met the criteria for Psychoactive Substance Dependence for this substance.

Reprinted with permission from the *Diagnostic and Statistical Manual of Mental Disorders,* 3d ed. rev.; copyright 1987 by the American Psychiatric Association.

The DSM-III-R makes a distinction between alcohol abuse and dependence. Operationally the difference between the two is of little importance in the workplace. Therefore, this chapter refers to both as if they were one. Regardless of whether the alcoholic employee suffers from alcohol abuse or dependence, the consequences seen in the workplace can be one or more of the following: absenteeism, lateness, impaired decision making, temper tantrums, accidents, carelessness, failure to complete assignments on time (often accompanied by myriad excuses), sexual harassment of fellow workers, irritability with clients, and reduced employee morale.

WORKPLACE DETECTION

Case Study 1: Success, Anxiety, and Self-Sabotaging Alcoholism

When Tom Hayes graduated from law school, he was offered a position with a prestigious law firm. He advanced mercurially in the liquidation department and was in the running for junior partner within a year. His heavy law school drinking continued into his legal career. Drinking had not interfered with his work before, but business lunches with clients steadily increased his daily alcohol intake. Tom developed considerable tolerance to alcohol. However, by the time he arrived home, he had usually consumed two scotches and two glasses of wine with lunch. With more drinks to unwind, wine with dinner, and a brandy or two afterward, Tom was drunk by bedtime.

Gradually, his job performance began to show the effects of his drinking. He would arrive at the office pale and slightly nauseated. Clients complained because of his forgetfulness, especially after lunch. The head of the liquidation department asked him to improve his job performance and suggested that Tom had been drinking excessively. Tom was given a leave of absence and went to a rehabilitation center. Psychiatric evaluation there revealed no underlying medication-responsive anxiety or depressive disorder. He stopped drinking there, but seemed immune to attempts at psychotherapy.

When Tom returned to work, he attended Alcoholics Anonymous (AA) faithfully for several months and was soon offered a partnership in the firm. He forgot that his recent first career setback had been caused by drinking. Proud of his new partnership, Tom lulled himself into thinking that drinking had no adverse effect on his life. After maintaining abstinence, he considered himself "normal" and decided that a controlled approach to drinking would be better than complete abstinence. He started one evening with two glasses of wine at dinner. Since he did not find himself wanting more on that night, he tried drinking wine with dinner again. The habit continued for several weeks, until Tom convinced himself that before-dinner drinks would be okay too. His drinking increased steadily, and he again began to sabotage his work performance. A major case was transferred to another partner and Tom was sent back for treatment. He was told that any further relapses would result in loss of his position with the firm.

Psychotherapy was now more helpful for Tom. His therapist stipulated that for treatment to proceed, Tom must remain sober and attend Alcoholics Anonymous regularly. Tom did remain abstinent from alcohol and maintained a high performance level at work while he worked toward uncovering the conflicts that had thwarted his recovery and career.

In discussions with his therapist, Tom gradually learned that he suffered from guilt surrounding chronic, unconscious anger at his father, who died shortly after Tom graduated from law school. Tom remembered his father as domineering, cold, and impossible to please. His father's education was limited, and at his career peak he became a factory foreman. Though his father always encouraged Tom to press for success, obtaining greater success than his father unwittingly felt like some sort of angry retaliation. Tom revealed a fantasy that his law school graduation was his father's death blow. Each time Tom reached a new level of success at work, his anxiety increased, he drank more to cover it, and he sabotaged his career as a result. His drinking and unreliability also caused discomfort and resentment among co-workers. So, without any conscious awareness, Tom had set up defeat with the aid of alcohol to "take back" his success, and thus reduce his anxiety.

The more he understood the roots of his problem, the more Tom learned how to adapt. When he no longer perceived achievement as an aggressive, patricidal act, he could accept praise, promotion, and increased responsibility. His work became reliable and productive. With the help of AA and psychotherapy, he maintained abstinence from alcohol.

When to Refer for Treatment

Although an odor of alcohol emanating from a worker might heighten suspicion, confrontation at that point would be premature. One key to effective intervention is timing. A clear pattern of decline in job performance must be documented. Several weeks of lateness and/or absenteeism or months of diminished productivity need to be on record. There are some exceptions, including (1) omissions of procedure that endanger others (particularly in the cases of pilots, train engineers, or physicians) and (2) obvious intoxication at work or work-related events.

Referral Strategy

Confrontation should proceed gradually. At first the worker receives verbal warnings about his or her behavior. This should be done privately and quietly. The first warning can be empathic: "You seem to be having trouble arriving on time for work. It's a problem for us and I wonder if you could improve on this." The warning is made by the worker's immediate supervisor. If the behavior does not change, a written warning is issued and placed in the worker's confidential file. Human resource departments usually have a policy stipulating a set number of warnings about a given behavior before taking a next step. For example, three written warnings about failure to arrive at work on time would justify mandating that the worker consult the human resources department, consulting psychiatrist, or employee assistance program.

Workers are referred for treatment when their behavior at work, poor attendance, or impaired performance is intolerable to management or to the worker. After the required number of warnings, workers should be informed unequivocally that their job is on the line unless they are willing to accept treatment. The employee is made to understand that the job will remain available until treatment is completed. Often, it is useful to enlist the aid of family members in confronting the employee regarding the need for treatment. Spouses and children will often mistakenly protect alcoholism through a conspiracy of silence. Empathic support from mental health professionals can ultimately lead to treatment intervention for the family, as well as for the alcoholic worker.

Case Study 2: Alcoholism in the Executive Suite and Treatment Referral by Management

Sam Janus was head of sales for the northeast region. For 10 years he had been a super salesperson and an excellent manager of the other sales personnel in his division. For the past year, though, he was less attentive, often arrived at the office 2 hours late, and took very long lunch breaks. In the afternoons, he was less alert and often forgot transactions. After one 3-hour lunch, he had a phone conversation with an important business contact and completely forgot the details of a contract. The client reported this to the company president. There had also been two incidents where his brusqueness had reduced his secretary to tears.

The vice-president in charge of sales had noticed a sharp profit drop for the northeast region. He called Sam in for a conference, thought that Sam looked seedy, and found Sam remarkably defensive about the decline in profits. The vice-president also talked with the human resource department. Sam's job performance had been evaluated not only by interviewing Sam but also through confidential discussions with his directly reporting subordinates. There was a major decline in office morale, coinciding with the changes in Sam's behavior. Sam's boss concluded that action was needed. He and the human resource director called Sam in for an interview. The director gave Sam two options. Either he get help, or he should look for work elsewhere. Clear point-by-point documentation had been available about Sam's absenteeism, lateness, forgetfulness, irritability, and profit decline.

Although Sam was initially resentful, he agreed to enter a rehabilitation program. He was treated on an inpatient basis, because he had shakiness, perspiration, and nausea whenever a few hours elapsed between one drink and the next. Sam thus needed 24-hour monitoring to prevent alcohol withdrawal seizures. In addition, his behavior had alienated his office staff to the point that they didn't really want him back in the office. Removal from the work environment was his best option. While completing the inpatient portion of treatment, the vice-president and the human resource director met with Sam, his alcoholism counselor, and his psychiatrist. The treatment staff at the hospital noted a wonderful change in Sam. His initial defensiveness changed to refreshing candor and a deep commitment to continued sobriety with the help of AA. Sam was given a second chance with the company, but it entailed a lateral move to a smaller division in a new geographic location. Still sober and in treatment 3 years later, he had turned that division around and was commended for excellent leadership.

Case Study 3: Alcoholism in the Factory: EAP Self-Referral and Family Treatment

Sven Harris was a welder at a factory that manufactured home appliance parts. Although a reliable worker, he had spent much of his weekly paycheck on alcohol. Every Friday, when his shift was over, he and his buddies converged on the local tavern. Although Sven arrived home intoxicated and verbally abusive, he said he didn't understand why his marriage was strained. He felt that his wife was nitpicking about alcohol and that she didn't understand how men relaxed. For a long while, his binges were short-lived and he was always on time Monday morning. Sven's two young sons watched plenty of screaming between their mother and father. The 4-year-old was having trouble playing with the other children in nursery school. Sven saw no connection to his drinking.

Steadily, the interval between binges became shorter. He started drinking all weekend, and then midweek. He started to stay out all night and show up at work still drunk. His welding precision deteriorated and his defective output was increasingly returned to the factory. Eventually, the defects were traced to Sven. His supervisor called him in and pointed out that the change in Sven's performance was endangering the company's reputation. Sven promised to improve, but mostly just called in sick when his hands were too shaky or his mind was too cloudy. Sven had always been proud of his welding skills and he was alarmed at his new work problem. Sven became less vehement in his denial of alcoholism. He saw an EAP counselor and accepted referral to the medical department for medical assessment and treatment selection. It was decided that Sven didn't require inpatient detoxification. Because he worked the day shift and drank at night, he was referred to a 6-week, 5-day-a-week intensive evening program.

The peer pressure and support of group therapy and chemical dependency education paid off. He began attending AA meetings daily and enthusiastically. After his return to work, he attended an evening aftercare program and stayed in AA. Sven's family behavior was different now. In sobriety, Sven was a more sensitive and attentive father and husband. With the help of Sven's EAP department, he and his family were referred to family therapy. His wife attended Al-Anon, a self-help organization for adult relatives of alcoholics. Sven and his wife increased their understanding of normal childhood growth and development and corrected their earlier disciplinary mistakes. With the guidance of the family therapist, the children could discuss their father's alcoholism openly. The level of communication between all family members improved, and the children started to recover from the emotional trauma of Sven's drinking days. Later, they attended weekly meetings of Al-Atot and shared experiences with other children of alcoholic parents. His son's social and academic adjustment improved. Sven remained sober, a masterful welder, and a happier family man.

CAUSES AND EFFECTS OF ALCOHOLISM IN THE WORKPLACE

There is a reciprocal relationship between the worker and the workplace. Alcoholic behavior jars and demoralizes co-workers. Workers who show up late, or who delay completion of their work, will increase the workload of more conscientious co-workers. Intoxication on the job causes personal conflict and sometimes physical risk. Co-workers become resentful, tense, and fatigued. When they think that the problem will not be addressed, they may feel considerably less motivated to arrive on time or to finish their own work. And their resentment in turn feeds their colleague's alcoholism. Alcoholic workers cause problems for everyone.

On the other hand, insecure or unpleasant working environments often trigger depression and anxiety. Some workers might respond with just a drink or two to unwind. But the susceptible worker might develop accelerating alcohol intake and problematic behavior. Growth, mergers, and layoffs produce anxiety and depression (see Chapter 7). Overly critical, irritable supervisors or co-workers are another source of workplace tension. Hypercritical supervisors are often guilty of lambasting a worker in front of others and yet never praising work well done. Workplace change, work relationships, and individual traits can lead to a sense of futility. Workers perceive that no matter how hard they try, it will not please the boss. Many such workers become angry and depressed, will stop trying to excel, and frequently will overstay the tavern on their way home.

Unfortunately, alcohol abuse and alcohol withdrawal produce depression and anxiety states. After just one or two drinks, there is a pleasant euphoria and an easing of inhibitions. But as more and more alcohol is consumed, the central nervous system depressant effect of alcohol predominates, and feelings of pessimism and hopelessness are exacerbated. Severe depression can result, with a corresponding high risk for suicide. While alcohol initially calms the nervous system, its removal has the opposite effect. If there is physical dependence on alcohol, then even a brief abstinence can produce withdrawal anxiety, palpitations, sweating, and tremulousness. While most suicide attempts occur while intoxicated, withdrawal anxiety can also increase suicide risk. For these reasons, psychiatric management should include careful evaluation for underlying depression and anxiety symptoms when the worker is in an alcohol-free, detoxified state.

Situations that promote drinking with co-workers and clients can permit the development of alcoholism in susceptible workers. In many businesses, the worker perceives that there is an expectation of alcohol consumption at business meals. Office parties, business conventions, on-the-job alcoholic refreshment, and business air travel are other opportunities to drink and behave inappropriately on the job. The susceptible worker may overdrink at lunch, reducing afternoon performance. Afternoons are often the time that supervisory sexual harassment takes place. The intoxicated supervisor is disinhibited and is perhaps in an alcoholic blackout as well. There may be no recollection the next day. Staff will often cover for an alcoholic boss by making excuses and making sure the work gets done. This tense, demoralizing, unproductive situation is typically left unrectified until a crisis supervenes.

PSYCHIATRIC MANAGEMENT

Diagnosis

There are nine symptoms in the criteria for alcohol dependence, and an individual must suffer from at least three of them for diagnosis of alcohol dependence (DSM-III-R alcohol and drug criteria are identical). According to DSM-III-R, alcohol abuse consists of "continued use of alcohol despite knowledge of having a recurrent social, occupational, psychological, or physical problem that is caused or exacerbated by use of the psychoactive substance" (here, alcohol) or "recurrent use in situations in which use is physically hazardous" (e.g., driving while intoxicated). With both abuse and dependence the symptoms must "have persisted for at least one month or have occurred repeatedly over a longer period of time."

Corporate medical departments can sometimes identify alcoholism by the use of specific liver function tests and complete blood counts. Often chronic maladaptive use of alcohol cannot be determined by laboratory tests. Urine screens are reliable only within a day of alcohol use. They may detect no alcohol in a binge drinker who did not imbibe alcohol within the previous 12 hours. In addition to impaired work performance, alcoholism can be suggested by such characteristics of alcohol intoxication as slurred speech, unsteady gait, red face, trembling, and, of course, an odor of alcohol on the breath.

Dual Diagnosis

Polydrug Dependence
Alcoholics are often dependent on sedative hypnotics like diazepam, alprazolam, or phenobarbital, or on "uppers" like cocaine or amphetamines. Urine tests for sedatives are often equivocal. Sedative hypnotics typically remain positive in urine for 2 to 4 weeks after last use. Occasional or regular prescription use for insomnia or a diagnosed anxiety disorder can also cause a positive urine test. Heroin, which is also sedating, can be detected by urine screen for 4 days after use. Cocaine and amphetamines are used for stimulation rather than sedation. Cocaine remains positive in the urine for at least 4 days after use. Joining the cocaine abuse of the 1980s, the early 1990s have seen heroin and cannabis abuse become frequent companions of alcoholism. Employees who abuse sedative hypnotics and stimulants in alternation present a confusing clinical picture. Although a urine screen is not definitive for alcoholism, the presence of heroin or cocaine in the urine of a person suspected of alcoholism suggests dual or polysubstance use.

Comorbidity with Other Psychiatric Disorders
In addition to polydrug dependence complicating diagnosis, there are certain psychiatric disorders that occur quite commonly among alcoholics. These comorbid diagnoses can contribute to alcoholic behavior, emotional distress, and failure of alcoholism treatment. Proper psychiatric diagnosis and treatment are essential. The more common diagnoses are personality, affective (depressive), and anxiety disorders (see Chapters 12, 13, and 14). Antisocial personality (sociopathy) and other personality disorders are commonly encountered. Counterintuitively, antisocial personality is more common among alcoholics than other drug addicts. Major depression, dysthymia, and bipolar disorder are commonplace, as are panic disorder, social phobia, and eating disorders (particularly bulimia), and less frequently, obsessive-compulsive disorder. Some women binge drink in combination with premenstrual syndrome. War veterans and physical or sexual abuse victims often have posttraumatic stress disorder as a contributor to alcoholism.

Central nervous system effects of alcohol and alcohol withdrawal mimic such psychiatric disorders as depression and anxiety. As a result, accurate diagnosis of coexisting psychiatric problems is nearly impossible during active drinking or during detoxification. While taking a detailed history, a psychiatrist can make an educated guess if symptoms of other illnesses predated the onset of alcohol dependence or were clearly present during a dry period. A coexisting diagnosis should always be suspected. If there is any suggestion of comorbidity, referral should be made to a psychiatrist with expertise in evaluation and treatment of alcoholic comorbidity, or the employee should be sent to a dual diagnosis rehabilitation center. Since comorbidity often helps determine the preferred type of alcohol treatment, it is a central concern of the treatment selection cases that are presented in the case studies that follow.

Detoxification

Alcohol withdrawal symptoms start to appear anytime from 24 hours to 10 days after the last drink. Most commonly, withdrawal occurs within 72 hours. Objective signs of withdrawal include increased blood pressure, pulse, respiration rate, and temperature. Other symptoms include shaking (tremulousness), nervousness, nausea, and visual, auditory, and tactile (skin crawling) hallucinations. The hallucinations are an extreme manifestation of withdrawal, called *delirium tremens.* If not promptly treated, delirium tremens can lead to convulsions, coma, and death.

Alcoholics usually have mild withdrawal symptoms that can be controlled with two or three doses of chlordiazepoxide (Librium) over a 24-hour period. Binge drinkers, who can have intervals of days or months when they do not drink, often have no withdrawal symptoms at all. If patients have been drinking daily for months or years, have experienced nausea or shaking hours after the last drink, have a history of hypertension, or have had withdrawal seizures in the past, hospitalization is advisable. Any one of these factors is potentially significant. Both hypertension and history of a previous withdrawal seizure merit round-the-clock monitoring.

Alcohol withdrawal symptoms are the mirror image of alcohol's effect on the nervous system. Initially, alcohol has a calming effect, lowers inhibition, and in overdose, depresses heartbeat and respirations. After the body's nervous system has become accustomed to alcohol, abrupt removal leads to withdrawal symptoms. Benzodiazepines cross-react with alcohol, and thus have a similar effect on the nervous system. Some benzodiazepines, such as chlordiazepoxide and diazepam, have a long half-life. A single dose remains active for 48-72 hours before it is metabolized (broken down into components and eliminated). Since alcohol is metabolized much faster, the longer-acting benzodiazepines are used for detoxification. They prevent convulsions and lower the blood pressure and pulse. When liver function tests are abnormal, or if the liver is enlarged upon physical examination, oxazepam is often preferred for detoxification. Since oxazepam is not metabolized by the liver, it is less likely to cause additional liver damage. The following detoxification admission orders are a sample of inpatient treatment procedures:

1. Chlordiazepoxide (Librium) 25 mg every 2 hours orally prn (as needed) for signs and symptoms of alcohol withdrawal. (Chlordiazepoxide 50 mg prn if there is a history of hypertension or previous seizure. Scheduled doses of chlordiazepoxide 50 mg four times a day should be ordered in addition to prn doses.) The next morning, the total amount of chlordiazepoxide given in the preceding 24 hours is calculated and then administered in four divided doses over the next 24 hours. Chlordiazepoxide is then tapered by 25-33 percent of the total daily dose each day.
2. Tigan 250 mg orally, or 200 mg by rectal suppository, for nausea and vomiting, every 4 hours prn, not to exceed four doses in 24 hours.
3. Laboratory tests: complete blood count, chemistry panel (including alkaline phosphatase, SGOT/PT, GGTP, bilirubin, total protein, fasting blood sugar, BUN, creatinine, electrolytes), vitamin B12, folate, thyroid panel, electrocardiogram, chest x-ray.

Medical Complications

While the screening blood tests are not specific for alcoholism, certain findings suggest some common medical complications. For example, the blood count might indicate anemia. This may reflect alcohol's toxic effect on bone marrow production of red blood cells. Alternately, alcoholism can lead to anemia from dietary deficiencies of iron, vitamin B12, or folate, or from alcohol-related bleeding disorders. With anemia and depressed white cells, the alcoholic has a poor immune system for fighting infection. Unless the alcoholic is in liver failure, mildly abnormal liver function tests are best managed by total abstinence from alcohol. Advanced cirrhosis, pancreatitis, peptic ulcer, and esophageal varices (dilated veins around the esophagus that frequently bleed) are complications that should be treated in conjunction with an internist, gastroenterologist, or liver specialist. Alcoholic cardiomyopathy (flabby, damaged heart muscle) and diabetes are other frequent complications.

Common nervous system manifestations of alcoholism include memory loss and peripheral neuropathy (nerve and muscle damage causing loss of such sensations as pain and temperature sensitivity, or causing muscle weakness). Peripheral neuropathy represents local damage to muscles and nerves of the hands, feet, or eyes. While complete paralysis of an arm or leg does not occur, the neuropathy often causes a very wide-based gait. Loss of sensation limits spatial awareness, and thus walking with legs close together would cause loss of balance. Memory loss and peripheral neuropathy can be prevented with large doses of thiamine (vitamin B1). Thiamine should be added to the admission order sheet whenever the neurologic exam or mental status exam suggests cortical damage or peripheral neuropathy.

Another type of nervous system damage is cerebellar atrophy. The two cerebellar hemispheres govern eye and arm movement. Intoxication induces a temporary cerebellar malfunction and consequent inability to walk in a straight line. When chronic alcohol exposure produces cerebellar atrophy (wasting), the lack of coordination becomes permanent. Importantly, neurologic symptoms should never be automatically attributed to alcohol. Unsuspected alternate causes must also be considered. Similarly, seeming alcohol withdrawal symptoms can actually have such other causes as thyroid disease.

Inpatient Versus Outpatient Treatment

Recent years have seen controversy over the possible increased efficacy of inpatient versus outpatient treatment programs. While many patients can be readily treated as outpatients, certain circumstances do require hospitalization. As the cases in this chapter demonstrate, inpatient treatment is necessary in situations that would make treatment outside of a hospital dangerous or ineffective. It should be noted that there are many variations of both inpatient and outpatient treatment models, and wide variations in treatment quality. Outpatient treatment in particular, can range from simple brief counseling, to comprehensive medical, psychiatric, and psychotherapeutic evaluation and treatment. The criteria for inpatient and outpatient treatment are as follows:

Inpatient Treatment	*Outpatient Treatment*
Risk of withdrawal seizure	No risk of withdrawal seizure
Severe medical complications	Healthy or medically stable
Severe coexisting psychiatric problem	Not psychotic, not suicidal
Pathological environment at home or work	Supportive environment

Case Study 4: Inpatient Treatment:
Medical Management and Major Depression

Millicent Gillespie, a single woman of 42, is the adult child of two verbally and physically abusive alcoholic parents. Until she finished high school, Millicent was the designated caretaker of her younger sister. More than once, she stopped an intoxicated parent from beating her sister. Her father was fired from job after job, and the family was often on welfare. Millicent vowed that she was never going to drink.

Despite everything, Millicent excelled academically, obtained full scholarship support at an elite private college, and was then immediately hired by a large accounting firm. She earned her CPA by studying at night and advanced to a high-level position. Millicent avoided emotional commitments. She devoted herself to her work and to her now alcoholic younger sister. When many of her company's clients left the metropolitan area, the company merged with another. Millicent was kept on, but she no longer reported directly to the CEO. Her new boss was uncomfortable working with women above the level of secretary and did not agree with Millicent's approach to client relationships.

Millicent depended solely on her work for emotional stability. She had no other sources of support to offset her reduced prestige and increased interpersonal stress. Since she had learned in childhood to keep feelings inside, and her parents' behavior kept her from having friends to her home, her social life in adulthood was not much different. After the merger, walking into her empty apartment at night became a dreary experience. In former times, she brought projects home, knowing that her efforts would be recognized. Now there was nothing to do except eat heat-and-serve dinners and watch television. She dreaded each workday, barely had the energy to get through her diminishing assignments, and had little hope for the future. She developed insomnia with early-morning awakening and lost 10 pounds without dieting. Although Millicent had no specific suicidal plans, she wondered why she was alive.

One day was particularly stressful. Her boss vetoed her proposal at a breakfast meeting and clearly put her down. She decided to try some wine with dinner, just to relieve the tension. She felt a little better and decided that one or two glasses of wine with dinner would do no harm. Soon, Millicent nipped wine all day on weekends, having four glasses with dinner and a bit more in the middle of the night. Counting the hours until she could return home and start drinking, she began to drink wine at lunch. The local trattoria opened at 11:30 and Millicent was soon the first customer each day.

It was the ten A.M. shaking that frightened Millicent out of her doldrums. When the tremulousness kept her from signing documents, she remembered how her mother's hands would shake in the morning. Although she had before suppressed any concerns about alcoholism, she now made an appointment with the EAP department. Because her tremulousness and elevated blood pressure suggested that she might risk seizure without medical supervision, inpatient treatment was advised. Moreover, her insomnia, weight loss, lethargy, decreased pleasure in her work, and passive suicidal ideation suggested the probability of a coexisting depression that would need attention. The depression, her work environment, and her lack of social supports all pointed to relapse risk in outpatient treatment. Millicent was referred to the dual diagnosis unit of a psychiatric hospital that merged psychiatric expertise with a deep respect for AA.

Upon admission, Millicent had a blood pressure of 170/110 and a pulse of 120. Her last drink had worn off and she clearly needed detoxification. Upon physical examination, her liver was enlarged, so her psychiatrist chose to detoxify her with oxazepam (a benzodiazepine that is not conjugated by the liver). Blood tests confirmed moderate but reversible liver damage, as well as dietary iron and folate deficiencies. Iron and folate were added to Millicent's daily orders.

Millicent's depression was still there after detoxification. With her electrocardiogram normal, imipramine 50 mg three times a day (an antidepressant medication) was added. Medication response was not expected for at least 2½ weeks. She attended daily group therapy and educational groups that taught about AA and stress relapse prevention. Her counselor and her psychiatrist also sent her to an Adult Children of Alcoholics (ACOA) educational group. Because of her depression, it was difficult for Millicent to concentrate, and she was feeling hopeless about her ability to stay sober. Finally, as the imipramine started to work, she began to derive comfort from AA meetings, group therapy, and ACOA.

Millicent had an on-site meeting with her EAP counselor, her psychiatrist, and her hospital alcohol counselor. Together, they suggested that a lateral move to another department of her firm would take her out of the environment that had triggered her depression and alcoholism. Human resources agreed and Millicent returned to work. She began to use AA instead of her job to compensate for her lack of affectionate supports. She enjoyed the new relationships she developed with her sponsor and other women in AA, and she learned to take criticism better at work. She continued to see a psychiatrist monthly for medication monitoring, supportive psychotherapy, and to watch for reemergence of depressive symptoms. Within a few months, Millicent's job performance matched her earlier level, and she was even a bit better with clients.

The case of Millicent Gillespie illustrates the importance of combining medical, psychiatric, and AA approaches. An inpatient dual diagnosis unit is designed to combine these approaches and to allow for close cooperation with outside EAP and human resource departments. Millicent's alcoholism, depression, medical problems, alcohol withdrawal, and emotional concerns were assessed, monitored, and treated in a safe, coordinated, and effective way. The hospital psychiatrist and alcohol counselor worked together with Millicent's EAP and human resource departments to arrange a new work environment that would not readily trigger a relapse.

Case Study 5: Inpatient Treatment: Alcoholism and Pathological Environments

Pamela Martin was the director of public relations for a dress designer. Her manager sent her on two or three overnight trips a month to cultivate department store buyers. It was stipulated that she should entertain buyers by inviting them to join her for cocktails and dinner. She had developed alcoholism, and her absenteeism and lateness had jeopardized her job. Nevertheless, she convinced herself that drinking with potential buyers was mandatory. She figured that they would feel awkward if she drank mineral water while they sipped martinis. Her boyfriend used cocaine recreationally, had encouraged Pamela to partake, and supported her belief that she was not an alcoholic. When she attempted to present a progress report at a monthly staff conference with markedly slurred speech and unsteady gait, there was no question that she had been drinking. Her manager, together with the human resource department, informed Pamela that she would be fired if she did not enter a residential rehabilitation program. Because of her unsupportive home environment and her continued conviction that drinking was required at work, Pamela was a poor risk for outpatient treatment. A residential chemical dependency program was advised.

Case Study 6: Inpatient Treatment: Alcoholism and Panic Disorder

Chris Brompton was a management trainee who began having panic attacks at age 25. While riding the subway, his heart suddenly started to beat rapidly, his arms went numb, and he was afraid he was having a heart attack. He had three similar attacks that week and they continued in the following weeks. He was convinced that these attacks were a sign of weakness. He didn't want to be laughed at, and he told no one. He discovered that the only way he could contain himself during a panic attack was to belt down some alcohol. Gradually, he developed alcoholism secondary to the panic disorder. He started calling in sick to work, so that he could stay home and nurse his panic and/or his hangover.

His office manager and co-workers became fed up with his unreliability. Although he didn't understand what was causing the frequent absenteeism, the office manager told Chris to get help. Chris was referred to a rehabilitation center for evaluation. The psychiatrist in charge listened to Chris's story from the beginning. He noted the recent-onset panic disorder and the resulting early signs of alcoholic self-medication. He decided to hospitalize Chris to be certain that the panic symptoms were not compounded by alcohol withdrawal. Since Chris had anticipated his panic attacks by drinking to try and prevent the attacks, he was now drinking every day. As a precautionary measure, he was prescribed chlordiazepoxide as needed for elevated blood pressure above 140/90 and for pulse rate over 120 for the first 10 days. Chris's thyroid function tests were normal, which eliminated the possibility that his symptoms had been due to hyperthyroidism.

After the detoxification period, Chris was no longer given chlordiazepoxide because the psychiatrist did not want Chris to become dependent on benzodiazepines. He initiated a trial of imipramine (an antidepressant with antipanic effects), and used blood levels to gradually increase the dose into the therapeutic range. Six weeks after starting imipramine, Chris's attacks were just about gone. AA plus an evening aftercare program reinforced abstinence. Chris returned to work after his inpatient hospitalization. His attendance could now be relied on, his performance shot up, and he was still a bit leery of the subway.

Panic disorder is a common psychiatric problem, especially in alcoholism. Panic symptoms are frequently misdiagnosed as mitral valve prolapse, atypical chest pain, asthma, esophageal conditions, vertebral column injury, cerebral vascular disease, and previously undiagnosed epilepsy. Accurate diagnosis is crucial to recovery. If panic symptoms are misdiagnosed, ignored, or otherwise unrelieved by accurate pharmacotherapy, then abstinence from alcohol is often unattainable.

Case Study 7: Outpatient Treatment: Alcoholism and Social Phobia

Paul Fox, an advertising executive in the creative department, was having palpitations and faintness every time he had to make a presentation. The symptoms didn't come on suddenly, but there were times when his throat was so dry that he could hardly speak at all. He had always hated reciting in class, but this was worse than anything he had previously experienced. Once, when his presentation to a client was scheduled after lunch, he experimented with drinking wine before presenting his new concept. He was more relaxed at that presentation and his concept was accepted for the next advertising campaign. He tried drinking before each presentation and, each time, he was more relaxed.

Unfortunately, there was a family history of alcoholism. Paul's father had died of alcohol-related causes and Paul may have inherited a tendency toward alcoholism. In any event, his alcohol intake increased from two glasses of wine before a presentation, to four glasses at lunch and a drink or two after work, and more wine with dinner. Paul's wife complained that he was quite irritable after work and he fell asleep right after dinner. At work, Paul's improved presentations were now becoming sloppy. In addition, he was having trouble coming up with new ideas.

Paul remembered that his father's drinking had also started with after-work drinking, irritability, and then dinnertime crying and screaming. Paul's father lost one job after another. Paul could see that he had a problem, but he didn't know how to make presentations without a few drinks to steady the nerves. After talking with his wife, he explained his plight to the company medical director and was referred to a consultant psychiatrist with expertise in alcoholism and dual diagnosis. Paul's public speaking anxiety was diagnosed as social phobia, and he was not physically addicted to alcohol. Paul tried AA, but was terrified at the prospect of telling his story. Most AA meetings begin with an assigned speaker, who has been sober for several months to several years. Other members comment on the speaker's depiction of his or her drinking career and subsequent recovery. Paul's social phobia interfered not only at work but even at AA meetings!

Paul's psychiatrist was concerned about substituting an addicting drug for alcohol, and so avoided the antianxiety benzodiazepines. Since Paul's symptoms were discreetly confined to public speaking occasions, the psychiatrist chose not to use a regular daily antidepressant that was effective for social phobia. Instead, he suggested that Paul use 20 mg of propranolol (a beta-blocker) just a half hour prior to presentations. Propranolol has long been used by musicians to reduce shaking, perspiration, and palpitations during performance. Paul was relieved to find that the propranolol allowed him to speak publicly without alcohol. Two years later, Paul still attended AA, avoided alcohol, and took propranolol before presentations at work.

Merging Psychiatric Treatment with AA Philosophy

There is nothing about the philosophy of Alcoholics Anonymous that is incompatible with good psychiatric treatment. AA is an organization of recovering alcoholics that originated in the 1930s. Bill W., a stockbroker suffering from multiple alcohol relapses and business failures, discovered that he could maintain sobriety by helping others become sober. Along with Dr. Bob, an alcoholic physician, he held group meetings of alcoholics, with the desire to give up alcohol being the sole membership requirement. Although AA has many references to spirituality and God, it has no specific religious affiliation. Agnostics and atheists can and do become sober through AA.

Relapse prevention comes about through recognition of alcohol craving triggered by three external circumstantial cues—people, places, and things— and by four internal psychological cues—hungry, angry, lonely, and tired (HALT). Discussion of these cues as they occur takes place in psychotherapy and in discussions with a sponsor. AA advises that all members should work with a supporting AA sponsor who has at least one year of sobriety. The sponsor is an experienced buddy who has learned how to manage craving successfully, and who can spot the hallmarks of impending relapse, rationalization, and denial in the more newly sober "sponsee." AA meetings and sponsors are available 24 hours a day. Psychotherapists should encourage reliance on sponsor support for relapse prevention.

Historically, AA members have been suspicious of all psychoactive medications. That problem was not helped by psychiatrists who dismissed AA as a cult, and who overprescribed cross-addicting medications for insomnia and anxiety. Fortunately, most psychiatrists now recognize the value of AA for maintaining sobriety, and they are far more careful in prescribing addicting medication to alcoholics. Correspondingly, most AA members have come to recognize the value of appropriately prescribed psychiatric medication. Should a sponsor advise a patient to avoid necessary antidepressants, antianxiety, or other medication, the psychiatrist can educate both sponsor and patient about the medication's actions and properties.

AA accepts no donations from benefactors. Financial support comes from voluntary member contributions. To emphasize member anonymity, no last names are given at meetings, and publicity focused on celebrity members is discouraged. To avoid factional rivalry and splintering, AA is completely apolitical.

No diagnosis coexisting with alcoholism can be treated successfully unless the patient is abstinent. Before AA existed, psychoanalytic attempts to treat the underlying emotional conflicts were most often defeated by continued drinking. Even today, the benefits of psychiatric medication and psychotherapy can be blocked or hidden by the effects of alcohol. Psychiatric assessment always includes specific screening for alcoholism and drug addiction, and treatment plans give careful consideration to AA referral.

RETURN TO WORK

Organizations are always worried about the back-at-work alcoholic. Although most recovering alcoholics are productive contributors to their companies, the early stages of returning to work often need enlightened supervision. If the right attention is given to continuing treatment, sobriety, and workplace factors, the odds of relapse are greatly reduced.

Case Study 8: Alcohol Relapse: Premature Resumption of Business Travel

Jim Parker stayed at work while he attended an evening chemical dependency recovery program. After only 4 weeks of sobriety, Jim blandly announced that he would take a 6-day business trip. This met with more than a little surprise from his group therapy peers, his counselor, and the group facilitator. Jim misinterpreted everyone's warnings. He heard a mistrust of his conscious intentions, rather than the wisdom of past experience. Jim was sure that he could maintain sobriety on his own, and out of state. The counselor spoke regularly with the program psychiatrist, but there was no communication with the human resource department at Jim's company.

Jim didn't want anyone at work to think that he couldn't travel, and he insisted on making the trip. Although his panic attacks had just recently stopped (the psychiatrist had prescribed desipramine), Jim still retained a fear of flying. He had always "treated" the fear with a few in-flight martinis, but he managed to avoid alcohol on the bumpy outgoing flight. He arrived at the hotel in time to meet some work buddies from other company branches, who invited him to the bar. Jim was angry with his treatment group for advising him not to travel, and he wasn't completely convinced of the need for total abstinence. He figured he was "stronger" than other alcoholics, and he decided to test his strength with a few drinks at the bar. Unconsciously, Jim also sought a reward for not drinking during the bumpy flight. He had three martinis. Since nothing terrible happened, he had a half liter of wine with dinner, and then retired to the bar until closing time. He slept through his alarm clock and arrived at an important breakfast meeting just as it was ending.

Rehabilitation centers usually advise keeping out-of-town assignments to a minimum for at least 6 months. There are several good reasons for this. For one, establishing a new habit of AA meeting attendance provides a foundation for a solid support network. This habit is easily broken when a newly recovering alcoholic travels. Even if the employee is diligent in finding and attending meetings out of town, local group members know the employee best, and they are more likely to notice the subtle changes in attitude that lead to relapse. The histories of relapsed patients show a pattern of complacency about meetings that precedes a return to drinking. When employees return from a business trip, they may be less attentive to recovery and may rationalize that AA attendance is not really essential for sobriety. Also, alcohol is all but poured down airplane passengers' throats, and first-class seats are almost like a flying bar. The temptation worsens when flights are lengthy or delayed. Finally, it is not easy for the newly sober alcoholic to be alone in a strange city. No matter how motivated, the craving for alcohol becomes intense. And with craving comes the unconscious rationalization that, "I'm out of town, so no one will know."

It is also important to address workplace factors that can trigger alcohol craving. The most significant stressors are often problematic interpersonal tensions. These tensions can be heightened by employee, peer, superior, and subordinate personality traits, by organizational change and stress, and by the lingering relationship effects of alcohol abuse. Sometimes, a lateral job transfer can remove the employee from a difficult set of relationships. Human resource departments play a pivotal role here and should always keep in mind the employee's highest level of past performance. It is counterproductive and far too simplistic to overlook true career potential, or to fire the sober alcoholic outright. On the other hand, offering promotions too early in recovery can trigger relapse. Inadvertently, it sends the message that the employee has somehow gotten away with drinking.

Returning employees are apprehensive about co-workers' knowledge of their problem. It is of vital importance that management, human resources, and mental health professionals respect employee confidentiality. Treatment centers typically advise patients to offer very little information about their absence to nonintimate acquaintances and co-workers. Excuses and lies compound themselves into ever more elaborate and unconvincing stories. The resulting atmosphere of deception not only creates mistrust but also encourages rationalization, denial, and thus relapse. Recovery should be accompanied by complete honesty. This does not mean that returning employees should say they have been in a rehabilitation center. "I'm fine. Thanks for asking," is more than enough. More open discussion is reserved for family, therapy, AA, and supportive intimates at work.

Patients with psychiatric comorbidity should be followed by a psychiatrist, with continuation of appropriate medication for at least several months. Many depressive and anxiety disorders have long-term intermittent courses and will often eventually recur. If an employee has a history of recurrent symptoms prior to alcohol treatment, or if symptoms recur when the medication dosage is reduced, follow-up should continue for an extended period of time. Periodic psychiatric assessment helps to prevent relapse and to preserve high-level job performance. It is likely to save far more money than it costs. For a small number of employees, treatment refractory alcohol abuse may make return to work impossible.

Case Study 9: Treatment Resistance: Alcoholism and Antisocial Personality

Mark Roberts had been sent to alcohol rehabilitation centers three times. In spite of his employer's repeated willingness to take him back, he had no loyalty to the company. He did not see alcohol as a problem, and he said that the company picked on him by sending him for treatment. Although he said he no longer drank, he was spotted a few times in a bar on the far side of town, and he called in sick at least once a week. Mark was also chronically low on cash. He would borrow money from co-workers but never offer to repay them. They were furious about this exploitation. When reminded of a debt, Mark exploded with rage, or he made an insultingly lame excuse. The company bookkeeper also began noticing that the cash at the end of the day was less than expected. One time, she noticed Mark lingering near her desk while she was in another room, and she later found that her ledgers had been altered. She reported this to her boss. In a slow market, they had both noticed profits that were even lower than expected. The drop in profits coupled with evidence of Mark's embezzlement led to his dismissal. Even so, there was no specific proof that he was drinking again.

SUMMARY

In this chapter, diagnosis, workplace detection, and management of alcohol dependence are discussed. Case examples are presented to illustrate how and when to refer patients and how to select the correct treatment. Return-to-work strategies for preventing relapse are outlined and are illustrated with case examples.

Although most of the coexisting psychiatric diagnoses commonly found among alcoholics are discussed, some diagnoses are not included, particularly bipolar disorder, atypical depression, generalized anxiety, psychosis, and personality disorders other than antisocial personality (see other chapters for details).

Bibliography

Blum, K., E. P. Noble, P. J. Sheridan, et al. 1990. Allelic association of human dopamine D2 receptor gene in alcoholism. *Journal of the American Medical Association* **264:**3156–3160.

Cloninger, C. R. 1987. Adaptive mechanisms in alcoholism. *Science* **236:**410–416.

Cloninger, C. L. 1991. D2 dopamine receptor gene is associated but not linked with alcoholism. *Journal of the American Medical Association* **266:**1833–1834.

Comings, D. E., B. G. Comings, D. Muhleman, et al. 1991. The dopamine D2 receptor locus as a modifying gene in neuropsychiatric disorders. *Journal of the American Medical Association* **266:**1793–1800.

Frances, R. J., and S. I. Miller (eds.). 1991. *Clinical Textbook of Addictive Disorders.* New York: Guilford Press.

Gallant, D. M. 1988. *Alcoholism, A Guide to Diagnosis, Intervention, and Treatment.* New York and London: W. W. Norton.

Gerlenter, J., S. O'Malley, N. Risch, et al. 1991. No association between an allele at the D2 dopamine receptor gene and alcoholism. *Journal of the American Medical Association* **266:**1801–1807.

Miller, N. S. (ed.). 1991. *Comprehensive Handbook of Drug and Alcohol Addiction.* Marcel Dekker, Inc.

Nace, E. 1987. *The Treatment of Alcoholism.* New York: Brunner/Mazel.

National Institute on Alcohol Abuse and Alcoholism. 1990. *Alcohol and Health,* seventh special report. Rockville, Md.

Schuster, C. L. 1988. *Alcohol and Sexuality.* Part VII in Monograph Series, H. I. Lief (ed.), Sexual Medicine. New York, Westport, London: Praeger Press.

Zimberg, W. J., and S. B. Blume. 1982. *Practical Approaches to the Psychotherapy of Alcoholism,* 2d ed. New York: Plenum Press.

17

Psychosis: Peculiar Behaviors and Inflexible Bizarre Beliefs

Richard H. Gabel, M.D., F.A.P.A.

ABSTRACT

Psychotic disorders comprise an important subgroup of psychiatric entities with far-reaching impact on workers and the workplace. The need for those involved with work settings to understand the causes and treatments available for these conditions cannot be overstated. It is important to recognize that although these disorders can have dramatic presentations, there are effective treatments available. This chapter provides professionals who encounter employees with psychotic disorders with a guide to understanding the implications of those illnesses for the worker and the workplace. Schizophrenia, delusional disorder, psychotic mood disorders, drug-induced psychosis, and psychosis caused by medical conditions are presented. Each diagnostic entity is discussed in the context of an illustrative case vignette with a description of epidemiology, phenomenology, treatment options, and expected outcomes. A description of workplace precipitants and possible interventions is provided.

INTRODUCTION

An essential goal of modern psychiatric practice is to help patients maximize their ability to reach the highest level of performance in all areas of living. The ability to work successfully carries benefits that extend far beyond the paycheck, into areas of family life and self-esteem. The worker who carries the burden of a psychotic disorder has the same aspirations as anyone else. Knowing the causes, manifestations, treatments, and expected long-term outcomes of psychotic conditions allows better management of potential impact on worker and workplace. This can be a struggle and is more difficult in adverse employment environments. Medical care and supervisory input sensitive to the specific needs of the worker and workplace are likely to yield benefits for employee and employer alike.

Psychosis has many general characteristics: a tendency to misinterpret environmental cues in a notably unrealistic, idiosyncratic or peculiar way; personality changes that can make relationships difficult; auditory or visual hallucinations. These symptoms are seen during active illness, but are not generally present during remission.

While there are many general symptoms of psychosis, it is important to remember that the symptoms are not specific. Just as fever can accompany many physical illnesses, psychosis can accompany many psychiatric disorders. The scope of this discussion includes schizophrenia, paranoid disorders, mood-related psychoses (bipolar disorder and depression), drug-induced psychosis, and psychoses caused by covert medical illness. Historically, schizophrenia has been commonly confused with these other psychotic illnesses. This confusion persists even today. Special attention must be paid lest schizophrenia be misdiagnosed when the actual cause lies elsewhere. Optimal treatment requires careful and specific diagnosis.

SCHIZOPHRENIA

Diagnostic Overview

Schizophrenia, or schizophrenic spectrum disorder, is a grouping of chronic, often relapsing illnesses that influence perceptions, thinking, social relationships, and judgment. Schizophrenics, in the acute phase of illness, may have the feeling that their thoughts are being monitored, that people around them can either read their mind or manipulate the thoughts they are having. They may hear voices that can seem to emanate from either inside their head or from the environment. These voices are often in the form of harsh commentary on every action of the schizophrenic, but on occasion they can be experienced as friendly or soothing in times of stress. At times, schizophrenics may become preoccupied with clearly irrational beliefs about their abilities, their bodies, or about religion. Schizophrenics may develop idiosyncratic mannerisms or rituals. They generally experience massive anxiety or fear when symptoms are very active and can become quite withdrawn as a result. Age of illness onset is variable, but it is most often in early adulthood.

DSM-III-R DIAGNOSTIC CRITERIA

295. Schizophrenia

A. Presence of characteristic psychotic symptoms in the active phase: either (1), (2), or (3) for at least one week (unless the symptoms are successfully treated):

    (1) two of the following:

        (a) delusions
        (b) prominent hallucinations (throughout the day for several days or several times a week for several weeks, each hallucinatory experience not being limited to a few brief moments)
        (c) incoherence or marked loosening of associations
        (d) catatonic behavior
        (e) flat or grossly inappropriate affect

    (2) bizarre delusions (i.e., involving a phenomenon that the person's culture would regard as totally implausible, e.g., thought broadcasting, being controlled by a dead person)
    (3) prominent hallucinations (as defined in [1b] above) of a voice with content having no apparent relation to depression or elation, or a voice keeping up a running commentary on the person's behavior or thoughts, or two or more voices conversing with each other

B. During the course of the disturbance, functioning in such areas as work, social relations, and self-care is markedly below the highest level achieved before onset of the disturbance (or, when the onset is in childhood or adolescence, failure to achieve expected level of social development).

C. Schizoaffective Disorder and Mood Disorder with Psychotic Features have been ruled out, i.e., if a

Major Depressive or Manic Syndrome has ever been present during an active phase of the disturbance, the total duration of all episodes of a mood syndrome has been brief relative to the total duration of the active and residual phases of the disturbance.

D. Continuous signs of the disturbance for at least six months. The six-month period must include an active phase (of at least one week, or less if symptoms have been successfully treated) during which there were psychotic symptoms characteristic of Schizophrenia (symptoms in A), with or without a prodromal or residual phase, as defined below.

Prodromal phase: A clear deterioration in functioning before the active phase of the disturbance that is not due to a disturbance in mood or to a Psychoactive Substance Use Disorder and that involves at least two of the symptoms listed below.

Residual phase: Following the active phase of the disturbance, persistence of at least two of the symptoms noted below, these not being due to a disturbance in mood or to a Psychoactive Substance Use Disorder.

Prodromal or Residual Symptoms:

(1) marked social isolation or withdrawal
(2) marked impairment in role functioning as wage-earner, student, or homemaker
(3) markedly peculiar behavior (e.g., collecting garbage, talking to self in public, hoarding food)
(4) marked impairment in personal hygiene and grooming
(5) blunted or inappropriate affect
(6) digressive, vague, overelaborate, or circumstantial speech, or poverty of speech, or poverty of content of speech
(7) odd beliefs or magical thinking, influencing behavior and inconsistent with cultural norms, e.g., superstitiousness, belief in clairvoyance, telepathy, "sixth sense," "others can feel my feelings," overvalued ideas, ideas of reference
(8) unusual perceptual experiences, e.g., recurrent illusions, sensing the presence of a force or person not actually present
(9) marked lack of initiative, interests, or energy

Examples: Six months of prodromal symptoms with one week of symptoms from A; no prodromal symptoms with six months of symptoms from A; no prodromal symptoms with one week of symptoms from A and six months of residual symptoms.

E. It cannot be established that an organic factor initiated and maintained the disturbance.

F. If there is a history of Autistic Disorder, the additional diagnosis of Schizophrenia is made only if prominent delusions or hallucinations are also present.

Reprinted with permission from the *Diagnostic and Statistical Manual of Mental Disorders,* 3d ed. rev.; copyright 1987 by the American Psychiatric Association.

The risk of both suicidal and homicidal behavior among schizophrenics is real, but it is difficult to quantify. Among those who are well enough to reliably hold jobs and do well, the risk is small. For the employer it is important to note that one of the best predictors of future behavior is past behavior. An awareness of the employee's history and the knowledge that outpatient treatment is continuing should be ample reassurance in these obviously important areas.

Case Study 1

Linda Mason, a 26-year-old female clerical worker with no history of psychiatric illness, came to the hospital emergency room with her parents. They had previously brought her home from a psychiatric hospital in another city. Three weeks before her initial hospitalization, she moved to the other city to meet new people and get a job. She made an abrupt decision to move because, after holding many office jobs in her hometown, she began to believe that prior bosses were in love with her. When the list of secret lovers started to include sports and movie stars, she became afraid that other women were so jealous that she was in danger. In her first attempt to live away from home, she became preoccupied with the thought that a man from a restaurant was secretly in love with her. Although she had never spoken with him, she became convinced that newspaper articles and television broadcasts were messages of love and devotion from him.

Linda began to spend free time alone in her room. She became frightened of the man's increasing ardor. She thought her food was poisoned and she became afraid to eat. Finally, she began to hear threatening voices and was convinced that her apartment was no longer safe. On the night before her hospitalization, she stayed wide awake in the lobby of a downtown hotel. The next morning, she found herself running through rush-hour traffic to escape her imagined pursuer. The police took her to an emergency room for hospitalization, and Linda's parents then brought her to a hometown hospital.

During hospitalization, psychotherapy started to help her make more sensible moves toward independence and to improve her relationships with men. Haloperidol (an antipsychotic, or neuroleptic, medication), 5 mg three times a day, was used to control her paranoia and hallucinations. She was discharged to a psychiatric rehabilitation program designed to help her reenter the work force. There she had job skill training and a volunteer job. Linda lived in a halfway house where peer interactions occurred in a therapeutic environment, and she saw her psychiatrist regularly for supportive psychotherapy and continued antipsychotic medication. After successful completion of the rehabilitation program, Linda found part-time clerical work in a small manufacturing company, and was soon offered a full-time position.

Six weeks later, an unexpected change in work duties required new interactions with many co-workers from another department. While Linda was able to complete her new assignments, she began to think that her co-workers "knew" about the man who had been her imaginary pursuer. She withdrew socially, stopped having lunch with co-workers, and left work silently at the end of the day. Linda's supervisor was aware of the psychiatric history and spoke to her promptly when her behavior changed. At the supervisor's suggestion, Linda reported the problem to her psychiatrist. During the psychotherapy session, she explored and clarified feelings about the new job situation, and her haloperidol dose was slightly increased. Her difficulties abated over the next 6 weeks.

Diagnosis

The classification of schizophrenia includes hebephrenic, catatonic, paranoid, latent, acute, residual, chronic undifferentiated, and schizoaffective subtypes. A detailed description of the differential symptomatology for each subtype can be found in DSM-III-R and is beyond the scope of this chapter. It is always essential to differentiate schizophrenia from the other causes of psychosis detailed in this chapter.

Workplace Recognition, Management, and Referral

The case of Linda Mason has several implications for understanding the employee with schizophrenia. In reaction to a subtle interpersonal change in the workplace, she suffered a mild increase in symptoms. There are many potential signs that can predict an acute worsening of illness. There can be subtle changes in self-care, such as not changing clothes or not washing as often as appropriate. There may be slight changes in relationships at work, often with early signs of social withdrawal. Work productivity, quality, or punctuality may deteriorate, sometimes with a new defensiveness or inappropriate reaction when confronted. There may be a worried call from family members. These changes and others can signal a need for intervention. When there is a good preexisting relationship with the employee, a supervisor can give feedback about the observed changes and can suggest psychiatric consultation or follow-up to review the situation. Additionally, the supervisor can refer the employee to the medical department for independent psychiatric opinion. In some instances, the human resources department or employee assistance program can help through its consulting psychiatrist.

Causes

The etiology of schizophrenia is not fully understood, but appears to include alterations in brain chemistry. Recent advances in clinical research have cast doubt on earlier theories that schizophrenia was caused by maternal child-rearing practices. For instance, if identical twins are raised separately from infancy and one develops schizophrenia, there is a likelihood that the second twin will also develop it. There is a general consensus for biological and genetic causes rather than errors in child rearing. Once the biological predisposition for schizophrenia exists, the disease may be triggered by stressful life events. These trigger events would not evoke a schizophrenic syndrome without the predisposition.

The biochemical problem in schizophrenia lies in dopamine transmission within the brain. Dopamine is one of the chemicals found in brain tissue that is responsible for sending signals from one nerve cell to another. Excess dopamine is thought to cause alterations in the perceptual process and consequent thinking problems in the schizophrenic patient. Antipsychotic (neuroleptic) medications reduce the dopamine detection ability on the surface of the receiving nerve cell, and are the fundamental pharmacologic tools against this illness.

Linda's supervisor did very well by noting signs of a problem. Future episodes might also be forestalled by handling changes differently. For instance, the supervisor could give the employee a longer lead time for workplace changes and could provide clear explanations to avoid misunderstanding. It is equally possible that unknown personal changes outside the workplace could trigger a worsening of the illness. A family member moving away, marriage, the birth of a baby, or a death in the family can have substantial clinical effects. It is a widely accepted clinical paradox that both positive and negative life events create stress. Even a long-sought job promotion can be stressful enough to precipitate an emotional illness.

Effects

Schizophrenia can often mean a reduction in social and occupational abilities, but not usually as much as people think. Function can be impaired by interpersonal difficulties, delusional preoccupation, and mental confusion.

Compliance with appropriate treatment will greatly reduce impairment. Inadequate treatment can lead to crisis (see Chapter 10).

Schizophrenic patients are especially susceptible to stigmatization in the workplace, further reducing their functional abilities. Though American society prides itself on the principle of equality for all, the emotionally ill are sometimes regarded as less equal than others. Stigma can come in many forms: a subtle decision to withhold a challenging assignment, a well-meaning decision not to prematurely stress the worker with news of impending cutbacks or changes, or a genuinely unconscious decision by co-workers to exclude the employee from unofficial after-work activities.

Allowed to go unchecked, stigma also affects co-workers through their fears, anger, guilt, and avoidance of maximal teamwork. The process of stigmatization requires that someone be seen as obviously different, and fear of the perceived difference makes the process all the more powerful. Familiarity with the meaning of emotional illness is a key neutralizing factor, with benefits for employee, co-workers, and employer. Line supervisors and human resource officers can track endemic elements of stigma and provide reassuring education to other employees.

Treatment

The treatment of schizophrenia has changed dramatically over the past 30 years. In what psychiatrists call "the premedication era," treatments for schizophrenia were few. Verbal psychotherapies sometimes offered certain limited results. Now, however, they are considered appropriate only for the least severely affected patients. Earlier enthusiasm for the use of verbal psychotherapy in the treatment of schizophrenia has been replaced by skepticism for its value without appropriate medication.

Early medication treatment relied on nonspecific sedatives. Although they had a calming effect, they did not have much real impact on such active symptoms as hallucinations and paranoid thinking. Many patients were too ill to function in the community and were forced to spend months to years in chronic psychiatric hospitals.

With the advent of specific antipsychotic (neuroleptic) medications, psychiatrists can more specifically and effectively target the symptoms of schizophrenia. Initially, the major benefit of antipsychotic medication is a reduction in "positive" symptoms such as paranoid delusions and hallucinations. There can be a long time lag between initiation of pharmacotherapy and the beginning of a good clinical response. Once the right medication is found, it can take anywhere from several days to weeks for a meaningful abatement of symptoms. Optimal return to work can sometimes mean an extended medical leave for treatment. More recent advances in psychopharmacologic research have offered new medications that can also make inroads against "negative" symptoms such as social withdrawal, "flattened" emotional response, abnormal inward preoccupation, and a tendency toward apathy.

Unfortunately, as with most medications, adverse side effects can occur from antipsychotics, even while correcting the excess dopamine transmission that underlies schizophrenia. Parkinson's disease is a common illness that is known to result from decreased dopamine transmission in a particular area of the brain. Antipsychotic drugs typically cause Parkinson-like symptoms because they decrease overall dopamine transmission. If simple precautionary measures are not taken by the prescribing physician, these side effects usually begin within the first week of therapy. The more sedating antipsychotics have self-correcting anticholinergic effects that reduce Parkinsonian symptoms. However, they are more likely to cause such anticholinergic side effects as sedation, slowed urination, and constipation.

Antipsychotic medications (Table 17-1) carry the long-term risk of a disorder known as tardive dyskinesia. Characterized by involuntary repetitive movements of the face, tongue, and large muscle groups of the body, tardive dyskinesia can itself be a socially disabling disease. It results from a nearly permanent change in the pattern of nerve conduction caused by longstanding dopamine blockade. Since there are limited treatments for tardive dyskinesia, careful use of antipsychotic medication is crucial. Clozapine, a new antipsychotic, may have less risk for tardive dyskinesia.

Treatment of schizophrenia is heavily reliant on medications, but should always include some form of psychotherapy. Insight-oriented psychoanalytic

TABLE 17-1   Common Antipsychotic Medications and Side Effects

	Potency	Sedation	Anticholinergic	Parkinsonism
Haloperidol (Haldol)	++++	+	+/−	+++
Trifluroperizine (Trilafon)	++++	+	+	+++
Fluphenazine (Prolixin)	++++	+	++	+++
Thiothixene (Navane)	+++	++	++	++
Perphenazine (Etrafon)	+++	++	+++	++
Thioridazine (Stelazine)	+	+++	++++	+
Chlorpromazine (Thorazine)	+	+++	++++	+

Note: The number of symbols indicates the level or intensity of side effects in the area noted.
Key: +/−, negligible; +, low; ++, mild; +++, moderate; ++++, major.

psychotherapy is too stressful or anxiety-producing for schizophrenic patients. Exceptions to this rule must be carefully selected. More typically, a supportive, interpersonal therapy is used. Group psychotherapy is often a treatment of choice for schizophrenia. It offers a nonthreatening atmosphere for sharing feelings and providing feedback from both therapist and other patients. In particular, it is helpful to discuss the often alien feelings and experiences schizophrenics have with others.

Psychoeducation is a common thread running through all forms of verbal psychotherapy for schizophrenia. Patients and families become familiar with the concept of stressful life events, their impact on illness, the importance of compliance with treatment regimens, and the warning signs of relapse. These are vitally important in the outcome for any given patient.

Return to Work

While the workplace hopes for an unimpaired return to work after treatment, the hope must be tempered with a sense of reality. Since the return to work can be stressful, consideration must be given to an adjustment period. Given this opportunity for renewed self-confidence, and appropriate continuing treatment, employees with schizophrenia should again be able to perform job responsibilities at the level of their peers.

DELUSIONAL DISORDER

Diagnostic Overview

Delusional disorder, sometimes called paranoid disorder, is a condition characterized by delusions with a content that makes them seem partially reasonable or believable. People with this condition do not generally behave in a bizarre or strange manner. They may not give any outward evidence that their thinking is influenced by delusional themes. It may come as a surprise to friends or co-workers to learn that they have delusional beliefs.

DSM-III-R DIAGNOSTIC CRITERIA

297.10 Delusional (Paranoid) Disorder

A. Nonbizarre delusion(s) (i.e., involving situations that occur in real life, such as being followed, poisoned, infected, loved at a distance, having a disease, being deceived by one's spouse or lover) of at least one month's duration.

B. Auditory or visual hallucinations, if present, are not prominent (as defined in Schizophrenia, A[1b]).

C. Apart from the delusion(s) or its ramifications, behavior is not obviously odd or bizarre.

D. If a Major Depressive or Manic Syndrome has been present during the delusional disturbance, the total duration of all episodes of the mood syndrome has been brief relative to the total duration of the delusional disturbance.

E. Has never met criterion A for Schizophrenia, and it cannot be established that an organic factor initiated and maintained the disturbance.

Specify type: The following types are based on the predominant delusional theme. If no single delusional theme predominates, specify as **Unspecified Type.**

Reprinted with permission from the *Diagnostic and Statistical Manual of Mental Disorders,* 3d ed. rev.; copyright 1987 by the American Psychiatric Association.

Case Study 2

Joan Green is a 46-year-old female laboratory technician who was referred to the psychiatric clinic of the hospital where she worked. One hour before, she had complained to her supervisor that a co-worker was diluting her chemical control solutions. Joan offered no evidence, but told her supervisor that the problem had started some weeks earlier when the co-worker was selected over her for a promotion. Joan felt certain that her co-worker, supervisor, and husband were conspiring to limit her career success, in order to keep her under their control.

Leaving her family halfway across the country, Joan had married a local man and moved to the area 18 months earlier when her husband lost his job. She told the psychiatrist she was also having difficulty adjusting to her new neighborhood, and that she severely missed her friends and relatives. Historically, Joan had been dependent on family members for guidance and support and had never before ventured away from home for more than 2 weeks. She had no prior psychiatric history, no symptoms suggesting either depression or schizophrenia, no history of drug or alcohol use, and no other unusual thoughts.

In discussing the situation with Joan's supervisor, the psychiatrist learned that there had been no deviation from her usual high quality of work, nor had longstanding tensions with the co-worker ever needed intervention. The psychiatrist advised

Joan to accept a psychotherapeutic treatment intended to help her to successfully adjust to her new surroundings. A mild antianxiety medication was suggested for the interim to reduce delusional preoccupation.

Joan felt insulted by the referral to a psychiatrist. Since she believed that the workplace problem was real, any attempt to link the treatment recommendation with the job problem evoked anger. And since she had incorporated the psychiatrist into her delusional belief, she was unable to accept suggestions for treatment. She asked to be excused from the interview because she felt that time away from her work would only worsen her difficulties and give her co-worker more of a chance to undermine her performance. There was no follow-up between the employee and the clinic after the initial contact. Some weeks later, the supervisor reported that Joan was fully functional. She no longer complained, but she had moved her workstation across the room and often looked angry or withdrawn.

Diagnosis

There are important differences between schizophrenia and delusional disorder. In contrast to schizophrenia, delusional disorder is less likely to include significant hallucinations, reductions in interpersonal skills, global expansions of delusional beliefs, or gradually increasing impairment over time. Most often the delusions remain encapsulated. Delusional disorder is a relatively uncommon condition, affecting less than one percent of the population. There is a roughly equal male-to-female distribution, with onset usually in middle life.

There are erotomanic, grandiose, jealous, persecutory, and somatic subtypes. Each is characterized by fixed beliefs that have no foundation in reality. For example, the jealous subtype might manifest itself as an unshakable belief that a spouse is unfaithful. The delusional conviction remains in place even in the face of ample disproof. The persecutory subtype is characterized by the delusion that the sufferer is the subject of the misdeeds of others. The persecution can come in the form of the belief that one is being cheated, followed, undermined, or maligned. These individuals sometimes think that the remedy lies in the legal justice system, and delusionally motivated lawsuits may follow. Because of their beliefs, they can be hostile and driven to retaliation within their delusional context. The erotomanic subtype is characterized by a delusion of a romantic relationship when none exists. This condition occurs more often in women than in men. The grandiose subtype involves a conviction of secret powers, talents, or attributes. The abilities may include a divine mission, or secret relationships with famous people. Individuals with delusional disorder are generally unshakable in their beliefs and can become demonstrably upset when confronted with the reality of the situation.

Workplace Recognition, Management, and Referral

The very nature of delusional disorder mitigates against early detection. Individuals tend to mask their closely held beliefs until the complete syndrome suddenly blossoms. In Joan's case, her supervisor became alarmed by what was revealed. The referral for evaluation occurred almost immediately, and Joan did not participate in the decision.

Another approach might have included more exploration of the problem, to establish the foundation for Joan's belief, and might have offered some basic reality testing to determine whether her work quality was impaired. A psychiatric evaluation might then be suggested or, in some cases, required as a condition of further employment. These cases require tactful management, as there is always a risk of incorporation into the delusional belief system.

Causes

Although the exact cause of delusional disorder is not known, there are some general predisposing factors. These can include preexisting personality disorders, social isolation, relocation to an unfamiliar environment, and sensory deprivation (caused by deafness or blindness). These factors can impede flexible responses to severe emotional stress, and thus predispose to delusional thinking. In any of the subcategories, the specific delusional type is the result of interaction between preexisting personality style, delusional vulnerability, and acute stresses.

Effects

The effect of delusional disorder on worker and workplace can be as varied as the myriad manifestations of the disorder. Once the delusion is revealed, the employee will have the impulse to conceal it again. Treatment will often encourage just this result. In the more florid cases of jealous or persecutory delusions, it may not be possible to cover over the false belief. In these cases, there can be serious disruption of the work environment for worker and co-worker alike.

Employees with relatively isolated or encapsulated delusions can carry them secretly inside for years without any outward signs. It is also possible for someone with a predisposition toward delusional thinking to remain symptom-free for a lifetime, in the absence of the right combination of sufficiently stressful precipitating events. In addition to the stigmatization that accompanies major psychiatric disorders, a delusional employee can become disruptive, litigious, accusatory, or infrequently even aggressive.

Treatment

The key to successful treatment of delusional disorder lies in the early formation of a solid therapeutic alliance. In other words, the treating psychiatrist must quickly become the ally of the aggrieved employee and must form a trusting relationship in which the beliefs are acknowledged but neither challenged nor confirmed.

Through careful questioning and reality testing, the psychiatrist may be able to gain a toehold from which to begin an in-depth exploration of the delusion's psychological causes. Antipsychotic, antidepressant, or antianxiety medications are sometimes used. They will soften the firmly held belief and allow further objective investigation. Through this process the employee will be able to gain enough emotional distance from the delusions to refrain from acting on his or her beliefs.

Return to Work

The timing of the return to work of the employee with delusional disorder should be guided by a consulting psychiatrist. This method helps to avoid inclusion of the treating psychiatrist into the delusional beliefs. If the delusion is not connected to the work environment, there is little intrinsic to the condition to prevent prompt and full return to work. However, if the employee has a fixed delusion about a co-worker or the work environment, he or she should not return until the delusion can be kept under adequate control.

As with other conditions, the workplace hopes that returning workers will be able to function without impairment. Again, this hope must be tempered with reality. Delusional disorders can be chronic, relapsing conditions. Employees with delusional disorder should reasonably be expected to remain compliant with prescribed treatment. Therefore, return to work is sometimes conditioned on periodic confirmation of continuing treatment.

PSYCHOTIC MANIA (BIPOLAR DISORDER WITH PSYCHOSIS)

Diagnostic Overview

Bipolar disorder is a disease characterized by cyclical changes in mood that may or may not be related to the circumstances of the patient's life. One key feature of bipolar disorder is the occurrence of both manic and depressive episodes. Unipolar major depression does not include manic episodes (see Chapter 13).

While cyclical changes in mood can be seen in the general population, as well as in other psychiatric conditions, a distinguishing feature of bipolar disorder is the presence of extreme elevations of mood during the manic phase. Psychotic mania can frequently have symptoms that closely resemble schizophrenia. Following the onset of a manic episode, a psychotic picture may begin to emerge. What had been an overestimation of ability can become the delusional belief of divinely engendered special powers. Questioning glances from observers can become woven into a paranoid delusional system that people are trying to undermine a project developed in the midst of a delusional scheme. As the manic employee becomes absorbed in the elaborate imaginings of the mind, auditory hallucinations can develop. The risk of assaultive behavior by a hostile, psychotic manic patient should not be underestimated. Equally so, there is a high risk of suicide or self-injury if a manic employee becomes convinced that he or she has been endowed with the power of invulnerability.

Case Study 3

David Somers is a highly successful 35-year-old married insurance salesperson, who was referred to his psychiatrist after he had not slept for five nights. Further history revealed that David had spent his nights secretly writing a novel sure to win the Nobel prize. The psychiatrist learned that David was "too busy" with his many new business ventures to keep up his regular job performance. David refused to accept any medication, because he did not think anything was wrong. To the contrary, he insisted things were far better than ever before.

He did continue twice weekly psychotherapy sessions. It soon became clear that David was planning his business ventures with the help of divinely inspired voices. David soon believed that his employer did not approve of his new endeavors, that obstacles were being placed in his path, and that his boss had hired men to follow him. He stopped going to the office, began to spend most of his time at home, and began to drink vodka to reduce his anxiety about the growing conspiracy. With his consent, his wife and psychiatrist talked in general terms with his human resources officer, and he was placed on disability leave.

David's condition worsened as he paid less and less attention to the details of daily living. He stopped bathing, skipped meals, and withdrew further into his web of delusionally motivated projects. Finally, when it was clear that David could no longer safely maintain himself, he was hospitalized under protest.

Treatment initially focused on pharmacotherapy with lithium carbonate (an antimanic medication) and chlorpromazine (a sedating antipsychotic medication). David was less irritable within 10 days, and in psychotherapy he started to recognize the grandiosity of his multiple far-flung schemes. He agreed to continue both psychotherapy and medication. In family psychotherapy sessions, David and his wife discussed the impact of his illness on their marriage. Finally, because of the outcropping of alcohol abuse, David was also seen by a substance abuse specialist. Over the course of a month, David's mania and psychosis resolved, and he returned to his preillness level of functioning.

Two weeks after discharge, he returned to his usual job responsibilities. Over the course of the next 3 years, he had two minor episodes of elevated mood with hyperactivity. On both occasions he was able to continue work and his usual functioning with the help of intensified psychotherapy and medication adjustment. Attuned to David's illness, his supervisor confirmed each time that the early symptoms had been treated promptly.

Diagnosis

See Chapter 13.

Workplace Recognition, Management, and Referral

It is vital to remember that bipolar disorder is a common condition. In any work environment, there will likely be someone with inapparent bipolar disorder. Detection, referral, and management of the nonpsychotic individual is covered in Chapter 1. When psychosis accompanies the presentation, there is a higher degree of urgency. Where the employee's behavior is flagrantly inappropriate, call his or her attention to the objective evidence. Point out that something is wrong without ascribing blame or making an on-the-job diagnosis. Since mania and psychosis undermine employees' ability to realistically evaluate their circumstances, it often falls to the employer to insist that psychiatric evaluation take place as a condition of returning to work. Where there is evidence of mania or psychosis, the definite course of action is referral for evaluation and treatment. Diplomatically accomplished, based on objective criteria, and accompanied by clear assurance of return to work after medical clearance, there are strong odds of a good outcome.

Causes

It is not known why mania will sometimes progress to more overt psychosis. Presumably, the predisposition to mania itself is complicated by an interplay of personality style, genetic endowment, and current psychosocial environment. Further research to clarify the influence of such variables is necessary.

Effects

The lifetime course of illness with psychotic mania is variable. These patients are vulnerable to relapse, and might cycle between high and low moods every few years to months if not treated. Fortunately, most of these people can be stabilized with a combination of maintenance medication and psychotherapy. In cases of psychotic mania, future episodes of mania are more likely to be psychotic than not. Some patients have a relatively uncomplicated course, few episodes, and require relatively modest maintenance medication and supportive psychotherapy. At the other extreme are patients who are noncompliant with treatment and who develop a progressively deteriorating illness that resembles severe schizophrenia.

Treatment

For acute psychotic mania, an antimanic agent is often insufficient. Instead, lithium or carbamazepine is combined with an antipsychotic medication. In relatively few cases, the medications cannot control the chronic cycles of episodes, or psychosis may dominate the clinical picture. In these instances, an antipsychotic medication is used as part of the maintenance regimen as well. Medications require continuous monitoring for efficacy and side effects.

Psychotherapeutic treatment of psychotic mania must be structured to meet the specific needs of the patient. The decision-making process that the treating psychiatrist goes through requires a complete evaluation of the patient's history, including any genetic elements. The ability of the patient to accept the need for treatment and to accept the reality of illness is a key element to successful treatment. In cases where psychological conflicts play an important role in triggering mood cycles, a limited insight-oriented psychotherapy is indicated. At other times, as with the psychotherapy of schizophrenia, a more psychoeducational approach is appropriate. Whatever the case, combined psychotherapy and pharmacotherapy provide the best treatment result.

Return to Work

The guiding principle in the return-to-work phase of this illness is that readiness for return should be determined with the help of a consulting psychiatrist. In most cases, the treating physician will want to limit contact with the workplace for reasons of confidentiality (see Chapter 3). No employee who has left the workplace for treatment of mania with psychosis (either voluntarily or at employer insistence) should return without such a determination.

Follow-up supervision of the employee should include observation for such reemergent symptoms as elevated mood, irritability, and impaired job performance. When needed, short sick leaves can limit the impact of an episode and shorten the course of treatment. The overall prognosis is very good when compliance is high, and patients can expect a return to their preillness level of functioning. Future episodes can generally be handled on an outpatient basis.

MAJOR DEPRESSION WITH PSYCHOSIS

Diagnostic Overview

Major depression with psychosis is distinguished from the nonpsychotic form by exaggeration of symptoms to psychotic proportions. As symptoms lose their connection to reality, the depressed employee with guilty preoccupations may develop an unshakable conviction of wrongdoing, or appetite may be diminished to the extent of conviction that food is rotten or poisoned. Weight loss may be misinterpreted as proof that body parts are dead or decaying. The fundamental principle is that any depressive symptom can become enlarged to psychotic proportions, limited only by the resourcefulness of the human imagination. In these situations, the delusions of guilt may become paranoid and may include accusatory auditory hallucinations. Hallucinations also become persecutory as psychotically depressed employees believe that their own wrongdoing has induced a scheme to either punish or do away with them.

Case Study 4

Thomas Mannes, a 62-year-old successful machine manufacturer and employer of several dozen factory workers, was referred to a psychiatrist by his internist after a physical examination revealed no apparent cause for a 15-pound weight loss. Over the past month, the weight loss had been accompanied by poor sleep, decreased energy, increasingly low self-esteem, and hopeless feelings. Thomas reported that he had no reason to go on living and that he was a useless burden to his family. The depressed feelings had started developing soon after the death of his twin sister.

When Thomas saw the psychiatrist, he felt guilty for countless shortcomings. He said he had been thinking of suicide and had been saving up his heart medication for a possible overdose. After careful consideration, Thomas and his wife agreed that he should continue treatment as an outpatient. A 3-day supply of nortriptyline (an antidepressant medication) was supervised by his wife. Two weeks later, Thomas acknowledged that he had been spitting out his medication, because he thought his wife had substituted poison. He felt she agreed with his belief that he was useless and without hope for improvement. Furthermore, he thought his weight loss was caused by an undiagnosed case of advanced cancer that was causing his internal organs to deteriorate. He said he had given up on his suicide plan because he was doomed to suffer a slow death from his condition.

He was hospitalized and therapy was initially directed at placing his feelings of worthlessness into a more realistic perspective. Pharmacotherapy was intensified through the use of haloperidol (an antipsychotic medication) in combination with his nortriptyline. Developmental history revealed that Thomas had suffered the early childhood loss of his maternal grandmother, who had been his principal caregiver. He was left with the unresolved childhood fantasy that he had done something wrong to make her go away. These feelings recurred after his sister's death. He felt he deserved to die.

After 2 weeks of treatment, he showed some improvement in psychotic symptoms. However, continued psychotherapy and intensified medication over the next 6 weeks did not substantially resolve his severe depression. On the advice of two psychiatrists, a course of electroconvulsive therapy (ECT) was started. Nine ECT treatments over 3 weeks effected a full resolution of the depression, including his delusions of worthlessness and suicidal thoughts. Maintenance antidepressant medication and psychotherapy were continued. He was discharged, and he returned to a full schedule of work activities within 2 weeks. He continued to function well, but with mild nonpsychotic depressive recurrences about every 2 years. These episodes required only briefly intensified psychotherapy and medication adjustment.

As a consequence of his own experience, Thomas was able to provide greater support and direction to his employees suffering from psychiatric illness. In addition, his insight-oriented psychotherapy enhanced his awareness of the impact of emotions on behavior and strengthened his skills as a manager.

Diagnosis

See Chapter 13.

Workplace Recognition, Management, and Referral

Major depression with psychosis should be considered on a continuum of severity with nonpsychotic major depression. Depressed employees in the earlier, nonpsychotic phase of illness will often be more accepting of referral advice. Employees with psychotic depression may appear withdrawn and depressed, or openly psychotic. Major depression with psychosis is a serious illness with many ramifications for the worker, family, and workplace. Early intervention can limit the adverse consequences of illness.

Causes

As with psychotic mania, it is likely that some people have a predisposition to depression that is combined with personality, life stress, or biological predispositions to psychotic complications.

Effects

The impact of nonpsychotic depression on the worker and workplace is discussed in Chapter 13. Because psychotic depression is more severe, all of the adverse effects are magnified. Notably, suicidal ideation is both more common and harder to detect in psychotic depression. The chance that a psychotically depressed patient might act on these feelings cannot be underestimated, and the symptom must be reassessed frequently. Risks are notably high when suicide is seen as an escape from delusional persecution.

Treatment

The psychological treatments available for the nonpsychotic forms of depression are applied to the psychotic forms as well. However, the patient who is delusionally convinced of guilt or wrongdoing may be noncompliant and may not benefit from psychotherapy alone. In such cases, psychotherapy alone is contraindicated and must be combined with medication. Medication without psychotherapy is also usually insufficient to effect full remission of symptoms. The most effective medication approach is usually a combination of an antidepressant and an antipsychotic.

Another important treatment for psychotic depression is ECT. This therapy involves a brief period of anesthesia and deep muscle relaxation. A small, computer-controlled electrical stimulus is used to induce a physically silent seizure within the brain, manifested only on an electroencephalogram. The resulting changes in brain chemistry lead to improvement in depression.

Return to Work

As with nonpsychotic major depression, there is usually a restoration to full and normal functioning after treatment. However, some employees with severe and recurrent psychotic depressions can become more difficult to treat as they get older. They may also develop a chronic state of slightly depressed mood and subtle social withdrawal.

DRUG-INDUCED PSYCHOSIS

Diagnostic Overview

The American workplace has fallen prey to the influence of the drug epidemic. Drug-induced psychosis includes any disorder of thinking that is directly attributable to either acute or chronic drug abuse.

Case Study 5

Allen James is a 35-year-old married rising middle manager of a high-technology company. Over the past 18 months of employment, his meteoric rise began to stall out. His supervisor noticed an unattractive weight gain, increasing dishevelment, and plummeting job performance. The supervisor was concerned, but uncertain about how to approach an employee who had become his friend over the course of many successful projects. Things came to a head when Allen requested a one month advance on his salary. When his request was denied, he began to express his belief that there was a grand scheme to oppose his rise. When Allen told his wife that he knew his supervisor was an FBI agent, she became alarmed and called the company.

The supervisor gathered his courage and patiently elicited the facts of Allen's cocaine addiction. Allen reluctantly accepted a referral to an inpatient substance abuse program. He spent 3½ weeks in highly structured treatment, which included individual psychotherapy, group therapy, family therapy, and initial antipsychotic medication. Upon discharge he was immediately able to return to work, continued in outpatient treatment, and resumed a highly successful and drug-free career.

Diagnosis

Diagnostic considerations for drug abuse are covered in Chapters 15 and 16. Drug-induced psychosis can look like schizophrenia or psychotic mood disorders. Substance abuse should always be considered in the evaluation of psychotic patients, even if previously attributed to schizophrenia, depression, or mania.

Workplace Recognition, Management, and Referral

Drug-induced psychosis can be initially indistinguishable from any other form of psychotic illness. Delusions and hallucinations are surprisingly similar, although drug-induced psychosis is more likely to include visual hallucinations. As with any substance abuse, the employee may begin to show changes in job performance, frequent lateness or absences, reduced ability to relate to co-workers, unexplained extended breaks, and decreased attention to personal grooming. Such subtle personality changes as indifference, irritability, and inappropriate shifts in mood may progress to suspiciousness, frank paranoid thinking, and elation or hyperactivity.

Causes

Common drugs of abuse that can cause psychosis include cocaine (powder or crystal-form crack), phencyclidine (PCP), amphetamines, and hallucinogens (LSD, mescaline, and others). Employees predisposed to psychosis are at greater risk for drug-induced symptoms.

Effects

Drug-induced psychoses have effects that are similar to other psychoses, as well as to drug abuse. In addition, drug-induced psychoses are more likely to include the potential for hostile or violent behavior.

Treatment

The immediate treatment for drug-induced psychosis includes abstinence from the offending agent and prescription of antipsychotic medication. Care must be taken to avoid drug withdrawal symptoms. Reduction in psychosis will enable the patient to cooperate in psychotherapy (see Chapters 15 and 16).

Return to Work

The principles that apply to drug dependence are applied to drug-induced psychosis. In general, drug-induced psychosis is a one-time event provided there is no further abuse of the offending agent. Some evidence suggests more rapid onset of recurrent psychosis with subsequent drug abuse. Treatments that enhance abstinence will effectively prevent recurrence of this form of psychosis.

PSYCHOSIS SECONDARY TO MEDICAL ILLNESS

Diagnostic Overview

Medical illness, diagnosed or hidden, can also manifest symptoms of psychosis. Psychiatric symptoms can be the first sign that something is wrong. The myriad medical conditions that can present psychiatric symptoms include endocrine disorders (hyper or hypothyroidism, Cushing's disease, Addison's disease, and diabetes), central nervous system tumors and infections, stroke, heart disease, pneumonia, and vitamin deficiency.

Case Study 6

Jane Ross is a 62-year-old married real estate agent and grandmother of three. A well-documented recurrent major depression has always responded promptly to routine treatment, and she has never had any other health problems. The owner of Jane's agency has been aware of her depressions, has learned to recognize early signs, but has never needed to suggest treatment.

Her career has been successful, but a recent downturn in the market has greatly diminished Jane's commissions. One of her grandchildren suffers from newly diagnosed epilepsy. Over the course of 5 months, Jane became more and more depressed, overweight, sluggish, and fatigued. She had diminished interest in her work and personal hygiene. Her depression did feel a little different than usual, and she became suspicious that other agents in the office were stealing her calls and real estate listings. Jane began to think that she could hear her co-workers talking about her and plotting to the destruction of her commission income. She stopped coming to the office, put a new business phone in her home, and refused to give the number to her boss.

Jane's boss and family got worried and wondered why she didn't call her psychiatrist. When Jane began to make accusatory phone calls to other agents, the boss insisted that she reenter treatment and get medical clearance before resuming work. Jane grudgingly complied, and told her psychiatrist that the situation was hopeless.

Since the symptoms were different than usual, Jane was sent for laboratory tests that included an endocrine profile. Jane was suffering from a serious case of hypothyroidism (underactive thyroid gland). She was referred to her internist, who diagnosed the hypothyroidism and corrected it with thyroid medication. No antipsychotic or antidepressant medication was necessary. Jane was able to readjust her thinking when her hypothyroidism was corrected and she understood the medical cause of her recent difficulties. With psychotherapy, Jane was able to make amends with her boss and colleagues, and effect an uneventful transition back to the office. Although the real estate market remained in the doldrums, Jane was able to see the reality of the situation and function appropriately.

Diagnosis

In the case of psychosis secondary to medical illness, it is essential to detect associated medical problems, or to recognize the nonpsychiatric origin of seemingly psychiatric symptoms. The possible contribution of medical conditions to behavioral change must always be kept in mind. Early detection in these cases can be life-saving.

Workplace Recognition, Management, and Referral

While patients commonly delay treatment for all medical conditions, the problem is intensified when presenting symptoms are emotional, and more so when there is a known history of psychiatric illness. Because Jane had an excellent work record despite her recurrent depressions, her boss expected her to seek treatment. So, the problem was not addressed in the workplace until it reached a near crisis.

Causes

Where medical illness is recognized as the underlying cause, it is best to avoid emphasizing workplace-related emotional stresses. This case illustrates the confusing clinical course that psychosis secondary to medical illness can take.

Effects

Any loss of touch with reality can cause devastating loss of confidence and demoralization. In this instance, the impact was limited because of the history of excellent job performance and good preexisting peer relations. However, the accusatory attitude of a psychotic employee can induce fear and anxiety among co-workers. The burden for the returning employee can be great. This can be lessened by understanding the medical illness and fostering acceptance in the workplace.

Treatment

Psychiatric management of psychosis due to medical illness requires recognition of underlying medical causes and patient compliance with proper treatment. Where psychiatric symptoms are more active, paranoia or agitation may require psychiatric medication until the underlying medical condition comes under control. Such cases require careful consideration of psychotherapeutic, psychopharmacologic, and general medical knowledge.

Return to Work

Return-to-work issues are similar to those for other psychotic disorders. The return can often be facilitated by a simple and nonjudgmental explanation of the condition's cause. Prognosis is generally excellent, so long as the underlying condition remains in control.

SUMMARY

This chapter deals with commonly encountered categories of psychotic illness, manifestations of the illnesses, treatment options, and guidelines for the workplace. The entities included in this chapter are not an exhaustive list. Real or apparent psychotic symptoms can also be produced by dementia, conversion disorder, dissociative disorder, and factitious disorders. There are striking overlaps between disorders mentioned in other chapters and the psychotic disorders. It is always important to properly diagnose psychotic symptoms and to apply optimal specific treatment.

Bibliography

American Psychiatric Association. 1987. *Diagnostic and Statistical Manual of Mental Disorders,* 3d ed. rev. Washington, D.C.: American Psychiatric Association.
American Psychiatric Association. 1989. *Treatments of Psychiatric Disorders.* Washington, D.C.: American Psychiatric Association.

Cancro, R. (ed.). 1971. *The Schizophrenic Syndrome: An Annual Review.* New York: Brunner/Mazel.

Day, M., and E. U. Semrad. 1978. Paranoia and paranoid states. In *The Harvard Guide to Modern Psychiatry,* A. Nicoli (ed.). Cambridge, Mass.: Harvard University Press.

Jefferson, J. W., and J. H. Greist. 1977. *Primer of Lithium Therapy.* Baltimore, Md.: Williams and Wilkins.

Kaplan, Harold I., A. M. Freedman, and B. J. Sadock (eds.) 1980. *Comprehensive Textbook of Psychiatry/III.* Baltimore, Md.: Williams and Wilkins.

18

Emotion and Illness: The Psychosomatic Interface

Brian L. Grant, M.D.

Organic Behavioral Syndromes
  Chemical Toxicity
  Drug Toxicity
  Organically Induced Depression and Psychosis
  Organically Induced Dementia and Delirium
Summary

ABSTRACT

Only in recent years has a systematic approach started to unravel some of the age-old questions about the linkages between emotions and illness. Emotional distress causing physical symptoms (somatoform disorders), falsely represented symptoms (malingering), physical symptoms of other psychiatric disorders (panic disorder and others), controversial medical illness (multiple chemical sensitivity syndrome and others), emotional causes of true physical disease (coronary artery disease and others), and toxic causes of behavioral symptoms is a fascinating but sometimes confusing field. Specific diagnosis and effective treatment depends on full awareness of the complex interaction between medical, psychiatric, psychodynamic, family, and cultural determinants. Similarly, workplace managers need to be sensitive to these issues in order to make appropriate decisions about employees with confusing physical symptoms. Even when the cause or severity of physical ailments is hotly disputed, the patient/employee may still be suffering from a psychiatric disorder that requires professional attention.

INTRODUCTION

Personality and physical factors have a reciprocal relationship with important workplace implications. Although modern medicine tends to distinguish and separate the mind from the body, this distinction is partial at best. In fact, true psychiatric and emotional conditions can be manifested through physical symptoms, while true physical disorders can be announced by emotional symptoms. This chapter examines these concepts by first reviewing the psychiatric classification of the somatoform disorders. Among the five somatoform variants described in this chapter are hypochondriasis, conversion disorder, somatoform pain disorder, somatization disorder (Briquet's syndrome), and epidemic (mass) hysteria. Factitious disorders and malingering are the intentional false representation of symptoms. Attention is also given to the controversial medical illnesses, syndromes of uncertain and possibly mixed physical and emotional origins. The controversial illnesses fall into a group of medical diagnoses that do not meet ordinary criteria for existence, but are nonetheless often attributed to purely physical causes. Concluding the chapter, there is a discussion of the emotional conditions associated with physical disease and toxic chemical causes of psychiatric symptoms. Case examples for selected diagnoses illustrate the interrelationship of emotions and physical illness.

SOMATOFORM DISORDERS: PHYSICAL SYMPTOMS OF EMOTIONAL ORIGIN

Case Study 1: Somatoform Pain Disorder

John Hawkins, a 53-year-old logger, experienced low back pain while moving a piece of machinery. When evaluated in an emergency room he received a diagnosis of lumbosacral sprain. He left his job because of the pain and has not returned in the intervening 7 years. John's pain complaints have progressed to his upper back, but multiple diagnostic evaluations have failed to produce conclusive evidence of physical pathology. When examined, John's complaints of pain were dramatic and presented in a pattern inconsistent with the anatomical distribution of back pain. He recoiled in apparent pain to a light touch on the skin and to direct downward pressure on the neck. He enrolled in a multidisciplinary pain unit, which resulted in a brief but unsustained symptomatic improvement. As a tenth-grade dropout, John had limited intellectual skills and equally limited work opportunities in sedentary occupations. His pain symptoms would increase when sitting or standing for prolonged periods, prompting him to drop out of vocational retraining programs. John confined his activities to his home, light recreation, and visits with friends and family. His wife and children assumed the tasks of home maintenance. Worker's compensation benefits partially replaced his lost earnings. A multidisciplinary consultative examination concluded that John had a somatoform pain disorder.

Case Study 2: Somatization Disorder (Briquet's Syndrome)

Sonia Thomas, a 34-year-old woman, worked for one year as a bench mechanic for a large electronics company. In that year, she missed 5 weeks due to various illnesses. This was viewed as excessive absenteeism, so she was referred to the company physician for consultation. Sonia had complaints in many organ systems, including gastrointestinal complaints, chest pain, dizziness, frequent faintness, trouble walking at times, painful sexual intercourse, and extremely painful menstruation, to name but a few of her health concerns. She has been steadfastly ill since her early twenties, despite various diagnostic procedures and even exploratory surgery. She has vehemently resisted psychiatric referrals, citing the many physical problems that physicians had been unable to effectively treat. When she did finally go, the consultant diagnosed a somatization disorder (Briquet's syndrome). Realizing the importance of a good clinical relationship, he referred Sonia to a skilled and empathic family practitioner. In this way, unneeded and potentially dangerous medical interventions might be avoided.

Case Study 3: Epidemic Hysteria and Controversial Medical Illness

Over the course of several months, several dozen flight attendants for a major airline were partially overcome while flying in a particular type of jet on various routes. The first episode followed the leakage of a solvent and detectable fumes that entered an air intake. The odor did not disturb passengers or the pilots, and only some of the attendants on that flight were affected. Although the condition was quickly corrected, the attendants continued to be overcome. Kindled by media attention, the problem ignited the animosity that remained several years after a long and bitter strike. Management had exacted major labor concessions at that time. Independent industrial hygienists, toxicologists, and physicians retained by the airline and government were unable to account for the symptoms on a physical basis, but felt that the incident was consistent with epidemic hysteria. Some of the flight attendants consulted with a clinical ecologist, who felt that they were afflicted with multiple chemical sensitivity syndrome. This incident resulted in losses totaling many thousands of dollars in medical and legal fees, and in lost productivity.

Five Somatoform Disorders

Each of the preceding cases illustrates a somatoform disorder, in which the predominant physical complaints have a psychiatric background. Five somatoform disorders are discussed here. First, hypochondriasis consists of a fear or preoccupation with having a serious disease, a misinterpretation of physical sensations or signs, and a lack of medical evidence to support the self-diagnosis. The so-called hypochondriac may seek multiple medical evaluations and investigations to validate these concerns. Second, conversion disorders present with discrete alterations in neurologic motor or sensory function that have no physical cause, and that serve to resolve unconscious emotional conflict. Third, a somatoform pain disorder is diagnosed when pain is the primary symptom. Fourth, somatization disorder is a specific diagnosis that requires multiple symptomatic complaints within a wide variety of organ systems, despite a lack of objective signs. And fifth, epidemic (or mass) hysteria is the simultaneous occurrence of similar physical symptoms in a group of individuals, but without physical cause.

As with many psychiatric disorders, the somatoform disorders likely represent a continuum of underlying emotional conflict in complex individuals. The several diagnoses may overlap in a way lacking clear criteria in any particular patient. Common to all of the somatoform disorders is the use of physical symptoms as an expression of underlying emotional state and personality. The presence of a somatoform disorder does not rule out the coexistence of other medical and psychiatric problems. Despite their confusing or overlapping presentations, these are very real problems that will often respond to appropriate treatment. The evaluating physician should take care to neither reject nor devalue the veiled emotional distress that these conditions often represent. Because somatization occurs without conscious intent, it is distinct from malingering, where conscious deception is the primary goal. Malingering is not considered a somatoform disorder and it is addressed separately in this chapter.

The incidence of somatoform disorders as a group is quite high. While patients who meet the rigid formal criteria for somatization disorder may be rare, those who exhibit somatization traits or elements of somatization disorder are more common. Studies of family medical practices reveal a very high incidence of patients who express physical complaints when their primary problems are actually emotional in nature. In the workplace setting, the prevalence may be higher still.

Hypochondriasis
Hypochondriasis is the fear or belief that one has a serious disease despite medical reassurance that no such disease is present. Appropriate physical evaluation does not support the diagnosis of a physical disorder and cannot account for the reported physical signs or symptoms.

DSM-III-R DIAGNOSTIC CRITERIA

300.70 Hypochondriasis (or Hypochondriacal Neurosis)

A. Preoccupation with the fear of having, or the belief that one has, a serious disease, based on the person's interpretation of physical signs or sensations as evidence of physical illness.

B. Appropriate physical evaluation does not support the diagnosis of any physical disorder that can account for the physical signs or sensations or the person's unwarranted interpretation of them, **and** the symptoms in A are not just symptoms of panic attacks.

C. The fear of having, or belief that one has, a disease persists despite medical reassurance.

D. Duration of the disturbance is at least six months.

E. The belief in A is not of delusional intensity, as in Delusional Disorder, Somatic Type (i.e, the person can acknowledge the possibility that his or her fear of having, or belief that he or she has, a serious disease is unfounded).

Reprinted with permission from the *Diagnostic and Statistical Manual of Mental Disorders*, 3d ed. rev.; copyright 1987 by the American Psychiatric Association.

Conversion Disorder

The diagnosis of conversion disorder requires a loss or alteration in physical functioning that suggests a physical disorder, but with no physical or neurological condition that can account for the symptoms. The presentation may often include neurological symptoms, such as paralysis (but not simply pain). When such physical symptoms arise at times of psychological stress or exceptional interpersonal conflict, emotional contributors are often present.

DSM-III-R DIAGNOSTIC CRITERIA

300.11 Conversion Disorder (or Hysterical Neurosis, Conversion Type)

A. A loss of, or alteration in, physical functioning suggesting a physical disorder.

B. Psychological factors are judged to be etiologically related to the symptom because of a temporal relationship between a psychosocial stressor that is apparently related to a psychological conflict or need and initiation or exacerbation of the symptom.

C. The person is not conscious of intentionally producing the symptom.

D. The symptom is not a culturally sanctioned response pattern and cannot, after appropriate investigation, be explained by a known physical disorder.

> E. The symptom is not limited to pain or to a distur-
> bance in sexual functioning.
>
> **Specify: single episode or recurrent.**
>
> Reprinted with permission from the *Diagnostic and Statistical
> Manual of Mental Disorders,* 3d ed. rev.; copyright 1987 by the
> American Psychiatric Association.

Somatoform Pain Disorder

Somatoform pain disorder may exist when a predominant complaint of pain is unsupported by any known cause. It may exist when an actual medical problem cannot account for the severity of the reported pain resulting in social and occupational impairment. Some cases share the same psychodynamic and emotional underpinnings as conversion disorders.

> **DSM-III-R DIAGNOSTIC CRITERIA**
>
> **307.80 Somatoform Pain Disorder**
>
> A. Preoccupation with pain for at least six months.
>
> B. Either (1) or (2):
>
>   (1) appropriate evaluation uncovers no organic pathology or pathophysiologic mechanism (e.g., a physical disorder or the effects of injury) to account for the pain
>   (2) when there is related organic pathology, the complaint of pain or resulting social or occupational impairment is grossly in excess of what would be expected from the physical findings
>
> Reprinted with permission from the *Diagnostic and Statistical
> Manual of Mental Disorders,* 3d ed. rev.; copyright 1987 by the
> American Psychiatric Association.

Somatization Disorder (Briquet's Syndrome)

A true somatization disorder is rare and requires specific criteria. Physical complaints or the belief that one is sickly should be a well-established pattern before the age of 30. There must be at least 13 symptoms that have prompted medical evaluation or treatment, or alterations in life-style. There must be no organic disorder that can account for the symptoms or for their severity when actual pathology is observed. The symptoms may be centered in the gastrointestinal, cardiopulmonary, genitourinary, or female reproductive systems. They may take the form of conversion or pseudoneurological disorders.

DSM-III-R DIAGNOSTIC CRITERIA

300.81 Somatization Disorder

A. A history of many physical complaints or a belief that one is sickly, beginning before the age of 30 and persisting for several years.

B. At least 13 symptoms from the list below. To count a symptom as significant, the following criteria must be met:

   (1) no organic pathology or pathophysiologic mechanism (e.g., a physical disorder or the effects of injury, medication, drugs, or alcohol) to account for the symptom or, when there is related organic pathology, the complaint or resulting social or occupational impairment is grossly in excess of what would be expected from the physical findings

   (2) has not occurred only during a panic attack

   (3) has caused the person to take medicine (other than over-the-counter pain medication), see a doctor, or alter life-style

Symptom list:

Gastrointestinal symptoms:

   (1) **vomiting (other than during pregnancy)**

   (2) abdominal pain (other than when menstruating)

   (3) nausea (other than motion sickness)

   (4) bloating (gassy)

   (5) diarrhea

   (6) intolerance of (gets sick from) several different foods

Pain symptoms:

   (7) **pain in extremities**

   (8) back pain

(9) joint pain
(10) pain during urination
(11) other pain (excluding headaches)

Cardiopulmonary symptoms:
(12) **shortness of breath when not exerting oneself**
(13) palpitations
(14) chest pain
(15) dizziness

Conversion or pseudoneurologic symptoms:
(16) **amnesia**
(17) **difficulty swallowing**
(18) loss of voice
(19) deafness
(20) double vision
(21) blurred vision
(22) blindness
(23) fainting or loss of consciousness
(24) seizure or convulsion
(25) trouble walking
(26) paralysis or muscle weakness
(27) urinary retention or difficulty urinating

Sexual symptoms for the major part of the person's life after opportunities for sexual activity:
(28) **burning sensation in sexual organs or rectum (other than during intercourse)**
(29) sexual indifference
(30) pain during intercourse
(31) impotence

Female reproductive symptoms judged by the person to occur more frequently or severely than in most women:
(32) **painful menstruation**
(33) irregular menstrual periods
(34) excessive menstrual bleeding
(35) vomiting throughout pregnancy

Note: The seven items in boldface may be used to screen for the disorder. The presence of two or more of these items suggests a high likelihood of the disorder.

Epidemic (Mass) Hysteria
This rare but fascinating syndrome may occur when a group of people, exposed to a common stimulus, simultaneously present with common physical symptoms of psychological origin. Typically, those afflicted are highly suggestible and in a situation where they feel vulnerable or powerless. In a work setting the stimulus may be a perceived toxic substance, noxious odors, an environmental stress such as extreme heat, or even an environment charged with prior emotional conflict.

Psychological Causes of Somatization

The somatoform disorders are outward manifestations of emotional distress, as determined by certain personality traits and cultural influences. Somatization is a psychological defense mechanism that provides some relief of emotional discomfort and simultaneously displays the discomfort outwardly through physical symptoms. Diseases of the body are regarded as fickle, uncontrollable things that happen to a person, rather than as problems generated from within. Thus, physical symptoms permit a comforting perceived detachment from both underlying emotions and outward behavior.

Somatoform disorders are often associated with early or midchildhood emotional trauma. The resulting intolerable feelings are suppressed from conscious thought to retain emotional equilibrium. When this suppression is incomplete, emotional conflicts and feelings may later emerge as physical complaints. The underlying trauma and resulting conflicts cannot be brought out and resolved without psychotherapy or a similar corrective experience. Somatization defenses and other maladaptive behaviors may become even more evident personality traits when a pattern of abuse reoccurs.

Cultural and Familial Causes

Somatoform disorders also have cultural determinants. Every individual exists within the cultural framework of the greater society, a particular subculture, and a unique family. The family, that most compact and intimate cultural unit, defines the limits of interpersonal experience for the newborn and infant. The spoken and behavioral language of the family is the earliest form of communication for a child. The child learns to communicate by watching, listening, and imitating. Over time, this process widens to include playmates, classmates, friends, and even co-workers.

To understand the meaning of illness to the somatic patient, it is important to learn about the illness behaviors of that person's family. Often there is a history of particular illnesses, pain disorders, and disability among family members. The expression of somatization may be a learned behavior, in addition to being a communication form determined by individual emotional defense structures. Verbal expression of emotional states and psychological discomfort is not well accepted in many families and cultures. In both the present and historical past, psychiatric disorders have often been attributed to other bodily organ systems. For instance, Western tradition has attributed depressed mood to "black bile," while some non-Western languages have limited psychological vocabularies. Explanatory models of disease causation are developed in a manner consistent with the cultural or psychological experiences of the individual.

Workplace Relevance

The larger world cultural and emotional determinants of somatization are important for understanding the workplace problems of health, productivity, and disability benefits. Since true somatoform disorders are not conscious, the primary gain for the individual is initially a reduction of emotional distress. Secondary gains may soon also accrue to the employee with symptoms, including reduced workplace demands and otherwise unavailable emotional and financial supports. When there is a social or cultural resistance to the concept of psychological illness, the individual who uses somatization will feel especially entitled.

Workplace problems and relationships offer a fertile field for the expression of emotional interpersonal conflict through somatization. With little alteration, workers bring their unique personalities, experiences, and problems to work. A worker abused as a child might unwittingly experience even normal supervisory advice as a reminder of past abuse. This could lead to profound emotional distress around the supervisor and workplace. Somatic symptoms might then develop as a way of reducing the emotional distress and finding an external explanation (primary gain). The symptoms can also be a way of countering supervisory pressure through the presentation of physical limitations, or of finding co-worker sympathy or disability benefits (secondary gain).

Workplace somatization takes on a new twist when it becomes entangled in formalized employee health and safety laws that call for sure and certain relief for the injured worker. A simple leg fracture due to a fall is a relatively unambiguous workplace injury. The bone is set, the fracture heals, and the worker returns to the job after a normal convalescence. Complications can set in when a worker predisposed to unwitting somatization (or to conscious malingering) sustains even such a straightforward injury. The worker may attribute the injury to a cause that others perceive as inconsequential. Inexplicable and disabling physical complications may unexpectedly appear, often leading to a medical disability claim. Employers then find themselves with legal and economic responsibility for a confusing medical condition.

Here, too, the symptoms have the effect of diverting the worker's attention from hidden emotional concerns, while attributing distress to externally caused physical symptoms.

Effective Assessment

Diagnosis and treatment of somatoform disorders is not easy. There are inherent difficulties in identifying specific syndromal patterns from a confusing clinical picture. It is always essential to look carefully for other true medical and psychiatric diagnoses, yet these commonly coexist with real somatoform disorders. For instance, depression is a common concomitant of both incapacitating physical paralysis and conversion disorder pseudoparalysis. To ensure a cooperative effort at diagnosis and treatment, physicians must offer patients a mutually acceptable explanatory model of the disease. Most importantly, emotional needs for a physical explanation require special expertise in diagnostic interviewing. When there is persisting ambiguity, confusion, or overt conflict about the nature of the problem, effective treatment may be difficult or even impossible.

Consider the somatizing patient who takes problems that are emotional and experiences them as physical. That patient engages in one form of what can be called resistance. Resistance springs from a desire to avoid the uncomfortable emotions associated with traumatic early experiences. The physician who deals only with the presented physical symptoms, while discounting any emotional basis or concomitants, may unwittingly heighten hidden emotional fears. For instance, at the same time that treatment sincerely addresses the physical complaints, inattention to emotional factors may reinforce a hidden fear of emotional abandonment. Moreover, invasive treatments can leave physical scars, while paradoxically increasing distress. And on the other hand, correct but premature presentation of an emotional cause will also leave patients feeling rejected by the physician. They will likely seek their care elsewhere.

The art of the effective physician involves an understanding of the factors that bring about a somatoform presentation. Diagnosis and treatment must be handled in a way that is both acceptable and helpful to the patient, but without unwitting collusion or further harm. It is unrealistic for a physician to assume that a patient with a somatoform illness will readily acknowledge a psychological explanation for the problem. Because the patient's beliefs are often deeply held and not easily altered, the physician should consider working within the context of the patient's beliefs. For instance, recognizing the real, if partial, benefits of nonmainstream health care models and treatments will leave the patient feeling better understood and more comfortable with continuing medical care.

Diagnosis and Treatment

Once the possibility of a somatoform diagnosis is raised, a psychiatric consultation can address the specific diagnostic possibilities. In addition to assessing comorbid psychiatric disorders, there are important differences between the various somatoform disorders. Effective treatment requires specific diagnosis, as well as a constant recognition of the patient's somatoform explanatory model for his or her distress.

Treatments must be selected for specific diagnoses, and individually for each patient. Commonly, treatment will simultaneously address the physical symptoms per se, as well as the emotional concerns. Pain and physical impairment can be treated with physical therapy and behavioral pain therapy. Psychotherapy typically starts with a focus on the practical and emotional consequences of physical symptoms. The possibility of emotional causality is allowed to arise only much later, when the patient starts to wonder about that possibility. Ultimately, psychotherapy seeks to uncover and thus relieve the hidden emotional fears that underly the somatoform symptoms. As always, the psychotherapeutic process should be specific but gradual.

Conversion disorders represent a special case, where the specific symptom offers anxiety reduction through physical incapacity, as well as a symbolic representation of emotionally unacceptable hidden impulses. A classic example is of the angry worker (from an angry family) who has an impulse to punch his boss. Rather than hit the boss and suffer the retribution of getting fired, he unwittingly develops a paralysis of his arm. Unable to hit, he has less need to worry about punching or getting fired, and he may actually earn sympathy from the boss or others.

Somatization disorder (Briquet's syndrome) is another special case. Studies have shown that female Briquet's patients have a high prevalence of male sociopaths in their families (see Chapter 14). This finding is consistent with the clinical observation that somatization disorder is highly resistant to psychotherapy, and that symptoms will sometimes persist in the face of a patient's willing agreement that no medical cause exists. Some cases of somatization may thus involve a degree of factitious symptoms or malingering.

FACTITIOUS DISORDERS AND MALINGERING: FALSELY REPORTED SYMPTOMS

The factitious disorders form a curious group of psychiatric entities. They are characterized by the intentional feigning of physical or psychological symptoms, in order to fulfill an inner emotional need to assume a sick role. This is done without external incentives such as greater economic status or improved well-being. These disorders thus differ from malingering, where symptoms are also falsely reported, but in an effort to gain external rewards.

Case Study 4: Malingering

George Casey, a 38-year-old steelworker, slipped on some grease, hit his head, and twisted his neck. Over the course of 5 months, he presented a left-sided partial paralysis requiring the aid of a cane, and exhibited an inability to think or communicate clearly. His wife accompanied him to each examination, reporting that he had severely impaired memory and did little more than sit on the couch and watch television.

Upon examination, George appeared to be a very impaired man. He would respond in a nonsensical and childlike way to the examiner and would fall if not supported while walking. Some of those who examined him were perplexed by symptoms suggesting a serious head injury. The fall itself was not severe and was not accompanied by loss of consciousness or immediate symptoms. Diagnostic examinations did not reveal any evidence of stroke or cerebral mass.

The employer chose to investigate the claim further. A private investigator set up video surveillance of George's activities. The investigator recorded George repairing a sloped roof and clearing land with a backhoe, all requiring the use of four limbs and full neck motion. George was able to engage in animated conversations. The videotapes supported a conclusion by the attending and consulting physicians that George was plainly malingering. The cost of George's claims to the employer and to the federal Social Security system exceeded $100,000 for medical benefits and time loss. George was prosecuted by civil authorities for fraud.

True malingering is not an emotional disorder. When found in a medical setting, it can be considered lying. The primary criteria for malingering are (1) the intentional production of grossly exaggerated physical and psychological symptoms and (2) a desire for external gain, such as the avoidance of work or prosecution, access to medications, or monetary compensation. Malingering may be present when the physical findings are unsupported by objective measures, but such inconsistencies also may be found in the somatoform disorders. The somatoform disorders differ in that they assume a consistent presentation, even in unobserved private settings. A malingerer feigns symptoms only as needed to attain certain conscious goals and might have normal functioning in unrelated settings.

Proving the existence of malingering is challenging and distasteful. Medical practitioners assume a spirit of mutual trust in the physician-patient relationship and often resist a search for dishonesty. Moreover, a resolution to the problem is more likely to lie in the employer's hands or legal action than in psychiatric treatment.

DSM-III-R DIAGNOSTIC CRITERIA

301.51 Factitious Disorder with Physical Symptoms

A. Intentional production or feigning of physical (but not psychological) symptoms.

B. A psychological need to assume the sick role, as evidenced by the absence of external incentives for the behavior, such as economic gain, better care, or physical well-being.

C. Occurrence not exclusively during the course of another Axis I disorder, such as Schizophrenia.

300.16 Factitious Disorder with Psychological Symptoms

A. Intentional production or feigning of psychological (but not physical) symptoms.

B. A psychological need to assume the sick role, as evidenced by the absence of external incentives for the behavior, such as economic gain, better care, or physical well-being.

C. Occurrence not exclusively during the course of another Axis I disorder, such as Schizophrenia.

V65.20 Malingering

The essential feature of Malingering is intentional production of false or grossly exaggerated physical or psychological symptoms, motivated by external incentives such as avoiding military conscription or duty, avoiding work, obtaining financial compensation, evading criminal prosecution, obtaining drugs, or securing better living conditions.

Under some circumstances Malingering may represent adaptive behavior, for example, feigning illness while a captive of the enemy during wartime.

Malingering should be strongly suspected if any combination of the following is noted:

(1) medicolegal context of presentation, e.g., the person's being referred by his or her attorney to the physician for examination;

(2) marked discrepancy between the person's claimed stress or disability and the objective findings;

(3) lack of cooperation during the diagnostic evaluation and in complying with the prescribed treatment regimen;

(4) the presence of Antisocial Personality Disorder.

Malingering differs from Factitious Disorder in that the motivation for the symptom production in Malingering is external incentives, whereas in Factitious Disorder there is an absence of external incentives. Evidence of an intrapsychic need to maintain the sick role suggests Factitious Disorder. Thus, a diagnosis of Factitious Disorder excludes a diagnosis of Malingering.

Malingering is differentiated from Conversion and other Somatoform Disorders by the intentional production of symptoms and by the obvious, external incentives. The person who is malingering is much less likely to present his or her symptoms in the context of emotional conflict, and the presenting symptoms are less likely to be symbolically related to an underlying emotional conflict. Symptom relief in Malingering is not often obtained by suggestion, hypnosis, or an amobarbital interview, as it frequently is in Conversion Disorder.

Reprinted with permission from the *Diagnostic and Statistical Manual of Mental Disorders,* 3d ed. rev.; copyright 1987 by the American Psychiatric Association.

PSYCHIATRIC DISORDERS WITH FREQUENT PHYSICAL SYMPTOMS

It is important to remember that there are several distinctly psychiatric disorders that may present with somatic components. For instance, the many common misdiagnoses of panic disorder include coronary disease, asthma, hypochondriasis, and generalized anxiety disorder. Such misdiagnoses will lead to inappropriate and ineffective treatment for a real and treatable disorder. The psychiatric disorders below are discussed elsewhere in this book, but they are briefly reviewed here to emphasize their importance when evaluating physical symptoms.

Panic Disorder

Panic disorder is a discrete form of anxiety whose features include attacks of great distress with at least four of the following physical symptoms: shortness of breath, dizziness, palpitation or fast heart rate, trembling or shaking, sweating, choking, nausea or abdominal distress, depersonalization or derealization, numbness or tingling sensations, hot flashes or chills, chest pain or discomfort, fear of dying, or fear of going crazy or doing something uncontrolled. If untreated, the disorder may progress to agoraphobia, the fear of going out in public. The physical presentation of the disorder, especially its unnerving cardiovascular symptoms, may prompt strenuous examinations for cardiac pathology. Panic disorder is readily treatable with certain medications and adjunctive psychotherapy.

Schizophrenia

Schizophrenia is a thought disorder characterized by persistent psychotic delusions, hallucinations, loose associations flat or blunted affect, and impaired social functioning. A wide variety of commonplace and bizarre physical symptoms can be reported. Schizophrenic patients will sometimes believe that they are victims of poison or other malevolent forces directed at them by family members, employers, or co-workers. It is nearly always unwise to dismiss such expressed concerns as delusional, without an objective look at the facts. In particular, care should be taken not to discount legitimate concerns and job-related complaints because of known psychiatric illness. On the other hand, it is equally remiss to overlook the potential influence of psychological factors on the concerned employee.

Depression

Depressed patients commonly present for treatment of such physical complaints as weakness, anorexia, insomnia, or light-headedness. This is especially prevalent in non-Western and lower socioeconomic groups. Chronic pain disorders such as headache, musculoskeletal dysfunction, and gastrointestinal distress also deserve special assessment for depression as a possible contributing factor. Chronic, vague, or nonspecific physical complaints should never be attributed to depression without appropriate medical examination. It is equally inappropriate to exclude depression from the diagnostic possibilities. When this diagnosis is overlooked, the continued distress can lead to needless suffering, unnecessary medical procedures, and even suicide.

CONTROVERSIAL MEDICAL ILLNESSES

This is an emerging group of illnesses and syndromes that are controversial in terms of their existence and purported causes. It is not yet certain that they represent true physical illnesses with a significant population prevalence. They present with ill-defined features and frequently ascribe a cluster of subjective symptoms to some bodily organ or system.

Several features make these syndromes controversial. First, there is disagreement about their existence as distinct entities, their prevalence, or their presence within a given patient. Second, there are healers and patients who feel quite strongly that real physical syndromes have been ignorantly or intentionally disregarded by the traditional medical establishment. Medical proponents of the syndromes may attract a great deal of attention. Afflicted patients often are elated that someone at last recognizes their physical and therefore "real" problem. Ironically, these same practitioners are often criticized professionally for alleged bad science and patient exploitation. Since careful research cannot clearly verify either consistent physical findings or psychiatric syndromes, the controversy continues.

Even a modest selection of controversial medical illnesses will not meet with universal agreement or approval. The debate about the names, causation, and even the very existence of these diseases attracts strong advocates and detractors. Some take an organic approach, some psychological, and others come from a middle ground. On the one hand, there is the problem of hastily attributing a syndrome to an organic or external cause while ignoring or downplaying the cultural and psychological basis of causation. On the other hand, it would be dangerous to ascribe all symptoms to a psychological origin. This would foreclose exploration and discovery of true physical pathologies that might cause or complicate a patient's presentation. In the workplace this could obscure the environmental factors that may cause or enhance symptoms of illness. Workplace factors can be both physical (physical conditions and substances) as well as social (corporate culture and employee relationships).

Case Study 5: Multiple Chemical Sensitivity Syndrome

Rebecca Greenson, a 43-year-old woman, worked as a laboratory technician at a college. Rebecca developed a respiratory distress syndrome that she attributed to the formaldehyde preservative she used in the lab. She left her job and filed a worker's compensation claim. Supporting her claim was a physician who called himself a clinical ecologist. He diagnosed multiple chemical sensitivity syndrome, and attributed it to Rebecca's sensitivity to formaldehyde, as well as to most synthetic chemicals found in urban and industrial settings. He prescribed treatment including vitamins, natural diet, and avoidance of synthetic fabrics and building materials. Rebecca left her urban home and settled in a cabin on the flanks of a mountainside. She became reclusive, but made some friends in a support group of individuals with similar problems of hypersensitivity. When she made her rare trips to the city, usually for medical visits, she wore a carbon filtered gas mask to trap airborne contaminants.

Multiple Chemical Sensitivity Syndrome (MCSS)

MCSS carries a primary complaint of inability to tolerate exposure to even small amounts of synthetic substances. Exposure may lead to a variety of severe, recurrent, and baffling toxicological reactions. The syndrome often follows an occupational or environmental exposure to chemicals, with substances such as formaldehyde frequently implicated. Consensus does not exist as to the definition of the syndrome, but certain diagnostic features have been observed. The onset of symptoms appears to be related to a documentable environmental exposure, insult, or illness; symptoms involve more than one organ system; the symptoms recur and abate in response to predictable stimuli; symptoms are elicited by exposures to chemicals of diverse structural classes and toxicologic modes of action; symptoms are elicited by exposures that are demonstrable; noxious exposures are at very low levels (i.e., many standard deviations below "average" exposures known to cause adverse human responses); and finally, symptoms cannot be explained by any widely available test of organ system function.

MCSS may be considered a subclass of the so-called environmental illnesses, or twentieth-century disease, falling within the self-defined purview of clinical ecology. It describes itself as "an orientation in medical practice dedicated to maintenance of health by recognition, management, and prevention of ecologic illness." Ecologic illness is usually described as "a polysymptomatic, multisystem chronic disorder manifested by adverse reactions to environmental excitants, as they are modified by individual susceptibility in terms of specific adaptation" (Brodsky 1987).

Without judging causation, it is fair to say that some highly disabled people are among those who are thought to suffer from MCSS and other environmental illnesses. Many mainstream medical practitioners, lawyers, and administrators still harbor doubts as to the existence of the syndrome, much less its potential for causing disability. One must distinguish between the debatable syndromal label and the person involved. For whatever reason, many of those afflicted are extremely uncomfortable and severely limited in their ability to function.

It is likely that MCSS and environmental disease are in reality a subclass of a psychiatric disorder, containing elements of somatization and anxiety disorders. Patients with the syndromes are indeed ill, but not in a way that is acceptable to them. In fact, they would vehemently reject the possibility of any emotional component. Psychiatric illnesses are generally thought to originate within the individual, due to some combination of biological, genetic, developmental, situational, and personality factors. Although the symptoms and suffering are real, the explanatory model for MCSS deals with responses to environmental factors, while failing to consider the psyche.

Chronic Fatigue Syndrome (CFS)

Chronic fatigue syndrome appears as a constellation of symptoms, including a marked level of fatigue lasting longer than 6 months and frequent physical complaints including fever, sore throat, muscle aches, and impaired cognition. It is highly controversial and has enjoyed considerable attention in the lay media and scientific literature. The debate about CFS extends to the question of a still undiscovered physiological cause, whether it represents a form of conversion or somatization of emotional symptoms, and whether it is a variant of depression. Physical theories include infectious causes, notably the Epstein-Barr virus, and speculation about immunologic responses caused by exposure to toxic agents.

However, a recent scientific study (Gold et al. 1990) that compared unaffected matched control groups to groups with CFS failed to demonstrate markedly different immunologic or viral states. Despite subjective reports of cognitive loss and dysfunction, these have not been demonstrated by objective measurements. It is more interesting that depressive illness has been observed with a high frequency among those with the disease, although the question of depression as cause or effect of CFS remains unresolved. It is possible that CFS is not a distinct entity, but that it is comprised of several conditions with common symptoms. In some cases, an infectious condition might predominate, while in others, the cause may be primarily psychological. Clinical observation suggests that atypical depression (dysthymia) is a common contributor, and is often responsive to monoamine oxidase inhibitor and serotonin reuptake inhibitor antidepressants in accepting patients (see Chapter 13).

Fibromyalgia may be an emotionally related subset of CFS. This disorder includes widespread musculoskeletal pain, high tender point count, and nonrestful sleep. Psychological causes may be at work when this disorder is the primary complaint and when no other medical illness can be documented (46 medical conditions have been associated with fibromyalgia). In one British study where 21 cases of primary fibromyalgia were followed for 5 years, all cases showed either a psychiatric disturbance or thyroid dysfunction (Forslind, Fredriksson, and Nived 1990). Women working in manual jobs were overrepresented and none had been able to return to full-time work. A U.S. study reported CFS subjects who were totally work disabled, but included subjects who retained a general ability to work in modified jobs (Wolfe 1990). The disability associated with this disorder seems to be affected, positively and negatively, by social and psychological factors. As CFS and its variations become more popularized, ill defined and controversial as they are, they are likely to become a more common source of disability claims and occupational dysfunction.

Effective Assessment

In whole or in part, these disorders frequently represent a somatization of psychological symptoms, as shown in their physical manner of expression and concurrent denial of emotional issues. Those who diagnose controversial illnesses, as well as their patients, typically are quite resistant to a psychological explanation. Unfortunately, such resistance may be the strongest among mainstream physicians. Medical practitioners, due to their own biases or blind spots, may fail to recognize emotional factors in patients who present with vague or poorly defined physical complaints. They will scrupulously seek a physiological solution to the problem, while sometimes neglecting an emotional line of inquiry.

The approach to such patients is made more difficult by their practiced resistance to emotional inquiry, much less psychiatric intervention. Psychiatric evaluation or consultation should be considered at the onset of syndrome presentation. The treating physician or manager should present the idea of a referral in a way that neither minimizes nor challenges the patient's theory about the problem. It is best to suggest that psychiatric consultation can help the patient to better understand the meaning of the illness, while helping others to understand the problem in a way that would not be possible with a traditional medical approach. By taking an empathic approach to the patient, it may be possible to reach a shared alternate understanding of the cause of the problem, and with that, symptom reduction. Efforts to dissuade patients from their explanatory models are likely to fail, both in terms of reducing symptoms and in maintaining a treatment relationship.

Diagnosis and Treatment

Diagnosis and treatment rely on understanding the interactions of patient belief systems, nonmainstream therapies, medical illness, psychiatric disorders, and optimal interview technique. It is important to find common ground with patients who espouse an alternative disease theory by listening to them, by expressing an understanding of how they feel, and by agreeing that they suffer from a significant problem. Culturally acceptable treatment alternatives will not usually impede effective treatment. Some conditions are self-limiting and responsive to suggestion. Suggestion can take the form of placebo medication or symbolic interventions.

It is always important to fully explore possible medical and psychiatric diagnoses. A long history of MCSS or CFS does not eliminate the possibility of a new or previously undiagnosed anemia, vitamin deficiency, hypothyroidism, anxiety disorder, or depression. Such disorders require specific and accurate diagnosis, but are readily responsive to treatment. At the same time, care must be taken to avoid prolonged or unnecessary medical diagnostic procedures. The psychiatrist's diagnostic interview and treatment selection keeps in mind the importance of the patient's beliefs, and the realization that those beliefs will remain important even after medication response. Common psychiatric disorders in these patients include major depression, atypical depression (dysthymia), and panic disorder (see Chapters 12 and 13).

At some point, it may become possible to effect psychotherapeutic exploration of illness meaning and effects. Initial psychotherapy is dedicated to the reduction of distortions and to increased self-capacity and understanding. During a session, there may come a point where the focus can be shifted from disease and external factors, to internal meanings and personal options. Ultimately, this may build self-esteem and reduce helpless feelings. While patients will not soon change their firm beliefs about symptom causality, they will more quickly feel less distressed and more in control of their situation.

It is important to recognize when an illness belief is consciously or unwittingly used to avoid personal responsibility and accountability. In those cases, both the illness and the patient's complaints may be pernicious and persistent. For example, family members and others may have some interest in perpetuating the illness. When this happens, symptoms and disability become a patient's passport to external emotional, physical, or financial rewards.

Patients will often seek primary health care from nonmainstream alternative health practitioners. Typically, these healers offer an explanatory model for disease along with a set of culturally acceptable treatments. With a different explanatory model for each patient or cultural group, the result can be a profusion of nonmainstream therapies. Scientific biomedicine does not enjoy a monopoly in the hearts and minds of all patients. Many regard biomedicine as impersonal and dangerous. Nonmainstream therapies that sometimes replace medical care include naturopathy, chiropractic, curanderismo, shamanism, iridology, reflexology, faith healing, and Christian science.

Exclusive reliance on these therapies can leave important illnesses undiagnosed and untreated, and underlying emotional distress largely intact. But, the therapies persist because they do offer some helpful and socially acceptable benefits. Each approach is based on a theory of disease origins, which may be venerated in one culture but abjectly dismissed in another that reveres "big science." However, many patients will concurrently accept and use multiple theories, for example, combining antibiotics with traditional herb medicines. Healing is an art and a science, success in either mode depending on the self-limiting nature of disease and the patient's sense of psychological well-being. Many nonmainstream therapies use therapeutic touch, which creates a human contact and bond between patient and therapist. This physical touch, often applied as a laying-on-of-hands, or a spinal manipulation, may have effects that go beyond any physiological reaction. It can have a nonspecific but substantial positive psychological effect.

EMOTIONAL ASPECTS OF PHYSICAL DISEASE

Until now, this discussion has focused on conditions that are primarily of psychiatric origin, most often known through physical symptoms, or as syndromes of uncertain or multideterminant origin. It is also commonly accepted that emotions can bring on physical disease and, conversely, that physical disease can cause emotional disorders. Even the most mundane accident, cardiac failure, or tumor has direct psychological consequences and meaning to the patient. Often these disease processes gain momentum from life-style factors that are personality driven, and there can be causal emotional determinants. Specific diseases that have been widely studied for possible psychosomatic components include coronary artery disease, peptic ulcer, essential hypertension, asthma, thyroid disease, rheumatoid arthritis, irritable bowel syndrome, cancer, and ulcerative colitis.

While discussion focuses on three physical disorders that have interactive relationships with emotional or psychiatric factors, knowledge of specific causal mechanisms remains limited. Much can be learned from illness in the workplace, a unique environment that is charged with experience and meaning. It provides an ideal backdrop for viewing the interactions of mind and body. The selected diagnoses and case study are presented as a brief introduction to this important topic.

Case Study 6: Coronary Artery Disease (CAD) and Type A Behavior

Samuel Bowden was an attorney who founded and managed a small law firm with several employees. As a young man from a working-class family, he drove himself very hard in school and work (summers, vacations, and during school). He graduated in the top quarter of his law school class, even while holding a full-time job. In time he was offered a partnership in a large law firm, but he chose to go into practice alone. Considered an excellent business attorney, his clients were nearly as devoted to him as he was to them. Over the years, however, his pace and demanding personality burned out several attorneys and staff members. He had a low tolerance for the universal incompetence of those around him.

Sam married in his early twenties, his wife assuming the traditional roles of supportive mother and homemaker. Their four children were born within a 7-year period, but never spent much time with Sam. Not content with the practice of law, Samuel invested in several working enterprises and maintained an active management role in each one. These included a small construction company and a cattle ranch with a second home. He typically spent more than 80 hours a week on his practice and businesses. At the age of 42, he had his first of several extramarital affairs. His wife saw them as typical behavior for a man of her husband's energy and drive. She tolerated these diversions as long as he did not let them "interfere" with their stable, though emotionally distant, home life.

Samuel avoided both long vacations and doctors, also tending to ignore occasional injuries, aches, and pains. He overlooked stabbing chest pains, since they would go away in a few seconds. One day, at age 53, while dining with a client, the pain returned and persisted. The client insisted on bringing Samuel to an emergency room, where a myocardial infarction was diagnosed. While in the coronary care unit, the hospital staff found him to be highly resistant to rehabilitative guidelines for moderation and life-style changes. He didn't think he had a serious illness. Upon release from the hospital, he returned undeterred to his work, mistresses, and family distance. At age 59, Samuel suffered another myocardial infarction. Suddenly conscious of his mortality, he became profoundly depressed. Upon recovery, he religiously followed his cardiologist's advice, and joined a Type A behavior therapy group for heart attack survivors. Over many months, he gradually learned a more relaxed approach to work and attached a greater importance to his family life. He realized after a while that his fellow group members were really the closest "buddies" he had ever had.

Coronary Artery Disease (CAD) and Type A Behavior

Coronary artery disease has received considerable attention as a model of the interaction between stress, environment, emotions, and disease processes. Many theories have linked the onset of CAD with certain character traits, and with the experience of external stress. In addition, loss of physical capacity and sick role demands of the cardiac patient can cause profound changes in activity, self-esteem, and economic status. Those changes can contribute to significant depression and anxiety.

One major theory of CAD describes a process that starts with repeated coronary arterial spasm and consequent damage and scarring of the arterial lining. Atherosclerotic plaques then obstruct blood flow. Finally, the restricted blood flow provides inadequate oxygen, with resulting angina or myocardial infarction. Risk factors for CAD include hypertension, increased serum cholesterol, smoking, age, family history, male gender, and Type A (coronary prone) behavior.

Type A behavior traits include hostility, chronic impatience, overcompetitiveness, and excessive job involvement. These signs may be most evident when there are job-related time and responsibility pressures. Furthermore, Type A behavior is associated with denial of illnesses, avoidance of medical care, and premature return to work after myocardial infarction. While many Type A behavior traits appear to serve the interests of an employee and employer, it is very important to distinguish the successful hard worker from the sometimes less successful hard-driving Type A.

Moreover, Type A behavior is accompanied by increased physiological stress reactions. For instance, Type A behavior may be associated with increased coronary arterial vasoconstriction in response to stress. It is also possible that Type A behavior predisposes to such other risk factors as smoking and serum cholesterol. Preventive measures are commonly used to lower the risk of CAD. These include efforts to reduce or stop smoking, to lower blood cholesterol levels, and to relieve hypertension. Workplace-based efforts at risk factor reduction include programs for smoking, diet, hypertension, exercise, and cardiovascular risk assessment.

Low Back Pain (LBP) Syndrome

The study of pain is a rich field that draws inspiration from the basic sciences of anatomy and physiology, as well as psychiatry and the social sciences. Researchers disagree as to the relationship of psychiatric disorders and pain. Some studies suggest that pain causes psychiatric symptoms, and others suggest that psychiatric symptoms cause pain. In reality, either approach may be valid to a greater or lesser degree, depending on the particular setting.

Pain is defined by the International Association for the Study of Pain (Seattle, Wash.) as "an unpleasant sensory and emotional experience associated with actual or potential tissue damage, or described in terms of such damage." Emotionally determined pain can sometimes exist without a specific physical focus. Whether it has a physiological cause or a purely emotional origin, pain is experienced subjectively in the mind. Pain cannot exist independent of the brain and cannot be measured except by indirect means, such as the skin, muscle, and neurologic responses that occur with painful stimuli.

Many pain syndromes exist, but low back pain (LBP) is by far the most prevalent in the workplace. It may be called a crypto-illness, not because it is illusory but because LBP is an inclusive term for an illness that defies categorization. Although LBP syndrome is not confined to the workplace, it is the most frequent cause of occupational losses, occurring in over 40 percent of the adult population in any given year, at an annual cost approaching $16 billion. In most cases, the LBP syndrome is self-limiting, with little or no social or occupational disruption. Most of the staggering losses can be attributed to a small percentage of the people afflicted.

Like other pain syndromes, LBP presents a wealth of diagnostic possibilities, ranging from disorders with clear anatomic causes, to complaints of pain that are unsupported by evidence of tissue pathology. In those cases where objective pathology is clearly present, LBP will frequently abate or improve with appropriate treatment and the passage of time. Treatment may include directed physical therapy, life-style modifications such as weight loss and exercise, postural and lifting training, and job modification. At times, specific medication or surgical intervention may be indicated, but bed rest is not considered a desirable treatment in most LBP cases. It may lead to deconditioning, prolong recovery, and contribute to a self-concept of disability. Pain medications can be useful and are often essential, but their substantial potential for abuse makes it important to carefully weigh risks and benefits.

It is very important to consider comorbid and underlying psychiatric diagnoses. Depression and other psychiatric symptoms should be actively diagnosed and should never be written off as understandable consequences of physical pain. Major depression commonly presents with pain symptoms, and chronic physical pain can often lead to major depression, with further exacerbation of pain. Proper treatment of depression will greatly enhance pain response to other treatments. In fact, studies have shown that tricyclic antidepressants can be effective for subjective pain relief, even in the absence of diagnosed depression.

Somatoform pain disorder is described above at length, but the LBP syndrome is the most frequent form of workplace somatization. It often serves to communicate other issues about the patient, especially when the complaints are chronic in nature. When an individual fails to recover or substantially improve after the initial stages of LBP, emotional factors should be considered. An episode of LBP syndrome could make it possible to avoid an unpleasant or intolerable workplace or supervisory situation. LBP symptoms might grant permission to avoid work, or might sanction an unwitting desire to perform in an unacceptable way. For example, a young mother who wants to care for a new baby may be burdened with expectations that she will hold a job. If she develops a persistent case of LBP, she might obtain implicit permission to stay home.

A further inducement for disability is the availability of wage-loss protection if LBP syndrome can be imputed to a work-related injury. In physically demanding trades, advancing age and the normal degenerative processes reduce the ability of older workers to tolerate everyday demands. An episode of LBP syndrome provides a way out. Another incentive for chronic LBP might be a declining labor market in a declining industry or depressed region. A poorly educated or illiterate worker may have few, if any, options for transfer or for retraining in a physically less demanding occupation. Even less strenuous jobs for poorly educated LBP sufferers tend to be in lower-paying service industries at little more than a minimum wage. Often the experienced manual tradesperson has enjoyed wages that were two or three times greater. Large disparities in potential income can act as a further disincentive to LBP sufferers who must recover in order to be reemployed. Clinical findings can be especially confused by malingering, when financial and other rewards are sought through conscious deception.

Irritable Bowel Syndrome

Irritable bowel syndrome is the most common gastrointestinal disorder encountered in the general patient population and in the workplace as well. While the definitions and the symptoms vary, it is a continuous or recurring condition that involves abdominal pain. This distress is accompanied by defecation that varies in terms of appearance, frequency, composition, form, urgency, and sensations, and by other physical evidence of bowel disturbance. The validity of any diagnosis may be open to debate, since there may be an overlap with other medical or psychiatric illnesses.

Irritable bowel syndrome may reflect several forms of biological vulnerability to gastrointestinal distress, more likely to be active when there is a psychological predisposition. Patients thought to have irritable bowel syndrome often exhibit symptoms of autonomic arousal. These symptoms include weakness, dizziness, sleep disturbance, and other pain. While these symptoms have long been thought to suggest associations with anxiety and depression, research efforts have yielded inconsistent findings. More recently, though, there has been increasing clinical recognition of panic disorder in general, and in irritable bowel patients. As a result, more recent studies have looked specifically for panic anxiety and have shown a high prevalence in irritable bowel syndrome. The gastrointestinal symptoms may represent specific physiological concomitants of panic anxiety, unlike the more emotionally complex symptoms of somatoform disorders and controversial medical illnesses. As a result, patients are often more accepting of psychiatric referral, medication, and psychotherapy.

ORGANIC BEHAVIORAL SYNDROMES

Many significant medical illnesses can often present with emotional or behavioral symptoms. Failure to diagnose the organic cause of such illnesses only sets the stage for a progression of the untreated problem. The workplace is a common site for initial appearance of the behavioral symptoms of medical illnesses. Underlying syndromes can be infectious, neoplastic (cancerous), metabolic, or toxic. Toxic syndromes can be induced by industrial chemicals, by alcohol or illegal drugs, and by prescription medications. This overview of some common presentations presents some basic considerations (see the Bibliography for further detail).

Chemical Toxicity

Undue exposure to common industrial and agricultural chemicals can induce behavioral change in the form of organic impairment. The effects of toxins on the central nervous system vary according to substance and dosage, and may include dementia, delirium, psychosis, and depression. These toxins may enter the body by ingestion through the mouth, skin, and respiratory tract. Potentially harmful workplace substances include heavy metals such as lead, mercury, and arsenic.

Of these, lead takes on the status of a general pollutant, found in many older homes and apartments, and in certain water systems. The effects of lead on the central nervous system include headache, dizziness, sleep disturbance, impaired memory, and personality changes such as irritability. Mercury intoxication can produce irritability and tremors of varying intensity that can resemble symptoms of multiple sclerosis. Arsenic is a common and biologically important substance, present in much living tissue. The greatest occupational risk is in its inorganic form. In high doses, arsenic toxicity can produce acute abdominal pain, restlessness, cramping, stupor, and paralysis, preceding death in a comatose state. In lower doses, arsenic can cause giddiness, headache, light-headedness, vertigo, and vomiting of blood.

Other more complex poisons include the organic solvents, organophosphates, and certain gases. Thousands of organic compounds play a familiar role in everyday life, and at times in contamination episodes. It is no small task to verify a toxic exposure, and then to distinguish its purported effects from baseline personality and neurological functions. The difficulty is greater in cases involving only one person at low levels of exposure. A careful exposure history should accompany the toxicological screening whenever a previously healthy individual exhibits behavioral or neurological abnormalities. The likelihood of toxic exposure and appropriate treatment can be determined by correlating the findings with a sophisticated toxicologic data base.

Drug Toxicity

Alcohol, illegal drugs, and prescription medications can all elicit a toxic response (see Chapters 15 and 16). Depending on the type of drug, common primary effects or side effects can include confusion, excessive stimulation, depression, anxiety, or psychosis. Drugs may have a synergistic effect if used in combination with other prescribed drugs or self-administered substances. For example, alcohol may potentiate the sedative effects of various antianxiety and antidepressant medications. Adverse drug responses may ensue not only from excessive dosages but at therapeutic and even subtherapeutic levels. Prescribed medications commonly known to affect the central nervous system should be used with extreme caution in settings where physical safety can be compromised, as in work involving heavy machinery or transportation. Potential drug toxicity must be considered by all who use or prescribe drugs, with potential benefits weighed against the risks to general health, safety, and performance in a particular job setting.

Organically Induced Depression and Psychosis

Among the physical diseases that can produce depressive symptoms are thyroid disorders, several infectious and neurological diseases, malnutrition, and cardiovascular disease. In the elderly, depression may be among the presenting symptoms of dementia. Treatment is complicated by the fact that depressive symptoms are a side effect of many commonly used medications. These medications include central nervous system depressants, such as barbiturates, drugs used in treatment of hypertension, such as the beta-blockers (propranolol), and various sedatives, including alcohol. Undesirable side effects, such as depression and confusion, can result from combinations of therapeutic medications. While drugs can induce psychosis, it can also appear as a component of several physical conditions, including lupus erythematosis, cerebral tumors, hyperthyroidism and hypothyroidism, and other endocrine abnormalities (see Chapter 17). Attempts to treat organically induced depression or psychosis through psychotherapy and/or antidepressant medications alone will not only fail but will also delay appropriate treatment of an underlying disorder.

Organically Induced Dementia and Delirium

Slowed thinking, impaired decision making, reduced reaction times, confusional states, and memory lapses can all have profound effects on performance and safety. Surprisingly, those symptoms can often progress gradually and quietly, until one day they have a dramatic effect. Too often, co-workers and employees notice early symptoms and assume a dementing process or some sort of understandable demoralization. Only the occurrence of an industrial accident, major judgment error, or clearly disturbed functioning will force action. While major depression is commonplace, primary dementia (Alzheimer's disease) is infrequently encountered in workers under age

65. Drug abuse, including opiates and alcohol, is a far more common cause of cognitive symptoms. Confusion can also result from impaired cerebral blood flow, brought on by arterial disease or stroke-inducing conditions. Toxic exposures, including those occurring in the workplace, may result in chronic and acute impairments of cognition, and are a particular source of potential concern in some industries.

DSM-III-R DIAGNOSTIC CRITERIA

ORGANIC MENTAL SYNDROMES

Delirium

A. Reduced ability to maintain attention to external stimuli (e.g., questions must be repeated because attention wanders) and to appropriately shift attention to new external stimuli (e.g., perseverates answer to a previous question).

B. Disorganized thinking, as indicated by rambling, irrelevant, or incoherent speech.

C. At least two of the following:
   (1) reduced level of consciousness, e.g., difficulty keeping awake during examination
   (2) perceptual disturbances: misinterpretations, illusions, or hallucinations
   (3) disturbance of sleep-wake cycle with insomnia or daytime sleepiness
   (4) increased or decreased psychomotor activity
   (5) disorientation to time, place, or person
   (6) memory impairment, e.g., inability to learn new material, such as the names of several unrelated objects, after five minutes, or to remember past events, such as history of current episode of illness

D. Clinical features develop over a short period of time (usually hours to days) and tend to fluctuate over the course of a day.

E. Either (1) or (2):
   (1) evidence from the history, physical examination, or laboratory tests of a specific organic factor (or factors) judged to be etiologically related to the disturbance

(2) in the absence of such evidence, an etiologic organic factor can be presumed if the disturbance cannot be accounted for by any nonorganic mental disorder, e.g., Manic Episode accounting for agitation and sleep disturbance

Dementia

A. Demonstrable evidence of impairment in short- and long-term memory. Impairment in short-term memory (inability to learn new information) may be indicated by inability to remember three objects after five minutes. Long-term memory impairment (inability to remember information that was known in the past) may be indicated by inability to remember past personal information (e.g., what happened yesterday, birthplace, occupation) or facts of common knowledge (e.g., past Presidents, well-known dates).

B. At least one of the following:

(1) impairment in abstract thinking, as indicated by inability to find similarities and differences between related words, difficulty in defining words and concepts, and other similar tasks

(2) impaired judgment, as indicated by inability to make reasonable plans to deal with interpersonal, family, and job-related problems and issues

(3) other disturbances of higher cortical function, such as aphasia (disorder of language), apraxia (inability to carry out motor activities despite intact comprehension and motor function), agnosia (failure to recognize or identify objects despite intact sensory function), and "constructional difficulty" (e.g., inability to copy three-dimensional figures, assemble blocks, or arrange sticks in specific designs)

(4) personality change, i.e., alteration or accentuation of premorbid traits

C. The disturbance in A and B significantly interferes with work or usual social activities or relationships with others.

D. Not occurring exclusively during the course of Delirium.

E. Either (1) or (2):

    (1) there is evidence from the history, physical examination, or laboratory tests of a specific organic factor (or factors) judged to be etiologically related to the disturbance

    (2) in the absence of such evidence, an etiologic organic factor can be presumed if the disturbance cannot be accounted for by any non-organic mental disorder, e.g., Major Depression accounting for cognitive impairment

Criteria for severity of Dementia:

Mild: Although work or social activities are significantly impaired, the capacity for independent living remains, with adequate personal hygiene and relatively intact judgment.

Moderate: Independent living is hazardous, and some degree of supervision is necessary.

Severe: Activities of daily living are so impaired that continual supervision is required, e.g., unable to maintain minimal personal hygiene; largely incoherent or mute.

Reprinted with permission from the *Diagnostic and Statistical Manual of Mental Disorders,* 3d ed. rev.; copyright 1987 by the American Psychiatric Association.

SUMMARY

This chapter examines a remarkable class of disorders: Each involves the interaction of physical symptoms with emotional factors. To complicate the task of the physician or psychiatrist, these disorders often have complex cultural and familial origins. For effective diagnosis and treatment to take place, it is necessary to be aware of these factors, and to use them in constructing an approach to underlying problems. So, too, workplace managers need to be sensitive to these issues to make appropriate decisions regarding employees who present with psychosomatic disorders. Even when the cause or severity of physical ailments is hotly disputed, the patient/ employee may still be suffering from an emotional or psychiatric disorder that requires professional attention. Factitious disorders and malingering present the additional problem of willful falsification of symptoms. The psychosomatic disorders are real physical illnesses that may have emotional or behavioral determinants. It is vital to recognize that emotion and illness are bidirectionally linked. Just as emotional states can evoke physical distress, a physical ailment can itself instigate psychiatric symptoms.

Bibliography

Alemagno, S. A., S. J. Zynanski, K. C. Strange, et al. 1991. Health and illness behavior of type A persons. *Journal of Occupational Medicine* **33**(8):891-895.

American Psychiatric Association. 1987. *Diagnostic and Statistical Manual of Mental Disorders,* 3d ed. rev. Washington, D.C.: American Psychiatric Association.

Brodsky, Carroll M. 1987. Multiple chemical sensitivities and other "environmental illness": A psychiatrist's view. In *Occupational Medicine: Workers with Multiple Chemical Sensitivities,* M. R. Cullen (ed.), pp. 695-704. Philadelphia: Hanley & Belfus.

Blackburn, H., L. O. Watkins, W. S. Agras, et al. 1987. Task force 5: Primary prevention of coronary heart disease. *Circulation* **76**(suppl. 1):1164-1167.

Cullen, M. R. (ed.). 1987. *Occupational Medicine: Workers with Multiple Chemical Sensitivities.* Philadelphia: Hanley & Belfus.

Deyo, R. A. (ed.). *Occupational Medicine: Back Pain in Workers.* Philadelphia: Hanley & Belfus.

Forslind, K., E. Frederiksson, and O. Nived. 1990. Does primary fibromyalgia exist? *British Journal of Rheumatolology* **29**(5):368-370.

Gold, D., R. Bowder, J. Sixbey, et al. 1990. Chronic fatigue. A prospective clinical and virologic study. *Journal of the American Medical Association* **264**(1):48-53.

Kahn, J. P., A. S. Perumal, R. J. Gully, et al. 1987. Correlation of type A behaviour with adrenergic receptor density: Implications for coronary artery disease pathogenesis. *The Lancet* **ii**(8565):1937-1939.

Kleinman, A. 1988. *The Illness Narratives.* New York: Basic Books.

Rom, W. N. (ed.). 1983. *Environmental and Occupational Medicine.* Boston: Little, Brown and Company.

Shepherd, J.T., T. M. Dembroski, M. J. Brody, et al. 1987. Task force 3: Biobehavioral mechanisms in coronary artery disease: Acute stress. *Circulation* **76**(suppl. 1):1150-1157.

Tollison, C. D. (ed.). 1989. *Handbook of Chronic Pain Management.* Baltimore: Williams & Wilkins.

Valciukas, J. A. 1991. *Foundations of Environmental and Occupational Neurotoxicology.* New York: Van Nostrand Reinhold.

Walker, E. A., P. P. Roy-Byrne, and W. J. Katon. 1990. Irritable bowel syndrome and psychiatric illness. *American Journal of Psychiatry* **147**:565-572.

Weiner, H. 1977. *Psychobiology and Human Disease.* New York: Elsevier.

Wolfe, F. 1990. Fibromyalgia. *Rheumatic Diseases Clin. North America* **16**(3):681-698.

Zenz, C. (ed.). 1988. *Occupational Medicine: Principles and Practical Applications,* 2d ed. Chicago: Year Book Medical Publishers.

Index